MANAGING FOR EXCELLENCE

Dr. A.K. Gavai

M. Com., Ph.D.

Himalaya Publishing House

MUMBAI • NEW DELHI • NAGPUR • BENGALURU • HYDERABAD • CHENNAI • PUNE • LUCKNOW • AHMEDABAD • ERNAKULAM • BHUBANESWAR • INDORE • KOLKATA • GUWAHATI

First Edition : 2013

Published by : Mrs. Meena Pandey for **Himalaya Publishing House Pvt. Ltd.,**
"Ramdoot", Dr. Bhalerao Marg, Girgaon, **Mumbai - 400 004.**
Phone: 022-23860170/23863863, Fax: 022-23877178
E-mail: himpub@vsnl.com; Website: www.himpub.com

Branch Offices :

New Delhi : "Pooja Apartments", 4-B, Murari Lal Street, Ansari Road, Darya Ganj, New Delhi - 110 002. Phone: 011-23270392, 23278631; Fax: 011-23256286

Nagpur : Kundanlal Chandak Industrial Estate, Ghat Road, Nagpur - 440 018. Phone: 0712-2738731, 3296733; Telefax: 0712-2721215

Bengaluru : No. 16/1 (Old 12/1), 1st Floor, Next to Hotel Highlands, Madhava Nagar, Race Course Road, Bengaluru - 560 001. Phone: 080-32919385; Telefax: 080-22286611

Hyderabad : No. 3-4-184, Lingampally, Besides Raghavendra Swamy Matham, Kachiguda, Hyderabad - 500 027. Phone: 040-27560041, 27550139; Mobile: 09390905282

Chennai : No. 8/2, 2nd Madley Street, Ground Floor, T. Nagar, Chennai - 600 017. Mobile: 09345345055

Pune : First Floor, "Laksha" Apartment, No. 527, Mehunpura, Shaniwarpeth (Near Prabhat Theatre), Pune - 411 030. Phone: 020-24496323/24496333; Mobile: 09370579333

Lucknow : House No 731, Shekhupura Colony, Near B.D. Convent School, Aliganj, Lucknow - 226 022. Mobile: 09307501549

Ahmedabad : 114, "SHAIL", 1st Floor, Opp. Madhu Sudan House, C.G. Road, Navrang Pura, Ahmedabad - 380 009. Phone: 079-26560126; Mobile: 09377088847

Ernakulam : 39/176 (New No: 60/251) 1st Floor, Karikkamuri Road, Ernakulam, Kochi - 682011, Phone: 0484-2378012, 2378016; Mobile: 09344199799

Bhubaneswar : 5 Station Square, Bhubaneswar - 751 001 (Odisha). Phone: 0674-2532129, Mobile: 09338746007

Indore : Kesardeep Avenue Extension, 73, Narayan Bagh, Flat No. 302, IIIrd Floor, Near Humpty Dumpty School, Indore - 452 007 (M.P.). Mobile: 09301386468

Kolkata : 108/4, Beliaghata Main Road, Near ID Hospital, Opp. SBI Bank, Kolkata - 700 010, Phone: 033-32449649, Mobile: 09883055590, 07439040301

Guwahati : House No. 15, Behind Pragjyotish College, Near Sharma Printing Press, P.O. Bharalumukh, Guwahati - 781009, (Assam). Mobile: 09883055590, 09883055536

DTP by : Athurva Graphics, Mumbai - 400 002.

Printed at : Geetanjali Press Pvt. Ltd., Nagpur. On behalf of HPH.

ll Shree ll

Dedicated Humbly,
to My Guru,

Prof. Late K.B. Gavai,

Who taught me, that,
Excellence is a continuous journey.

— Dr. A. K. Gavai

PREFACE

Excellence is a continuous journey. When one goal is achieved, we have to again strive hard for another higher and more valuable goal. Goals and their achievement are less important. What matters most is the efforts to improve, enhance and make things better than earlier. This thinking style and practice constitute the core of the philosophy of excellence. Excelling is an unending process. Then, sky is the limit. But this process is not automatic. It needs an appropriate mindset and level of thinking. We must view every task as an opportunity to make the best use of our potential and better things around. This mindset and line of thinking induces us to consider each of our job seriously and perform sincerely. This is our first step towards excellence.

Progress requires integrity. This integrity must be reflected in our thoughts and actions. We should feel extremely sad and annoyed for our mistakes and also should learn from them, for a bright future. Similarly, we should never stick to our achievements and should not be happy with our glorious history. We must develop an unsatisfying thirst to move ahead on the path of improvement and progress all the time. We should think less of our achievement and more of the achievables.

Life is lively if we move ahead, stagnation, passivity and lethargy is death. So long as we actively work with passion, we truly live the life.

— Dr. A.K. Gavai

CONTENTS

CHAPTER 1

WHAT IS EXCELLENCE?

INTRODUCTION

Excellence is the word we use to describe something which is uniquely the 'Best'. Normally our description and positive appreciation of something starts in the ascending order of 'Good', 'Better', 'Best' and thereafter 'Excellent'. We thus use the word excellence to tell about something which we think is marvelous.

The Oxford Dictionary explains that to excel means to surpass, to be pre-eminent and excellence means great merit, when, we use this term in management context, we have the same meaning and connotation of excellence as achieving and preserving and presenting great merit. We wish to make ourselves and our institution or organisation as pre-eminent. We intend to obtain merit and remain always meritorious.

This is not a simple job. It can neither be achieved in a single day, nor can it be an achievement for a single day. It is a matter of continuous improvement and upgradation. It is not in the form of a fixed, particular, certain target, which, once accomplished the problem is over and so one can rest comfortably. It is not a single achievement but achieving and accomplishing higher and higher targets consistently. Managing for excellence, therefore, should be understood as an unending, explorative and joyful journey rather than a preconceived and preplanned destination. This does not mean that planning and targets are meaningless and irrelevant in excellence management. In fact these two things bring focus, economy, purpose and direction in the working of an organisation and streamline its operations and channelize its resources to their optimum productive use. In excellence management the plans and targets are flexible and directional and not narrow and restrictive. They are treated as useful tools for bettering the performance continuously. So plans are revised and targets reset from time to time. The objective is to surpass and get ahead. So excellence management concentrates on improving, enhancing, upgrading, innovating and progressing endlessly.

Further excellence management is an explorative process. Because innovation is the key to progress and excellence. An orgainsation striving for excellence should never be afraid to accept novel ideas, work methods, organizational techniques and resources. New combinations of resources, work focus and new managerial styles will lead to development of excellence in performance. The static work culture emphasizing on routinisation and regimentation places the big hurdle in the development of proper attitude for excellence management. So the organisations should encourage creative thinking and passion to do everything in the best way. If the present system and methods are limiting the performance, then those system and methods should be replaced by more purposeful and relevant systems. This is possible when creative thinking and work passion is appropriately nurtured, supported and apprehended.

A search for excellence is a joyful process also. This is in the sense that searching and developing something that enhances oneself is really enjoyable. Excelling one's competitors and when there are no competitors, excelling one's past performance, is not a matter of compulsion. An urge for excellence is self-imposed. In certain situations, due to intense competitions, a company will have to essentially, improve itself for survival, But this external pressure for improvement and upgradation is only a symptomatic cause for developing the corporate culture for excellence. The basic drive to better oneself and one's performance should be original self-emergent. Competitors and own past performance are useful for the purpose of benchmarking only. The real germ is a strong achievement drive and self-motivation. The pleasure in seeking and reaching to new heights is the purpose as well as the reward of the search for excellence.

Sir Edmund Hillary, after his conquest of Everest, was questioned in an interview, what made him go to the Everest and he plainly replied. **Because It Is There.** This is the secret of striving for excellence.

THE FOUNDATION OF EXCELLENCE

Corporate excellence is not a matter of chance or simple, situational, discreet tricks and tactics. It is the result of systematic thinking and prudential efforts. Corporate strategy and corporate culture are the two sound pillars of excellence management. A judicious corporate strategy takes into account the customers of the organisation, the competitors of the organisation and the strength and weaknesses of the company itself. A strategy which is blind about the customers, competitors and company can become effective only by chance and the probability of this chance element is next to nil. Further, a culture suitable and supportive to excellence management has three important aspects, namely, commitment, competence and consistency.

Kenchi Ohmae, defines a strategy in terms of the three key players (Corporation, customers and competitors) as follows. A strategy is the way in which a corporation endeavors to differentiate itself positively from its competitors, using its relative corporate strengths to better satisfy customer needs. Kenchi Ohmae calls the corporation, customers and competition as the main players who collectively formulate the strategic triangle. The strategist has to prepare such form of strategy which will help the corporation to achieve superior performance than its competitors. A strategy that does not provide a competitive edge will be called ineffective and therefore useless. The basic objective of formulating and implementing a strategy is to surpass the competitors and win the competition. Now a company can make superior performance and win competition only if it is able to catch up more customers and capture a larger market share. For this purpose a company will have to serve the customers in a better manner than its competitors. This is possible only if the company's strategy can properly match its strengths with the clearly defined market. The strategist has to always think and devise plans and actions which will use the full strength of the company to satisfy customer's needs in a manner relatively superior than its competitors. The key question which a company should ask itself is how it should become unique in serving the customers and attending to the needs of the market. This thinking has to become the basis of a strategy.

A strategy provides an action plan. This action plan is put to practice by the people. People are the cornerstone of success of every organisation. Even the best strategies become fruitless without active and sincere participation of people. The integrity of the members of an organisation can grow when a supportive work culture is developed. Involvement is the key to best performance. When one is mentally involved in the work he does, then the quality of his performance not only improves, but sometimes reaches to the level of a miracle. Greater the involvement, higher is the level of one's performance. When people are truly involved in their jobs, success comes to them automatically. Such people astonish others with their remarkable and outstanding performance and become ideal for others. Commitment and competence make oneself a mark of excellence. A strong sense of commitment develops from a deep involvement in the job. Former us **President John F. Kennedy** says, that, 'I don't mind if my son chooses drilling roads as his occupation, but he should be the best at that. When one is physically and mentally involved in the job completely, the work becomes the labour of love. Then one never feels tired, bored or spent for the lot of efforts and energy, one has put in the job-accomplishment.' Every such exertion is looked and felt as a constructive contribution by oneself. Working becomes meaningful and one is, therefore, self-motivated. Then, there is no separation between the work and the individual as well as the individual and the organisation. For such people work is passion and they pose themselves as organisational men. In fact, there is lot of difference in saying that I work for XYZ ltd and I am a XYZ man. In the former case the person exhibits a contractual relationship which is somewhat in the transactionary form. In the latter case, the person expresses an emotional and mental involvement in the organisation which is rather deep rooted and relatively permanent and gives the person an identity which is inseparable from his organization. Such people are prepared to do anything and everything, constructive and productive, for their organisation. So to achieve excellence, an organisation needs committed people. Therefore the management should focus on devising ways and means and developing an atmosphere which will generate, nurture and nourish the sense of commitment and responsibility among people.

Commitment can help to develop capability and competence. If you have devoted yourself for a particular cause, then you start taking more and more interest in it. As a result you become more alert in serving the cause to the best of your ability. You also become keen about your performance. Commitment develops emotional bonding and a sense of responsibility. Once people love their jobs and take them as their personal obligations, then they are ready to make all efforts to do the best in their jobs. At such a situation completing the quotas and achieving the work targets does not remain a problem. People make achievements even beyond their assigned work targets. The competence of an individual depends upon the skill or expertise and integrity of the individual. One must possess the knowledge and capacity to do the job in the best possible manner. This develops expertise. But simply the skill or expertise is not sufficient. It must be supported by integrity and then only the true competence will rise up. Integrity teaches the person to offer his best skill and efforts to the assignment. It tells the person that this is 'your' job and so you should devote yourself to it completely. Integrity develops the positive attitude and preparedness to strive hard for the work and goal accomplishment. However integrity cannot be injected. Like a particular skill it cannot be inducted. It can be nurtured by developing suitable work-ethics and work-environment. It is a matter of cognitive learning as well as social learning. Therefore the company should develop appropriate culture wherein commitment and competence will be regarded as high values which everyone should try to imbibe.

The efforts for excellence should be consistent. So besides commitment and competence, consistency is the third element of the corporate culture necessary for excellence.

Prof. Bala Balchandran-Kellog, Professor of Accountancy, Information and Management at North Western University, has given the following formula for business excellence.

Business excellence = 4C + 5E + 6P where – 4C means Customer, Change, Cost and Competition. 5E means Economy, Environment, Education, Empowerment and Equity. 6P means Profitability, Products and Services, Productivity, Processes, Performance measures and Preferred Partnership.

If we take up of these 15 factors and pay sufficient attention to them, then we will be able to achieve excellence in our business. The factors are mostly self-explanatory and their importance is so well understood that they do not require any further clarification.

Mckinsey 7S model is one more popular model for organisational effectiveness. The model explains the interrelationship of 7 key elements which determine the organisational effectiveness.

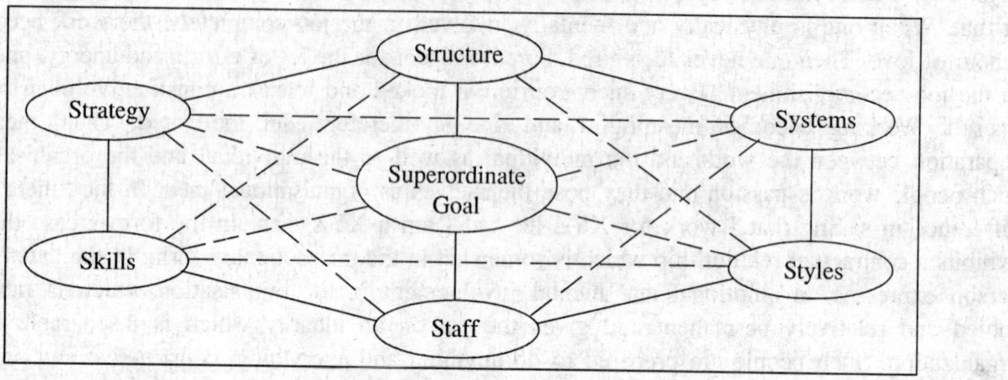

Fig. 1.1 : Mckinsey 7S Model

Mckinsey 7S model displays describes that excellence effectiveness cannot be solely attributed to one single factor. It is a total effect which, can be brought by a suitable and wise combination of 7 elements, namely, organisational goals, organisational structure, the employees of the organisation and their skills, managerial styles, strategy and the organisational system relating to decisions and actions. However when we look behind these 7 elements, we find only one determinative factor and that is the human being. The human element in organisation is a basic root factor for all its performances as well as problems. People decide goals, develop systems, prepare strategies, form structures, choose styles and use skill. So we must focus to develop the right attitude of people. Right attitude means positive attitude. People with positive attitude do not see situations as problems, difficulties, hurdles and obstacles. They even welcome problems because they treat them as opportunities to prove one's capabilities, learn new things which are more useful and to grow further against all odds. Positive attitude induces and inspires people to convert the problems into opportunities. **Richard Bach** has made a typical comment in this regard. He says that there is no such thing as a problem without a gift in its hands. We seek problems because we enjoy their gifts.

We must never forget that there is no reward without risk. However the risk to be accepted should be moderate and well-calculated. Analysis and research is essential for this. However intuition and judgement also has a very significant role to play in this context. Analysis tells you that a particular project involves a specific volume of risk; but your intuition and judgement may say that you are capable to handle this risk factor successfully and so embark on the project. This multidimensional approach is most needed for problem solving in the modern business world. An organisation wishes to achieve excellence requires such type of people and their development on this line should be made thoughtfully. Progress and upgradation requires a purposeful and continuous change. When the external environment is changing relentlessly, the rate of change inside should be greater than the rate of outside change. We have to build a receptive and responsive mindset of people. A responsive mindset teaches to hold all the time reasonable optimism. It trains to take success as well as failure in a balanced manner. Success should not breed over-optimism and failure should not cause pessimism, lethargy and depression. After, every failure there should be introspection and reorganisation of all strengths to overcome the situation. And after every success there should be a desire to scale new heights. This desire should not take the form of a dream or over-ambition, but should become a regular and normal habit to strive for new heights. We should always avoid over-defensiveness and over-offensiveness if we wish to move ahead on the path of excellence. An objective analysis of the situation as well as of self-capabilities combined with a strong determination to overcome all obstacles and difficulties to reach the goal is the foundation of the efforts for excellence. The objectivity in analysis brings fairness in self-evaluation and self-assessment. At the individual or organisational level when one is making self-examination, one has to note down all the strengths and weaknesses of the examinee without any positive or negative bias, we have to be factual all the time. We must remember that facts cannot be altered or ignored anytime. Doing so, will lead to self-deception. At the same time, we should understand that the situation can be improved. If we are strong in certain respect, we can enhance our strength and develop superiority. If we are weak in certain areas, we can plan to work harder to improve and with consistent and wise efforts we can overcome our limitations and remove our deficiencies. Thus if we are open, objective and analytical; we can expand our capabilities, build up new capabilities and successfully eliminate our defects and deficiencies. Our blind faith in self-merit or fear of failure due to exaggeration of weaknesses can result only in deadlocks and stagnation.

Analysis provides us an accurate self-picture whereas determination to march ahead gives us motivation. The strength of such determination depends upon the value of the goal. What we wish to achieve (goal) always acts as a parameter to judge the validity and relevance of our efforts. When the goal is noble, outstanding and invaluable, our efforts become more systematic and persistent because the urge to achieve is the strongest. So commit yourself to a cause beyond self-interest. The nobility of such a cause mobilize people more effectively than anything else. Then people are ready to put in all efforts to achieve the goal. For example, when a steel company, in their advertisement, writes in bold letter that we build the nation and below it is written in a bit smaller letter that we manufacture steel too; it definitely makes an impact. The noble goal of nation-building which becomes its mission, brings more meaning and value to the steel production activity which then becomes an important way and effort to build the nation. Such noble objectives effectively direct and motivate the people in organisations to do their respective work and jobs. Therefore always see a big dream and then work hard to make it real. In fact, such a dream itself will make you to put in all your efforts and work hardest continuously, to bring it into reality.

EXCELLENCE-WHAT IT REQUIRES

From the above discussion and further analysis we can shortlist the essential elements for excellence.

(1) A mission to do something noble and work for a cause beyond self-interest.

(2) Acceptance to the social obligation to contribute substantially to the economic and social progress of the nation and thereafter, to the progress of entire mankind.

(3) Development of pride for work and profession.

(4) Cultivation of a strong achievement drive to become the best performer in terms of quality, expertise, customer-service and financial results.

(5) Development of leadership for excellent performance at all levels of management and organisation.

(6) Clear vision about the future and work.

(7) Development of positive attitude. Teaching people to see the opportunities in problems and winning such opportunities.

(8) Involvement in work and organisation, commitment to the goal and moderate level optimism.

(9) Objective self-assessment and building up suitable strategy to make the best use of self-strength and overcome limitations.

(10) Developing strong team spirit and 'we' attitude in place of 'I' attitude.

(11) Creation and continuous nurturing of 'Excellence Culture', emphasizing on values like continuous improvement and upgradation, research and modernization, progress and development, quality orientation, cost reduction and rejection of *status quo*, stagnation and lethargy.

From a Good organisation to a Great Organisation

The philosophy of excellence is based on the foundation of continuous improvement and upgradation. So excellence is not a destination. It is an eternal journey. Every performance should excel the earlier performances and achievements. Thus the theory of excellence intends to convert a good organisation into a great organisation. From poor to a good, is no doubt an achievement. But from good to great is a more spectacular and magnificent achievement. This requires a strong burning desire for progress and consistent efforts in the right direction.

The need to improve is felt either due to external pressure or due to internal urge. The competition many times forces the organisations to alter, modify and revise their plans, strategies, targets, work methods and processes. Where a modification and improvement programme is undertaken due to such external pressure or environmental compulsion, an organisation may become and remain a good one, but cannot reach the height of a great organization. A great organisation internalises improvement and upgradation as one of the basic routine functions. It instills, develops and fosters an urge to improve as an essential element of its work culture. The members of such organisation always perceive the need for improvement, even though there is no such external pressure. Then innovation becomes a rule and progress becomes a habit.

Great organisations have certain prominent common features, which are as follows:–

(1) Trust is a dominant character of great organisations. Such organisations are found to treat their employees in a fair way. A vibrant democracy, allowing employees to express their ideas and views regarding work and methods fearlessly is observed in most of these organisations.

(2) Great organisations are found to provide physically safest work environment with suitable facilities that create and develop the right ambience to motivate for the best work and use of the complete potential for the organisational achievements.

(3) Great organisations pay enough attention to maintain proper work-life balance for employees. They look to their employees as 'whole persons' and accept them as human beings. These organisations fully realise that they hire people and not their skills alone.

(4) Great organisations take care of employee development and advancement. They provide training to employees for their career advancement. Employees in such organisations have pride for their organisations.

(5) Great organisations typically pay more attention to excellence in execution for which they do the following things:

(a) They always set realistic and achievable goals.

(b) They provide adequate resources and people to accomplish the goals.

(c) These organisations make precise planning and adhere to their plans in all situations.

(d) They divide their goals into smaller definite time-bound targets and such targets are set for each and every person and workgroup in the organisation.

(e) They set deadlines for task-completion and thereby build focus in actions and implementation.

(f) Great companies emphasize on participatory decision making. They believe in decentralization and team decisions. This automatically in return develop commitment, alignment, work-focus and initiative among employees.

(g) Great companies are found to be always positively responsive to environmental changes. Employees in these organizations are habituated to pay special attention to all details in planning and execution.

(h) Great companies have a strong customer-orientation and market focus which is reflected in all their decisions and actions.

Are We Really Managing for Excellence?

It is essential to make self-assessment. We must question ourselves regularly to find out whether we are actually following the philosophy of excellence. This introspection requires an examination and evaluation of our objectives and policies, organisational culture and values, HR management and work organisation and the process of decision making and communication. These are the important elements which largely influence the work style and effectiveness of an organisation.

(A) Corporate Objectives, Strategies and Policies: They have a deep impact on the performance and progress of the organisations. Their suitability largely contributes to organisational success. The judgement about the apporiateness of corporate objectives, strategies and policies can be formed by raising the following questions and searching their replies.

(i) Do the corporate objectives go beyond quantified goals and encompass the strategic vision of the future environment?

(ii) Does the company identify its opportunities in the market clearly and capitalize on them effectively?

(iii) Is there any consistency in the functional policies of the company?

(iv) Does the company respond promptly and efficiently to the changes in the external environment?

(B) Values and Culture: The work-culture and values deeply influence the performance and work-related behaviour of employees. How strongly the employees are motivated to give their best performance depends upon the kind of work-culture and value-system which the organisation has developed. Following questions should be asked to check out, as to how far the organisational culture and value-system is suitable to strive for excellence.

(i) What kind of values and aspirations form the guiding force for the company?

(ii) How the organisational values motivate the employees to put in their best efforts and use their complete potential?

(iii) How the work ethics in the company reinforce high standards of performance?

(iv) Is the culture rule-bound and bureaucratic or is it giving encouragement to risk-taking and entrepreneurship?

(v) Does the organisation accept innovation as one of its prime values?

(vi) Has the organisation ingrained innovation as a value among the managers?

(vii) Does the company have customer-orientation? What is the degree of customer-orientation? Is it reflected in the operations, structure and systems of the company?

(C) Decision Making and Communication: Decision making and communication process contribute significantly to organisational effectiveness. How decisions are made and are communicated to the concerned employee has an effect on efficiency, teamwork and productivity. To test the quality of decision making and communication process, following questions are to be asked:

(i) To what extent delegation and decentralization is made and is encouraged in the organisation?

(ii) Do the superiors interfere in the tasks delegated to the subordinates?

(iii) What is the condition of communication? Is formal communication more encouraged or informal?

(iv) What is the quality of communication? Are there frequent communication gaps, miscommunication and noise?

(v) How much fast is the communication? How much delay occurs in communication and why?

(vi) How much value does the company place on time as a resource?

(vii) Is there team-leadership and grapevine communication in the company?

(D) Work Organisation and HR Management : The structure of the organisation and human resources management practices are the important factors from the point of view of goal accomplishment and fast results. A rigid organisational structure results into bureaucracy and impersonalisation. A tall organisational structure develops a large number of hierarchical layers making the administration more complex and causes decision-delays and operational delays. Acute division of labour, overspecialisation and departmentation makes job division into meaningless, repetitive tasks as a result of which monotony, boredom and fatigue is felt by the workers and their creativity gets suppressed. A line organisation develops obedience at the cost of initiative and a line and staff structure provides loopholes for shirking the responsibility. The point is that the company should develop such an organisational structure which will provide work-flexibility; encourage creativity, initiative and teamwork; facilitate easy work coordination and timely communication and bring greater result orientation and effectiveness in collective efforts.

Besides the structure of the organization, the HR practices in respect of employee recruitment training, placement, motivation, performance appraisal, promotion, compensation and grievance settlement have an impact on the employee attitude and employee loyalty. For achieving excellence the employees should possess strong positive attitude, work-commitment and loyalty to the organisation. Only appropriate HRM practices can develop and create the suitable work environment in which such things will breed up automatically.

To check the appropriateness of the organisational structure and HRM practices, one has to find out the answers to the following questions.

(i) Does the structure provide simplicity and ease in managing the work, workers and managers.

(ii) Does the structure clearly explain the working relationship, lines of authority and responsibility and work-related interdependence of people and work groups?

(iii) Does the organizational structure provide scope for collective thinking and problem solving, team-leadership, initiative and entrepreneurship?

(iv) Does the company emphasize on merit as the sole criterion for recruitment and promotion?

(v) Does the company employ performance-based and efficiency-linked remuneration system?

(vi) Does the company allow and show active interest in employee development?

(vii) What is the kind of motivation and level of employee morale?

(viii) What is the condition of employer-employee relations (industrial relations)? What is the past record of the organisation in this regard?

(ix) What is the situation of employee-commitment, job-involvement and company loyalty? What is the rate of employee attrition? What are the causes?

(x) Does the company accept and practice sincerely the concepts like employee empowerment, participative management, collective decision making, autonomy and decentralisation and open communication and team leadership?

(xi) Do the employees share credit and recognition for accomplishing the company's goals? Is the employee-commitment self-generated?

(xii) Does the company offer more value and importance to group or individuals? What special effort does it take to develop the spirit of co-operation and collective work?

(xiii) How much importance does the company give to human values and human relationship? Does the company follow a task-centred management style or employee-centred management style?

❑❑❑

CHAPTER 2

STRATEGY AND CULTURE THE CORNER STONES OF EXCELLENCE

STRATEGY AND STRATEGIC THINKING

The term 'strategy' is used in defence science is to describe the art of planning and directing large military movements and the operations of war. In business, 'strategy' helps to plan for future as it sets out that the products and services a company should make and sell to which market and how. **Laurence Jauch** and **William Glueck** define a strategy as a unified comprehensive and integrated plan that relates to the strategic advantages of the firm to the challenges of the environment. A strategy is designed to ensure that the basic objectives of the enterprise are achieved through proper execution by the organisation.

According to **Arthur Sharplin,** a strategy is a plan or course of action which is of vital, pervasive and continuing importance to the organization as a whole.

In the view of **James Brain Quinn,** a strategy is the pattern or plan that integrates an organisation's major goals, policies and action sequences into a cohesive whole.

Alfred Chandler defines strategy as the determination of the basic long-term goals and objectives of an enterprise and the adoption of courses of action and the allocation of resources necessary to carry out these goals.

Ingor Ansoft explains that strategy is the common thread among the organisation's activities and products market that defines the essential nature of business that the organization was or planned to be in future.

In the view of **Michael E. Porter** the core of general management is strategy. Strategy develops and communicates the company's unique position, makes trade-off and forges fit among activities.

Porter's definition highlights the following aspects of a strategy which point out its utility, validity and necessity.

(1) A strategy, in simple sense, is a plan or a course of action or a set of norms for decision making forming a pattern and creating a common thread.

(2) This common thread which a strategy develops is related to the activities of the organization.

(3) Such activities are derived from the policies, objectives and goals of the organization.

(4) When these activities are pursued properly and prudentially, the organization is able to move forward to its desired future position. Strategy makes this perusal possible and effective.

(5) Strategy suggests the best and most beneficial way of resources allocation.

(6) Strategy helps the enterprise to acquire the competitive position by making trade-offs among different activities and creating a fit among them.

Strategy is necessary to win the competition. If there is no competition, then, a strategy is hardly required. Every business strategy thus is aimed at obtaining a competitive advantage. So a strategy to become effective must describe the following three essential elements.

(a) Most important objectives to be achieved.

(b) The most significant functional policies (such as the production policy, marketing policy, finance policy and HR Policy) guiding or limiting the actions.

(c) The most important and relevant actions which are essential to accomplish the desired goals. To decide wheather a strategy can prove to be effective or otherwise, we have to test it on the following criteria.

(1) Clarity of objectives.

(2) Attainable goals.

(3) Decisiveness and focus.

(4) Freedom of action and development of commitment.

(5) Flexibility, competitiveness, speed and resourcefulness.

The strategy must have clear-cut objectives, ambiguity, in respect of objectives results into haphazard actions and wastages. It should be made clear what the strategy aims at. The objectives should clearly specify whether the strategy intends stability, growth or retrenchment. Such clarity brings focus and decisiveness. The organization is then able to concentrate on more suitable, relevant and selective tasks and activities, which in turn develops and enhances organizational competitiveness. Further the goals and targets set should be attainable. Unattainable goals cause frustration and kills initiative and speed of decision and action. The successful accomplishment of one goal motivates automatically to strive for another higher level goal and this creates an environment and culture of making efforts continuously for improvement, upgradation and enhancement; which is a prerequisite for managing for excellence. Flexibility and autonomy are another two important elements which increase the effectiveness of a strategy. The freedom of action and the freedom to revise, modify and alter the course of action to suit the circumstances brings flexibility in the strategy. A rigid strategy many-times proves ineffective, unwanted and obsolete. The most important thing in strategic thinking is goal accomplishment. If due to changed circumstances the chosen course of action is not adequate and efficient to accomplish goals, it should be modified and the strategy should provide scope for such changes. The strategy should help in developing an environment of commitment in the organisation. Further the competitiveness, resourcefulness and the speed to deliver the results are other important elements which act as the criteria of an effective strategy.

In fact a strategy, maps out the future and decides which products and services the organization will take to which market and how. It provides a plan for selling the products and services to specific markets competitively and excellently. The success of strategy therefore depends on supplying the excellent service to the customers and thereby making good financial returns. When these returns are more attractive than your competitors, your strategy is successful and effective.

If we try to read the mind of the strategist, we observe that an effective strategist looks at what is happening around him presently in the context of where he wishes to go. He analyses the situation to work out a plan to achieve the future targets. A strategist reacts positively to the problem and sees them as the opportunities to improve. He balances the short-term needs and long-term needs precisely and inspires people to use their full potential to achieve the targets. An effective strategist is a good communicator and efficient and loyal team-player.

The strategic framework has the following important steps.

(1) Analysis of information to understand the position of self (organisations).

(2) Pinpointing the competitive advantage.

(3) Defining the scope of the company's products and their markets.

(4) Making decisions regarding area of business and focusing of resources. Decide where to focus the resources.

(5) Identifying, prioritizing and implementing change.

(6) Continuously monitoring the performance and reviewing strategy.

The stages of strategic thinking are described as follows :

Phenomena → Grouping → Abstraction → Determination of approach → Provisional formulation of hypothetical solutions → Validation or rebuttal of hypothetical solutions by in-depth analysis → Emergence of conclusions → Giving a concrete form to conclusions → Draft plan of action → Implementation by line managers.

Now we have properly understood that the object of strategic thinking is to bring about the conditions most favourable to one's own side. A strategy involves the precise judgement about the right time to attack or withdraw assessing the limits of compromise correctly. In the process of strategic thinking from the stage of phenomena to the stage of giving concrete conclusion, the thinking is made to develop a solution on the problem. And from the draft plan of action the planning for implementation of the solution starts. In fact, analysis is the critical starting point of the strategic thinking. The events, trends or situations which takes the shape of a problem are dissected by the strategist into their constituent parts. The strategist then studies each such constituent in depth to understand its significance and then reassembles them in such a way, so that, his advantage will be maximized. Thus the strategist converts a problem into an opportunity. This analysis is combined with the intellectual elasticity or flexibility which enables the strategist to come up with realistic responses to the changing situations.

Strategic thinking differs from conventional thinking. The conventional mechanical approach is based on linear thinking. The strategic thinking is also different from intuitive thinking. Intuitive thinking takes everything on intuition and reaches to conclusions without any real breakdown or analysis. In strategic thinking the strategist first develop a clear understanding about the character of each element of a situation/event/problem and then uses fully his brain power to restructure the elements in the most advantageous way. Strategic thinking makes a combination of rational analysis based on the real nature of things and imaginative reintegration of all different items into a new pattern using the non-linear brain power.

The first stage in strategic thinking is to pinpoint the critical issue in the situation. Unfortunately many times we fail to differentiate the real problem from its symptoms. And then we focus on the symptoms and search out remedies. As a result the symptom disappears, however the real problem remains undetected and so the losses and worries continue. Therefore, we have to precisely identify and pinpoint the critical issue, which is the root cause of the problem. Otherwise we will not be able to develop effective solution. Strategy aims at altering, improving and enhancing the strength of the enterprise relative to that of its competitors and so it involves such decisions and actions which will help to serve this purpose. So we must distinguish the strategic decisions and actions from those which are aimed at achieving operational improvements. The decisions and actions made to streamline the organization or to increase profitability or to improve training or to increase the speed and efficiency of management procedures have the basic objective of improving the operational efficiency.

According to **Kenchi Ohmae** (mind of the strategist), there are 4 types of decisions and actions which can be termed as strategic actions and which intend to strengthen the company's position relative to its competitors. Ohmae calls them the four ways to strategic success.

They are as follows:

(a) KFS – Intensify the key factor of success.

(b) Aggressive initiative.

(c) Relative superiority.

(d) Strategic degrees of freedom.

A strategy based on **intensifying the key factor of success** emphasizes on functional differentiation or functional diversification. With this thought the company readjusts the allocation of its resources in such a way as to increase its market share and profitability. The company searches out and identifies the key factor of success in the business and then concentrates its resources into a particular area where it sees an opportunity to achieve the most significant strategic advantage over its competitors. In any business, there are some selective handful of factors which determine the outcome and result of one's efforts. These factors are called the key factors of success. For example in banking industry the key factors are collecting the money at a cheap price and lending it at a higher price. If a banker is able to collect deposits by offering a lower interest and give loans at higher interest, then he will be successful. Thus if the banker can get money at a rate which is cheaper than the rate at which he lends them, then his business as well as profitability will increase and if he is doing this more efficiently than his competitors, then his market share will expand. So the key factor of success in banking industry is to get cheap money and lending it at a higher rate. In steel industry, economies of scale is the key factor. Operating on a large-scale is more profitable there. In Ice-cream industry the ability to control the seasonal variation in supply and the ability to provide economic refrigeration throughout the distribution process are the key factors. In housing construction industry, control over the cost and speed of completion of the building are the key factors. In hotel industry quality and freshness of food items along with promptness of service are the key factors of success. Thus the strategy based on the key factor of success suggests to concentrate the scarce resources like capital, people and time on key functional or operating areas which are decisive for success of a particular business. An organization following a strategy based on KFS has to identify the key areas and apply the right mix of resources to get a superior position in the market compared to the competitors.

There are two major approaches to identify the key factors – (1) Dissection and (2) Distinction. According to the first approach the strategist dissects the market imaginatively to identify its key segments. As per the second approach the strategist distinguishes the winner companies from the losers and then analyses the difference between them. The strategists thus attempts to pinpoint the causes of their success as well as failure. For this purpose the strategist scrutinizes the whole vertical chain of business systems involving various activities right from the procurement of raw material to the supply of after sales services. Such a scrutiny will provide the inputs for developing the insight to recognize the key areas and activities to be focused for success.

The strategy based on relative superiority focuses on exploiting the competitor's weakness. It tries to achieve a relative advantage by exploiting any difference in competitive conditions between the company and its rivals. For this purpose the strategist compares the products of the own organization with those of the competitors – systematically. By this systematic and methodical comparison, he is able to identify the unique strength of his products. Thus the strategist can find out where the relative advantage for his products stand. Does this advantage exist in cost or in price? Accordingly the strategist develops activities to exploit this advantage. In this context there is a famous example of the photo-film makers Sakura and Fuji. By realizing the cost advantage, Sakura introduced a 24 exposure film at a price of 20 frame roll. So the user can pay the price of 20 frames and get 24 frames. Though the price for Sakura-roll and Fuji-roll is the same, still Sakura could attract customer by giving them more than its competitor at the same price. Thus, in order to achieve relative superiority the organization can cut down the cost and offer more to the customers in the same price, which its competitors too, are charging; or the organization can reduce the price (expand its customer-base) and offer the same or equal utilities which its competitors are also offering to the customers. So you can be a cost leader or a price leader either by keeping (controlling) the cost at the lowest or by offering a price less than your competitors. Thus organization can offer more benefits to the customers at the same price or benefits similar to its competitors in the same price and thus can prove its relative superiority over its competitors. The strategist can make use of the following means and accomplish this goal.

(a) He will make use of the technology, sales network and profitability of those of his products which are not directly competing with the target competitors.

(b) He will make use of any other differences in the composition of assets between the enterprise and its competitors.

The strategy based on aggressive initiative focuses on challenging the existing systems, methods and norms of making the business to promote creativity and flexible thinking. A strategy is effective only when it is original and is not the imitation of the competitors. So aggressive initiative focuses on asking 'why whys', i.e., on asking why should we do business this way? Why not the other way? The strategy of aggressive initiative is useful especially when (1) The industry is either stagnant or slow-growth industry and (2) your competitor is so well established that it is hard to dislodge him. Under such circumstances the only solution to get an edge over your competitors and win the competition is to adopt an unconventional strategy. Such an unconventional strategy should be aimed at upsetting the key factors for success on which the competitor has built the advantage. The competitor might have become a cost leader or a price leader. In both these situation, the competitor might have emphasized on the monetory saving which the customers will enjoy when they purchase his products. Now a company following aggressive intiative will focus on the quality of its product and propagate price as an irrelevant and unimportant factor in the purchasing decision process. It can do this by challenging and altering the different criteria for buying nationally. So it can raise a question publicly through its advertisements, as, do we purchase products and services to save money or to enjoy their utility and get maximum satisfaction. The strategist thus questions the importance and validity of price as a selling point and substitutes it by the product quality. He changes the key factor of the business and an important assumption that cost and price are the powerful tools to win the customers and replaces it by a new postulate that it is the quality of the products and services which matters most to the customers.

The strategy based on aggressive intiative has the starting point of challenging the accepted assumptions governing the way of doing the business. Thus the strategist follows the following methodology.

(1) He asks why whys? In other words he questions the utility, validity and indispensability of the then existing assumptions for making business successfully.

(2) He envisions and introduces new assumptions.

(3) He thus changes the rules of the game and upsets the *status quo*.

(4) By doing all this the strategist gains a novel and powerful advantage.

The strategy based on the strategic degree of freedom emphasizes on maximizing the user benefits. When the competition becomes more and more intense, then the company can win this competitive struggle by the deployment of product innovation. This innovation should intend to provide maximum benefits to the users. So the company should try to supply a product which will provide multiple services. For example, a milk-chocolate drink containing different minerals and vitamins and providing a complete diet and at the same time being sugar free and so having a low calorie-base, has multiple utilities for the consumers. A wrist-watch giving you accurate timing in digital form, working as a stop-watch or alarm-clock as per your need, supplying the information like altitude, atmospheric pressure, day and date, serving as a calculator is introduced to maximize the users-benefits. A mobile handset and phone, giving the facilities like sms, alarm, videography, FM radio, movie-clips, jokes-news-astrology, calculator, video-games works for the customers as a multi-use device or all-in-one device.

The innovations referred in this strategy may either modify the existing product or introduce a new product. Sometimes the strategist works to open up and develop a new market also. The intention is to exploit the market by vigorous measures in those areas which are so - far untouched by the competitors.

According to **Kenchi Ohmae** the principles governing these four methods of strategic success are as follows –

(1) Avoid doing the same thing on the same battlefield as your competitor.

(2) Adopt such measures which your competitors will find extremely hard to follow.

(3) Extend the advantage still further.

The strategic thinking by these 4 methods aims to achieve a relative advantage over the competitors by attending the competitive situation successfully. So the strategist should not imitate the strategy of his competitors. Because such an imitation will only reinforce the competitor's impact in the market. For example if your competitor is following a strategy of charging low product-price and if you imitate it by beating your drums in the same rhythm then you are in fact benefiting your competitor. Because, under such circumstances, customers will feel that there is nothing special in your product. The price advantage which you offer is already available with your competitor and is fully enjoyed by the customers. So the customers may not be interested in experimenting with your products unless there is something special for them which is different from the competitor's products. Thus repetition of the competitor's strategy does not work. In fact, by such imitation you remind the market what your competitor offers and push the customers to your competitor.

The strategist, therefore, should do something different. At the same time, this something different should be so unique and indigenous, that the competition should not be able to follow it easily. Your strategy should be very difficult for your competitors to adopt, then you can extend the competitive benefits on a large-scale for a long time.

A perfect strategy is not possible in the real world of business. Because the market is always dynamic and the business-situations change over time. Further the competitors take new steps each time and so developing a perfect and once for all strategy is impossible and is a logical fallacy. So in strategic management what counts is the good performance relative to your competitors and not the performance in absolute terms. Thus a good business – strategy is the one by which a company can gain a significant competitive advantage over its competitors at an acceptable cost. A strategist has to search out a way to do this.

SECRETS OF STRATEGIC VISION

There are certain important hints and dos and don'ts which the masters of strategic management provide as guidelines for making effective strategies. These are summarized as the secrets of strategic vision. They are as follows –

(1) **Always avoid the strategic tunnel vision –** This problem arises when the strategist start feeling more and more pressure of the competition. As a result his mental vision starts narrowing down. This situation is compared to the condition of a driver who is in great hurry and so is running the car at the highest speed. Automatically his vision gets converged on those things which are on the road ahead of him. He therefore can watch and perceive those front things, but cannot see the other things which are lying by the roadside. This happens more frequently when you are driving through a tunnel. There, you are straightway running your can in the direction of the other end of the tunnel and your vision is focused only on it. So you automatically ignore the things on the tunnel-wall. A strategist may pass through a similar situation. In strategic thinking when a broader view is needed, the view of the strategist might have been narrowed down. So he converges his attention on only one alternative and lose the sight of other various alternatives open for him to win the competition. This problem is more probable in case of those people who are obsessed with the idea of winning and so see everything in terms of success or failure. Therefore avoid this tunnel vision, develop a broader view and try to visualize mentally as many alternative solutions as are possible. The more the strategic alternatives one is able to think and envision, the greater is the possibility for development of a more effective, efficient and fruitful strategy.

(2) **Avoid all or nothing fallacy and perils of perfectionism –** Many a time, we expect hundred percent success and it becomes unattainable. Under such circumstances, we should not become disappointed and should not quit. A good strategist is always realistic and practical. So if the strategy does not bring the total success then see that at least it can bring the problem under control, overcome the obstacles and avoid the worst to happen.

Another important thing the strategist must remember is that there cannot be a perfect strategy so it is futile to try to draw a perfect strategy. Sometimes even a marginally superior strategy is sufficient to beat the competition. So avoid the perils of perfectionism. Because in trying for a perfect strategy one will ignore the time element and sometimes may remain inactive. It is said that too much analysis leads to paralysis. What is vital is timing. Therefore, even if you have a strategy giving you a slight edge over competition, it does not matter much, but, then, pay attention to put it into effect at exactly the right moment. It is not wise to go for an unending quest for ideal strategy. Do not make yourself the victim of perfectionism.

(3) **Develop flexible thinking –** Do not simply focus on few, selective strategic alternatives. Develop the full range of alternatives and constantly weigh the cost and benefits of each of them. Pay attention to the changes in the environment and respond to them earnestly. Pose the 'what-if' type questions to develop flexible thinking. For example, if the situation becomes such and such; what will be our best course of action.

(4) **Keep a watch on details –** A good strategist always keeps all details in proper perspective. He keeps an adequate watch on details before preparing the strategic plan. This helps to develop the complete understanding of the problem to be solved. Some problems are too complex and multisided. As such a clear-cut solution on such problems is hardly possible. So people avoid such problems to handle. This breeds up intellectual timidity in the organizations. Neglecting or leaving out certain problems simply because they are difficult to solve is not wisdom. This tendency causes the problem to get more momentum and to expand the sphere of its effect. So unbundle the different elements of the problem, look into all details, find out the pertinent factors building the problem, trace the interrelationship of these factors and thus get a complete grasping of the problem. Also calculate the uncertain events and estimate their positive and negative outcome.

(5) **Focus on key factors –** In every business there are certain key factors which are responsible for your performance, results and success in that business. These key factors are, in fact, handful of factors. They are not large in number but still their impact on the probability of success in that business is extensive and deep. A strategy becomes successful only if it can control these key factors enough effectively or if it can make use of these key factors skillfully for the benefit of the organization. For example in banking, collecting the money cheaply and lending it at higher rate, is the key factor. In ice-cream industry the ability to ensure economic refrigeration and to control seasonal variation is the key factor. In steel industry economies of scale in manufacturing is the key factor and in beer industry economies of scale in distribution is the key factor. Such key factors widely and deeply influence the performance and success of an organization in the respective business. So if a strategy can make their skillful application or if it can effectively control them, then such a strategy can bring more fruits to the organisation.

(6) **Challenge the constraints –** Every organization has certain limitations. These limitations form certain constraints on its performance. Such constraints and limitations are neither inevitable nor unavoidable. A change in the thinking style or approach or perspective can develop remedies on these limitations. A good strategist develops and propagates the kind of thinking which will focus on developing the ways and means to remove the constraints. The altitude to attack the limitations and make prudent efforts continuously is most needed. So the job of the strategist is to inculcate and strengthen such type of attitude and approach throughout the organization. The removal of the constraints can develop ideal state of affairs for the organization which are most beneficial. Creative and profitable lines of business activities are normally undertaken thereafter. Better fruits of the chosen strategy are then experienced. However the starting point of such a progressive step is the removal of constraints. For this purpose the strategist always has to remember the following three postulates.

(a) Constraints and limitations are the matter of our outlook, rather than the aspects of the situations. What we call as constraints, limitations or restrictions may be the simple factors of the case which we have taken negatively because these factors are not favourable to us.

(b) All constraints, limitations and restrictions are removable. There is nothing which is impossible in this world.

(c) To remove the constraints, we must develop the attitude to challenge the constraints. Those who dare, decide and determine the innovate courses of action and put them to implementation with concerted efforts; overrule the limitations and bring success to the organization. This is the indication of a good strategist.

(7) Avoid strategic schizophrenia – Sometimes different units of the company start thinking that they are independent entities and they are separate from one another. Such kind of thinking develops mutual conflict and distrust. Harmoney and team spirit, then, becomes weak. Such organizations cannot make a united concerted efforts for success. So, to avoid this strategic schizophrenia and its further effects, use a common database at the planning stage, so that, one-sided thinking and single-sided decision can be avoided. The formation of a superordinate goal, covering the objectives and targets of all different units, divisions and departments is necessary. Such a goal should consider the corporate aims and corporate benefits and it should possess the power to motivate all individuals and groups in the organization. The strategic plan should accommodate all units and divisions and should give each one of them a specific role to accomplish, which will contribute to the total organizational success. For successful strategic vision, always focus on what we can do and not on what we cannot do. The combination of the good strategic plan and sustained, wholehearted, united efforts are the pillars of corporate performance and output.

According to **Kenchi Ohmae** (The mind of the strategist), successful business strategies are the result of a particular state of mind. According to Ohmae the strategic-thought process is basically creative and intuitive rather than rational one. The rigorous rational analysis only stimulates this creative process. The insight and consequent drive of the strategist clubbed with the sense of mission fuel this thought process. This does not mean that rational analysis is totally useless in strategic thinking. Analysis, too, contributes to the strategic thinking process in the following ways:

(i) Analysis tests the ideas which are the outcome of the creative process.

(ii) Analysis works out the strategic implications of such creative ideas.

(iii) Analysis ensures the successful execution of these wild but high-potential ideas which (without analysis) otherwise would never be implemented.

Ohmae strongly believes that great strategies are like great 'Artwork' or great 'Discoveries'. The great artwork or great scientific invention, of course, requires technical mastery in respective areas; but such great things originate in insights. And these creative insights are beyond the conscious analysis of anybody. Ohmae refers to the outstanding performance of some of the Japanese corporations and accredits it to their super strategies. He points out that those strategies are the result of the great natural talent of their strategists. In the opinion of Kenchi Ohmae the good strategists have an intuitive grasp of the basic elements of a strategy. They have an idiosyncratic mode of thinking in which the company, customers and competition merge in a dynamic interaction. As a result of this; a comprehensive set of objectives and action plans eventually crystalise. The key to this strategic thinking process is insight. This process is intuitive, creative as well as disruptive. It is disruptive in the sense that it attacks and disturbs the *status quo*.

Developing a new strategy – There are normally three distinct phases in the development of a new strategy. They are

(a) Analysis.
(b) Planning.
(c) Implementation.

Analysis provides the basis for making choices, planning provides direction and implementation brings the results. During analysis, collect more and more background information. It is most necessary to collect wide information about the following matters.

(i) The happenings inside the organisation.
(ii) Information about what the customers want. (The pattern of their consumption, changing consumption style and priorities, etc.)
(iii) Information about the competitors and their operations.
(iv) Information about the research and development trends in the industry.

On the basis of this information and analysis, prepare the statement of strengths and weaknesses of the organisation. Then enlist the future opportunities.

The second phase is planning. The data collected and analysed should be used as basis to make decisions which will bring the company close to your aim. Then consider the advantages over the competitors and set the boundaries within which to operate. The strategist lists out the products and services which will be in demand in future. Also the strategist enlists the markets which will be available in future. The efforts to prepare the list of products, services and markets, make the strategist to foresee and predict the future business opportunities and possibilities. The strategist makes this prediction on the basis of the analysis of the information collected. After this the strategist chooses which of the markets he wish to develop with the existing products or new products. He also points out which markets are to be left out or vacated as they are not beneficial to the organisation. This helps the strategist to decide future position of the company and to work out a realistic budget.

Strategy implementation relates to determining what the company can do and how. For effective strategy implementation, it is necessary to communicate the strategy to everyone concerned. To achieve the strategic goal sometimes smaller changes are made in the techniques and methods of teamwork. On the other hand in some situations, strategy-implementation may require certain far reaching drastic changes in the organisation and learning of new skills.

SHORT-TERM AND LONG-TERM THINKING

Short-term and long-term thinking is an integral part of strategy formulation and development. Only thinking for long-term goals or thinking for short-term goals is useless. So the strategist should direct the company to work hard for the achievement of long-term goals and simultaneously make it strive for the immediate results. The strategist further should build strategic thinking in making day to day decisions and consider the long-term implications before commiting to action.

For good strategic thinking, it is essential to strike a balance between the short-term and long-term goals and planning. It is usually seen that some organizations focus only on short-term success and eventually risk the long-term failure. Short-term planning deals with the immediate future whereas long-term planning looks into the far away future. A company concentrating only on short-term gains is tempted to produce and sell its existing products and services without paying attention to quality improvement, product modification and innovation. Contrary to this view, a company fully focusing on long-term goals will ignore the present business opportunities and thus may lose the market and customer. So it is wise to foresee the future business opportunities, but at the same time, be realistic about what you can achieve presently. In order to ensure the good business of tomorrow, it is necessary to maintain a good market-share today. One should never forget that undue emphasis on long term planning may cause the present business to suffer. So focus on the present to achieve the growth you need now and also keep an eye on future to ensure that today's good decisions are equally beneficial tomorrow.

Balancing the short-term and long-term planning needs appropriate efforts and discipline. Sometimes more time and energy is used to attend the operational issues (short-term targets) and the long-term objectives are ignored. To avoid such things, follow the methodology given below.

(1) Prepare a timetable to produce and maintain your strategic plan. Follow the timetable strictly. Avoid getting distracted by operational issues.

(2) Allocate appropriate time and resources to strategy and operations. Stick to that plan.

(3) Strategy-development is a continuous process. So, even, when your plan becomes operational, do not neglect future planning.

(4) Set aside one day in a fortnight to discuss the issues relating to the development and implementation of the strategic plan with your team.

(5) Keep regular communication with your customers and accordingly review the roles of your team.

(6) Often keep the strategic plan fresh by revising the goals and methods of working from time to time. Ensure that the members of the team involved in strategy-development remain committed and focused.

(7) See that, every step in the planning process is practical and achievable. Decide precisely when to act. Do not spend time in over-analysis as it leads to paralysis.

(8) Do not jump to conclusions. Collect and review all pertinent facts before drawing any conclusion.

(9) Give sufficient chance to the team-members to air their views, comments and observations in the meeting. Encourage them to research the facts and brainstorm them for working out beautiful, original ideas.

(10) Maintain maximum flexibility in the strategic plan. As the failure market changes, your plan must be able to incorporate in it, suitable alterations.

An effective strategic plan has the following three basic elements

(a) Accurate information.

(b) Strong ideas.

(c) Committed people.

In every organisation, there are some people who have interest in the strategy or who can influence the strategy-development. They are the superior-executives, the staff-experts, key-functionaries, major suppliers and main customers. They can be collectively termed as strategy-stakeholders. All these stakeholders can provide valuable and useful advice, information and resources to the strategist. When more and more key persons are involved in strategic planning, the spirit of cooperation is automatically increased and so better results become possible. When the plan is ready, its implementation should be accurate and precise. This requires commitment of the staff which can be gained by developing a motivating atmosphere in the organisation. This motivating atmosphere requires two way open communication and participative managerial style.

The foundation of an effective strategic plan is the accurate and up to date factual information. Guesswork or prediction without a scientific basis cause a strategy to collapse. So it is essential to collect all relevant information before arriving to any conclusion. If some data is missing, then, consider the full range of probable facts, before making any decision.

Strong valid ideas are the outcome of realistic creative thinking. Wild imagination and too much rational analysis are the two mutually opposite extremes; between which, realistic creative thinking is the golden-mean. To combine creativity and realism together, (i) consider the key trends in the market which are tobe monitored. (ii) Pinpoint the possible product choices of the customers. (iii) Suggest (by using the two above) the new innovative ways to gain a competitive advantage.

Brainstorming sessions are the most useful tools to develop realistic creative ideas. In a brainstorming session, each member of the strategic planning team expresses his idea. The team leader gives his/her opinion, but does not dominate the debate. The spontaneity is to be encouraged. The team-members listen to one another, contribute their observations and suggestions without being critical to one another. In order to make the brainstorming most fruitful, create a comfortable and relaxed environment so that each member will feel free to express his ideas. Make the seating arrangement informal with all members facing each other. In the first instance, allow each member to speak out his ideas openly. In the second stage refine all these ideas and in the third stage sort out them into groups.

For developing a strong strategy, analysis of the business of the company is to be made at the beginning. This analysis includes the following.

(1) Assessment of environmental influences.

(2) Understanding fully the customers.

(3) Analysing the competitors.

(4) Identifying the opportunities as well as threats.

(5) Assessing own skills and capabilities.

Assessment of environmental influences includes making a detail and up to date analysis of political, economic, legal, technological and demographic environment. The changes in political governance, political system, political policy and international relations have widespread and deep impact on the business and industry as a whole. Economic policies and the reforms programme can produce an effect on the position of the company and its future growth. The industrial and labour laws as well as the role of government in economic development expands or restricts the possibilities of business expansion, foreign collaborations and the status and attractiveness of such economic activities. The pace of technological progress affects the cost and quality of the products and services. Changes in the size and composition of population affects the market potential. So the environmental analysis and assessment is the first task in pinpointing the position of your organisation.

Customer is the driving force behind all economic and business activities.

The process of understanding your customers involve following activities.

(i) Analysing why your customers purchase your products and services.

(ii) Researching out what is their ideal.

All customers do not have the same desires and expectations. So the research and analysis as above is needed. It provides information about the priority and preference of the customers needs. This helps the strategist to design a strategy which will serve the customers in a better manner. In order to create and develop loyal customers, one must know their preferential buying criterion. The preferential buying criterion contain the different aspects of a product or service which a buyer considers on a preferential basis while choosing a product or service and making a buying decision, such as quality of the product, price of the product, company patronage or satisfactory customer service. So, it is seen that, normally, there are four buying criterion which a buyer uses in his own preferential way. They are – (i) Product-price (ii) Product-quality (iii) Customer-service (iv) Company patronage – Every buyer may use these criteria in a different order. For some buyers quality may be an important consideration, for some price and for some other customer-service. – So try to know what your customers prefer – Quality? Economical price? Prompt customer service? Company relations? Then find out what your customers see as ideal offering in respect of the three Ps, namely, Product, Process and Price. So assess –

(i) What do you supply – which products of what quality?

(ii) How do you deal with the customers?

(iii) What price do you charge? How much do your products cost to your customers? The answers to these questions tell us that –

(1) Customers want error-free products

(2) Customers usually prefer the user-friendly products, which do not require any special knowledge or training to use.

(3) Customers want prompt attendance, fast and efficient ordering and delivery, accurate invoicing and after sales service.

(4) Customers expect the sales people to possess full product knowledge. Further they expect satisfactory clarifications and explanations of their querries, doubts and objections.

(5) Customers want the product-price to be reasonable. It should not be exorbitant, exploitative or inflated. The price should relate to the product-quality. In the modern competitive market, the low-price product segment is expanding very fast. Nowadays, many customers look for cheap and best options.

(6) Credit facility and installment-purchase are becoming more popular. Customers now prefer those companies which offer them favourable credit terms and easy installment-payment for the products to be purchased.

Analysis of competitors is again an important pre-requisite for developing a strong strategy. When your performance is better than your competitors, then only you will become successful. So simply meeting your customers is not sufficient, but one has to do this in a manner much better than his competitors. Analysis and evaluation of the capabilities of the competitors will help to identify the potential opportunities and threats in the market. So in the first instance identify and pinpoint your key competitors. Then survey the changing requirements of the customers. Because such changes will have a lot of effect on the future market. Be sure that your competitor will also be thinking of exploiting these changes which give birth to new opportunities. Find out whether your competitors possess the necessary capabilities. If he has those, then, that constitutes a threat for you. If your approach and abilities are in no way different than your competitors, then you will not derive any competitive advantage.

Assessment of self-skills and capabilities enables the strategist to plan realistically. When a plan is prepared after a due and reasonable evaluation of the organisation's own resources, team-skills, information systems, work-methods and processes; then, it is more realastic and practical. In order to face the competition successfully, one must have a proper understanding of one's own capabilities as well as the capabilities of one's competitors. So besides the competitor's analysis; it is necessary to make self-analysis and self evaluation. It does not mean that one's own weaknesses should be allowed to limit the strategy. The organisation, therefore, should note the areas requiring improvement and build them into the plan. As the market is dynamic, no product or business process lasts forever. In this fast changing business, everyone therefore, is required to improve one's own skills and capacities. To improve the business-processes, the organisation has to follow the steps as under –

(i) Make a close examination of own business-processes. Focus on reviewing the process of receiving and confirming orders, distributing and delivering products, supplying after-sales-service, fixing the terms and condition of sale.

(ii) See whether there are – (a) duplications, (b) gaps or (c) complaints regarding any of the above business-process.

(iii) Check out your information-system. Find out whether it provides you – (a) right information, (b) at right time, (c) in right form and (d) at least cost.

(iv) Assess the skills and capacities of your team members. But do not play the role of an examiner directly. Encourage the team members to make a self-assessment. Ask them to review and discuss openly about their own strengths and weaknesses. Maintain an informal, friendly and cooperative atmosphere at such meeting.

(v) Locate the deficiencies, weaknesses and the areas requiring improvement. Enlist them according to their urgency. Find out, which areas require immediate correction, rectification and improvement. Also classify them as areas requiring minor improvement and major improvement.

(vi) Design improvement programmes in consultation with the concerned executives and officers in charge of related business-processes. Communicate the programme to the employees working at operating level.

(vii) Intervene the improvement programme in the strategic plan.

PLANNING THE STRATEGY

Strategic planning is a continuous process. The formulation of a strategic plan involves the following stages.

(a) Defining and deciding the purpose.

(b) Determining the competitive advantage.

(c) Developing focus and setting boundaries.

(d) Estimating budgets.

Every business has a primary as well as a secondary purpose. The primary purpose describes the cause of existence of the organisation. Why the organisation exists in the business? What is its main goal? The purpose of the strategy should fit with the purpose of the organisation. If the organisation aims at fast growth, then the strategic-purpose must support the fast-growth and must provide means and methods to accomplish the fast growth. The statement of strategic-purpose should be clear and brief. Further the strategic-purpose should be to the point and action-oriented.

Determination of an enduring competitive advantage is the second step of strategic planning. The organisation can decide its competitive advantage by identifying its distinctive capabilities. The organisation must be doing certain things so nicely that sets it apart from its competitors. e.g. A particular organisation is extremely efficient in innovation, another one is efficient in extensive and aggressive marketing, again some others in getting cheap finance, etc. This distinctive capability provides the competitive advantage to that organisation and acts as the backbone of its strategy. The competitive advantage must be enduring. That is to say that the competitive advantage should last for a considerably longer period. A particular organisation may be enjoying multiple advantages. However all of them may not be enduring. Further a tactful combination of these different advantages may result into the development of an enduring competitive advantage. So find out how your organisation can develop an enduring competitive advantage. For this purpose, do the following –

(1) Make detail review of your strengths. Remember that to qualify it as a true advantage a strength must be recognized as a strength by your customers.

(2) Summarise all your competitive advantages. Ask yourself a question for this purpose; - why your customers have not switched over to your competitors?

(3) Apply the test of time to trace the enduring advantage. A competitive advantage which will last longer is the enduring advantage. An advantage which will be lost in the near future is of no better use. So test all advantages on the basis of time. Ask yourself how long in future, will you enjoy a particular benefit and accordingly decide the durability of each such advantage.

Developing the focus and setting up the boundaries is the third step/stage in strategic planning. The development of focus involves indentifying the products and markets that are considered worthwhile area for giving more time, resources and attention. This focus and emphasis is required to be reviewed and revised from time to time, because of the change in circumstances.

In the process of focusing, the organisation concentrates its efforts and resources on some of its products and markets which will prove tobe more profitable and productive to it in future. The organisation decides where to focus in the light of the analysis of competitive advantage. It has to select those products and markets which will give it the enduring competitive advantage. Similarly focusing is alligned with setting the boundaries. Setting up the boundaries relate to planning and deciding what you are not going to do. In other words it is a process which brings more preciseness and specificity in your focus. It sharpens the focus and develops an acute convergence in it. Focusing decides as to which products and markets, we will serve and boundaries setting determines as to which products and markets, we will not attend in future. In one way, boundaries setting is the corollary of focusing. Boundaries setting is essential because there are different product and market options available to the organisation. The organisation may not be able to make and serve all these products and customers with the same level of efficiency, economy and effectiveness and so it becomes most essential to choose the products and markets to be attended as well as to be left out. This choice helps to utilise the physical and nonphysical resources in the most profitable manner. Boundaries-setting prevents people from wasting their time and energy on unwanted and comparatively less beneficial opportunities. It helps to choose those markets and customers who will provide an enduring benefit to the organisation. In other words it will help to focus on those products which will have a longer utility-life and so which will be demanded in the market for a long time. Also it will help to focus on those customers who will be there in the market for a long term. Setting up the boundaries bring greater ease and definiteness in fixing and deciding the target markets. Trying all things for all people leads to lack of focus, thin spread up of resources and ultimate failure. Boundaries setting and targeting the customers is described as a rifle approach as against the nonfocussed shotgun approach. Focusing and boundary setting has following important benefits.

(i) Focus improves effectiveness. The more the organisation brings focus in its strategy and operations the greater is the effectiveness in its performance.

(ii) As the organisation starts concentrating on specific markets, it becomes more knowledgeable about its customers' consumption and buying behaviour.

(iii) Focussing and boundaries setting helps for making market-segmentation. Market can be segmented by region, size growth-potential, volume and value of buying, distribution channel, etc.

While setting up boundaries, try to avoid too many or too few boundaries. Because too many boundaries will narrow down the business opportunities of the organisation and thus restrict and limit the scope of business of the organisation. As against this, too few boundaries will cause to lack of focus, leading to lower level performance and profitability.

The fourth stage in strategic planning is preparation of budgets. At this stage, cost estimations and profit forecasting is made. The costs of allocating the resources for the chosen products and markets are predicted. The profit from this business is then forecasted. The estimated cost and profit is compared to calculate the net financial return. If this net-return is quite satisfactory and possesses a higher probability of realization, then the strategic plan is worth accepting and executing.

Two precautions are always to be taken during strategic – planning.

(a) Before making any decision regarding the strategic alternative, always consider its implications well in advance before finalising the decision.

(b) Do not make the assumption that, you are doing everything in the right way. So review, modify and update your strategic decisions and actions regularly.

IMPLEMENTING THE STRATEGY

Strategy implementation is a process of activating a strategy. It is a process of putting the strategic plan into action. Strategy formulation and strategy implementation are in fact intertwined processes. They are two types of linkages between strategy-formulation and strategy-implementation. They are – (i) Forward linkages and (ii) Backward linkages. Strategy formulation results into certain changes in the organisation which are required to be made for effective strategy-implementation. These are forward linkages. Further strategy-formulation is also affected by factors related with strategy-implementation. A strategist has to consider about the aspects of execution of the strategy while formulating it. Thus he should plan, what can be possibly executed. The strategist should not choose those strategic alternatives which cannot be executed due to organizational limitations.

With the formulation of a new strategy or modification of the existing one, certain changes are required to be made in the organizations. These changes may relate to the organizational structure, leadership style, resources allocation, etc. To activate the strategy, such changes are essential. However such changes, most of the time, are in the form of incremental changes or modifications. A strategy requiring a complete total drastic change in the organisational structure, leadership, work – culture, resources – allocation is very difficult to execute and so such strategic choices are normally left out. Usually, organizations tend to adopt those strategies, which can be implemented with the help of present structure and resources and a little more additional efforts. The changes which a strategy demands for its implementation, must be within the capacity of the organisation to incorporate.

The changes required for strategy implementation take the organisation from where it stands to where it wishes to reach. So these changes, mostly, are in the form of improvements. Thus strategic implementation involves setting those change-projects in motion which will achieve the objectives of the strategy. These changes/improvements should be introduced in such a tactful manner that they will upgrade the future performance and at the same time will keep the present performance at the peak. This has to be paid special attention because usually when some changes are introduced, it affects the present performance and simultaneously give birth to resistance. The resistance to change is on account of psychological factors like fear and insecurity, economic factors like reduced income and more expenditure and social factors like loss of status, dismantling of group, changes in social relationship, etc. Whenever changes in the work, procedure, structure or system in the organisation are suggested, the first reaction, many times, of the employees is fright and tension. A feeling of insecurity develops *en masse*. People have the fear that they will not be able to cope up with the changed environment, their earnings may reduce and cost of living may increase, their social bondings and relations at work place and outside may get disturbed, etc. This automatically breeds up the resistance to change. Such a negative feeling and resistance can be reduced and removed, through proper and timely communication of the change-projects and through persuasion and counseling. However, besides resistance, there is an adverse effect on the performance. This happens due to the indifference and carelessness which minutely springs up due to proposed change. People feel that the proposed change will alter my job-position, role and responsibility, the status and importance of my work and department, the nature of my job and many more such things. Then, under such circumstances, they lose their interest and inclination for their present job.

They ask a simple question, that anyhow if our works and methods are going to change, why should we make more efforts in the present job. If I am going to be transferred to a new position/location/department with next few days, then why should I waste my energy in the present job? This attitudes deteriorates the quality of work, lowers the performance level and spoils the spirit of excellence. Therefore it is necessary to maintain and elevate the present performance by usuing tact as well as the motivational and control skills.

For effective implementation of strategy, systematic execution of improvement-programme (change project) is very much needed. For systematically making the required improvements, following three functions are to be made. They are –

(i) Prioritising the changes/improvements.

(ii) Listing out the improvements.

(iii) Identifying gaps.

To prioritise improvements, firstly, identify the areas of improvement. For this purpose, the strategist has to compare the current situation with the ideal. This comparison will give the strategist the idea about the gaps between the ideal and the current. On the basis of this comparision, the strategist can group all those very important and critical changes, which are to be immediately made for good implementation of strategy.

Listing up of improvements include preparation of a comprehensive list of about 50 to 100 critical issues, which need improvement for the success of the strategy. The strategist, while listing up the improvements, has to deal with the most important areas for improvement first. Always think of the ideal to get an insight to make improvement in respect of your own business processes, technology and people. Always look for the best that you can do in each area.

The review of current situation and its comparison with the ideal will reveal the gaps. The strategist then should focus on the major gaps. Major gaps are those gaps in respect of which the corrective action is must. To identify the major gaps, do the following –

(i) Look at your customers handling processes. Are you attending your customers' orders, enquiries, service – requests or grievances promptly and positively ? Think – what further steps can be taken up to improve these processes.

(ii) Assess your technology and resources. Does the technology need upgradation? Are the resources sufficient and efficient?

(iii) Evaluate the skills, experience and abilities of your staff. Have you given right job to the right person? Do your people need extra induction and training to work under changed circumstances?

When the listing of different areas for improvement is made, it is useful to classify and catagorise them as high medium and low on the basis of impact and urgency. The following illustrative matrix can provide sufficient idea in catagorising and prioritising areas requiring improvements.

IMPACT		**High**	**Medium**	**Low**
	High	Product Quality	Product Price	Technology [upgradation]
	Medium	Customers Service	Cost control and Cost reduction	Product (New) Development
	Low	Sales-promotion and Advertising	Employees' Training	Dealers' Training
		High	**Medium**	**Low**

Urgency

Fig. 2.1 Activities in an organisation

The above matrix displays the different activities in an organisation requiring improvement. All these areas have different impact and urgency. As per this matrix product-quality is the area which requires immediate attention and improvement and this area and the improvements have high impact on the organisation and its strategy. Next is the area of product price, then technology, then customer-service, cost control and cost reduction, New product development, sales promotion and strategy, employee training and the area having least impact is dealers-training. The high impact areas require improvements to be made necessarily, whereas the low-impact areas may not require major or drastic improvements. However, certain minor improvement are to be made in respect of these areas on the basis of urgency.

When urgency is taken as a sole criterion; product quality, customer service and sales promotion and advertising are the areas requiring immediate improvement, weather major or minor; depending upon their impact. Product pricing, cost-control and cost reduction and the employees training even though do not require immediate improvement have tobe dealt with at the second level of priority. Technology upgradation, New product development and dealers' training are the area which have lowest urgency in respect of introducing any change or improvements.

The strategist has to deal with those changes which have high urgency and high impact and thereafter the other areas according to urgency and impact. It is always better to make necessary changes well in advance and before they become most urgent.

For effective improvements, a disciplined approach is necessary. A planned change plays a vital role in successful implementation of the strategy. Therefore to bring discipline and efficiency in change-projects, workout action plans with objectives, milestones and time-scales. As change-projects are, mostly, aimed at improving long-term operational effectiveness, their complete execution may sometimes take one and half years to two years depending upon their complexity and wide application, so each change – project should be broken up into action plans. Each action plan must have a predecided time-scale with the starting and completion dates. Further each action plan must have a definite, specific objectives.

When an organisation effects changes and improvements for future at the same time, it is continuing its present operational plans and targets, that rules its today's business. When the change – projects and improvements are underway, the organisation has to review its operations and processes to accommodate the changes. Each change project has a goal which is divided into specific objectives for action plans. These objectives must define what the action plan is trying to achieve and when. The objectives must have the following characteristics –

(i) **Stretching capacity (or challenging capacity):** The objectives must be challenging, enough so that, the managers and their teams will enjoy thrill in trying to achieve them.

(ii) **Measurable:** The objectives should be quantifiable, then only they can be precisely measurable. Remember that, what we measure; we value and of course what we do not measure; we do not value.

(iii) **Achieveable:** The objectives must be realistic and practical, so that, the team is able to achieve them. Unachieveable objectives cause frustration and develop a feeling of failure which has a demoralizing effect.

(iv) **Relatedness:** The objectives must be related to the customers and so they should improve service to them The objectives must talk about better customers' services.

(v) **Time targets:** The time for achieving the objectives must be specified. The end-dates, i.e. the dates by which the objectives are to be achieved; should be prescribed.

In short the objectives of the action plan should be 'SMART' objectives (Stretching – Measurable – Achievable – Related – Time-targeted). Furthermore a particular manager should be given the overall responsibility of the action plan. This will bring greater accountability in implementing the change – projects or improvements. The manager will further allocate specific jobs and roles to the members of his team.

The change-projects are time-taking and so we divide them into action plan. To bring greater speed and preciseness in implementing the action plan, we have to set out milestones. The milestones are events or small achievements which help to measure the progress in implementation. They also help to check out whether the actions and task are made in the right direction. Milestones break down the work into a series of tasks and thus keeps a watch whether the change-project is on the right track. Milestones provide direction for the progress of the change-projects.

Besides milestones, setting up of time-targets is another important thing to be done to bring discipline, definiteness and disposition in implementing change-projects. The specific time allotted to each improvement, makes possible the introduction of improvements systematically and timely. As we know that some changes have high impact and some have low impact. So, sometimes, the low impact changes may be sidetracked and ignored due to other important operational issues. Specific accountability for improvements and time-scale helps to avoid such situations of indisciplined and haphazard implementation of change-projects. At the same time it is useful to record the progress of change-projects. This will provide the tool for introspection and also will give the direction for further progress.

Strategy implementation has following important aspects.

(1) Project Implementation.

(2) Procedural Implementation.

(3) Resources Allocation.

(4) Structural Implementation.

(5) Behavioural Implementation.

(6) Functional and Operational Implementation.

In fact strategy implementation covers nearly all aspects of good organizational management and administration. Strategies lead to plans which leads to programmes and programmes lead to projects. A programme covers goals, policies, procedures, rules and actions to activate the plan. A project is defined as a highly specific programme for which time-schedule and costs are predetermined. Projects create the infrastructure needed for day to day operations in an organisation.

Project Implementation: The **Project Management Institute of United States** defines a project in the following words – A project is a one-shot, goal-directed, major undertaking requiring commitment of varied skills and resources.

According to **Newman, Summer, and Warren,** a project is a cluster of activities which are relatively separate and clear-cut. A project typically has a distinct mission that it is designed to achieve and a clear termination point which is the achievement of the mission.

Gittinger defines project as the whole complex of activities involved in using resources to gain benefits.

According to **Dr. Vasant Desai** a well-planned project includes the following –

(a) A correct consideration of alternatives.

(b) Identification of key issues.

(c) Broad participation.

(d) Compactness and enforceability.

Project-implementation is defined as a process of expeditious completion of the project within the budgeted resources. Now for the proper implementation of the project, it must be –

- Nice,
- Neat,
- Clear-cut and
- Specific.

The key issues in project implementation are

(i) The pattern of investment.

(ii) Benefits or gain.

(iii) Time-limit and

(iv) Coordination of activities leading to effective and efficient implementation of the project.

Procedural Implementation: This deals with studying and following different legal provisions, govt. orders, rules and regulations. Some of the important legislations and regulations to be paid due attention are – Company Law – rules and regulations, SEBI requirements, MRTP Labour Legislations, Patenting and Trademark requirements, Consumer Protection requirements and Environmental Protection and Pollution Control requirements.

Resources Allocation: This aspect of strategy implementation deals with procurement and distribution of resources to strategic tasks. Financial resources are primary source which are needed to create, develop and maintain physical and human resources. Finance is the life-blood of any organisation without adequate financial support, no strategy can work well. Finance is required for long-term as well as short-term purposes. The **long-term finance** is used for acquisition of capital assets and **short-term finance** is used for working capital. Finance is raised through internal or/and external sources. **Internal sources of finance** include retained earnings, reserves like general reserve, development rebate and investment allowance, provision for depreciation, provision of taxation. **External sources of finance** include shares, stocks, debentures, bonds, loans and advances from banks and financial institutions, public deposits, bills of exchange, trade credit, etc. Normally for strategies involving modernization, diversification and expansion; external sources of finance are tapped. Because such strategies require huge capital for long-term. For stability and slow growth strategies internal sources are tapped. However while choosing a particular source of finance, the cost of capital is an important consideration.

After the procurement of financial resources the next step is their allocation. There are two approaches to resources-allocation which are exactly opposite to one another. They are – (i) Top-down approach and (ii) Bottom up approach. In the **top-down approach** of resources-allocation the top-management (consisting of Board of Directors, Managing Director or CEO) decides the requirements of different operating units and accordingly makes the distribution of resources. As agains this in the **bottom up approach** each operating unit intimates its need for resources through requisition and all these requisitions are collected and aggregated for resources-allocation. Therefore bottom up approach is described as aggregation method of resources allocation whereas top-down approach is called as segregation method of resources-allocation. Some organizations combine both approaches for resources-allocation. This combination approach is termed as strategic budgeting. It takes into account the strategic factors like environmental changes, core competencies, marketing capability of the organisation and past performance and their likely impact on strategy implementation and objectives achievement. This budget considers resources – availability and corporate policy while formulating the budget. The traditional budget puts stress on accounting whereas strategic budget is a dynamic tool of the management for more tactful and purposive allocation of resources.

There are various **means of resources-allocation** besides the above mentioned strategic budget. They are as follows –

(i) BCG matrix : The Boston Consulting Group provides a graphic representation of the different businesses of an organisation on the basis of the relative market share of each business and the industry growth rate. The vertical axis denotes the industry growth rate which is the rate of growth in sales in percentage for a particular industry. The horizontal axis shows the relative market share which is calculated as the ratio of a company's sales to the sale of industry's largest competitor.

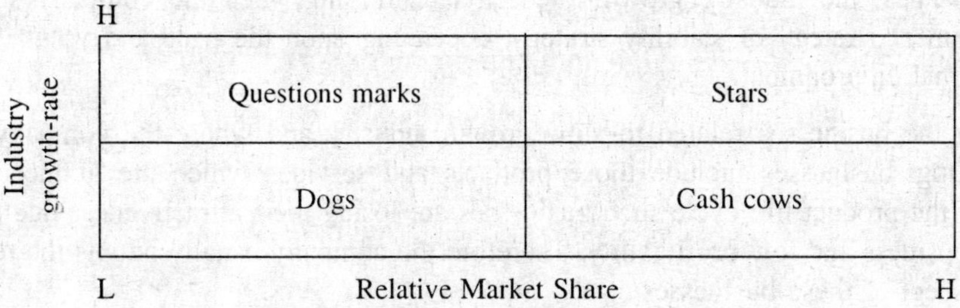

L – Low, H – High

Fig. 2.2 BCG Matrix

Relative Market Share

(i) Stars are the products (businesses) of the organisation which have high market share and where the industry-growth-rate is also high.

(ii) Cash cows are the products (businesses) of the organisation which have high market share but the growth of the industry is at a low rate.

(iii) Dogs are the products (businesses) which have low industry growth rate and low market share.

(iv) Question marks are the products (businesses) in respect of which the industry growth rate is high, but the market share of the organisation is low.

Now a company pursuing expansion strategy will focus on 'star' products as the industry for 'star' business is growing at a fast rate. Naturally more resources are required to be allocated for star-businesses to acquire a strong competitive position. Because presently stars have below our expectation, market share, which can be further improved by well-planned efforts.

Cash-cows businesses are giving maximum income to the organisation presently, because the market share of the organisation in respect of them is sufficiently large. They are the most profitable businesses of the organisation today. However the growth rate that industry is low and so the future of these businesses is dim and uncertain. So the organisation should adopt the stability strategy in respect of these businesses. This means that no more further investments in these businesses. The resources-allocation for them will be moderate and with a view to maintain the current optimum profitability. But no expansion in respect of these businesses. There another probable danger in respect of cash cows businesses. Such businesses may lose their utility, validity and relevance in future and they may, then, start making losses. So, by analyzing the future of these businesses with the help of sales forecasting, trend analysis and market surveys, a strategy of phased retrenchment should be adopted in respect of them.

Question marks are the business with high industry growth rate, but low market share. Question marks are the new products or services with good potential. They can be converted into 'stars' by making enough investments. The company can acquire a dominant market share by being aggressive in respect of question marks. It can focus on cost reduction or product differentiation to get the market leader position. Since question marks have good business potential due to the high growth rate of the industry – expansion – strategy in respect of them is more preferable. However if due to the external environmental factors such as govt. policy, political instability, economic changes and demographic changes, the industry growth-rate starts decreasing; then the company should better adopt a retrenchment strategy or stability strategy, depending upon the pace and volume of adverse changes in external environment.

'Dogs' are the businesses related to slow growth industry and where the company has a low market share. Dogs-businesses include those products and services which are at the declining or sinking stage of the product life cycle such businesses are losing their attractiveness due to high cost of running the business and low profitability. Therefore the company usually adopts the retrenchment – strategy in respect of these businesses.

The BCG matrix thus, provides guidelines and direction for resources allocation.

(ii) PLC based budgeting: This method of resources-allocation links up the distribution of resources with the stages in the product life cycle. The product life cycle explains that a product passes through, generally, four stages namely, introduction, growth, maturity and decline. At the stages of introduction and growth more resources are to be allocated to the product. Because at these stages the product requires proper nurturing through resources – support. At these stages the product is moving towards getting established in the market. It can become the market leader and can acquire number one position. At this stage the customer-response to the product is increasing. Especially at the introduction stage, greater resources support is needed to bring brand awareness. Because the product is new. At the growth-stage again more resources should be allocated to the product because at this stage the product is becoming more and more popular and customers response and sales are increasing. However, still, the product is facing competition and so it needs a greater resources support for making extensive and aggressive marketing sales-promotion and advertising.

The product at the maturity stage is an established product and is having the highest sale. In other words it is a cash cow product. Therefore the company, simply, has to match its production and sales with the demand in the market. At this stage though the product-sales is at its maximum level, there is nil growth or a very thin marginal growth in sales. So it is not useful to invest more resources in this product. A stability strategy is, therefore, preferable.

A product at the declining stage is a sinking product. The sales are fast decreasing, the customer response is negative and the product is losing its attractiveness and utility. Therefore, retrenchment strategy is the best option in respect of such products.

(iii) Zero-based budgeting: Zero-based budgeting is a kind of budgeting technique which requires fresh calculation of costs, for resources-allocation, each time. In traditional budgeting, the expenditure of the previous year is taken as the basis for allocation of resources for the current year.

The zero-based budgeting, on the other hand, adopts, a different approach. It uses 'zero ground' as the basis. It makes a start right from the scratch. It asks that if the activity is to start for the first time, then how much resources should be allocated to them. It considers the validity of the activity and then decides whether it has got any relevance or not and accordingly is it worthwhile to spend money and allocate resources for such an activity. Zero-based budgeting is on the line of perfect budgeting and so insists on making fresh calculation of costs and other estimates each year instead of using costs of the preceding year as the basis. It also suggests that while making such fresh calculations; the validity, need and usefulness of the activity, task or operation should be considered and reconsidered each time. Thus zero-based budgeting questions the validity of each item of cost and does not accept it simply because the said expenditure is incurred in the previous year and so should be allowed and made for the current year. Zero-based budgeting brings greater rationality in budgeting. It points out that the budgetary estimates should be made on the basis of the analysis of the factors of cost and not on the basis of the assumptions about the costs. Because circumstances and situations change over the time and so past calculations and predictions may not now remain as realistic and relevant. Some costs might have increased and some might have decreased. Further some tasks and costs might have now become unnecessary. Therefore spending money on them is unwise and wasteful. The resources allocation should always be purposeful, productive and useful. This objective is achieved more precisely with the help of zero-based budgeting.

(iv) **Parta System :** This is a control device for management control. It is a daily budgeting and financial reporting system. It makes daily assessment of net cash inflows from operations, before tax and dividend. This is useful to keep an up to date knowledge about the cash resources. The daily recording of cash inflows provides the precise information of cash balance on a daily basis. This is useful for appropriate allocation of cash resources on the basis of urgency and impact. Again there is a concept of budgeted parta which is a predecided amount of net cash inflow. The budgeted parta is forecasted and decided by the chairman and the incharge of the strategic business unit. This budgeted parta or forecasted cash inflow gives idea about the cash position in the near future, which provides necessary direction for the resources allocation. A comparision between the budgeted and actual parta can help to evaluate the changing condition of the business of the organisation.

Though there are different techniques and methods of resources-allocation; in actual practice it is a very complicated job. Several internal and external factors affect the process of resources-allocation. Among the internal factors, the priority of the strategic tasks, the internal politics in the organisation and the preference of the dominant strategist are the major factors. The different strategic tasks have different priority from the viewpoint of the company management. Naturally resources are allocated according to that priority. Moreover the internal power politics affects resources-allocation. Each department tries to pull more resources. Because more resources are equated with more power. Again the preference of the CEO to different strategic tasks and departments has an effect on resources-allocation.

Besides the internal factors, again there are external factors affecting resources-allocation. The major external factors are government rules and regulations, expectations of the shareholders and the restrictions imposed by the financial institutions. Government sets rules for pollution control, waste disposal, labour welfare. Accordingly the company has to set aside resources and spend money for their compliance. Sometimes the expectations of the shareholders in respect of dividend, rise up and so the company has to pay higher divided which results into a greater outflow of cash resources. The financial institutions which lend huge loans and participate in the capital of the company imposes restrictions on the company regarding disbursement of resources or making of investment. This also affects the resources-allocation of the company.

□□□

CHAPTER 3

STRATEGY IMPLEMENTATION

STRUCTURAL IMPLEMENTATION

An organisational structure in the simplest sense is the way in which different tasks and subtasks are arranged. The diagrammatic display of on the organisational structure is made on the organisational chart. But a chart simply shows the skeleton of the organisation but does not depict the mechanism of organising. The strategist has to create the structure, activate it and redesign it to suit it for strategy implementation. A strategist therefore has to look deep upto the process of organising and thus create a good and sustainable structure. For this purpose the strategist has to do the following:

(i) Identifying and describing the major tasks which are vital for strategy implementation.

(ii) Classifying and grouping the tasks on the basis of the skills required for their performance.

(iii) Delegation of authority and determination of responsibility to complete the task.

(iv) Developing and maintaining appropriate communication and coordination among the departments, work groups and employees to build up teamwork.

(v) Designing, developing and administering the supporting systems such as information and planning system, motivation and appraisal system and control and development system.

Organisational structure is the hardware of the strategy and so precisely matching it with the strategy is utmost important. **Chandler** is of the opinion that changes in the strategy requires changes in the structure to achieve economic efficiency. Therefore, if a particular structure does not fulfill the requirements of the strategy then it has to be redesigned. Again **Salter, Thain** and **Scott** are of the view that as an organisation grows in size and diversity, it moves from a simple to a complex form. In the **first phase** organisations are small enterprises and as such they are managed by their owners who are entrepreneurs. Such organisation have simple operations. In the **second phase,** there is functional specialisation and departmentalisation. These organisations have a size bigger than those in phase I. The work is organised here through departments based either on function or process. The **phase III** organisations are large in size, widely scattered and have units/different divisions, normally on the geographic basis. Each division is functionally independent and is linked directly to the headquarter. Thus each division enjoys semi-autonomy. These semi-autonomous divisions again, may adopt functional structure. The **phase IV** organisations have the most complex organisational structure. They are large, multiproduct, multiplan organisations. The organisations which adopt related or unrelated diversification to reach this stage. The organisations at this phase, too have a divisional form. However this divisional form is larger in size, more complex and more sophisticated as each division may be a subsidiary company a functionally autonomous profit centre or a strategic business unit. [A Strategic Business Unit (SBU) is defined by **Sharplin** as any part of business organisation which is treated separately for strategic management purpose.] The corporate headquarter of phase IV organisations provides strategic direction as well as policy-guidelines to all divisions, through corporate level strategy.

There are several types of organisational structure. The major types are as follows -

(1) **Entrepreneurial Structure –** It is the most elementary structure where the owner himself is the manager. Such organisations are small in size, offer a single product or service and normally serve the local market. The owner is the manager and there is quick decision making, timely and prompt response to changes in environment and simple systems and methods of work. But such organisations are unsuitable for future expansion. Further such organisational-managements have more emphasis and concentrations on day to day operations and negligence to strategy development.

(2) **Functional Structure –** Here the principle of functional specialisation and departmentalisation is followed. This organisation has a higher level of efficiency due to specialisation and delegation of authority. But at the same time it suffers from the problems of difficulty in work coordination, conflict between the staff and line officers, narrower specialisation leading to higher cost of operations.

(3) **Divisional Structure –** Under this method work is divided on the basis of product line, geographic area covered or type of customers to be served. Thus product-diversification market segmentation or geographic expansion of business proves the need of divisional structure. In such situations functional structure is found as inadequate and unsuitable. so there may be area-wise divisionalisation or product-wise divisionalisation or customer-segment wise divisionalisation. These separate divisions will have a functional structure within them. Each division normally will have the marketing operations (production and processing) and personnel departments. The finance and legal services may be centralised. Each division is functionally separate and independent. Each division is semi-autonomous. Each division is linked directly to the headquarter. This structure is useful to organisations which are large, have scattered business and own different units/plants. Divisional structure can follow the strategic management style more effectively than functional or entrepreneurial structure. The focus on specific area or product or customer class brings acuteness in performance. The changes in micro as well as macro environment are promptly perceived and suitable corrective action is immediately initiated. However, divisional structure faces the problem of resources-allocation among divisions and corporate office. Sometimes corporate overheads increase. The sharing of authority and responsibility between the corporate office and division has to be precisely defined and described. otherwise conflicts arise. At the same time, there may be disagreement and diversity in the style of functioning among different divisions due to the inconsistent policies. Therefore, consistency and comprehension in policy-matters should be carefully preserved.

(4) **SBU Organisational Structure –** According to **Hale C. Bartlett** a Strategic Business Unit (SBU) is a discrete element of the business serving specific products and markets with readily identifiable competitors for which strategic planning is conducted. Again in the views of **Sharplin,** Strategic Business Unit (SBU) is any part of business organisation which is treated separately for strategic management purposes.

A SBU organisational structure is created by adding another level of management in the divisional structure. The divisions are grouped on the basis of common strategic intent and an strategic business unit thus comes into existence. A SBU is thus a group of divisions having a common strategic intent. The concept of strategic intent is very broad and there is hierarchy of strategic intents. At the corporate level it takes the form of the vision and mission. At the business level it is reflected through goals and objectives and then at the operational level the objectives are subdivided into functional-objectives which are required to be fulfilled to serve and accomplish the strategic intent. In the simplest words, a strategic intent is the purpose or goal of the organisation. It is the aim of the organisation strategic intent points out what the organisation is set to achieve. strategic intent lays down the framework and the organisation operates within this framework. In the eyes of **Hamel** and **Prahlad** strategic intent is the obsession to win at all levels of the organisation. It envisions a desired leadership position and establishes the criteria which the organisation will use to chart its progress. **Hamel** and **Prahlad** states further that the strategic intent encompasses an active management process which includes –

(i) Focusing the organisations attention on the essence of winning.

(ii) Motivating the people by communicating them the value of the target.

(iii) Leaving room for individual and team contributions.

(iv) Sustaining enthusiasm by providing new operational definitions as circumstances change and

(v) Using intent consistently to guide resources-allocations. In SBU organisational structure, the divisions are grouped on the basis of common strategic intent. Normally, SBU organisational structure is adopted when the divisions increase in size, number and diversity. SBU-organisational structure establishes coordination and facilitates control of large and diverse divisional organisations. SBU organisationtional structure prescribes accountability at the level of business units. But it creates difficulty in defining autonomy and responsibility of each SBU and its head.

The major disadvantage of SBU structure is that it forms an additional layer between the corporate and divisional management. Additionally, in large and diverse organisations, several difficulties arise in handling the different SBUs efficiently and effectively.

(5) **Matrix Structure –** Matrix organisational structure is a combination of project or product structure and the functional structure. In large organisations there is often a need to work on different projects/products and each one of these projects have some kind of importance from the business point of view. So such organisations need to develop the matrix structure.

The matrix structure is developed by forming a team of functional specialists from different areas and making them work on a special project or product. During the project these specialists work on the project and report to the project leader. After completion of the project they revert back to their parent department and continue their routine departmental duty. The matrix structure makes the best use of the individual specialist talent for the most important need and thus makes its fullest utilisation. It fosters creativity by pooling up diverse talent and by making them work collectively. It gives more exposure to functional specialists. However, it creates confusion among individual team members regarding their responsibility and accountability due to dual accountability. So there is a need to provide the clear-cut instructions to the functional specialists about their role, responsibility and reporting authority. The matrix structure is more complicated also. It needs vertical and horizontal combination to form project teams consisting of diverse talents. Again matrix structure requires to prepare a detail prescription of authority to who will order and instruct whom for what purpose, under what circumstances and for what period otherwise shared authority will lead to confusion, miscommunication and conflict.

(6) Network Structure – It is also called as spider's web structure or virtual organisation. According to **J.G. March** the network structure is composed of a series of project groups or collaborations linked by constantly changing non-hierarchical cobweb-like networks. Network structure has emerged due to the following two reasons. (i) The emergence of knowledge-based industries. (ii) The rising volatility of business-environment.

In the network structure, there is a small headquarter of the organisation which acts like a broker connecting the suppliers and the autonomous teams performing the specialised functions. The core organisation is thus simply a shell. The network structure is highly decentralised. It is organised around customer groups or geographical regions. The business functions are scattered far and wide. Network structure makes extensive use of outsourcing. It has very few internal resources and it relies largely on outside specialists in respective areas. It mostly outsources the support services which are necessary for the production and marketing of goods and services.

Network structure is suitable for the continually changing environment. It has a high level of flexibility. It is adaptive to cope up with the changing environment. The network structure enables the firm to focus on its core competencies. However, it faces difficulties regarding the coordination and control of functions. Also it involves high cost due to duplication of resources and risk due to overspecialisation.

The different types of structures available have to be studied carefully by the strategist and the suitable structure is to be selected. Since these different structures have relative merits and demerits, it is really difficult to decide as to which structure should be called as suitable one. The suitability of the structure should therefore, be decided in the light of the requirements of the strategy. So a structure which will be most helpful for the effective implementation of the strategy can be decided as the best option. Normally, the structure evolves as the organisation grows from one stage to another. The internal and external environment also affect the suitability and choice of the structure. A functional structure is most preferred in the stable environment whereas a divisional or matrix or network structure is more suitable in a volatile environment. Now, for a competitive environment a strategist has to design and develop the structure which is not only suitable from the environment point of view, but is also helpful for achieving the strategic objectives. So the strategist should make the organising process more focused. For this purpose identify the activities which are critical for achieving the strategic objectives and group them accordingly. The structure which has been designed on the basis of the requirements of the strategy and develop its core-functions from that viewpoint is more suitable.

The experts on organisational design **B. Macy and H. Izymi** describes the characteristics of the emerging thinking in organisational design. According to them, the traditional large size organisations with centralised decision making is replaced by organisations with small business units having cooperative relationship and decentralised participative decision making. Traditional organisations have the vertical communication patterns which now organisations replace by introducing the horizontal communication system. Outsourcing, autonomous work teams and cross functional work teams are the important features of modern organisations. The traditional organisations, as against this, used to opt for vertical integration, functional work teams and quality-based work teams. It does not mean that modern organisation do not pay attention to the quality aspect on the other hand they are more quality conscious. For this purpose they offer extensive training, emphasize on value-chains and design the jobs accordingly. Traditional organisations have individual focused specialised job design. The concept of virtual organisation is very fast entering in business world and many business houses are accepting the same. The changes in organisational design are in one way, indicating the changes in the competition and environment which have necessitated these structural changes. So in this new, globalised and highly competitive economy, the organisations need to be customer-focussed, flexible and adaptive to the environment, quality-driven preferring participative decision-making, result-oriented, performance-based and possessing learning attitude. The structural implementation has to consider these needs to develop the suitable organisational design. In fact irrespective of any strategy the structure has to be flexible and adaptable to the environmental changes. Many a time, the strategy implementation also requires certain modifications in the major systems of the organisation, namely, information system, control system, appraisal system, motivation system and development system and planning system. Every organisational structure involves units and subunits in the form of departments, divisions, sections and business-units, etc. Each such unit is assigned certain tasks and activities and so there is always a need to bind these different units and authority positions together so that there will be a well-coordinated, symphonised performance of all units unidirectionally. We know, that structure is the way in which the tasks and subtasks in an organisation are arranged. So it is necessary to see that the structure fulfills to develop such a structure which will match with the changing environment and strategy. Changes in environmental affects the strategy and the alterations and modifications in response to them, in turn requires changes in organisational structure. We do not have a structure which can be termed as the most superior structure and which will satisfy all needs of all types of strategies at all times. Because different types structures have relative merits and demerits. So the strategist has to assess the special needs of the strategy as well those of the organisation to decide the suitability of the strategy. Delaying and flatter organisational design is suggested more emphatetically nowadays. It has advantages of quick communication, decentralisation, prompt decision making and action orientation, for rapid-growth strategies it is useful. But can it claim the same degree of suitability for stability or retrenchment strategy? The point is that structural suitability has to be decided in the light of strategic needs and environmental changes. Following are given some tips to design a more time relevant, compatible and environment-suitable structure.

(i) As the participative management style is more preferred today, design such a structure which allows open, quick and two way communication at all levels.

(ii) Design such a structure with system which will build up result-oriented review and control mechanism.

(iii) Design the structure having systems of such a type that will encourage professionalism and result-oriented performance among employees.

(iv) Design such a structure involving system which will provide sufficient guidance and full scope for career development for employees along with a responsive motivation system for job-related as well as other creative meritorious performance.

(v) Make customer-focussed design, which will have the capability to serve the customer in a better way.

Behavioural Implementation – To make a successful and effective implementation of a strategy, we have to consider the behavioural aspects of the people who participate and play active role in strategy implementation. If the behaviour of the employees and managers is such which acts as hurdle in the progress of implementation, all earlier efforts will become futile. For example, if we intend to achieve cost leadership and so want to offer the least cost products which are priced lowest in the market; then we have to focus and make special efforts to reduce our operating cost, avoid all types of wastages, make minimum expenses and increase efficiency and productivity. This requires changes in the attitude and behaviour of employees. Unless and until the employees become cost-conscious and wholeheartedly accept their role and responsibility in respect cost-reduction and cost-minimisation, the strategic objective of cost-leadership cannot be attained. Behavioural implementation, therefore, focusses on directing and developing employee behaviour in such a way that it will suit and support more acutely for strategy-implementation.

The major issues relating to behavioural implementation are:

(a) Leadership (b) Corporate culture (c) Corporate politics and use of power (d) Personal values and business ethics (e) Social responsibility.

(a) Leadership : According to **Gluek and Jauch** leadership affects organisational performance. It plays a critical role in success and failure of the enterprise leadership for the manager, is the focus of activity through which organisational goals and objectives are accomplished. Development of leadership and assigning the leader crucial role in strategy implementation is an aspect of behavioural implementation. Different theories are put forward by the researchers on leadership. A brief summary of them provides us the idea as to specific theme of leadership has focussed on certain capabilities and actions of leaders. Personality theme of leadership believes that leaders become so due to certain traits and qualities. Behaviour theme suggests that actions make the person a leader. A leader is a leader because he acts like a leader. A leader can influence because of his behaviour and so it is not important what a leader possesses, but what a leader does. Situation theme suggests that situational factors decide the leadership. So in different situations different persons having different personality-traits become leaders. Transactional theme of leadership discusses the role-differentiation and society interaction between the leader and subordinate. Transformational leadership states that a leader is a transformationist.

In essence the behaviourist state that leadership is the influenceability. Leadership exists because there are followers. A leader remains a leader so long as he has followers. When his influence disappears his followers disappear and there the leadership comes to an end. So it is said that leadership is alive moment by moment. There is the acceptance theory of authority behind leadership which describes that the collective acceptance of the followers gives someone the position of a leader.

The leader plays a significant role in strategy implementation. His influence on the followers can make them work hard and work honestly for the accomplishment of the strategic goal. The **power** of leader is more meaningful and effective in this regard than the **authority** of the manager. So the development of appropriate leadership automatically becomes an important aspect of behavioural implementation. A visionary leader who develops new qualities and skills in subordinates who welcomes the change and builds confidence among followers to act as change agents, who delegates them authority and transforms them as leaders; can take the organisation along way on the path of progress and prosperity.

A leader is able to lead and motivate the organisation and people to achieve the desired results. For this purpose which particular style he follows matters more. Because the leadership style has a far-reaching effect on the organisation and its performance. The leadership style, in fact, is the way in which a leader uses his power. There are three popular leadership styles, which are as follows:

(1) Free rein or *Laissez-faire* style.

(2) Autocratic style.

(3) Participative style.

The leaders following **free-rein style** avoids authority as well as responsibility and depends totally on his team to set the goals and chalk out the programmes and procedures. A free rein leader prefers to occupy the back seal and plays a minor role and uses minimum power. An **autocratic leader** is authoritative in attitude and centralises the power to direct and decide in his own hands. He, expects the perfect and total obedience from his subordinates. Some autocratic leaders are benevolent and offer rewards to followers for their specific satisfactory performance. However, the attitude to hold power to decide and control is common among all autocratic leaders. The leaders who follow the **participative style** are democratic in nature and so delegates and decentralises the authority and encourage the subordinates to express their views in decision making. They discuss issues with subordinates, listen to their views and try to develop collective decission process.

Again there is **transactional** style and **transformational** style of leadership. The transactional leaders use rewards (like pay, fringe benefits, higher job status) to motivate the subordinates. Transformational leaders involve subordinates in a mission by inspiring them through a noble goal of higher order. Transformational leaders help the followers to transcend their own limitations as well as self-interest and contribute more significantly in accomplishing the goals of the organisation. Transactional leaders are task-oriented whereas transformational leaders are relationship-oriented. The studies conducted at the university of Michigan describes two important leadership styles. One is job-centred leadership style and another is employee-centred leadership style. Job-centred leaders are strongly task-oriented and emphasize on task completion by hook or crook. Employee-centred leaders are relationship-oriented and emphasize on developing and maintaining cordial relations with followers and through that achieving task completion. Hard task masters having least concern for human relations are successful in the short run and their's is limited only with completing the given targets. In the long run the subordinates develop strong annoyance and bitter reaction against such leaders and so non-cooperation, reducing productivity and increasing disputes become the frequent happening and result of this style. On the other hand employee-centred leaders motivate the subordinates to cross their self-limit and give the best performance output which will be ascending each time.

Hersey and Blamchard describe four styles of leadership. They adopt a situational approach and suggest that selection of any of these four styles will depend upon the maturity of the employees. The level of employee-maturity is described by the following three factors collectively:

(i) The degree of achievement motivation.

(ii) The willingness of the employees to accept responsibility.

(iii) The level of their education and experience.

The above three factors together determine the maturity level of the subordinates. How as per the maturity level the leader can choose any of the four styles, namely telling, selling, participating and delegating style.

(a) Telling Style : It is a style having high orientation. This style is suitable for employees having lowest maturity level.

(b) Selling Style : It is a leadership style having high task as well as relationship orientation. This style is effective for employees having low maturity level.

(c) Participating Style : This is a high relationship and low task style. It is effective when employees maturity level is high.

(d) Delegating Style : This leadership style is having low task and low relationship orientation. It is effective when employees are having highest level of maturity.

For the implementation of the strategy the leader has to act as a motivator, problem-solver, figurehead, negotiator and consensus-builder. A strategic leader has to sit on the top of the situation and observe how well things are managed. For controlling the situation and for achieving the strategic goals; he has to energize the organisation and make it positively responsive to the opportunities emerging in the changing conditions and develop innovative ideas. Strategy implementation is effective and fruitful when there is teamwork for which the leaders has to build up the consensus and the spirit of cooperation and unity among the subordinates and followers. Sometimes success becomes the only criterion and hence people try to reach to the goals, fulfil the objectives by hook or by crook. The values and morality is sidelined in the reach for accomplishing targets. Such an environment is detrimental to the organisation in the long run. So the strategic leader has to communicate consistently the organisational values to the subordinates and enforce the clinical standards. Moreover, feedback and rectification are the important tools which the leader should use prudently. The leader should keep a personal contact with the key subordinates, different work groups and people who are playing crucial roles at operational levels in strategy implementation. Some management experts suggest that the leader in such situation, should manage by walking around. By doing that he can keep a precise control on the situation and the progress in implementation. As and when the implementation activities are deviating from the goals, immediate corrective action should be initiated. This is possible when the leader has uptodate information about the progress of implementation and so he can issue orders and instructions for modification and can initiate immediately the rectification process. A leader has to develop the strategy supportive corporate climate and culture in the organisation.

(b) Corporate culture : Corporate culture distinguishes a good organisation from a bad one. Experts on corporate culture describe it as a set of assumptions which the members of the organisations share in common. Through these assumptions are usually unstated explicitly, they have powerful influence on the behaviour of the managers and employees.

C.D. Pringle, D.F. Jenning and J.G. Jogencker *(Managing Organisations – Function and Behaviours)* state that corporate culture refers to the values and patterns of beliefs and behaviours that are accepted and practiced by the members of the organisation. Thus, values and beliefs are the important components of culture. Values are the assumptions about the ideals. These ideals are worthy and desirable for the organisation. Values describe what are valuables. Values direct what are worth achieving and retaining. Beliefs on the other hand, are assumptions about reality and these assumption get reinforced by the actual experience. Values and beliefs are the cornerstones of the corporate culture. To what extent, employees share these values and beliefs in common, will decide how much strong or weak the corporate culture is. In a strong culture, the thinking pattern, expressions, feeling and actions of the employees have greater commonness. The people working in such organisations understand the objectives and strategy of the company much better than people in organisations having weak culture. Further employees in strong culture precisely know their strategic roles and a strong culture is more powerful in channelling the concept of appropriate employee behaviour and thus enables employees to do their jobs in a more strategy supportive manner.

Corporate culture affects the implementation of the strategy. This effect may be positive or negative. It is most necessary to bring a close culture–strategy match. If the culture and strategy are mismatching to one another, a lot of hurdles arise in strategy implementation.

In such situations, the employee behaviour is not strategy-supportive and this causes the strategy to fail. If culture is perfectly matching with the strategy then, such a situation automatically energises the employees and make them work and act suitably and supportively.

(c) Corporate Power and Politics : Politics is the art of getting and usuing power. We perceive politics and power, many times, negatively. Whenever we hear the term politics, we associate it with manipulation, domination, suppression, subjugation, exploitation and falsification. But this is neither completely correct nor realistic. **A. Sharplin** *(Strategic Management)* defines politics as the carrying out of activities not prescribed by policies for the purpose of influencing the distribution of advantages within the organisation. The tactics to be used to influence this distribution are political and relate to the use of power. When the policies are inadequate, politics has to be used. Every corporate culture has a political components and politics exists in each and every type of organisation.

Power is indispensible in politics. Power is described as influenceability, i.e., the ability to influence corporate politics and use of power, personal values and business ethics social responsibility. Power makes the individuals and groups to follow a particular course of action which the powerful (the holder of the power) desires. Power and authority are the two separate concepts. Though sometime power and authority are correlated; power is distinct from authority. Some people in the organisations are powerful though they possess very little authority or no authority is positional. The source of authority is the position and designation which one is having. Authority is delegated by the superior to his junior. The sources of power are multiple and varied. Power is earned. Power is neither delegated nor conferred upon a person.

According to **JRP French and B. Raven** there five different sources where from power in the organisation is derived and thus there are five types of power which are as follows:

(1) **Reward Power :** It arises from the authority of the manager to reward the employees for their positive outcome.

(2) **Coercive Power :** It emerges from the authority of the manager to penalise and punish the employees for negative outcome and wrongdoings.

(3) **Expert Power :** It arises from the knowledge, expertise, competence and capability of the manager which are accepted, respected and acknowledged by others, i.e., employees, colleagues and subordinates.

(4) **Legitimate Power :** It is gained by the manager through his ability to use his position in the organisation to influence the behaviour of other employees.

(5) **Referrent Power :** It arises from the ability of the manager to develop favourable and positive feelings about himself among the employees, with the help of his own personality or charisma. The more the employees like their manager, the greater the referrent power the manager possesses.

Politics is concerned with the use of power. **Henry Mintzberg** is of the opinion that corporate politics is not inherently good or bad. The division and partition among people is made by politics which is wrong. This leads to weakening down the unity, morale and team spirit of the employees. When the people in the organisation start thinking in a piecemeal way and look to the organisation as distinct parts which are separate from one another, then the organisational performance and effectiveness starts declining under such circumstances the employees are not able to view the organisation as a whole. Naturally the decisions, actions and behaviour does not become harmonious and complementary to each other. If each work group does not try to relate his job and work with other groups and departments and simply views his job as a separate one and complete in all respect, the unity of direction and unity of purpose will be lost. The organisation then will not exist as a cohesive organisation. So politics leading to partition and division is completely bad. However politics in organisation can yield good results if it is prudently used as a tool to implement the change programme in the organisation. When the organisation is passing through a phase of stagnation and *status quo*, then it needs to be shaken up thoroughly. This is where corporate politics can be used as an effective and useful tool. The basic changes which are necessary in such organisation can be very well incorporated by using corporate politics as a mean strategy implementation is mostly concerned with change-management. So corporate politics can be of great use in strategy implementation. **Mintzberg** views that politics can be used to develop required tension in the first phase and a political harmony in the next phase. The strategist must understand when and how to encourage politics to create an atmosphere supportive to change and when to discourage politics and shun it off to boost up the spirit of unity and harmony. **Mintzberg** says that the organisation must be pulled apart before it is pulled together. Thus in order to reorganise the corporation better for strategy-implementation it has to be first segregated. The group think mentality, the old and unsuitable roles and functional relationships, the traditional presumptions and convictions about jobs and achievements are required to be wiped out and dismantled. The jobs should redesigned and the roles responsibilities and relationships among individual employees and work groups are to be reset. Many times the organisation passes through a process of complete, transformation. Even a partial transformation faces resistance, then we can imagine how strong and concerted resistance the employees can show to a complete transformation programme or to a scheme of total reorganisation. So political tactics can ease down the problem and helps to weaken down the collective resistance. Developing coalition and building consensus for accepting and implementing change have proved to be comparatively effective in this regard.

If politics and power are the indispensible elements in the organisation. A question springs up as to how they can be used for the best advantage of the organisation. This relates to the strategic use of power and politics in the organisation. For strategy implementation politics and power play in the organisation can be utilised to the best advantage of the organisation. Coalition and consensus building which are basically the political tools, help effectively to obtain the cooperation and contribution of employees and work groups for strategy implementation. Issues relating to resources-allocation, work distribution, conflict-resolution can be very well handled by using the political tricks and tactics. As **J.B. Quinn** *(Strategies for Change – Logical Incrementalism)* observes that most strategic decision and most strategic thrusts in large enterprises emerge as a part of an evolving continuous political consensus-building with no precise beginning or end. So to make the best strategic use of power and politics, first of all, the strategist has to accept the existence and inevitability of politics in the organisation. He has to understand who wields the real power in the organisation. He has to search out those individuals and groups whose opinions and views carry weight among others and who influence the thinking and actions of others. The strategist has to be sensitive and receptive to the political signals emanating from different parts of the organisation and has to understand the political structure and relationship in the organisation. A strategist has to lead the strategy for consensus is necessary. He should not dictate the strategy. Dictation will result in strong reactions and negative actions from the employees. This will ruin the purpose of the strategy and will create number of hurdles in strategy implementation. The mental preparedness, consent and cooperation of the employees for the change programme incorporated in strategy implementation is essential. This develops employee-involvement and encourage employee-participation which is the foundation for successful strategy-implementation. When the negative decisions are made through mutual consent and collectively their intensity and adverse effects are not that way felt seriously. When employees themselves discard the unviable and unacceptable ideas, then the probable ego-clash does not arise. The ideas which employees accept voluntarily are easier to put to practice. If the strategist starts playing the role of the autocratic leader, then he narrows down the possibilities of winning the confidence and cooperation of colleagues and subordinates. Furthermore, the strategist has to offer rewards and incentives for responsiveness and impose penalties for aloofness. This will boost up the spirit of cooperation on one side and simultaneously put threat for non-performance. When organisational commitment is properly rewarded, a tendency to show it and act accordingly develops automatically. So politics and power can be used cleverly for strategy-implementation. However, unprincipled politics should be avoided strictly, otherwise it will lead to selfish motives, nepotism, disharmony and neglect of the organisational interests and objectives.

(d) Personal Values and Business Ethics : Personal values influence the individual behaviour and throughts and actions. The organisation consists of large number of people and all these people possess different personal values which influence internal environment in the organisation as well as strategy implementation.

A personal value, in the simplest senses is what is valuable to the person. It is a concept of an individual about the desirable. According to **Christenesen C.G.** *(Business Policy – Text and Cases)* a value is a view of life and a judgement of what is desirable which is very much a part of person's personality and a group's morale. According to late **Prof. K.B. Gavai** a value is the criterion for right and wrong, good and bad, undesirable and desirable. A value provides direction to decide and describe – (a) What is right and what is wrong (b) What is good and what is bad (c) What is desirable to the individual as well as to the society and what is undesirable.

All people have and many times they are different from one another. As people are very much sensitive and assertive about their own values, a value clash arises as a result of this situation. A conflict which emerges from difference in values is difficult and complicated to resolve and settle. Because both parties have different conception about the right and wrong behaviour and they endorse their separate thinking and interpretation rather religiously, without preferring any idea of compromise. Therefore, the strategist has to see that the changes and implementation programme is compatible with the values of the employees. Rather the organisation should try to develop and communicate such values among its employees which are helpful in improving the organisational performance and effectiveness. The values like integrity and honesty, dignity of labour and dignity of people, self-dependence and hard-work, cooperation and team spirit, freedom and autonomy, quality consciousness and research-orientation, progress and modernisation, customer-orientation and service motto, thrift and productivity are essential for the modern organisations to cultivate among its employees. Without them the organisation will very hardly survive in the present business world where intense competition is the rule. The strategist has to plan and select suitable activities to nurture and cultivate the appropriate values in the organisation and among its employees. If the organisational values are properly communicated and implanted in employees cleverly and tactfully then there is a greater possibility for the unanimous efforts for strategic success. On the other side, when the organisational and personal values differ and if this gap is considerably broad; then value-confusion, value-contradiction and value-clash is inevitable. The employee will be totally confused about giving priority and importance to the values. Which values, he should adhere to? Personal or organisational? In such a situation he may, possibly, resort to a contradictory value as a result of which his actual behaviour will be contrary to the expected behaviour. This will create a value-clash giving birth to a dispute between the individual and the organisation where the entire issue will be the propriety of a value. For example, if the individual views obedience and conformity as a good value, whereas the organisation treats independence and freedom to decide and act as a more valid and useful value; then confusion, contradiction and clash is bound to arise. Because what the individual feels as a good behaviour in the light of his value system may be abused as inefficiency and passivity by the organisation from its viewpoint. The organisation expects the individual to take initiative and decide and act independently as per the situation without waiting for the specific orders and instructions from the superior. Contrary to this, the individual acts exactly opposite to this. So, then misunderstandings and disputes start. Therefore, communication and transmission of suitable values among employees is a must. The employees should thoroughly understand, what the organisation values and accordingly should internalise and imbibe that kind of thinking. The organisation should provide the conducive environment and facilities for this process. There must be proper blending between individual and organisational values. Additionally, the employees should learn to prioritise the organisational values to individual values.

Besides the personal values, business ethics also plays an important role. Business ethics refers to the development of ethical practices in business. It attempts to awaken the ethical insight in business dealing. According to **L.N. Nash** *(Good Intentions Aside – A Managers Guide in Resolving Ethical Problems)* business ethics is the study of now moral norms apply to the activities and goals of a commercial enterprise. It is not separate moral standard, but the study of how the business context passes its own unique problems for the moral person who acts as the agent of this system. This clarifies the fact of the moral dispute which is faced by the businessman. While making the business decisions. As most of the time business goals are economical and focus on wealth creation; they may neglect the moral elements involved in the process. Especially, the strategic thinking is more prone to this risk. In the strong urge, to win competition and maximise strategic advantage, the strategist may opt for the ethically questionable practices, which are rather short-cuts to success. Business ethics is a lamp that throws light on the moral aspects of business. It operates as a system of values and is primarily concerned with checking how the business goals and practices serve the human end. Therefore, those decisions and actions of business which produce harm to the human ends and which injure the public interest should always be avoided by the strategist. In fact the strategist should pay attention to the moral side of all problems and their solutions. Nowadays, there is an increasing awareness, all over the world, about ethical practices in business. Under such circumstances, if a particular company engages unethical practices; then it will have to face lot of public criticism, besides loss of image, reputation and finally business-standing. Honesty of purpose, sincerity in action and transparency in dealings is expected by different stakeholders from business organisations all over the world. Corruption and malpractices are always condemned and criticised. Nobody, dares to support, canvass and follow the unethical and immoral practices.

However, the strategist has to face a typical complicated dilemma in respect of ethical practices and their perpetuation in organisations. On one side there certain elements involved in the accomplishment of a particular business target, which can be called as the practical or pragmatic demands of the work. They influence possibilities of work fulfillment and target achievement. These practical demands distort the value-system and to satisfy them, the organisation has to compromise on its ethical stance and sideline its ethical practices. On the other side, there are certain good values and ethical are certain good values and ethical ideals in the organisational working which gives it a distinctive identity and develops its work culture. Those values and moralities may be a matter of pride and dignity for the organisation. However, practically it may not be possible to adopt and follow them due to their higher cost and less utility in the changed environments. Its your competitors who are offering kickbacks and personal gifts to obtain purchase orders or to settle the bills, how long can you, afford to keep yourself away and aloof from such practices. If you follow them, they you are neglecting your ethical ideals and if you reject them, then you may be losing the business and giving your space to your competitors. This is a big dilemma before the strategist. The strategist, therefore, has to handle such situations skillfully and tactfully. At several instances the views of the decision maker influences the decision-process. His own value-system and personal integrity impacts the quality and content of decisions. Ethical practices and their reference should be policy-consideration. A kind of commitment to ethics must exist in the organisation. The top management must take this stance that come what may, we will never abandon our ethical viewpoints and ethical practices. Even if loss occurs, the top management should insist on business ethics. This undeterred commitment to ethics tells effectively to all others, how much the organisation values ethics. It may be possible that such a strong support to ethical practices by the management may cause losses and difficulties in the short run. But in the long run, it carves out the good image of the organisation and will develop and strengthen the credibility of the organisation. The strategist has to maintain this view and so should lay down certain do's and dont's in the implementation of the strategy which will clarify ethical perception of the organisation and will prohibit the objectionable behaviour. This will avoid confusion about practically clever behaviour and ethically wise conduct. It is a well understood fact that the ethically managed organisations have outperformed the organisations engaging unethical, manipulative, dubious, suspicious and so called shrewd and pragmatic practices. Business ethics sets out a value-system which will provide guidelines for morally correct decisions and actions that will uplift the credibility as well as business prospects of the organisation. The strategist has to make the following three important functions in this regard.

(a) Inculcating the value system.

(b) Reconciling the divergent personal values with the organisational values.

(c) Blending the strategic intentions with the organisational value system. This will include the modification of values as well as the strategy. The purpose of this is to bring a congruence between the thoughts and actions.

(e) Social responsibility and strategic management – Social responsibility of business is an important issue in the present days. Should a business organisation accept social responsibility? This question which ultimately express exactly opposite two views. According to **Adam Smith** and **Milton Friedman** who advocate the first view, the only responsibility of business is to perform its economic functions efficiently and provide goods and services to the society and maximise the profit. This view has always been criticised as narrow and short-sighted. There is another view which is exactly opposite to this. According to the second view business is an integral part of the society. And as such it has a basic social responsibility. It has to serve the interest of the society first. Profit is always a secondary consideration. Profit cannot become the objective of business. Rather it is the reward for efficient business performance. Not simply profit, but profit through service is what matters most. The society entrusts the valuable scarce resource to the business for their optimum utilisation for the best social benefit. The business can combine its economic interests with its social responsibility objectives. The business can work to achieve its self-enlightened interest, where the business will pay attention to the different aspects of its social responsibility while trying to accomplish its economic goals. Modern concept of social responsibility is related to the accomplishment of stakeholders interests. The concept of stakeholders is broader than that of stockholders. Stockholders or shareholders are the suppliers of capital and therefore partial owners of the organisation. As such most of the time the organisational management is interested in protecting and nurturing their interest. So it pays them good dividend, looks after the safety of their investment and tries to enhance the shareholders worth. However social responsibility does not mean taking care of the interests of the shareholders only. The concept of stakeholders include shareholders, employees, customers, suppliers, dealers and marketing intermediaries, government and public at large. All these stakeholders should get due rewards for their support and contribution to business.

Therefore, the employees should be given fair wages, healthy working condition and human treatment. The customer should get quality products at reasonable prices and uninterrupted product supply. The suppliers should get their payment promptly without any unnecessary delay. The dealers and marketing intermediaries should get their return, commission and other remuneration as per agreement without any form of embarrassment. The business should pay taxes and other dues to government honestly and should follow the government policy, directives rules and regulations sincerely. The general public should not be ignored. Their consent and cooperation helps the business organisation to exist, survive, grow and become prosperous. So the organisation should pay attention to the consequences of its business activity on the society in general. There should always be positive effects of business on the society such as supply of quality product; use of natural, physical and manual resources in the socially desirable manner, generation of employment doing everything to enhance public well-being. At the same time business should avoid and reduce its negative effect on the society such as pollution, poverty and disparity, wealth concentration and monopoly creation, restrictive and unfair trade practices, black-marketing and dumping, etc. The society should always be at an advantage due to business activities.

So, in a nutshell there are three Cs of social responsibility of business. They are –

(1) Compliance.

(2) Contribution.

(3) Consequences.

Compliance aspect relates to obeying the law, following the policy measures and directives of the government and complying the rules and regulations. Contribution aspects focusses on the benefits of business to the society and the efforts of business in achieving the public well-being. Consequences look into the positive and negative effects of business on the society. So these 3C's collectively can highlight the social responsibility of business in the shortest and simplest way. But the next question arises, a strategist can incorporate this social responsibility aspect in the strategy and make it acquire competitive success.

We should never forget that good business always have social and ethical elements. Successful companies have neither rejected their social responsibility, nor have ignored or skipped it away. Because they know that when they conduct their business in a socially responsible and responsive manner, it produces a good effect on their corporate-image. Image-building is a complicated and critical activity. It requires well planned and carefully designed wise activities and sustained efforts. Image-building is further a multidimensional activity. It expects the corporation to do a lot of activities in different mutually related as well as unrelated areas. As a business organisation, to develop good corporate image, you have to supply quality products at reasonable prices, you have to pay fair wages to your employees and treat them with justice and humanity, you have to pay government dues honestly and timely and see that you contribute to government revenue significantly. More, you have to act as a good corporate citizen. All these activities and behaviours made with an intention to build and develop good corporate image are nothing but different aspects of social responsibility and social responsiveness. A good corporate image is the true asset of every business organisation. It is an intangible asset, but it pays or causes to pay rich dividend in the long run. Because good image helps significantly, to develop and enhance credibility of the organisation. This Credibility and trustworthiness will assist the organisation to influence and command more resources, greater market share and higher public response. Everybody would like to associate with an honest and responsible organisation and collaborate in its activities. Then business success follows you automatically. There is no greater loss to anybody in personal and professional life than a tarnished image. You may be an individual or an organisation and you may be in business or elsewhere, but in all walk of life you require a good image to survive and succeed in a competitive environment. And when day by day competition is becoming more acute, intense and widespread, no business organisation can afford to loose or deteriorate its good image. Because that will risk its existence and survival in business.

Modern organisation pay attention to the social responsibility aspect. They try to become more social responsive and so decide seriously which social activities they should take up, how much resources should be allocated to them and how this social responsiveness should become an integral part of their business objectives. Nowadays, organisations not only fulfill their duties and responsibilities towards stakeholders; but also voluntarily engage themselves in programmes and activities which social content and social motives, e.g, the polio eradication programme AIDS awareness programme, mass literacy, eye donation and blood donation, wild life protection and preservation, sports and cultural activities, poverty alleviation and self-employment, prevention of women abuse and child battering, running old home and orphanage centers, etc. The socially enlightened organisations actively support such programmes and even sometimes take initative in them. The strategist can cleverly integrate these social responsibility activities of the organisation with its business strategy. He can prepare the mission statement in such a manner that it will make clear explicitly the role of the organisation in the society. Naturally the objectives will also incorporate these social elements. The strategist usually makes the appraisal of the organisation as well as that of environment. Organisational appraisal is made with an intention to know about the strengths and weaknesses of the organisation and environmental scanning is made to identify the opportunities and threats in the environment. Though normally, this is done with a business purpose, it can be made with some wider objectives also. The organisational and environmental appraisal can be done to trace the organisational capabilities to tackle the social problems and to forecast social concerns and issues which need highest attention, respectively. The strategist then can choose an alternative action which can serve the business as well as social purpose. **C.R. Christensen** *(Business Policy – Text and Cases)* suggests that the inner coherence of a strategy can be extended by choosing social issues most closely related to the economic strategy of the company, to the expansion of its market, to the health of its immediate environment and to its own industry and internal problems.

Strategy implementation mainly deals with resources-allocation. When the organisation decides to include social activities in its business activities, then the pattern of resources-allocation changes. The strategist will have to spare human, capital and technical resources to discharge the social responsibility activities. Specific roles and responsibilities should be created and assigned to particular individuals. Policies, procedures and systems will be required to be reset to blend properly the economic activities with social activities. Suitable leadership should be developed to handle the social issues and business issues in a collaborative manner. In short the strategist has to align the social responsibility to the process of strategic management.

Functional and Operational Implementation : A functional strategy is described as a narrow plan providing goals and objectives of a specific function. It is useful for resources allocation among different functions within a particular functional area. Functional strategies are the part and parcel of corporate strategy. For every functional area there needs a strategy such as marketing strategy, personal strategy, finance strategy, etc. The activities in respective functional areas effectively contribute to the success of a corporate strategy. So they need to be focussed, coordinated and directed to accomplish the goals of the corporate strategy. Therefore, the functional strategies are necessary which are derived from the corporate strategies.

In functional implementation, two things are very important. The first is the horizontal fit and the second is the vertical fit. Here the term fit means to align the activities and capabilities of an organisation with its strategies. In any organisation, there are several strategies at different levels. At the corporate level there is some strategy. At business level again there is a strategy. At the SBU level there is some strategy. So strategies operate at different levels and there is the need to maintain proper co-ordination and congruence among these strategies. This congruence is called vertical fit. At the same time there should be congruence among different activities which are taking place at the same level. This is called horizontal fit.

For example, when a functional strategy is aligned with a business strategy, it is called vertical fit. Because, in this case a lower level strategy such as functional strategy is aligned with a higher level strategy like business strategy. Now, at the same time, there is a need to create the horizontal fit also because the vertical fit alone is not sufficient to integrate the strategic network, so we have to create this horizontal fit. For this purpose we have to develop congruence and coordination among activities of different functional areas like operations, finance, marketing, personnel and information-management. The activities performed in these functional areas should not work at cross-purpose. These activities should contradict one another. There should be an alignment in all these activities. Vertical and horizontal fit, both, together build the strong strategic network.

Vertical fit leads to functional implementation and horizontal fit leads to operational implementation. Vertical fit leads to define functional strategies in terms of their capability to contribute for the creation of a strategic advantage for the organisation. For example strategic marketing managements means aligning marketing management within the organisation with its corporate and business strategies. Thus, each functional management is aligned with the strategies at different levels to gain a strategic advantage. This strategic functional management (such as strategic HR management, strategic financial management or strategic marketing management) is carried out with the view of serving precisely the objectives and the strategies of the organisation.

The horizontal fit intends to bring the integration of all operational activities which are performed to supply the product of the organisation to the customers. These activities are the part and parcel of operational implementation. The operational implementation aims at achieving the operational efficiency. Now in order to achieve the operational efficiency, the organisation has to make its all value-creating activities in the best possible manner and also in a way much superior to its competitors. Then only it can beat its competitors and can win the competition. So ultimately operational implementation is related with the making of value, creating activities in the optimum manner. All such value creating activities are interlinked with one another and thus they form a set of activities. This set is called the value-chain. **Michael Porter** introduced this concept of value-chain, for the first time in 1985 *(Competitive Advantage-Creating and Sustaining Superior Performance).*

A **value-chain** is described as a set of interlinked value-creating activities performed by an organisation. An understanding of this series of activities is essential to assess the strengths and weaknesses of the organisation. If the organisation is trying to achieve excellence then it has to continuously evaluate its strengths and weaknesses in comparison with its competitors. It has to build new strengths and reduce its weakness to the minimum. This can be done by constantly analysing, improving and monitoring all its activities which are performed to produce and supply a product or service to the ultimate consumer. That is why the value-chain analysis occupies an important position in creating operational effectiveness. In a typical organisation these value-chain activities may begin the procurement of raw material and include all those operations which are performed for the conversion of raw material into finished products and marketing of these products to the end-users i.e., the consumers. According to **Porter** these value-chain activities of a manufacturing organisation can be divided into primary activities and support activities. Primary activities are those activities which are directly related to the flow of product from the producer to the ultimate consumer. Support activities, on the other hand, include all such activities which are performed to sustain primary activities. **Porter's** generic value chain precisely give the description and classification of primary and support activities. **Porter** further divides the primary activity into five sub-activities. They are inbound logistics, operations, outbound logistics, marketing and sales and service.

Inbound logistics include activities like warehousing, material handling, inventory control and scheduling operations include manufacturing, packaging, assembly and maintenance. These activities are performed for converting the raw material into finished products.

Outbound logistics include order processing, physical distribution, warehousing (finished goods) and transportation, etc.

Marketing and sales include product pricing, sales promotion, distribution, etc., Service includes after sales service, training, etc.

Besides the primary activities the value chain includes the support activities, which are procurement, human resource development, technology development and infrastructure. Procurement includes the activities like purchasing physical resources. Human resources development includes recruitment, remunerating, developing and retrenching the employees. Technology development includes equipping and assimilation staff functions like accounting, finance, general management, etc.

Porter's value chain provides for a series of all interrelated activities which are made to create a product and carry it to the consumer. The profitability and business success of the organisation depends on how this value-chain is managed effectively and efficiently.

In many organisations the activities in the value-chain are dispersed and are performed by different departments. For example marketing department undertakes outbound logistics, marketing and sales as well as service. Operations department looks after inbound logistics and operations. The procurement of different materials and operating supplies is made almost by all departments as per their specific needs. Some organisations follow the centralised procurement policy and so they set up a separate purchasing department and entrust it with the responsibility of material procurement for all departments and task-groups. Thus, we find that the departmentalisation and the classification of the value-chain activities match with one another normally. For proper implementation of functional strategies, we need to prepare the functional plans and policies.

Functional strategies operate at a level below the level of the business strategies. A company with multiple businesses require to develop appropriate functional strategies for each business division, so that it can have an overall higher productivity and profit. For example, a company may be engaged in the business of manufacturing and marketing of steel, cement, fabricated material and furniture Now its steel division has again certain functional areas, such as operations, sales, R & D, etc. Each such functional area has further a list of sub-functions. All these functions and sub-functions should be performed in tune with the business strategy, for which we have to prepare functional plans and policies. Functional strategies are always expressed in terms of functional plans and policies and operate within the business strategies. Functional plans and policies involve the tactics which make a business strategy work. plans select and decide a course of action and policies provide guidelines to those actions.

According **William Glueck,** functional plans and policies are needed for the following five reasons :

(i) To implement the strategic decisions by all parts of the organisation.

(ii) To provide a basis to control the activities of different functional areas.

(iii) To reduce the time spent by functional managers on decision making by laying down clearly what is to be done through plans and providing the discretionary frame work within which the decisions should be made through policies.

(iv) To maintain consistency in handling similar situations by different managers.

(v) To maintain coordination among the different functions.

Functional plans and policies help to perform the different key activities of the organisation smoothly, effectively and efficiently. However all these key activities are segregated in different functional areas or departments. This is done as per the principle of division of labour and specialisation. Such a division and specialisation helps to bring higher productivity and fuller utilisation of physical and human resources. However, there is a need to integrate all these activities, as all of them have been performed to achieve overall organisational objectives. Integration of functional plans and policies provide means for this aggregation. The strategists have to provide the mechanism for this integration. The mechanism usually take the form of an integration-committee. This committee consists of representative of top management and heads of functional divisions. The committee has the following three responsibilities to accomplish:

(i) To integrate the functional plans and policies.

(ii) To review the implementation of these plans and policies.

(iii) To make suggestions for revision and modification of these plans and policies in the light of strategic change.

According to **William Glueck,** certain considerations affect the integration and so they should be paid due attention. These considerations are

(i) Need for internal consistency.

(ii) Relevance to development of organisational capabilities.

(iii) Making trade-off decisions.

(iv) Determination of intensity of linkages.

(v) Timing of implementation of plans and policies.

The key organisational tasks are segregated and performed in different departments and therefore the need for internal consistency arises. The internal consistency ensures that different functional plans and policies do not work at cross purpose but operate in consonance. For example, if the sales promotion and advertising department is planning for an aggressive strategy to win the intense competition in the market, it will have to spend more money and use more resources. However at the same, if the accounts and finance department is following a policy emphasizing on thrift and strict control on spending, then under such circumstances sales promotions and advertising and accounts and finance departments are operating in dissonance and the result will be loss of the internal consistency and difficulties in the implementation of business strategy which aims at getting an edge on competition. So the functional plans of different functional divisions must be positively correlated, unidirectional and in tune with the business strategy of the organisation. This will develop and maintain internal consistency which is most essential for effective implementation of functional strategies.

The organisation should develop its capabilities relevant to the integration of functional plans and policies. These capabilities of the organisation offer if the competitive advantage. Normally, the organisation concentrates its resources in those functional areas where it wishes to build up its strategic competitive strength. Such a development of core competencies require synergy. Synergy is possible when different skills, efficiencies, talents and efforts of different functional areas are properly integrated. For example, when an organisation wishes to become a market leader has to pay attention to atleast, following four important things :

(i) Superior product quality.

(ii) Reasonable and affordable product price.

(iii) Efficient, prompt and economical product distribution.

(iv) Aggressive and attractive product promotion.

Now to give the best quality products, the operations department has to make the processing for conversion of raw material into finished products, precisely, accurately and the best possible manner. The finance department should work out the costing and fix the price in such a way that the best competitive price will be set for the customers. The product distribution dept should devise such methods and techniques as to keep the product supply to the market continuous and prompt. The sales promotion and advertising department should make the product campaigning, canvassing and publicity in the most attractive and influencing way. Thus, in order to become the market leader, the different functional divisions of an organisation have to work in a well organised, integrated and cohesive manner. And therefore all functional divisions will have to correlate their plans and policies and there must be the proper integration of the same. Then only the distinctive and effective organisational capabilities will be developed.

For effective functional implementation, certain trade-off decisions are to be made. The different functional areas have to work collectively and harmoniously. So the strategist has to place adequate and appropriate emphasis on all functional areas. Naturally each functional area has to sacrifice something, when emphasis is laid on the other areas. Such trade-off decisions are the part and parcel of functional implementation. However plans and policies should minimise the aberration due to trade-off decisions and optimise the implementation.

Further the strategist has to pay attention to the intensity of linkages. Though all departments should work in a coordinated and integrated manner, still there are some departments whose level of coordination of some specific strategies is required to be higher than other department. For example, an organisation adopting a cost leadership strategy and emphasizing on turning out low cost products will have to develop higher coordination among R & D department, operations department and marketing department. Further a strategy will have to develop a higher level of coordination among departments like R & D, product design, operations and marketing. Thus, we must remember that the intensity of linkages is not permanent and static and it may vary according to the need of the strategy from time to time. In addition to this timing of implementation is one more important consideration a functional policy to be implemented must be put to practice at the appropriate time, i.e., when it is most relevant. For example, if a company is trying to achieve the position of a market leader in a business where technical expertise of the employees is a critical factor of success, then it has to implement a development-oriented personnel policy. Otherwise it will fail to achieve the expected strategic goal. Further, in a market where competition is intense and so product development and innovation is the need of the time, a spending will be proved as untimely. Therefore functional policy implementation must have relevance to the time. Untimely implementation may result into weakening the corporate strategy or frustrating the corporate intent or failure in meeting the corporate goal.

Operational implementation is the last aspect of strategy implementation. Operational implementation refers to the approach adopted by an organisation for achieving operational effectiveness. It deals with all those nitty gritties of the strategy. It covers all details which are to be done practically in the organisation for strategy implemention. It relates to the tangible work which will put the strategy into an action with a focus. **Michael Porter** describes operational implementation in the following words. The operational implementation aims at achieving operational effectiveness which includes efficiency and which relates to performing similar activities better than your rivals. It refers to any number of practices that allows a company to utilise better its inputs by reducing defects in the product or by developing better products faster.

The scope of operational implementation and operational effectiveness is very wide. The science of management has developed and introduced several tools, techniques, radices and methods to improve operational effectiveness. The most critical areas of operational implementation and operational effectiveness are productivity, process, people and pace. Some experts view them as the 4 Ps of operational effectiveness. Productivity is usually described mathematically as the ratio of the quality of output to the quantity of input. It is the measure of output to input. Productivity will be said as higher when the desired output is obtained with less input and it is lower when higher input yields a lower output. Now the output is the organisational products and services, And the input is material and physical resources, monetary and manual resources, time and knowledge (technical know-how) resources and managerial resources. The use of all these resources as input incur some cost to the organisation. Now, when the company is able to turn up maximum output in minimum cost, it is achieving the higher productivity level and *vice versa*. To serve this purpose the organisation will have to avoid wastages, speed up the operations, reduce and eliminate the errors and mistakes and introduce such techniques and methods of work which will utilise the fully productive capacity of men and machines in the most efficient, effective and profitable manner for the short run as well as long run. Then only the productivity will be maintained at a higher level. Therefore the organisation will have to look into each and every detail of all kinds of work so that those can be done in the best possible way. Productivity upliftment requires detailing. Every smaller particular may add up to productivity or sometimes may adversely affect the productivity, if it is not properly attended to a mistake, defect or wastage by one may be very small and so may be treated negligible, but a cumulative effect of all these can produce a disaster. Infact, performance-deterioration is a gradual process. It begins with smaller errors and ends up into a situation of total loss and complete destruction. So at the operational level, things are to be watched out carefully. Productivity acts as an important criteria or degradation in the organisational working and accordingly the actual performance and actions are in tune with the strategy or otherwise.

The second area of operational effectiveness is people. People mean the stakeholders in the organisation. They constitute investors, customers, suppliers and employees. Among these stakeholders the employees play a direct and most crucial role in operational implementation. The capacity, skill, integrity and morale affect the operational effectiveness. If these elements are absent or in less proportion, then the operational efficiency and effectiveness is going to suffer adversely. Therefore the attention must be paid to develop the employee capacities to sharpen the employee skill to strengthen the employee integrity to boost up the employee morale then only the operational implementation will be effective.

The third area is pace, which means speed. Pace is always measured in terms of time. It is concerned with how fast a particular work is done. Efficiency is the parameter of pace. Efficiency is expressed as the ratio of work completed to time taken. Operational implementation has a time dimension. If the strategy is executed with all its details at proper time and within the reasonable time limit, then only its success is more probable. Decisions and actions delayed or prolonged are going to become fruitless and irrelevant. So one must do those things at the time when they are most needed. Second point to remember is that one has to make proper decision and action before his competitors do the same. You have to reach to a new market before your competitor goes there. You have to innovate and introduce a new product before your competitor starts thinking on that line so be the first and be the faster to become the first – this is the rule to win in a competitive atmosphere, so pace or efficiency of implementation has a great concern.

The fourth area of operational implementation is the processes. Processes making productive and fuller utilisation of their implementation methods involve procedure which are systematic and orderly procedures consists of steps which have a chronological order and which when followed gives the result of work-completion. So process involves methods, methods include procedure and procedure have a series to step or action which make the work to progress towards its completion. Proper procedure, correct methods and due processes contribute significantly to operational implementation.

Strategic evaluation and control : This is the final stage of strategic management. strategic evaluation operates at two levels : strategic level and operational level. At the strategic level the evaluation process aims at assessing the consistency of the strategy with the environment. At the operational level, the evaluation is made to check out how well an organisation is pursuing its strategy. This strategic evaluation has a broad purpose to assess and measure the effectiveness of the strategy in achieving organizational objectives. It also provides the direction for taking the corrective action whenever required. Strategic evaluation and control keeps the organisation on the right track. It tells us whether the strategy is producing the desired effect or not. Generally the strategic evaluation and control peeps into the following important questions and seeks out their answers.

(i) Are the premises on which the strategy is formulated proved to be correct?

(ii) Does the strategy direct the company towards its intended and desired goals?

(iii) Is the strategy implemented precisely and accurately or are there any flaws and defects in implementation?

(iv) Is there any need to change and modify the present strategy of formulate a new strategy?

(v) Does the strategy causes for fuller and proper utilisation of resources?

(vi) Is every decision and action being made as per the predecided schedule? What has caused for the delay? Strategy-deficiency or operational lethargy.

(vii) How the organisation has performed?

The strategic control and evaluation is important because it is able to co-ordinate the tasks performed by individual managers groups, division, SBU through the control of performance, strategic evaluation helps to keep a check on the validity of strategic choice. It assesses the suitability of decisions in the context of requirements of strategy. It takes a feedback of strategy implementation and thereby provides considerable amount of useful and valuable information which can give a sound base and direction for planning and developing new strategies.

The process of strategy-evaluation has four major steps, which are as follows:

(i) Setting standards of performance.
(ii) Measurement of performance.
(iii) Analysis of variances.
(iv) Corrective action.

The standards of performance are, in other words, the criteria of performance. These criteria are both qualitative as well as quantitative. The qualitative criteria try to assess a number of factors such as organisational capabilities, core-competencies, risk-bearing capacity, strategic clarity, flexibility and workability. **Glueck and Jauch** recommends three sets of qualitative criteria. They are

(i) Consistency.
(ii) Appropriateness and
(iii) Workability.

The criterion of consistency evaluates the strategy with respect to objectives, environmental assumptions and internal conditions. Then appropriateness assesses the strategy from the viewpoint of resources capabilities, risk preference and time horizon. Workability tests the strategy with regard to its feasibility and stimulation.

Besides this qualitative criteria, there are quantitative criteria also. An organisation can evaluate its performance quantitatively by two ways :

(a) It can compare its present performance with its past performance and thereby find out whether it is progressing or regressing.

(b) It can compare its performance with the industry average or with the performance of its major competitors – usually different financial criteria are used to make this quantitative evaluation. They are net profit return on investment, return on equity, earning per share, rates of dividend, market price of shares, sales–growth, market–share and productivity and efficiency, labour satisfaction index etc.

However, certain barriers occur in the process of strategic evaluation and control. Amongst the several such barriers the major barriers are as follows –

(i) Resistance to evaluation.
(ii) Short-term approach.

(iii) Limits of control.

(iv) Difficulties in measurement.

(v) Efficiency v/s effectiveness.

As the evaluation process makes an analysis of behaviour of managers and employees and tries to set a control on that, the manager and employees many times strongly resist it. At the same time, managers are interested in quick results and so they make the evaluation of all immediate activities, as it is easier and simpler. However the long term implications are ignored. So the extended effect of the strategy on the overall performance thus, remains unstudied and unscrutinised. Evaluation aims at setting the control. But the degree of control is very important and crucial issue. How much control the strategist should levy on the managers is a big question. Too much control will impair the freedom and ability of the managers to take initiative and to work creatively. Too little control will result into disharmony and lethargy will make the evaluation and control process infective and purposeless. So deciding an appropriate degree of control entailing disciplined performance and preserving the freedom to take initiative to introduce innovative ways and means to do the work in a better manner. Moreover the validity and reliability of the measurement techniques is again a questionable issue. This creates difficulties in measurement. The most debatable points in this regard are the problem of qualification of objectives or performance standards and the ability of the information system to provide valid and truthful information in time. If distortion occurs in the information, the evaluation can become incorrect and the control may become inadvertent. If performance standards are not set properly, the process of evaluation will lose its direction. So while setting the performance standards, the key areas of performance should be identified first and accordingly the key managerial tasks in these areas should be paid due attention. Such key tasks have some special requirements. Those should be considered well in advance. The performance indicator should very well express these special requirements. For example, if a company wishes to follow a market development strategy, then the key managerial task will be to improve and extend the identity of the products of the company in the market. For this purpose, the company will have to increase its material share, which is the special requirement of this strategy. Now, at the operational level the growth in sale will become the target and the increase in sales revenue will become a good performance indicator.

It is presumed, that once the performance standards are set appropriately, measurement becomes an easier task. But, this assumption is not 100 per cent correct. Because in an organisation, the activities are varied in nature and so demands different types of skills and efforts. For example, the contribution of a manager and that of a worker is always different in nature and importance. The later task can be quantifiable and so accurately measured. But how to measure the managers contribution precisely? A uniform standard for the managers and the worker cannot be set. In addition, to this difficulty, the timing of measurement and the periodicity in measurements also raises certain questions. The timing of measurement is concerned with the point of time at which evaluation is to be made. It should not be made either earlier or later, but should be made at the correct time. Normally a task should be evaluated when it is complete. However certain tasks are required to be evaluated during the process of their performance. So, in such cases the strategist has to set the critical points, when performance in respect of them is to be measured. This method is to be followed in respect of those activities of continuous and ongoing activities and which do not have a specific end-point. Another issue is the periodicity of measurement. It deals with the frequency of measurement. How often the evaluation should be made? This question does not have a definite quantifiable reply. It has to be resolved by applying the reason. For example, financial performance is measured quarterly, half yearly and annually. A strategic impact can be measured for the short as well as for the long-term. However, it should always be remembered that the frequency in evaluation should not disturb and intercept the performance. At the same time, see that the evaluation is not so much delayed, that its purpose is lost.

The fifth barrier in evaluation is the contrast between the concept of efficiency and effectiveness. Efficiency is described as doing the things rightly whereas effective performance emphasizes on doing the most appropriate and required things in the right manner. Effective performance avoids spending of time, energy and resources on doing unrelated, unwanted, purposeless task. Effectiveness brings for and direction in performance, whereas, efficiency brings economy.

These barriers in evaluation should be avoided. **Andrews** provide the correct line of thinking in this regard, when he says, that the true function of evaluation is to increase the perceptions of the problems limiting achievement.

Strategic control is another important activity which the strategist should carefully attend. Strategic control has the following three important aspects :

(i) To consider the changing assumptions that determine a strategy.

(ii) To evaluate continuously the implementation of the strategy.

(iii) To make the corrective action to adjust the strategy to the new requirements.

Strategic control differs from the traditional control system. Traditional control is a post-action control. Traditional thinking initiates control-measures when the action is complete. On the other hand in strategic control, the necessary steps to control an action are taken during the course of action. It is in the form of continuous control. Strategic control is in the form of an early warning system. **I D Hunger and T. L. Wheelen** *(Strategic Management)* have provided certain guidelines for effective control. These guidelines for effective control are as follows :

(i) Control should monitor only the managerial activities.

(ii) Control should be timely.

(iii) Control should aim at pinpointing exceptions.

(iv) Control should emphasize rewards for meeting/exceeding performance standards.

The strategic control is different from operational control. Therefore the emphasis in strategic control should be on monitoring the managerial activities. The managerial activities include decision making, planning, organising, co-ordination and communicating, directing and motivating and follow up. These managerial activities provide a system and set-up for operational performance. If the managerial functions are not properly done, the operational efficiency will definitely suffer. For, wrong or untimely decisions cannot be corrected by their precise execution. If a decision is wrong, an action following that decision is going to produce an unexpected and unfavourable outcome. The same rule applies to other managerial activities like planning the strategy or selecting the appropriate strategic alternative, developing, organising and allocating resource for strategy implementation, co-ordinating and communicating and giving direction motivation to employees to achieve higher targets and give their best performance. If these managerial functions are up to the mark, then their strict and disciplined implementation increases the probability of success. Therefore strategic control will have to pay more attention to managerial activities.

The timeliness in control is one more important thing to remember. Infact continuous monitoring and control is expected in strategy evaluation and control. Then only the control can be timely. So right from the step of strategic thinking prior to strategy formulation to strategy implementation at every control and monitoring is essential. Three questions should always be asked to test and check the validity of the strategy. They are :

(i) Is the strategy viable and workable?

(ii) Am I going in the direction of my goals and objectives? or Am I deviating from them?

(iii) Does the strategy give me any competitive advantage? How? When? Where?

Moreover, the rule of exceptions is advised. The control should pinpoint exceptions. This means that the strategist has to focus on the important activities which are the key activities and are more responsible for the organisational success. There is an eighty-twenty principle. This principle states that in every organisations, there are 20 per cent activities which are crucial and are responsible for 80 per cent achievements. Therefore If we carefully, handle watch, control, and monitor these 20 per cent activities, then 80 per cent achievements are guaranteed.

Rewards and penalties are two important tools of control. Rewards have a positive effect and they motivate people to perform better. Penalties have a negative and demoralising effect. Penalties discourage, whereas rewards encourage. However a clever combination of rewards and penalties is useful to direct and push up desired behaviour and to control and eliminate undesired actions. The performance should improve and enhance. This is done through rewards. At the same time, errors and bottlenecks should be removed and avoided further. Sometimes, only penalties are imposed for mistakes and for cost overruns. Hence, employee act with utmost care and caution. This improves efficiency to certain extent but the effectiveness is ignored. Thrift and economy must be maintained, but at the same time, results are also equally important. Efficiency focuses on getting the maximum by spending the minimum. Effectiveness emphasizes on doing the right think. This is possible by providing rewards. Efficiency is concerned with doing the thing in the right way, without making errors, mistakes and delays. This is done imposing penalties for wrongdoing. So by way of rewards and penalties an encouragement for both, to do the right thing and that too in the right way is given.

There are four basic types of strategic control. They are as follows :

(a) Premise control.

(b) Implementation.

(c) Strategic surveillance control.

(d) Special alert control.

Every strategy is based on certain assumptions in respect of the organisational and environmental factors. The changes in these factors can produce a very large effect on the strategy. Therefore it is essential to keep a track of such changes and assess their impact on the strategy. This is done through premise control. Premise control identifies the key assumptions and keeps a track of changes in them to evaluate their impact on strategy. The continuous testing of these basic assumptions to verify their validity, is an important job essential for the effectiveness of the strategy. And this job is done by the premise control. If the changes in the environment and the organisation are not properly studied, then the strategy will become ineffective and unrelated. For example, when the nature of competition (which is an important environmental factor) changes, the strategy has to be modified, because the previous assumption regarding the competition is no more valid now.

The second type is implementation control which is aimed at testing the plans, programmes and projects. These should guide the organisation towards its predetermined objectives. Implementation control checks out whether the plans, projects and programmes guide the organisation to its predecided objective or not. If at any moment of time it is felt that the allocation of physical, manual and time resources will not give the organisation the expected benefit, then immediately it can be revised. This becomes possible due to implementation control. Infact, implementation control leads to strategic rethinking. There are two methods of practicing implementation control. The first is milestone review method and the second is identification and monitoring of strategic thrusts methods. In the milestone review method critical points in the strategy implementation are identified. These critical points are in terms of events, important end-times and big allocation of resources. Thereafter a comprehensive review of these milestones is made to assess their continuous relevance in the achievement of strategic objectives. In other words, milestone review checks out and verifies as to how the events, project end-times and resources allocation which are the critical points in implementation are positively and sustainably contributing to the achievements of objectives. So, here we decide certain steps (milestones) in the implementation as more important and once we complete them then, we try to look into the progress towards objectives which is instituted and indicated by these milestones. In the second method of implementation control, the strategic thrusts are identified and monitored. For example, if a company wants to launch a new product, then under this method, it will conduct a pretesting and assess the possibility of market-success of this product. If this evaluation gives positive results. it will continue the product launching programme. But if the evaluation gives negative results, then it will abandone this programme and may take up another one.

Strategic surveillance is aimed at a more generalised and overreaching control and thus it is different from premise and implementation control which are more specific in nature. **Pearce II J A and Robinson Jr. R. B.** (Strategic Control – A New Perspective – *Academy of Management Review)* describe strategic surveillance as the one designed to monitor a broad range of events inside and outside the company that are likely to threaten the course of a firms strategy. For effective strategic surveillance we need to develop organisational learning and knowledge management system. Because strategic surveillance intends to monitor all those inside and outside events which will affect the company's strategy adversely. It is a broad-based control making general monitoring on the basis of selected sources of information. If some important piece of information is lost, then perhaps this type of control will collapse. So systematic and efficient management information system is essential. In this context, **David Aaken** (*Developing Business Strategies*) suggest that a formal, yet simple, strategic information scanning system can enhance the effectiveness of the scanning effort and can preserve much of the information now lost with the organisation.

Special alert control is based on what is called as trigger mechanism. It has a purpose of an immediate reassessment of a strategy. When sudden unexpectated events take place special alert control intends to give a rapid response to such unexpected events. With this view, it formulates contingency strategies and assign the responsibility of handling the unforeseen and unexpected events to crisis management teams. Crisis is described as a critical situation, which occur in an unexpected way and which threatens the course of a strategy. Certain events create such crisis; e.g., the sudden fall of a central government, a natural calamity, an industrial disaster, etc. When a crisis occurs, the organisation has to pay attention to minimise the losses and destruction. Crisis management has following important steps, as stated by **Mitroff II** *(Crisis Management–Cutting Through the Confusion)* :

(i) Signal detection.

(ii) Preparation for crisis and prevention.

(iii) Containment and damage limitation.

(iv) Recovery leading to organisational learning. ——— special alert control system performs the job of signal detection.

Strategic control is a complex process and in big organisations it makes use of sophisticated techniques for controlling purpose. Strategic control has a basic objective of continuously assessing and reassessing the environment and thereby detect and uncover all those events which significantly affect the strategy. It differs from operational control on several fronts. Operational control is concerned with actions and performance and is aimed at allocation and use of the resources of the organisation. Strategic control, according to **Pearce** and **Robinson**, is proactive in nature and is aimed at continuous questioning about the basic direction of the strategy. It is concerned with steering the future direction of the organisation. Strategic control, therefore has a focus on the external environment of the organisation, whereas, operational control focusses on internal environment and uses the techniques like budgets, schedules and MBO. Strategic control uses environmental scanning, information gathering, questioning and review as control–techniques.

The techniques for strategic control are grouped into two broad categories. This classification is made on the basis of the type of environment faced by the organisation. The organisation operating in a relatively stable environment uses strategic momentum control and the organisation in a relatively turbulent environment should use strategic leap control as it is more appropriate in that situation.

(a) Strategic Momentum Control: These evaluation techniques assure that the basic assumptions of strategy–formulations are still valid and tries to find out the ways and means to maintain the existing strategy momentum of the organisation. There are three techniques in this catagory. They are

(i) Responsibility control centres: These centres are of 4 types; namely, revenue, profit, expense and investment centers. They form the core of management control systems. Each of these centres is designed on the basis of measurement of input and output.

(ii) Examination of success factors: There are certain critical factors which are responsible for the success of the organisation as well as the strategy. These critical success factors (CSFs) are also referred as strategic factors or key factors for organisational success. The strategist has to identify these factors and manage them. By way of evaluation the strategist can assess whether these CSFs are helping the organisation to achieve its goals or not.

(iii) The generic strategies approach: This approach of strategic control makes a comparison between the organisations which adopt similar strategies. By this kind of comparison the organisation is able to know, how and why other organisations are adopting and executing the same strategy and whether our organisation is following the similar path.

In this regard, the concept of strategic group is the group of organisations which adopt similar strategies and use similar resources. It is observed that firms within the same industry adopt the similar strategies and thus belong to the strategic group.

(b) Strategic Leap Control: This type of control technique is useful for those organisation which are working in relatively unstable environment, such organisations have to make strategic leaps to introduce the significant changes. This control assists the organisation to define new strategic requirement and to cope up with the environmental realities. There are four types of techniques which are grouped as strategic leap control. They are as follows

(i) **Strategic issue management:** This technique is aimed at identifying the strategic issues and checking out their impact. on the organisation. **H.I. Ansof** *(Implanting Strategic Management)* defines strategic issue as the forthcoming development, either inside or outside of the organisation, which is likely to have an important impact on the ability of the enterprise to meet its objectives. The strategist can manage these forthcoming development i.e. strategic issue and thereby avoid the impact of surprising environmental changes. It can also design the contingency plans to make the strategy shifts, if so required.

(ii) **Strategic field analysis:** It looks into the synergies in the organisation. In the view of **P. Lorange, M. F. Morton and S. Ghoshal** *(Strategic Control)* strategic field analysis is a way of examining the nature and extent of synergies that exists or lacks between the components of an organisation. Thus, through this kind of analysis the strategist is able to trace out whether synergies exist in the organisation or not.

(iii) **Systems modelling:** It is a computer based model simulating the essential features of the organisation and its environment. This technique enables the organisation to exercise a pre-action control by assessing the impact of the organisation when particular strategy is adopted.

(iv) **Scenarios:** These are perceptions about the likely environment which the organisation will probably face in the future.

Besides the techniques of strategic control, following are some important techniques for operational control. They are grouped as – (a) Internal analysis (b) Comparative analysis (c) Comprehensive analysis

(a) **Internal Analysis :** It deal with the strengths and weaknesses of the firm in absolute terms. It consists of three types of techniques namely, value chain analysis, quantitatives analysis and qualitative analysis.

(i) **Value chain analysis:** It focusses on interrelated activities which are performed in a sequence for manufacturing and marketing the product or services. Value chain analysis is useful because it separates total tasks into identifiable activities and later on the firm can assess the effectiveness of these activities.

(ii) **Quantitative analysis:** It considers the financial and nonfinancial parameters. Quantitative factors bring ease and verifiability in evaluation. Ratio analysis, activity based costing, economic value addition, etc., are the financial parameters of quantitative analysis. The nonfinancial parameters include market ranking absenteeism, number of patents registered, rate of advertising recall, total cycle time for production, service call rate etc.

(iii) **Qualitative analysis:** Certain aspects of performance are such, that those cannot be measured with the help of numbers and figures and therefore qualitative analysis is necessary. Qualitative analysis supplements the quantitative analysis. The methods of qualitative analysis are based on judgement, intuition and opinions of experts. Surveys and experimentation are the commonly used techniques of performance-evaluation.

(b) **Comparative Analysis:** Comparative analysis consists of three methods, namely benchmarking, industry norms and historical analysis. Comparative analysis compares the performance of the organisation either with the organisation on with its own past performance.

(i) Benchmarking : Under this method the organisation finds out the best practices in a particular area and then follow those best practices and improve the performance. Best practices are the benchmarks and the organisations adopts them as the standards to exercise operational control. The organisation always attempt to bring its performance in line with these best practices in a particular area. The performance of the organisation is evaluated on a continuous basis, till the performance reaches the best practices or benchmark level. Now in order to excel, the organisation has to cross the benchmark and go beyond. Benchmarking can be done in any functional area like production, sales cost-control etc.

(ii) Industry norms : This method compares the performance of the organisation with its peers in the same industry. It makes a comparative assessment. The industry-norms method of evaluation makes the organisation competitive by enabling it to bring its performance to the level of its industry peers and then try to surpass it.

(iii) Historical analysis : Under this method the present performance of the organisation is compared with its past performance. As this method assesses the performance of the organisation over a given period of time, it also helps to analyse the trend or pattern of performance. It gives the organisation a better perception of its performance and so this method is used more frequently.

(c) Comprehensive Analysis : Comprehensive analysis adopts a total approach, rather than focussing on one function or one department or one activity. It includes following two methods.

(i) Balanced scorecard method : This method considers a wide range of parameters and thus follows a balanced approach to performance measurement. It identifies following four key performance-measures

(a) Internal business perspective.

(b) Customer perspective.

(c) Financial perspective.

(d) Learning and innovation perspective.

(ii) Key factor rating method : It adopts a holistic approach. It takes into account key factors in several areas and on the basis of them evaluates the performance.

Besides the above methods of performance–measurement **MBO** is another most popular and extensively used method for the same purpose MBO, i.e., Management by objectives is propounded by **Peter Drucker**. MBO is based on the regular evaluation of performance against the objectives set. These objectives are decided through the discussion between the superior and subordinate and are mutual agreed upon. Since the objectives are set through discussion and consultation, it develops a kind commitment in the workforce for their accomplishment and this automatically acts as a self-control system.

In India, the Marwari business firms follow, more usually, an effective system of operational control, which is called as the **Parta System.** It is an indigenous system which keeps track of daily cash generations. **S. Sharma** *(Management Control Systems – Text and Cases)* defines parta as the predetermined budget of the net inflows from operations before tax and dividend. Normally, the owner family and the company head and then a comparision is made between the budgeted parta and the actual performance on a daily basis.

Strategic control and evaluation plays a significant role in improving, upgrading and enhancing performance. Simply planning for excellence is not sufficient. Execution and follow up as well corrections of errors is equally important.

Kenechi Ohmae *(The Mind of the strategist)* views that insightful thinking, drive for achievement and a sense of mission is necessary to develop an effective strategy and effective strategy is the corner stone of excellence. Ohmae suggests that the determination of critical issue is an important central step in strategic thinking. Rather it is the starting point of strategic thinking. If we are able to pinpoint the critical issues of a problem, then we can devise more probably, the accurate solution! Now to pinpoint the critical issue we have to follow the process of abstraction. This process of abstraction has three stages namely.

(a) Concrete phenomena stage.

(b) Grouping stage.

(c) Abstraction stage.

The concrete phenomena stage begins with assembling the items in respect of which the company is at a disadvantage, e.g., there may be several events when the young employees are not readily responding to organisational goals or several products of our organisation are not fetching good returns. Such problems, are common in respect of different people and in different situations, they show some kind of similarity and relatedness on the basis of which they can be brought together. These problems are putting the company at a disadvantage and are also pushing it far back to its competitors. Once such problems are identified and gathered together, they are further classified according to their common factor. These are called, the concrete phenomena, e.g., the cases of young employees with reduced interest can be classified into the concrete phenomena under the title 'Declining moral among younger employees' or the cases of fall in profit in respect of different products and markets can be classified into a concrete phenomena falling profitability.

The second stage of the abstraction process is that of grouping. Grouping will bring all problems having common denominator into one group, e.g., the concrete phenomena like the declining morale among youngsters, low departmental mobility among workers, aged workforce and prolonged retirements, clash between merit and seniority at promotion can be grouped as personnel problems. Then falling profitability and increase in the number of unprofitable products can be grouped as strategic problems. Increasing selling and distribution cost, rising production cost, higher wages and material cost, increasing interest on borrowed funds can be grouped as costing problems.

The third stage is that of abstraction. At this stage, the strategist looks into each group as a unit and enquires into the crucial issue which the unit possesses. Abstraction enables us to bring the crucial issue to the light. It avoids the risk of neglecting the important aspects, e.g., all personnel problems may be due to the inflexible organisational structure and policies, all cost problems may appear due to the lower cost of operations of our competitors and all strategic problems may be due to rigid strategy and lack of revision and modification in it.

After abstraction the strategist has to decide the solution. If the abstraction is precise, then the strategist can develop a concrete and workable solution. The right solution always depends upon the correct, complete and comprehensive analysis of the problem. And therefore, the scholars of strategic management say persistently that, analysis is the first step of right strategy formulation.

Implementation brings fruits to the strategy. A strategy in itself is not effective unless it is put to execution. The unorganised and inefficient implementation can reduce and mollify the effectiveness of even the best strategies. Unless we act, we will not get what we have planned for and our actions should be disciplined and directed precisely towards our goal. So pay attention to implementation.

Strategy and plan are the two terms which are very close to one another. And so, sometimes people treat them as synonymous. However the nature and purpose of business planning and strategic management are different, through both relate to the determination of future action, planning is rather neutral whereas strategy is more focussed. The purpose of the business strategy is to gain the competitive advantage. Therefore if there is no competition, then there is no need for the strategy.

Kenechi Ohmae explains the four routes to strategic advantage. Thay are as follows –

(a) Identify the key factor for success.

(b) Relative superiority.

(c) Aggressive initiative.

(d) Strategic degree of freedom.

(a) Identify the key factor for success (KFS): In order to gain the competitive advantage, under this method, the strategist recognises and identifies the key factor of success in the or in the concerned business. Then he diverts and concentrates more and more resources into that particular area. Where the organisation perceives an opportunity to obtain a strategic advantage over its competitors. The strategy based on KFS has an objective to intensify the functional differentiation. Therefore the resource are concentrated in a particular area in such a way that it will build up and strengthen those capabilities of the organisation with which it will be able to increase its market share and its profitability.

For example, in food industry the KFS is the preservation of freshness and taste of the products. So a company in food industry which wishes to follow a strategy based on KFS, will pour more resources (monetary, mannual, physical and time resources) for preservation of taste and freshness of its products. Again the electronics industry the KFS is product novelty and reduced price, so a company adopting the KFS strategy, shall concentrate all its resources on product research and development function.

(b) Relative Superiority: This approach in strategy thinking is based on exploiting competitors, weaknesses. Relative superiority will be established when the company is able to create and obtain some kind of relative advantage, which its competitors are not able to obtain. A company is able to achieve the relative advantage by exploiting any differences in the competitive conditions between itself and its rivals. For this purpose the company can make use of its technology, sales network, profitability of its noncompeting products or any other difference in the composition of its assets and that of the rival.

(c) Aggressive Initiative: This approach in strategic thinking is based on innovative ways of thinking and doing. It suggests to upset the existing assumptions and equations of doing the business. It advises on attempting forcefully and effectively to change the rules of the game of business. Therefore it tells you to ask why-why? In other words it advises to challenge the existing styles of thinking and doing the business. Aggressive initiative expects your company to think and act in a revolting manner. For example, if your competitor well-established in a stagnant or slow-grow industry, then you can beat him by developing an unconventional strategy following the approach of aggressive initiative aimed at upsetting the key factors of success on which your competitor has developed his advantage, By doing this your company may shake up the *status quo*, stir up the accepted assumptions of doing the business and thereby gain a novel and powerful advantage. In aggressive initiative all that you have to do is to become innovative, revolting and creative.

(d) **Strategic degree of freedom:** This approach of strategic thinking is based on maximising the user benefits so product modifications, new product development, development of new markets are the different ways by which the company can reach to this goal.

Kenchi Ohmae views that, in all these four major approaches, the principle concern is to avoid doing the same things on the same battlefield. Do not copy down your competitor. Do not repeat what the others have done or are doing. Always do and make should be always totally of yours, which your competitors will find not only hard and difficult to follow, but nearly practically impossible to imitate easily and economically. So your strategy and its advantage will remain something unique and beneficial to you only. Then extend this advantage further and still further.

KFS approach Focussing on key functions or operations is useful and reasonable when your company is suffering from resources scarcity. Particularly when the resources like capital, human beings and time are limited, scarce and somewhat inadequate it is more wise to concentrate them on key functional or operational areas. These key functional or operational areas are those areas which are decisive for successful business of that type. So identify these key areas and then apply the right mix of the scarce resources. Do it differently than your competitor so that you can get an advantage over him.

To identify the key factors, the strategist can follow any of the following two methods.

(1) Dissect the market as imaginatively as possible and identify its key segments.

(2) Discover what distinguishes the winner companies from the losers and then analyse the differences between them.

Market Segmentation: Dissecting the market relates to market segmentation. Segment the entire market productwise and customerwise. By doing this the strategist is able to identify the wide range of product-market segments and also recognise which segments are strategically important. Then, product-market strategies for the crucial market segments can be developed. The strategist can assign specific responsibility to implement these segmentwise strategies. Now it becomes necessary to know the profitability of each such proposed strategy. So calculate the likely pay-off for strategy for each segment and also calculate the resources requirements of each strategy. This calculation will help to decide the economic justification of the proposed strategies and segments. On the basis of this evaluation, revise the segment-priorities in the light of corporate resources.

Highlighting the differences between the winners and losers: This is another method of identifying the KFS. This method makes a thorough study of winners and losers and discovers and analyses the points of differences between them. In other words, it searches out who are the winners as well as the losers in the particular business and then researches into the causes of their victory and defeat. That is, why the winners are the winners and the losers are the losers. Thus, it investigates about the factors which contribute significantly to the success of a company in particular business. The key factors of success in different industries may be different. The KFS may lie in certain functional areas, distribution channels, production technology raw material sourcing, economies of scale, quantity and quality of sales forces product range and product variety etc.

After identifying the KFS the strategist has to exploit in the most advantageous manner. In order to search out to the KFS, the strategist has to scrutinise the entire vertical chain of business-system involving the raw material sourcing as the first stage to the final stage of customer-servicing. This scrutiny will provide guideline for identifying the KFS in the business-operations. By this way the strategist will come to know as to which of the business operations can be strategically more important. If the strategist tries to develop a strategy covering every stage of business operations, then it will overstrain the company resources. So by controlling one or two stages of the chain of business operations the strategist can derive a competitive advantage for his company. Identifying the KFS is one part and exploiting the KFS through a suitable strategy is the another part. Simply, identification of KFS will not automatically yield the company a competitive advantage. So the strategist has to develop a strategy which will deploy the KFS fully and persistently. For example, if you have an advantage in material sourcing due to backward integration, this advantage has to be properly preserved and utilised to win them competition or if you have a strong sales team then utilise its full strength by being aggressive and covering up an extensive market area. Sometimes your competition too has the same and equal capabilities like you, then your consistent and effective utilisation and execution of your capabilities will distinguish you from your competitor.

Relative Superiority: Sometimes there are identical product lines. In such a situation the products of our company and those of your competitors will mostly appear similar to one another and so it becomes difficult to identify the distinctive and unique strength of our product on which we can develop a comfortable market share. Under such circumstances a systematic comparison between our products and competitors product analysing the differences in respect of every major and minor aspect of the product can provide direction to achieve relative superiority. This relative advantage may be relating to product price or product cost.

Aggressive Initiative: Aggressive initiative is an approach of strategic thinking which challenges the prevailing assumptions of doing a business, by asking why-why, i.e., why should we produces and sell things in this way. Why should we make business in this particular manner? In this way aggressive initiative identifies the fundamental bottlenecks of the fundamental improvements. Sometimes a statement occurs in business. This happens due to a particular situation in which the cost of the operations and the effectiveness of striving for the KFS reaches to the limit. In such a stalemated situation operational improvements do not produce any radical effect. The efforts of the organisation to enhance the KFS does not produce any increase in the market share or the profitability of the company. The company, over the years, is drifting slowly in one direction and getting deteriorated in this process. In order to bring the company out of this deteriorating process and to break the stalemate, drastic steps are to be taken up. As a first step of the aggressive initiative approach, the strategist should challenge the accepted common sense of the industry. With this purpose, the strategist should enquire, whether the KFS has remained unchanged over the years or not. The production or selling methods might have remained unchanged which act as KFS and form the common sense notions of efficient business.

In aggressive initiative approach, the strategist raises most startling, brainstorming questions which challenges the existing assumptions of making business and thereby opens up new, revolutionary ways of thinking. Aggressive initiative approach induces and encourages us to think what is unthinkable, e.g., Why should we see the movies always in darkness? Why should the photographs have to go through the negative stage before being printed? Why is it essential to visit the bank to make the transactions like deposit or withdrawal of money, during specific office hours? — Such questions at the first glance may look unrealistic, useless and hopeless. However they have introduced innovative thinking in related business-areas. New products, new methods and new process are invented in the process of searching out the answers to these questions. Therefore, now we can watch movies on a television-set, without darkness around us. We have digital cameras and printers which omit the negative stage and directly give us the photographs. Presently, several banks have established ATM centres and started home-banking services so that the customer need not have to visit the branch office of the bank during specific working hours to make a transaction. Further the just in time technique of inventory management, outsourcing, collaborations, commerce are again some more examples of breaking the situation which has become excessively rigid over a long period of time.

Aggressive initiative tells us, simply to shake up the things a little, by listing the basic assumptions of that business are still valid and hold good for that business and its continuity. Aggresive initiative brings a spectacular change in the direction of strategic thinking. The fundamental of this approach is to confront what is taken for granted in a business and challenge it by a simple question – Why? – This kind of continuous questioning (such as why? why? why?) will lead to the stage where the basic and fundamental problems and bottlenecks are lying. Infact, this type of questioning and the inquisitive mind is the origin of all inventions, innovations and discoveries. So make questions and moreover make the right kind of questions.

Strategic Degrees of Freedom (SDF) : SDF is the mode of thinking which is useful more to the manufacturers of consumer goods and low cost industrial goods.

When we expect a particular company to improve its performance at all operational levels, we presume that the company has unlimited resources. But this assumption can never be realistic. Infact, a good strategic plan is the one which considers the constraints on resources and which can be effectively worked out within the limited, finite resources. Therefore the strategist has to choose a particular direction for success. Now this choice is again influenced by an important critical factor, called the degree of strategic freedom. In other words the strategist has to calculate and consider the space or room for improvement of performance in the direction decided earlier.

The strategy based on KFS focusses on the key factors of success and the ways to find them. The strategic degree of freedom deals with the amount of freedom for strategic moves in the areas surrounding a particular key factor. The strategist never thinks of adopting all the theoretical possibilities of improvement, while formulating a strategy. Because one has always to be realistic. The strategist therefore, tries to select the few axes which can produce the desired results. Strategic degree of freedom designates such axes along which a strategy can be realistically and practically worked out. The objective of assessing SDF is to avoid the wastage of money time and labour which will definitely in advance the best direction for the improvements. In broader context, the theme of SDF tells us to try to grasp the direction to concentrate the resources which will give us the best possible chance to capitalise most effectively on the key factors.

We know that strategies are to be formulated at different levels, namely at the corporate level, at the business level, at the functional as well as operational level.

Grand Strategies : The corporate level strategies are called grand strategies. These strategies are basically about the choice of direction which a company has to adopt in order to achieve its objectives. These strategies are of following four types.

(a) Stability strategy : This strategy is adopted by a company which intends an incremental improvement in its functional performance. For this purpose it marginally changes one or more of its businesses. Thus it does by changing its customer group, customer function or technology. Stability strategy is less risky. It involves fewer changes so the employee-resistance to change does not occur normally. In a relatively stable environment and after a rapid expansion, in both these situations, stability strategy is preferable.

(b) **Expansion Strategy:** When an organisation expects high growth, then it follows the expansion strategy. In such a situation it broadens the scope of its business to improve its overall performance. The expansion strategy may take the form and shape of concentration, integration, diversification, co-operation or internationalisation strategy. Expansion strategy is suitable to business environment which demands increase in the pace of the activity. The organisation following expansion strategy has two major advantages, one is psychological and the other is the market advantage. The prospects of growth in the expansion strategy has a motivational and self-satisfying effect on the staff and managers. It develops a sense of pride in the organisation. Additionally expansion strategy increases the market share and market control of the organisation and provides it an edge over its competitors.

Retrenchment strategies : When an organisation aims at contraction of its activities, it follows a retrenchment strategy. Then, it substantially reduces or eliminates the scope of its business. Retrenchment involves a partial or complete withdrawal in one or more of the businesses of the organisation in terms of customer groups or customer functions. In other words, by following a retrenchment strategy the organisation can trim the unwanted fats and can slim itself. By this method it can get rid of its unprofitable businesses, customer groups and customer functions. The retrenchment strategies are of these types, *viz.*, turnaround strategy, divestment strategy and liquidation strategy. Normally the retrenchment strategy is followed when the environment is extremely threatening. If the organisation is facing continuous losses, then the management may express its reluctance to remain in the same loss-making business and may adopt the retrenchment strategy. Sometimes the organisation wants to achieve stability, so it follows the retrenchment strategy and thereby shifts and reallocates its resources from unprofitable business to the profitable business. Some organisations wants to streamline their functions and businesses and build a focus for which they follow the retrenchment strategy.

Combination Strategy: A combination strategy is the mixture of the stability strategy, expansion strategy and retrenchment strategy. An organisation may adopt this mixture in different times in the same business. If the organisation is conducting different business in different industries requiring different strategic response, then it prefers a combination strategy. Even for large organisations facing complex environment, combination strategy is more useful.

Business level strategies: These strategies are the courses of action by an organisation for its businesses separately. These strategies are prepared to serve identified customer groups, satisfy their needs and provide them the value. In this process the organisation uses its competencies to gain, sustain and enhance its competitive advantage. **Michael Porter** has made the pioneering work on business level strategies. This work is known as competitive strategies. According to **Porter** the choice of a competitive strategy depends upon two factors, (1) The industry structure and (2) The positioning of a firm in the industry. Porter views that industry structure is determined by five competitive forces, which are as follows – (a) the threat of new entrants, (b) the threat of substitute products or services, (c) the bargaining power of suppliers, (d) the bargaining power of rivals, (e) the rivalry among the existing competitors in an industry. The second factor is positioning of the firm within the industry. According to **Porter** positioning is the overall approach of the firm to competing. It is designed to obtain the sustainable competitive advantage. It is based on two variables. (a) the competitive advantage and (b) the competitive scope. Competitive advantage can arise due to two factors namely lower cost and differentiation. Competitive scope, similarly can be in terms of broad target and narrow target. **Porter** states that there are three basic competitive strategies. They are (i) Cost leadership (ii) Differentiation (iii) Focus

When an organisation can obtain a competitive advantage by manufacturing and selling its products and services at the lowest cost than its competitors, it is following a strategy of cost leadership. When prices of all firms are comparable, a cost leader firm makes more profit due to lower cost. Such a firm, to keep the cost low analyses the cost drivers and identifies the areas to reduce the cost of its operations. It uses several innovative techniques to lower the cost such as attaining the economies of scale, developing cost-saving technology, higher capacity utilisation, mass productions and distribution, product standardization, targeting average customer, etc. A firm chooses cost-leadership strategy. when price competition is intense, customer loyalty is low, products are standardised and differentiation is looked as superfluous. Through cost-leadership is initially beneficial, the lower cost advantage is not long-lasting. Very soon the competitors too, start developing cost-reduction techniques. Secondly, cost-reduction is not market friendly. It ignores experimentation and modifications in product attributes and customers interest.

Sometimes the firm derives the competitive advantage by adopting a strategy of differentiation. Then, the firm incorporates special features in its products and services which are demanded by the customers. The prices of such products may be higher, but the products are unique in their character. According to **Porter** lower-cost is based on the competence of the firm to design, produce and market a comparable product more efficiently than its competitors; whereas differentiation is based on the competence of the firm to provide unique and superior value to the buyer in terms of product quality, special feature or after sale service. Thus a differentiated product stands distinctive in the market and is preferred by the purchasers for its special utility or attributes. Buyers are ready to pay more for such product because of its valuable utility. A firm can achieve differentiation by incorporating special features in the product, raising the performance of the product, increasing its quality and utility etc. A firm following differentiation which can cover up the cost of differentiation and leave a positive margin. A differentiating firm can successfully distinguish itself from its competitors. It can develop its own loyal customer class. It can prevent the new entrants in the market as such a differentiation is an expensive task. Differentiation has a greater focus on the market and customer as compared to the cost leadership. Though differentiation has a number of advantages, it suffers from several limitations also. Differentiation does not fetch the expected advantage if it is based on something which is not valued by the customer. Over differentiation or addition of unwarranted and unrelated features to the product reduces the utility, validity and importance of differentiation. Differentiation tries to develop and project the uniqueness of the differentiated product. But in the long run this perception of uniqueness does not sustain. Gradually, competitors start introducing similar product features and the differentiation no longer remains distinguishing. The one who is the first in differentiation, therefore reaps out the benefits in the initial period. The price premium in differentiation too has a limited benefit. Too high price offsets the attractiveness of differentiation. In that case the buyers start making the cost benefit analysis. If this differentiation is not properly communicated to the buyers, then the buyers neglect the additional advantages of the product while making their own cost-benefit analysis.

The third type of competitive strategies are focus strategies which are niche strategies. They rely on cost-leadership or differentiation but cater to a narrow segment of the market. Focus identifies a narrow target in terms of market and customer. A firm develops focus by choosing specific niche and identifying the gaps that are not covered by cost leaders and differentiations. Then it creates superior skills to cater to niche markets and develops superior efficiency to serve them. Focus strategies work when the market segment has some kind of uniqueness. The special features and attributes of the product should be able to satisfy the needs of such markets. The needs of such market should be so special that the other common customers have not perceived them so far. This niche must be big enough to become profitable and should possess good growth potential. At the same time the major industry players should not be interested in this niche. A focussed firm can protect itself from competitors as the other firms having broader target do not possess the ability to cater to niche market. They cannot profitably provide the products and services to the niche market like the focussed firm. However, adopting a focussed strategy and serving a niche market require development of special capabilities which is a difficult process. Costs are higher in such cases, as market is limited and the sales volumes are small. Focus is in fact a commitment to a narrow market segment such firms have difficulty in moving to other segments. Moreover niches are often transient. They soon disappear due to development of technology or market factors. Technology may make production of niche products easier or the customers may switch over from the niche products to lower cost products of the cost-leaders. Sometimes the niches may become big to attract big players. So a focussed firm has to consider these risks.

Strategy is one cornerstone of excellence. The other is corporate culture. Strategy-making is an intelligent, thoughtful job which requires insight as well as foresight. Following are some of the tips for better strategy formulation and implementation.

(1) Time and content, both are equally important. what a strategy does and what affects its effectiveness and success.

(2) A strategy must hit the competitor where he has no escape rule and therefore he has to come down to his knees. So compete in that market, where the rival firm has weakest chance of the successful rescue or strong retaliation.

(3) Assess the potential impact of the strategy and also the risk of failure, periodically. Evaluate – Measure – Attack

(4) Remember victory at battles contribute to win the war; but a war is not as simple as a battle.

(5) Quality, novelty, economy and speed are the four wheels of the success chariot. Balance them always.

(6) Go for SWOT regularly. Business environment is dynamic. Once a strong player is not always so.

(7) Information is the heart of strategy. Upto date, comprehensive, accurate information pumps life and energy in the strategy.

(8) Execution is the ultimate decisive step. A strategy will be successful only when it is implemented with prudence and promptness. So do not decide only, but act strongly to win.

❒❒❒

CHAPTER 4

ORGANISATIONAL CULTURE

Organisations have different identity which is separate from its founders and owners. They are corporate citizens. Similar to individuals, organisations too have their own image. However this distinctive identity and image is not conferred on the organisation automatically. Till 1975, scholars and students of management viewed organisations as a structure through which the activities of a group of people are co-ordinated and controlled. The organisations were thought to have existence, form and shape as displayed on the organisational chart. Therefore, the organisations were thought to have vertical levels, departments, authority, responsibility, relations, work groups, etc. Thus organisations were looked as rational means, only. But later it was realised that organisations are more than simple means and structures. They have life and energy like individuals. They have a living which influences the surrounding and which is influenced by the surrounding also. Organisations are flexible or rigid, supportive or indifferent, innovative or supportive like individuals. So it is felt by all of us that each organisation has a unique character beyond its structure. Thus EACH organisation has its own culture which makes it totally distinctive from others. Organisational culture has its origin in the process of institutionalisation. **Institutionalisation** is defined as a process whereby an organisation takes on a life of its own, which is separate from any of its founders or members and thus acquires identity and immortality. An institutionalised organisation acquires its own value and status. It gets a self-recognition beyond its products and services. When its original goals become irrelevant, it redefines them and continues its stay in the business. Institutionalisation develops a common understanding among the members about the propriety and sensibility of behaviour. Under such circumstances desirable and acceptable modes of behaviour and performance become self-evident to members. Institutionalisation acts as the foundation of organisational culture. **Stephen Robbins** views organisational culture as a system of shared meaning held by members that distinguishes the organisation from other organisations. In the words of **Edgar Schein** organisational culture is a pattern of basic assumptions invented, discovered or developed by a given group as it learns to cope with its problems of external adoption and internal integration that has worked well enough to be considered valuable and therefore, to be taught to new members as the correct way to perceive, think and feel, in relation to those problems. **Turnstall,** defines organisational culture as a general constellation of beliefs, morals, value systems, behavioural norms and ways of doing business that are unique to each corporation. According to **Joanne Martin,** as individuals come into contact with organisations, they come into contact with dress norms, stories people tell about what goes on, the organisation's formal rules and procedures, its formal code of behaviour, rituals, tasks, pay system, jargon and jokes, only understood by insiders and so on. These elements are some of the manifestation of organisational culture.

According to **Fred Luthans**, following are the important characteristics of the organisational culture.

(1) **Observed Behavioural Regularities:** The members of an organisation, while interacting with each other use common language, terminology and other rituals that relate to deference and demeanour.

(2) **Norms:** Standards of behaviour as well as work performance exist in each organisation. They provide guidelines as to how much work to do. Organisations may express it as do not do too much or too little.

(3) **Dominant Values:** Organisations advocate certain major values and expect that its members should follow the same. Some of such values are high efficiency, customer care, best product quality, regularity and discipline, etc.

(4) **Philosophy:** Organisations lay down policies based on certain beliefs about how employees and customers are to be treated.

(5) **Rules:** Organisations set guidelines for members to get along in the organisation. The new members have to learn them and adopt them. Then only they are accepted as full-fledged members of the organisations.

(6) **Organisational Climate:** It is described as the overall feeling, that is conveyed by the physical layout, the way participants interact and the way members of the organisation conduct themselves with customers and other outsiders.

These characteristics, according to experts, exist on a continuum from low to high. Empirical research support them.

Stephen Robbins gives yet another list of primary characteristics of organisational culture, based on various research. They are

(1) **Innovation and Risk:** The degree to which the employees are encouraged to take risk and conduct innovation.

(2) **Attention to Detail:** The degree to which employees should attend to details, show the precision and make analysis.

(3) **Outcome Orientation:** The degree to which the management focuses on outcomes and results compared to the techniques and processes adopted to achieve these results.

(4) **People Orientation:** The degree to which the management considers the effect of its decision on people.

(5) **Team Orientation:** The degree to which work activities are organised around teams rather than individuals.

(6) **Aggressiveness:** The degree to which the members of the organisation are competitive and aggressive rather than easy-going.

(7) **Stability:** The degree to which organisational activities maintain *status quo* in contrast to growth and progress.

The organisational appraisal on the basis of these seven characteristics give a picture of its culture. These characteristics too exist on a continuum of low to high.

Organisational culture is a descriptive term. It is not evaluative. It is concerned with how employees perceive the different characteristics of the organisation's culture. It does not enquire whether the employees like it or not. Research on organisational culture seeks out how employees see their organisation. So organisational culture is the common perception which the members of the organisation hold.

The study of organisational culture is not complete unless we understand certain related important concepts such as dominant culture, subculture, core values, strong and weak culture. People having different background join organisations. So organisations do not have a uniform culture. All members do not share the common perception to the same degree. As a result of this, dominant culture and subculture exists throughout a typical organisation. A **dominant culture** expresses the core values which are shared by a majority of the members of the organisation. It is the macro view of the culture and it gives the organisation a distinct identity and personality. In fact, when we talk about the culture of an organisation, we are referring to its dominant culture. Besides the dominant culture, there exists a subculture in every organisation. A **subculture** is defined as the set of values which are shared by the minority members of the organisation. Usually it is a small minority and so subculture is in the form of mini-culture. Subcultures tend to develop in large organisations and are the results of the problems and experiences shared by the members of a particular department or unit. A subculture mostly has the core values of the dominant culture plus additional values unique to the members of the minority group. Core values are defined as the primary or dominant values that are accepted throughout the organisation. The subcultures can develop vertically or horizontally. Suppose a particular product division of a conglomerate has a unique subculture, different from other product division. Then we can call it a case of vertical subculture. Similarly, when the functional specialists like accountants, engineers, cost consultants, legal officers have a set of common shared understanding, then the horizontal culture develops. If the organisation has no dominant culture and if numerous subcultures exist within it, then the uniformity in the interpretation of the appropriate and inappropriate behaviour will be lost and so the value and significance of organisational culture as an independent variable will reduce. Culture acts as a powerful device to guide and direct behaviour. This is possible due to the aspect of shared meaning. If this aspect is absent, it automatically becomes nonexistent. Once different groups of people decide and accept different criteria (which sometimes contradict one another) for propriety of behaviour, then a standard uniform, well accepted meaning of appropriate and desirable behaviour is not developed. So the commonness of suitable behaviour is absent and the organisation becomes a cultureless entity. Groups and individuals start behaving in their own manner and according to their own personal philosophy. In such organisations the bonds of unity and togetherness which culture develops throughout the organisation are weak and sometimes completely fragile.

Further organisational culture may be strong or weak. In a **strong organisational culture** the core values are intensely held and widely shared. A large numbers of such organisation are seen to have accepted the core values and possess greater commitment to those core values. In an organisation with strong culture, the high degree of sharing and intensity creates an internal climate of high behavioural control. Thus a strong culture has a strong impact on the behaviour and performance of the employees of the organisation. The members of such organisations very clearly know what is expected of them and they are sure about what to do and how to do as a matter of an appropriate action. In a strong culture there is a high degree of agreement among the members for what the organisation stands for. This unanimity regarding organisational objective builds loyalty, cohesiveness and commitment. Thus a sense of unity and belongingness develops and so the propensity to quit the job and leave the organisation declines. So organisation with strong culture have less employee turnover. As against this, when core values are not shared with high degree of intensity, the result is the formation of **weak** organisational **culture**.

The degree of sharing depends upon two factors – (a) orientation and (b) rewards. Orientation programmes are organised for the newcomers. Through such programmes the newcomers are informed and trained in respect of the core values of the organisation. Informal orientation also can be done through day to day work habits, personal dialogues and examples. Rewards also play a vital role in building strong organisational culture. Promotion, incentives and growth opportunities as rewards to employees who understand and follow the core values better, encourage other employees to adopt the same practice. This automatically increases the degree and intensity of sharing.

Functions of Culture: Organisational culture brings identity and uniqueness to the organisation. Organisations distinguish themselves from others doing the same or similar business on the basis of their culture which is reflected in the performance and behaviour of its members. The other major functions which culture performs are as follows.

(1) Culture provides for shared patterns of understanding about organisational values and beliefs. This influences the thinking and behavioural process of the members of the organisation.

(2) Organisational culture draws a boundary that separates and differentiates one organisation from another. This boundary helps to identify and distinguish the members of the organisation from the non-members.

(3) Culture generates a sense of commitment to something larger than one's personal self-interest.

(4) Culture provides social stability to the members of the organisation, by providing them appropriate standards.

(5) It acts as a control mechanism to guide and shape the attitude and behaviour of organisational members.

(6) It makes the employees stick to the conformity by prescribing behavioural modes.

(7) Members of the organisations learn what to value and how to feel under different circumstances from organisational culture.

(8) Culture provides unity of direction and purpose to the members of the organisation.

(9) Subcultures help the members to deal with specific day to day problems. By way of social architecturing, subcultures are to be integrated in dominant culture to develop a strong organisational culture.

(10) Culture can create and nurture the spirit of excellence.

Organisations have either mechanistic or organic culture. Similarly organisational culture may be authoritarian or participative. **Mechanistic organisational culture** displays the values of bureaucracy and feudalism. Authority, then flows from top to bottom. Communication is restrictive and flows through prescribed channels only. Organisational work is conceived as a system of narrow specialisation. So there is strong departmental loyalty and interdepartmental animosity. The loaded terms like we and they acquire immense importance and feelings of separation prevail among groups and departments throughout the organisation. The organisation becomes machine-like, where each component part is separate from one another, has a specific place and particular function to do. Every part operates, but still there is very less spontaneous interrelationship. All groups and departments perform their specific functions in prejudiced manner though the attempts to bring integration and cohesion in them are least. Hierarchy, departmental boundaries, formalities, rules and regulations, procedures have more importance than task-accomplishment.

Organic culture, on the other hand, has a greater emphasis on task accomplishment, teamwork and free communication. It keeps away the formal hierarchy of authority, rules and regulations and prescribed norms of communication in a problematic situation. The thrust is then on solving the problem. Organic culture is like the human body which responds to any situation as a whole cohesive, unified entity. There is utmost integration and cohesion in the organisation. A typical wholeness and unity is observed in the organisation when it faces challenges, problems and difficulties. There exists a widespread understanding within the staff about the problems, threats and opportunities which the organisation is facing and there is willingness and preparedness to take appropriate roles to solve the problems. In such a culture, when problem arises the person with expertise assumes spontaneously the leadership position and wields far more influence than the formal boss. Organic culture emphasises on flexibility, teamwork, consultation, change and innovation. Mechanistic culture has a strong resistance to change. Organic culture is thus more live, enthusiastic and energetic. There is greater degree of relatedness, belongingness and involvement in work and people at all levels of the organisation.

In the **authoritarian culture** all the power and authority is concentrated in the hands of the leader. Obedience and discipline are great virtues and disobedience is severely penalized and punished. It is presumed that he knows very well what is good for the organisation and acts accordingly such a culture may result into development of 'Yes Boss' mentality in the organisation. In a **participative culture,** democratic management style is followed. Employees are encouraged and allowed to participate in decision making. The basic assumption underlying this practice is that, people are more committed to decisions which are participatively made than to those which are imposed on them by the authority. In a participative culture group-problem-solving methods are used. This induces collective thinking. Different, undiscovered aspects of a problem are also highlighted and studied minutely. Information-sharing and new and innovative thinking is mostly observed in the organisations having participative culture. Participative culture breeds equality, sharing and responsibility. Especially when, the members of the organisations are professionally qualified and expert, the participative culture is suitable.

Culture as a Liability: Culture has certain functional as well as dysfunctional impact. The functional impact or merits of the organisational culture include an enhancement in organisational commitment, consistency of employee behaviour and the reduction in ambiguity. However, there are certain dysfunctional impacts or demerits of the organisational culture which makes it a liability instead of an asset. The liability aspects of organisational culture are as follows:

(i) Culture acts as a barrier to change.

(ii) Culture becomes a barrier to diversity.

(iii) Culture works as a barrier to mergers and acquisitions.

Organisational culture develops the consistency in employee behaviour. This works as an asset in a stable environment. But when the environment is dynamic and is undergoing a rapid change, an entrenched culture of an organisation is not appropriate because then the culture makes it difficult to respond to the environmental change. Culture thus acts as a barrier to change when the business of the organisation is not as usual like the past.

Culture becomes a barrier to diversity. Workforce diversity becomes a reality today. Diversity arises when an organisation hires new employees of different race, religion, gender, language, nationality than the majority of the organisation's members. This may breed up paradox.

Management wants these employees to accept the core organisational values. At the same time, it wishes to extend its acceptance and support to diversity and differences to create its image as a liberal, generous, democratic management. Strong cultures, however, pressurise the employees to conform. They limit the range of acceptable values and styles. This acts as a barrier to diversity.

Culture becomes barrier to merger and acquisitions also. Mergers and acquisitions are normally made to obtain financial advantages or product synergy. But if the culture of amalgamating organisations do not match, then problems relating to performance, behaviour and teamwork arises. This eliminates the expected advantages of merger and increases complexity of management.

CREATING AND SUSTAINING ORGANISATIONAL CULTURE

According to **Fred Luthans**, the process of development of organisational culture has following important steps.

(i) The founder (usually a single person) has an idea of a new enterprise.

(ii) The founder brings in one or more key people and creates a core group that shares a common vision with the founder.

(iii) The founding core group begins to act in concert to create an organisation by raising funds, obtaining patents, incorporating, locating space, building and so on.

(iv) At this point, others are brought into the organisation and a common history begins to be built.

In the early stage of organisational formation, the founder and his core group establish the organisational culture. Their vision and mission about the organisation creates values and norms which is the core part of the organisational culture. In the early period, the small size of the organisation facilitates the founder to spread up and communicate his vision throughout the organisation and among all its members. The founders have typically some original idea about the organisation. These ideas are mostly free from the previous assumptions or biases. So some kind of unique culture of the organisation starts developing. This initial organisational culture is mostly influenced by the personal values and ideologies of the founder and his key associates. These values, ideologies, concepts, assumptions, biases and norms regarding the performance and behaviour set up the framework of organisational culture. This fixes the boundaries for all employees and expresses what is permissible and what is nonpermissible. This original culture gets modified and enhanced by the experience of the old members of the organisation who were initially employed by the founder and his core team.

After the organisation starts working, some critical incident takes place, which brings alteration and reform in the existing organisational culture. These critical incidents may have positive or negative impacts. Some incidents may be traumatic or undesirable. They produce anxiety or tension. Naturally certain norms and precedents are developed to avoid such incidents. Certain 'Don'ts' are decided to reduce and eliminate the possibility of future occurrence of such incidents. After a considerable period the precedents become the values and principles prescribing the particular culture of the organisation. Similarly. The critical incidents producing positive impact too, develop certain cultural norms. They set the 'Dos' in the organisation. They prescribe the desirable behaviour for the members of the organisation.

Sustaining the Organisational Culture:

Sustaining the organisational culture is a process of solidifying the acceptance of the core values and the ensuring of the maintenance of the culture by itself. There are several practices to do this. **Fred Luthans** describes the following sequence of the steps of the socialisation process for this purpose.

(i) **Selection of entry level personnel:** At the time of selection of an employee, besides his specific skills and job-related traits; his personal style and values are also screened to find out whether they fit with the organisation's culture. When this happens, there is greater organisational commitments and lower attrition rate among the employees. If the employees have a realistic job preview (popularly called as RPJ) of the organisation's culture, then they are found to be doing well in that organisation.

(ii) **Placement on the job:** This is the second step. At this stage the new recruit is subjected to a carefully orchestrated series of different experiences. Its purpose is to instigate the new recruit to question about the values and norms of the organisation and to decide whether he can accept them or not. For example, in some organisations the new entrants are purposefully given bigger targets and more work-load which are beyond their initial capacity. This is done to teach them humility and tell them that they are beginners and have to learn a lot. It also intensifies the group cohesiveness, as the employee under such situation is emotionally stirred up and so starts relating with his co-workers and colleagues.

(iii) **Job mastery:** At the second stage the new employees feel a cultural shock. This shock is reduced through training and field experiences offered to the new entrants to get a mastery on the job. This helps the employee to learn the organisation's culture, its values and norms.

For example, in Japanese companies promotion is seniority based and time-bound. The employee collects lot of job experience and develops considerable expertise before he is elevated to a higher post. When a newly hired worker learns this performance norm there, he is not tempted to search for a short cut or a political means for rise in the career.

(iv) **Measuring and rewarding performance:** This step consists of meticulous attention to the measurement of operational results and accordingly rewarding the individual performance. These systems should be comprehensive and consistent. They should focus on those aspects of business that are most crucial to corporate values, such as competitive success. In organisations with strong culture, the employees violating cultural norms are sent to, what is termed as, penalty box. This penalty box typically involves a lateral move to a less desirous location. This way the faulty employee is side-tracked. As a result of this, the career-progress of such a person either slows down or stops. Measuring and rewarding performance typically makes the employee to fit himself in the organisational culture.

(v) **Adherence to important values:** To sustain the organisational culture, there should be a careful adherence to the firm's important values. For this purpose the employees should identify themselves with the organisation's core values. Identification with values involves learning to accept these values and trusting them. There should be a strong integrity towards these values and a commitment that anything that harms these values will never be done. Identification with values not only consists of wholehearted acceptance of values but simultaneously the uncompromising loyalty and fidelity with them. Observation of these values then become the prominent purpose of one's decisions and actions. As **Pascale** feels that it is in one way of placing oneself at the mercy of the organisation. Because when the employee resorts to the organisational values, he is actually making a lot of sacrifice in terms of long working hours, inconvenient job-rotations and transfers, unfair criticism, etc. He accepts all these because he is convinced that he is serving a noble cause like availing the society in general and customers in particular goods and services of better quality and thereby, enhancing their consumption satisfaction. This compensates the sacrifices. The employee incurs a mental cost when he surrenders his personal life for organisational work. But then the important core values of the organisation which he adheres to gives him a relief and reward that he is doing a meaningful and socially useful activity. This results into an earning of appropriate price for the costs incurred. An organisational culture which builds the proper learning and understanding of its core values, helps the employees to internalise these values and identify themselves with these values. This helps to sustain and strengthen the organisational culture.

(vi) **Reinforcing the stories and folklore:** Folklore helps to explain why the organisation does things in a particular way. So the folklore need to be reinforced. One of the common forms of folklore is stories with those morals which the organisation wishes to reinforce. These stories of folklore more easily communicate the cultural values of the organisation among the staff as well as to outsiders.

(vii) **Recognition and promotion:** Recognition and promotion of employees doing their job well and who can become the role models for others is an important task in sustaining culture when such employees are honoured as winners, other employees are automatically induced to follow the behavioural and performance pattern. Recognition is a powerful reinforcer. When a particular decision, action, behaviour or performance is recognised, it is more likely to be repeated not only by the person concerned but also by other spectators. Because they too want that kind of reward. Formal recognition has a good motivational impact. Social recognition in the form of one on one attention, too, produces good results in this regard. Recognition and promotion of employees strictly adhering to the cultural values of the organisation can effectively build, spread and sustain organisational culture.

Stephens Robbins views that once a culture is in place, there are practices within the organisation, that act to maintain it by giving employees a set of similar experiences. According to him the following three forces play a particularly important part in sustaining a culture.

(i) Selection practices.
(ii) The actions of top management.
(iii) Socialisation methods.

The selection process typically assesses and identifies the knowledge, skills and ability of the candidate in the context of the expected level of performance on the job. However, at the point of final selection of the candidate, his precise suitability in the organisation is considered deeply and minutely. This suitability is judged on the basis of the value system of the candidate. A quest is made whether the candidate possesses values same or similar to the organisational values. Because in order to become a good match for the organisation, the aspiring candidate must possess at least a good portion of the core values of the organisation. Any mismatch in this regard becomes problematic further to both, the organisation and individual. So the management of the organisations makes such type of screening while selecting and recruiting new employees so that a judgement regarding their fitness in the organisational culture can be made precisely. Those who are fit from the point of view of the culture are selected and this is how the organisation sustains its culture.

The actions of top management produce a major impact on the organisation's culture. The decisions, actions, views and expressions of the chairman, the CEO, the Managing Director and such other similar top management people send a message for the employees about the organisation's culture. Through what these top people speak and how they behave, the senior executives establish norms that filter down through the organisation. These norms tell what is an appropriate behaviour, what should be avoided, what is more valuable in the organisation. Such norms strengthen the value-system in the organisation and make its culture sustain.

Socialisation is the third important force which helps to sustain the organisational culture. Socialisation is an adoption process. It is defined as the process that adapts employees to the organisation's culture. When new employees join the organisation, they are unfamiliar with its culture and so they are potentially likely to disturb the belief and customs in the organisation. Therefore they need to be indoctrinated in the culture of the organisation. Socialisation serves this purpose. The most critical stage of the socialisation process is the entry of the new recruit in the organisation. At this point the organisation seeks to mould the outsider into an employee in good standing. If the new recruit fails to learn the essential or major role behaviours, he is labeled as nonconformist or rebel. And then the organisation may expel him. Similarly the organisation is socialising every employee during the entire period of his career either explicitly or implicity.

Conceptually socialisation process has three stages, (1) Prearrival stage (2) Encounter stage (3) Metamorphosis stage. The prearrival stage encompasses all the learning that occurs before the new recruit joins the organisation. It recognizes explicitly that each individual joins the organisation with a set of values, attitudes and expectations.

These expectations are about the job and work to be done as well as the organisation. Prearrival stage is defined by **Stephen Robbins** as the period of learning in the socialisation process that occurs before a new employee joins the organisation. The training in schools and colleges play a significant and useful role in this respect. For instance Business Schools provide training that moulds attitudes, values and expectations suitable to work as managerial personnel in business organisations. In certain professions prearrival training is given to the aspiring newcomers to make them fit and suitable for that profession. For example, compulsory articleship in chartered accountancy course or compulsory internship in medical education. Besides such prearrival training selection process is also useful for prearrival socialisation. During this process of selection many organisations inform the prospective employees about themselves as a whole. The selection process ensures the inclusion of the right type of the employee in the organisation. **Van Maanen and Schein** writes in 'Career Development' that the ability of the individual to present the appropriate face during the selection process determines his ability to move into the organisation in the first place. The success depends on the degree to which the aspiring member has correctly anticipated the expectations and desires of those in the organisation in charge of selection.

The second stage of the process of socialisation is the encounter stage. It is the stage in the socialisation process in which a new employee sees what the organisation is really like and confronts the possibility that expectations and reality may diverge. When the new member enters into the organisation he brings certain expectations about the job, co-workers, boss and the organisation in general. The expectations may be fulfilled or may not be. Accordingly the perceptions of the employee formed earlier may either be reaffirmed or reality may totally differ. When the expectations and reality differ, the new employee must undergo socialisation that will detach him from his previous assumptions and conceptions and replace them by another set of them which the organisation deems desirable. If this socialisation fails and if the new employee is totally disillusioned with the actualities of the job; he may resign and quit the job in the extreme situation. Therefore, at the selection stage proper and careful screening and assessment of the adaptability of the candidate is important to the organisational culture.

The third and the last stage of the socialisation process is called the metamorphosis stage. **Stephen Robbins** views that this is the stage when a new employee changes himself and adjusts to the job, the workgroup and the organisation. This metamorphosis can be made in a number of ways. **Robbins** gives following options for this purpose.

(1) **Formal vs. Informal Socialisation:** In formal socialisation, the newcomer is segregated from the ongoing work setting and is informed about his role explicitly. Specific training programmes and orientation programmes are the examples of formal socialisation.

Informal socialisation puts the employee directly into his job without any special training.

(2) **Individual vs. Collective Socialisation:** Usually the professional firms socialise the new members individually. As against this in army camps the new members are grouped together and processed through an identical set of experiences.

(3) **Fixed vs. Variable:** This classification of socialisation methods is made on the basis of time-schedule. In case of fixed schedule, standardised stages of transition of a newcomer from outsider to insider are established. Training programmes and probationary periods are the examples of fixed schedule socialisation. Variable schedules do not have any fixed time-table or time-limit. It focuses on making the newcomer 'ready' for taking the assignment. Unless he becomes 'ready', the socialisation is not complete. As such there is no fixed schedule. Variable schedules do not give any advanced notice of their transition time-table.

(4) **Serial vs. Random:** In serial socialisation the role models are used, who train and encourage the newcomers. Apprenticeship and mentoring programmes are the examples of serial socialisation. In random socialisation role models are deliberately withheld. The newcomer is left on his own to figure out the things.

(5) **Investiture vs. Divestiture:** Investiture socialisation presumes that the qualities and qualifications of newcomers are essential for job success. So it confirms and supports them. Divestiture socialisation on the other hand tries to strip away certain characteristics of the newcomers.

It is found that more organisations adopt formal, collective, fixed-schedule, serial and divestiture socialisation techniques. They focus on stripping away differences and replace them by the standardised behaviour, which is more predictable. By the process of socialisation the organisation may breed up conformists or creative individuals. This depends upon the nature, purpose and direction of the metamorphosis process. This process shapes the newcomers as the organisation desires. Careful selection provides potentially suitable candidates. Socialisation moulds and carves out of them right type of employee personality. Socialisation is complete when the newcomer becomes comfortable with the organisation and the job. He has then, understood and internalised the norms of the organisation and work group and has accepted them. Then the newcomer becomes a trusted and loyal member of the organisation. His peers and superiors place confidence in him. He feels sure of his capabilities. He knows his job very well and is also aware of rules, procedures and formal as well as informal practices followed by the organisation. He knows the criteria of his evaluation and work-appraisal. He understands what the organisation expects from him and what constitutes a job 'well done'. He adopts what the organisation describes as the desirable behaviour. A newcomer then becomes perfectly fit and matching to the organisational culture. Metamorphosis converts a newcomer into an organisational man. Socialisation produces a positive impact on the productivity and commitment of the employee. It reduces their propensity to leave the organisation and go elsewhere.

Learning the organisational culture: Culture is transmitted to employees through several different means. The most important and effective means are stories, symbols, rituals, language and statement of principle. A brief discussion of these means is as follows.

(i) Stories: The newcomers learn about the organisational culture through well composed and remembered true stories about the founders, policies and practices of the organisation. A story about some critical incidence underlining the moral is also useful. Normally these stories are told by the seniors to the juniors on different occasions and thus pass over to generations. These stories pass the message what the organisation at values are and how these values were created and nurtured over the years.

(ii) Rituals: Rituals refer to any practice or pattern of behaviour which is repeated in a prescribed manner. According to **Stephen Robbins** rituals are repetitive sequences of activities which express and reinforce the key values of the organisation, which goals are most important, which people are important and who are expendable. E.g., daily singing of prayers or company songs by work-groups, annual conventions and performance appreciation therein, monthly get-togethers and celebrations of group achievements, probationary periods and assessments of newcomers, common lunch, regular sports and exercises, etc. These specially designed repetitive activities conveys the employees how their organisation is culturally different from similar ones in the same business. Rituals help the employees learn the culture of their organisation.

(iii) Material symbols: Certain material symbols play an important role in culture learning. The layout of corporate headquarters, the layout and size of offices, the elegance of furniture, dress, attire, executive perks, etc., are called material symbols. These symbols convey to employees who is important, the degree of egalitarianism desired by top management, the expected suitable behaviour, etc.

(iv) Language: Every organisation develops unique terms to describe equipment, offices, key personnel, suppliers, customers or products. New employees learn these acronyms and terminology and then start using the same. Thus they develop a feeling of being an integrated member of the organisation. This language is a special part of organisational communication. More fluency the employee acquires on this language, the stronger bonds they develop about their relationship with the organisation.

(v) Statement of principle: The culture is transmitted through statement of principle. Some organisations display their principles publicly. The moral values and principles which the organisation thinks important are formally and informally communicated to the employees. Principles and values are always central to any culture. Once they are properly understood by employees, automatically the employees start inheriting the culture. Some organisations prepare and publish the code of ethics and expect the employees to follow the same.

Impact of culture on the effectiveness of the organisation: The culture of an organisation has positive as well as negative impact on its effectiveness. The positive or functional impact of the culture produces good results such as unity, harmony, teamwork, productivity increase and reduced labour turnover. Strong culture develops strong emotional bonds developing steadfast loyalty, belongingness and relatedness. Organisational culture links up people and groups as the integral part of the organisation and transforms the employees into organisational members.

Similarly culture produces negative or dysfunctional impact also. These include group think, blind spots, resistance to change and innovate. Group think kills creativity, develops compromising attitude and works out mediocre solutions which can hardly solve a problem completely. Strong culture develops an attitude to protect and cover up inefficiencies and weaknesses under the mask of collegue-relations and togetherness. A typical kind of *status quo* and stagnation breeds up in organisations with strong culture which resists change, reforms and innovations. Culture forms a clan. And a clan always suffers from xenophobia, i.e., the fear of outsiders. Nepotism and separation becomes the worrying features of such organisations. Another problem emerging from a well-knit culture relate to the management of diversity. Modern organisations are characterised by workforce-diversity. People having diverse social, national, economic background, join the organisations as employees. Gender and cultural differences add to this diversity. Especially multinational companies face more acutely this situation of workforce-diversity. It has several merits like creative thinking, rationality in decision making, widening of perspectives, etc. Therefore many times the organistions encourage and support this diversity. Strong culture emphasises on conformity whereas diversity develops and displays different behavioural and thinking patterns and styles. Culture and diversity thus acts opposite to one another. Unless culture accepts diversity as a value and tries to build unity in diversity; conflicts may start in the organisation.

Culture may become a barrier for amalgamations and mergers. Previously experts used to consider only the financial matters to decide the suitability of a merger. In recent years cultural compatibility has become a prime concern. Initially, the financial position of the organisation to be acquired may become an attraction. But the mergers work successfully only when the cultures of the amalgamating and amalgamated company match with one another. If there is a mismatch, then, the merger is likely to fail.

Organisational culture affects the control mechanism, normative order, performance and satisfaction of employees. Culture directs behaviour and serves as control mechanism. Culture is diffused throughout the organisation. A strong culture is characterised by shared beliefs and values, which all members of the organisation are adhered to. Thus people understand what is described as the appropriate behaviour and what will become objectionable. This works as an automatic control mechanism. Only when the members deviate from the norms and expected behavioural pattern, the manager intercepts and initiates the necessary corrective actions.

Culture and employee satisfaction are correlated. When culture matches with the needs of the employees, satisfaction is highest. The satisfaction of employees depend on how they perceive the organisational culture. For example, if employees have a strong achievement drive, the culture where people are rewarded for their high achievements is most satisfying. It employees need adequate freedom and autonomy in their work, an organisational culture which is low in structure and has loose supervision will satisfy them. Further culture and performance are interrelated. It is observed that when culture is informal, creative and supports risk taking, then, employee performance improves. This happens when the technology used is non-routine. On the other hand, when routine technology is utilised then performance will be higher, if (i) leadership is task-oriented, (ii) organisation is formally structured, (iii) The management is risk-aversive and seeks to eliminate conflict.

John Kotter and James Hasket conducted a study on culture and performance. Their study confirmed the positive correlation between culture and performance. The major conclusions of this study are as follows.

(a) Corporate culture has significant impact on long-term economic performance.

(b) Corporate culture probably will be an even more important factor in the next decade.

(c) Corporate cultures that inhibit strong long-term financial performance are not rare; they develop easily, even in organisations that are full of reasonable and intelligent people.

(d) Although tough to change, corporate cultures can be made more performance enhancing.

In the view of **Stephen Robbins**, socialisation also has influence on performance. If an individual is properly indoctrinated into the organisation, his performance tends to be higher. Normally, the impact of culture on performance is favourable and productive. But this happens only when the culture is unique, value-based and inimitable. The positive impact of culture is the outcome of well-managed and sustained positive core-values by the organisation. If conscious and prudent efforts are not made then a culture stimulating and supporting negative values and disvalues emerges. A negative organisational culture becomes a liability for the productivity development efforts.

According to **Joseph Kotter and James Heskett** (Corporate culture and performance), the impact of organisational culture is the function of three important factors, namely, direction, strength and pervasiveness. **Direction** refers to the path indicated by organisational culture. The direction may be positive or negative. When the culture facilitates goal attainment it is said to possess positive direction. On the contrary when the culture hinders goal-attainment, it is said to have negative direction. **Pervasiveness** means homogeneity. Organisations are composed of divisions and departments. Each such division or department has its own subculture. If these subcultures are strong and distinct from one another, the overall organisational culture becomes less homogeneous and this reduces the organisational effectiveness. The **strength** of the organisational culture is the pressure it can exert on the members of the organisation. Strength of the culture depends on two factors (a) the longevity of the culture and (b) employee turnover. If a typical culture is existing in the organisation for a longer time, its strength is greater. Similarly if an organisation is having a stable labour-force and the employees-turnover is the least, then the culture becomes strong. On the other hand if a culture is new or short-lived and the employee turnover is higher then the organisational culture become weak to produce any effect on performance and behaviour.

Managing the culture: Culture-management has following three important elements.

(a) Deriving benefits of the prevailing culture.

(b) Teaching the culture appropriately to the newcomers.

(c) Changing the organisational culture.

Many times it is easier to take the advantage of the existing culture than to develop a completely new culture. Because creating new values, customs and norms are comparatively difficult. So the manager should try to derive benefits and more advantages from existing culture. For this purpose he should develop the complete understanding of the organisational values and the supportive behaviour. Then through proper communication he should spread the organisational values at all levels of management and encourage that type of employee behaviour which supports and strengthens these values.

Culture-teaching is normally done by senior employees to junior employees. Through dialogues, interactions, rituals and model behaviour, the seniors can place before the juniors the concept and characteristics of desirable and acceptable behaviour. The imitation of the some behaviour by the juniors helps to sustain and continue the culture.

Culture-change is rather a big issue of culture-management. Theoretically even though we favour the idea of a stable culture; in actual practice culture can never be stable and fixed. The value-system, the concept of desirable, the ethical principles, norms of behaviour undergo a continuous change. Life itself is a changing phenomenon. Further, as the organisations are social system, any change in its surrounding will also cause a need to change its functioning and internal environment. Thus culture-change is an inevitable and essential element. The real question therefore is how to introduce this change. There are five approaches to culture change, which are as follows:

(1) **Adding new members in the organisation:** At the higher level of management, addition of new member is an effective strategy for changing organisational culture. A new CEO, CFO, Managing Director, General Manager plays a significant role in changing culture by injecting new values, thoughts and views in the organisation.

(2) **Changing the reward system:** Culture-change is a learning exercise. When, new culture is introduced, new value system and behavioural norms which are an integral part of new culture are inducted in the organisation. Those are required to be learned and imbibed by the employees. Effective learning takes place through properly desired reward system. When desired learning is associated with suitable and attractive rewards for the same, learning takes place faster. Learning includes unlearning also. It is a process of both accumulation as well as elimination. New thoughts, views and principles are to be thoroughly understood and accepted by heart and at the same time old ideas and outworn norms and assumptions should be discarded and forgotten. A cleverly designed reward system for the same proves considerably useful in this respect.

(3) **Use of culture-shock as a tool:** A culture shock is an event or an incidence which forces an organisation to examine the validity and utility of its culture, seriously. It poses some important questions about the propriety and relevance of the organisational culture. A sudden fall in sales and profits, litigation by a major and prestigious customer, resignation of a top-boss or key person, etc., are negative shocking events which sensitises the organisation climate. If such events are attributed to the cultural deficiencies, a thought process of examining and revising the culture gets started.

(4) **Changing the structure and style of management:** Organisational culture can be changed by changing the organisational structure and managerial style. A tall and pyramid shaped organisational structure consists of a number of hierarchies. This not only concentrates decision power at top and lengthen decision process but it also discourages initiative, independent thinking and places excessive importance to obedience and work as per rule. A flat organisation gives more weightage to employee-empowerment and decentralised decision making. A change of organisational structure will strike the process of culture-change automatically. Again a turn around from an autocratic style of management to a participative style also causes cultural changes. Changed structure and/or changed management style thus commences cultural change. However, all further niceties relevant thereto should be properly attended. Culture change has to be a planned, articulated gradual process. It is different from the change in systems, methods and procedures. Those changes can be made overnight and implemented instantly and immediately. A change in culture is effectively implemented, only when, the mind-set of the employees is appropriately and methodically changed and suitably developed. This process does not possess any short-cuts. If due time and diligence is not paid, then the process will yield defective results. Without inculcation of the new desired values and ideals in the minds of employees, culture-development will become haphazard.

Every culture is deep rooted in our mind. Therefore whenever a new culture is introduced, resistance and a question about its suitability is born immediately. A major portion of our culture is related to our beliefs and value system. If the new cultural is challenging our old beliefs and values drastically and posing serious questions regarding their propriety and worthiness, it becomes very difficult to accept this, even though rationally and logically the new culture has evidenced and proved the deficiencies and demerits of the old culture. The general human tendency is nonreception of self-mistakes and so new culture-resistance is quite normal and obvious. Who will like to get acknowledged that he was wrong over all these years? Culture-management and change process has to go through a variety of resistances. Some of these resistances are rational and some are irrational. Most of the forces which resist change in organisational culture are as follows.

(1) Fear of the new value system. (2) Disruption of previous stable and well-groomed relationship. (3) Distrust about the intentions of management. (4) Threat to the present organisational power-structure. (5) Inertia of the organisational structure. (6) System relationship and effect thereon. (7) Vested interest. (8) Cost factor.

Changes often bring with it uncertainty and ambiguity. The new values are questioned because many people do not have a proper understanding of their necessity and validity in the first instance. It is always said that an old dog cannot easily be taught new things. The fear is a psychological resistance and as such, positive attitude to learn new values and behaviour is to be developed systematically. The distrust of management and the disruption of old personal relationships are the two important reasons of resistance when these forces get clubbed with the vested interest; the resistance becomes much stronger and organised. Employees may perceive that the management is using culture-change as a tool of exploitation. The new value system and work-ethics it is introducing may be suspected to be exploitative and with manipulative intentions. For example, an organisation insisting on meticulous efforts for quality-building may be looked as burdening the employees with extra-work and demanding more labour. Another management introducing a merit-based promotion system in place of the previous seniority-based system, again may be blamed in indulging in manipulative tactics by making the career advancement of employees uncertain and variable. Once the faith is lost, the relations become weak and disputable. In such situations things of normal nature also become difficult to manage and the agreements even on reasonable issues are hard to obtain. The changes disturbing the personal relations are usually not accepted smoothly. Vested interest and fear of social isolation develop such a resistance. A quotation-based purchasing method replacing the open market purchasing as per requirement and team leadership replacing a personal hierarchy has resistance normally from those whose vested interest get paralysed by these new work methods. Flexi-timing and home-office is opposed due to the fear of loss of social interaction among employees at work-places. If everybody is allowed to choose his own work-schedule or to work from his dwelling; then the chances of meeting each other at common places, rather collectively and of sharing with each other the matters relating to work-life and private life, automatically become dim. Naturally, such way annoyed people will record their resistance.

The threats to power, structure-inertia, system-relationship and rise in cost are the organisational resistance and not personal one. Many changes disturb the power structure in the organisation. Decentralisation and higher delegation of authority to people at the operating level will change the equation of power, control and status in the organisation. Change of tall organisation to flat one, job enlargement and job-enrichment, the introduction of task-group in place of the functional departments, development of cross-functional and self-managed teams, etc., are the changes which are restricted and resisted by the organisational structure itself. In a bureaucratic organisation with multiple layers of hierarchy and authority; the above changes are very difficult to incorporate. Because these changes are to be introduced as a series of changes and not as a single change. So the resistance will emerge at different levels from different corners. Any change has a domino effect. So a change in one system affects other subsystems also. So again the other subsystems need to change. Change in the functions of one department may requires the other departments to change their method of operations. This and other changes may burden the organisation with increased cost. Narurally objections and resistances are bound to arise.

The organisation has to, therefore, manage the resistance to change by adopting the following approaches to change.

(i) Appropriate communication and education of employees about the need and validity of change helps to soften the resistance.

(ii) Making participation of employees in the decisions regarding change has a positive response. It develops the employee-support to change, creates suitable awareness and builds commitment among employees to cooperate, respond and implement the change programme.

(iii) Negotiations, consultations and bargaining with employee unions or the influential groups of employees help to lift up the resistance to change. Especially the issues in the change programme which may affect the job-security and such other employee-benefits can be resolved through negotiations. A win-win situation can be developed through proper negotiations and bargains.

(iv) Manipulation and cooption are the less expensive and easier to use tactices to effect the desired change. Manipulations include all covert attempts to influence. For example, facts-twisting to make them more attractive, withholding the unpleasant information, spreading systematically the rumours favourable to change, etc., are such manipulative tactices. Cooption is a combination of manipulation and cooperation. In, cooption the leader of the resistance group is called to implement change. He is persuaded to make decisions and actions positive to promote change and not to go for bitter and obstructing behaviour. Cooption is based on the principle of making the friendship with enemies and thereby reducing their resistance.

(v) Coercion is again a typical approach in change management which is based on the use of power and pressure. Coercion is the last resort. When all the above approaches become unworkable, then only coercion is to be applied. The use of coercion can be justified when employees are adamant, stubborn, nonreceptive even to good proposals and non-cooperative for betterment. In such situations, the negativities of employees are not due to ignorance or immaturity but due to well conspired strategy of cornering the management and weakening down its power and authority. Especially when a change disturbs the vested interests, the aggrieved party resorts development of unreasonable resistance which does not have any strong foundation of logic and rationality. The resistance is on the line of opposition simply for opposition. The resisting group, by this way, wants to show its nuisance-value. So tough-stance on the part of management is required. Coercive tricks involve threats, penalties, punishments and negative reinforcement. For example, those non-cooperative employees are warned at first and if they continue resistance, then, transfer of the problematic employee to a remote place, loss of promotion, stoppage of increment, negative remarks in performance evaluation, etc., are the corceive techniques by which the resisting employees are taught the lesson for their wrong behaviour.

The different approaches of change management should be adopted in different situations. The approach of communication and education works well when the management has sufficient time and change is not urgently required. Though this approach is costlier and time-consuming, it gives proper enlightenment to employees regarding the nature and need of change and the roles of employees, therein. Participation and involvement of employees in change decisions are useful when change efforts require more commitment, on the part of employees. The management then has to form a task force to look after the change-project. Special efforts then should be made to develop the commitment. Negotiations become effective when the change is going to cause some loss. Then a give and take will work. When employees are convinced that they will get something for sacrificing something, their lookout towards change programme itself will 'change'. Coercion is always the last option. When other approaches fail, then only coercion should be thought of. Coercion has comparatively a swift effect. So in urgency, coercive techniques are employed. But coercion has negative effects, much stronger than its usefulness. A change implemented by way of coercion will never be accepted by the employees from their heart.

A change in culture is a crucial job. It requires proper planning, logical approach and systematic efforts. A change which is introduced in a haphazard manner does greater damage than the effects of stagnation and *status quo*. So the change-management requires all diligence and purposiveness. What is most difficult to do is to change the mindset of people. And in culture change, the organisation exactly tries to do the same.

Culture-strategy Match: As we know that culture consists of values, beliefs, the acceptable patterns of behaviour and the work-practices. Organisations have the cultural uniqueness. Even if two organisations are operating in the same industry, produce similar goods and services and serve the same market, still their cultures may differ significantly. The unique culture of each such organisation provides it the required strength and sometimes may become a burden also. Especially when, the culture is unsuitable for the strategy which the organisation desires to follow; then culture is looked as a liability and burden rather than an asset. In such a situation, strategy-culture mismatch results into frictions and conflicts in the first instance and total failure at the later stages.

Every organisation develops its own method of solving problems, building resources and capabilities, conducting activities–functions and operations and managing the entire show. As all these things get crystallised over the years, these become part and parcel of the organisational culture. When most of the employees accept the core values and norms of performance and behaviour developed by the organisation, wholeheartedly, it results into a strong culture. An organisation with a strong culture is proud of itself in a wholesome way. Therefore, there is a resistance to change. If such organisation follows a strategy which is unsuitable to its present culture, then difficulties and problems arise in its implementation. Again an organisation having weak culture, too, will face similar problems. Because in organisations having weak culture, most of the employees do not have a deep sense of the company purpose. Their level of organisational commitment and job involvement is very low. They simply look to their jobs as a source of income. Many of them have either no loyalty or divided loyalty. So such organisations are fragmented internally. They lack cohesion and team spirit which act as the cornerstones of strategy implementation. A good strategy fails when its execution is haphazard, untimely and unorganised. The unanimity of action and consistency of purpose in decision makes the organisation effective and powerful in achieving its strategic goals. Thus a culture whether strong or weak has an impact on the success of strategic management.

Terence F. Deal and **Allen A. Kenedy** (Corporate Culture) feels that a strong organisational culture is a powerful lever in channeling behaviour and helping employees in doing their jobs in a more strategy-supportive manner. This happens due to following reasons

(i) The system of informal rules and peer pressure which exists in strong cultures direct employees to follow the expected and desired behavioural patterns. As the weak cultures suffers from lack of strong company identity and purposeful work climate; there happens substantial employee confusion and wasteful efforts.

(ii) A strong culture motivates the employees by turning their jobs into the way of life. It does this by providing structure, standards, value system and strong company identity.

Culture-strategy match has the following positive effects

(i) It energises and motivates employees.

(ii) It helps to manage human resources efficiently and effectively.

(iii) It results into a powerful and effective strategy implementation.

(iv) It avoids confusion and conflict and improves and strengthens the company performance.

Corporate culture is influenced by environmental changes. What happens outside the organisation has an impact on the functioning and internal atmosphere of the company. A change in political, economic, social, demographic, technological and global situations will produce some kind of effect on the people who constitute the labour force of the organisation. The environmental change may result into a change in the value-system, attitude towards work and leisure, skills, life and work philosophy and preferences and priorities of people. This in turn may bring a new awakening among people. These people form the workforce. Naturally the expectations, views and ideals of this workforce gets changed over the period. The transitions and reforms in the society knocks the doors of the organisation and impacts its culture. Therefore, we should always remember that culture is a dynamic thing. It undergoes changes in its own way rather continuously. But many of such changes are so minute that they go unnoticed. When a particular strategy is to be practiced, the suitability and dynamism of culture gets illuminated. Because, then these two elements have a considerable importance and impact on the success of the strategy. Changes in strategy has to be accompanied by the changes in culture. **Schein** (Organisational Culture) observed that the effectively formulated strategies also fail if they are expecting to imbibe and follow assumptions, values and ways of working which are at a variance with the organisation's culture. If proper modifications in the cultural elements are not made, then employees do the same old things in the same old way giving importance to those old notions and priorities. All this ruins the purpose of the strategy and blunts down its sharpness and effectiveness.

R.E. Miles and C.C. Snow (Organisational Strategy, Structure and Process) made an extensive study of the impact of orgnisational culture on strategy-formulation. They classified different organisations into three types, namely, Defenders, Prospectors and Analyser. Defenders desire a secured and stable niche in the market. Prospectors have the objective of exploitation of new product and market opportunities. Analysers intend to match new ventures to present shape of business. Defenders normally prefer a strategy to defend its current business. Therefore they emphasise on coefficient production. Low price and customer-service such organisations have a thrust on centralised control, formal planning, cost efficiency and specialisaion. Prospectors want to exploit the market opportunities and so they prefer the growth strategies. They make product and market development on a continuous basis. For this purpose they constantly monitor the business environment and make use of multiple technologies. For fast growth they emphasise on flexibility, decentralisation and *ad* *hoc* measurement. Analysers wish to match the new ventures to the present shape of business. They expect the steady growth and for this purpose follow the market penetration strategies. They exploit the findings of applied research. Normally they do not attempt for market leadership. They act as followers in the market. Analysers emphasise on intensive planning and co-ordination of functions. The control system in such companies is very complicated.

The organisation, thus, has to first identify itself whether it is a defender, prospector, analyser or otherwise. There can be again different kinds of classification of companies. However, the fundamental postulate which guides and directs these efforts is that organisational culture and strategy must be matching one another. Two broad views exist. Either change the culture to suit the strategy or change the strategy to fit the existing culture. Both views are based on certain assumptions which theoretically are workable, but practically are very difficult to deal with. Certain part of culture and strategy is changeable. But some parts of organisational culture is unchangeable. Therefore, the strategist has to select such a strategy which fits the existing culture. Then, while implementing the strategy, the efforts are made to bring the culture and strategy close to one another. An alignment between culture and strategy requires the following things to be done.

(i) Diagnosing the facets of existing culture which are strategy supportive.

(ii) Identifying the facets of present culture which are to be modified to bring match with the strategy, and

(iii) Deciding the actions to be taken by the management to modify the cultural environment and create a stronger match with the strategy.

Organisational culture sometimes is like umbrella which gives a wide coverage. Naturally some part of it sometimes may be strategy-supportive and some part may require modification to suit to the chosen strategy. The strategy-supportive elements should be preserved and for the modification of the rest, appropriate actions are to be decided. Culture modification can be made in phases. Total transformation of culture is difficult and complicated and therefore, phased modification is more related. More complete change of an organisation's culture, in most of the cases is unwarranted. It may prove injurious to the unique identity of the organisation.

Culture modification to match with the strategy requires, usually, two types of managerial actions, namely, symbolic actions and substantive actions. Symbolic actions provide the indication about the kind of behaviour and performance which the strategist wish to encourage. The substantive actions provide the direct guidelines about desired behaviour. They are made by the strategist himself to reinforce the culture by words and deeds. Symbolic actions include the following

(i) Rewarding and honouring the employees whose actions and performance serve as role model.

(ii) Giving prizes and special incentives to the rate bursters and target bursters.

(iii) Conducting the ceremonies and functions during which the new values are directly and indirectly, formally and informally communicated to the employees through speeches, dialogues, group discussions, etc.

The substantive actions are to be made by the strategists themselves. The chief executive in such situations lead by example. He takes initiative and follows a pattern of behaviour and performance which is strategy-supportive. He may issue instructions and directives of the same for his subordinates. He takes a commanding position to introduce changes in actions and performance of people to bring a match between the culture and the strategy.

Most of the strategies are designed to acquire a competitive edge and as such expect high level of performance. So the culture of the organisation will have to develop and sustain the values which will raise the spirit of performance. The spirit of high level performance focuses on creating organisational excellence and effectiveness. For this purpose the organisation has to become human resource oriented. Following tips help to shape an organisation as human-oriented.

(1) Show concern for human dignity. Treat people as human beings and with respect.
(2) Identify the potential of people and induce them to use it singularly and collectively.
(3) Recognise and respect the differences among people regarding abilities and aptitudes. Adopt a confrontation technique to utilise them to develop creativity.
(4) Empower people. Give them adequate functional autonomy to encourage the spirit of initiative and leadership.
(5) Develop and declare champions who are the performance winners and make them the role-models.

Jack Welch views that the real and limitless productivity comes from the challenged, empowered, excited and rewarded teams of people. He provides tips to develop such teams which are as follows. (a) Engage every single mind in the organisation. (b) Make everyone part of the action. (c) Allow everyone to have a voice and a role in the success of the organisation. The present business environment is extremely competitive. This competition has now become brutal. Under such circumstances, employees always feel proud and excited to work in a productive and successful organisation which has got an edge over competition. This association is rewarding for employees in terms of monetary and job satisfaction.

Such a successful organisation has proper integration of culture and strategy. If the core values of the organisation are not supportive to the strategic objectives, then confusion and contradictions in the decisions and actions of people occur more often and in bigger scale. Culture provides a meaning to the actions of people. An employee may be doing any major and important action or a minor and unimportant activity in the organisation. However, how he views his job will give him the positive or negative motivation to perform. The quality of his performance will always relate to what that job means to him. Many people do their jobs which are mostly rudimentary and formal in nature rather over sincerely, because they feel that they are doing a meaningful, valuable and useful job. Such a perception in a collective form is the outcome of the organisational culture. If the culture and strategy are not mutually complementary and adaptive, the employees may ignore even the strategically more important actions and functions; simply because those are considered meaningless and marginal in the absence of the proper frame of reference of the suitable value system. Culture provides the background and customs and traditions. It gives contextuality to decision and action. It clarifies silently what the organisation desires and aspires for. It acts as a glue to hold people together and also as a lubricant to keep them moving towards the organisational goals. Culture is a sum total of ideas, interests, values attitudes, skills, communications, myths, expectations, experiences and even fears shared by the group of people. **Bary Phagon** (Developing Your Own Company Culture) feels that culture is the history expressed in present.

The study of successful organisations and their culture by experts reveal the following noteworthy facts.

(1) The work environmental in such organisation look relaxed and caused, (2) The managers are inclined to provide to the staff information and help all the time. They rarely issue order and

instructions. They act more as facilitators, than bosses, (3) The decision making is collective and through consensus. Managers prefer to guide the decision process instead of making decisions by self, (4) Employees at all levels feel mentally safe and secure. An element of mutual trust is systematically percolated throughout the organisation. Such things develop strong bonds of loyalty and commitment between management and employees, (5) The culture in such organisations is more permissive and liberal. Ranks, formal authorities, control issues do not matter more in such organisations, (6) The systems focus on self control and the power of people. Thus, they develop human corporate culture, (7) These organisations have workforce diversity which they take positively and build strengths there on, (8) Successful organisations behave like matured individuals who determine their own future and overcome their limits.

Michael Porter described the three important strategies for competitive success. They are (a) Cost leadership, (b) Differentiation and (c) Focus. Cultured modifications and adaptability are essential for their successful implementation. For example, to become a cost leader in the market, the organisation will have to develop cost consciousness among its staff. Economy and thrift then should be made the core values. In order to make people to think and act for cost control, they should be convinced to accept economy as a principle. The introduction of cost cutting and cost control tools and techniques will be limitedly useful, unless people internalise economy as a virtue and a way of functioning. When they do this, they will devise their own methods of cost cutting and avoidance of wastage. Thereafter, the organisation will effectively embark on cost leadership. Because the concept of cost does not have financial dimensions only. It has time and labour dimensions as well. So when monetary expenses increase, cost rise is obvious. Similarly the delays in project completions adds to time-cost and the excess labour exerted to correct errors and mistakes also cause an increase in labour-wastage. The time cost and labour cost ultimately affects the financial costs on one side and the marked opportunities and quality on the other. A differentiation strategy requires a culture of innovation and creativity. Because differentiation focuses on creation of products which are distinctive in terms of utility and quality. So unless the organisation places strong emphasis on research and development, a differentiation strategy can not be effectively implemented. For suitable research and development function, the organisation will have to provide special attention to innovation management. It has to develop innovation and creativity, as its core values. Finance, marking, personnel and production, i.e., all the four important function departments, play a vital role in this respect. The release of funds for research and product development, conducting the market surveys to provide for proper direction to research activity, training the employees to undertake research as a part of their functional responsibility and developing their suitable mindset and using the research and innovation in actually producing the products are the important aspects of innovation management which is at the heart of the differentiation strategy. If the organisation looks to the research as a discrete activity and treats it as an isolated function which is similar to other business functions but separate from them, then differentiation strategy will hardly become fruitful. Because when an organisation is following a differentiation strategy, it must have a clear idea as to what differentiation it will make and why? All the research efforts must be directed towards providing and inventing something useful to the customers. Thus the research must have a market orientation and a focus on the needs of the consumers. At the same it should consider financial availabilities, resource limitations and time constraints. Further the people should have adequate and proper motivation for participating in research and innovation activity. Focus is a marketing strategy. Cost leadership has financial orientation. Product differentiation has thrust on product development. Likewise focus has a market base. A focus strategy may employ cost leadership or product differentiation in selected markets.

Again a focus strategy need to have a culture in the organisation which should be market-oriented. A marketing culture expects flexibility, opportunism, speed and judgemental observation. Flexibility develops when there is an encouragement and support for lateral thinking opportunism and judgemental observation a decision system based on facts and figures, rather than intuition and the exceptional commonsense. Speed requires efficiency, delayering of the organisation and functional autonomy. Thus the culture is suitable for focus strategy specific and unique and the same rule applies to cost leadership and product differentiation.

Cultural suitability has to be considered from the point of view of the grand strategies also. **Lawrence Jauch and William F Glueck** (Business Policy and Strategic Management) provides for a classification of these grand strategies. From their viewpoint there are four grand strategies, namely, stability, growth, retrenchment and combination. The first three are independent and separate strategies whereas the fourth one is a mixture of the first three.

Some organisations prefer stability strategy. This they do either by maintaining the *status quo* or by adopting sustainable growth. The firms trying to maintain *status quo* attempt to keep their size and level of production and sale almost the same every year. They serve the same class of customers and operate the current line of business. Especially small firms with limited resources are usually more inclined to follow *status quo* strategy. Sustainable growth is a slow growth strategy. It is more practical than *status quo*. Because *status quo* theoretically means zero growth which is neither realistically possible, nor reasonably acceptable. Because in the present competitive markets each firm has to keep on moving ahead for its survival and stability. Otherwise its existence will be at a stake. When running, the one who stops will automatically lag behind and will be thrown out of the race eventually. Thus either through *status quo* or slow growth a firm can maintain stability.

However the organisational culture must be suitable for such a stability strategy. This suitable culture has the following important characteristics

(1) Risk aversive attitude of management and employees.

(2) A satisfactory level of profit is perceived as great success by the firm rather than growth.

(3) Strong resistance to change by every corner of the organisation with objections like change will upset smooth operations and disrupt the current working relationships, etc.

(4) The firm has either a small size with resources constraints or a superior market position with voluminous profits. In both situations the firm affords and prefers stability. In other words, one would love stability and *status quo* if either he possesses everything or finds no possibility of marching ahead to get something.

(5) The cost of growth seems to be higher than its benefits and therefore the organisation thinks it unwise to provide financial and managerial support for the same.

Stability preferred organisations place importance to routines and repetitions. These, later, become their important values. So such organisations feel that growth will cause harm to the quality of their products and customer services. This culture of only a 'carry forward' type thinking, attitude and actions, mostly matches stability strategy. The innovative thoughts and ideas, forward outlooks, aggressive developmental actions are abuses in such organisations. Because they emerge from creativity and progress, which such organisations disregard as disvalues. Stable firms value only continuation of the past like same trading volume, same customers and satisfactory earnings. Changes and revisions are made only when they are indispensable and inevitable. Such changes usually are marginal and superficial.

Similarly, some firms acquire dominant position in the industry due to their size and competitive ability. Such firms may like to opt for the stability strategy to avoid the abuse of the monopolistic organisation. Moreover smaller firms having product specialisation also go for stability strategy. Because such organisations, being speciality suppliers are too conscious about their product quality and customer service. Again firms whose top management has an inertia for change, are more inclined towards stability strategy. Thus stability strategy is suitable for those organisations whose culture value stability more than vibrant activism.

Growth strategies are suitable for firms which operate in extremely volatile environment. Such a fast changing environment poses a threat of obsolence before the organisation. Due to the fast changes in the firm environment, the products and services of the firm may soon become outdated and so useless. So the firm adopts growth strategy and tries to increase its performance objectives. It intends to increase its profit volume, sales volume and market share. For this purpose it broadens the scope of its customer group and customer functions. As we know, that, there are eight broad growth strategies. Those are (1) Internal growth strategy, (2) Concentration strategy, (3) Mergers, (4) Takeover and acquisitions, (5) Horizontal integration, (6) Vertical integration, (7) Concentric of conglomerate diversification, (8) Joint ventures. Each of such growth strategies needs suitable organisational culture for successful implementation. If the firm has a typical culture of preserving its identify, image and quality; it should adopt an internal growth strategy wherein the emphasis is on increasing the efficiency and capacity of its employees, production and sale.

In case of concentric growth strategy, the firm concentrates its efforts on a limited number of customers-groups, customer-functions, products or alternative strategies. For customer-related concentric strategies the firm requires a customer-focused work culture. Such a culture has to develop practices of attending to customers in all possible ways. Rules and procedures have to be kept aside in certain situations to serve the customer better. A concentric strategy with customer focus is successful in a customer-oriented culture. A bureaucratic organisation insisting upon the routines and standard practices does not possess the flexibility for customer service. For a customer-focussed strategy, the firm has to create customer-orientation throughout the organisation. Because customer service is not simply the concern of marketing department. When all functions and activities of the organisation are aimed at providing the best service/product to the customer; then a combination of all functions together make the customer-focussed strategy meaningful and effective.

A product-focussed concentric strategy tries to make product differentiation. The firm wants to position its products as the unique selling propositions. This can be done either in terms of product price or product utility or both. For making the product the best buys for the customers, the firm has to concentrate on the cost. A cost-effective, economical product can be supplied when cost-conscious culture prevails in the organisation. In such an organisation economy and thrift becomes a value and cost reduction, wastage elimination and control and saving and optimum resource utilisation becomes a regular and normal practice. Similarly a product strategy focusing on building product utility and enhancing the same, will have to carve out a culture of innovation. This is different from cost culture. An innovation culture will encourage and support creativity. In order to develop something new, the firm has to allow employees for experimentation. All experiments do not bring success. In fact, the unsuccessful experiments have to be treated as the cost of learning. If this kind of approach is taken by the firm, then only efforts for research and innovation will increase. A culture of innovation has to be liberal on the issue of cost and spending. So if the firm wants to adopt a product-concentration strategy with focus on increasing product utility, then it will have to be less cost-conscious and more innovation supportive. On the other hand if it wants to win on the ground of product pricing, it should concentrate on cost cutting and economising. Each of these strategies will be effective only if the organisation develops the suitable and supportive culture for the same.

Mergers, takeovers, acquisitions and joint ventures are those external growth strategies which have an element of co-partnership. In all these strategies the firm brings an outsider under its control or combines his business with their own. Under such circumstances confusion, contradictions and confusions are more often among the mixing or combining elements. Many times the stronger or the bigger partner has a negative attitude towards the junior or smaller partner. This is possible in mergers. Again in case of acquisitions or takeovers, the professionalisation of management may be replaced by money power. Such things may later cause the firm to revert its decision. So it is observed that after a few months of merger, again both partners decide to demerge and disband their relationships. In case of takeovers and acquisitions; reselling of acquired business is not a totally unusual phenomenon. These reversal of decisions take place because, the original decisions are made in a hectic or haphazard manner; mostly due to financial temptations. The acquiring firm or the big partner in merger wish to broaden their resource-base and so the suitability of merger is ignored. If both firms have disparate culture, the mergers and acquisitions become liabilities. Therefore, there is a need for proper planning before making these decisions. While making acquisitions or mergers; human considerations should be made along with financial one. The style of functioning of people of the joining firms may be different. Those should be made compatible. Unless the employees of both firms work together, harmoniously and with team spirit; the desired rise in efficiency and productivity is not achieved. Mergers and acquisitions should result in creation of synergy. A synergical effect is produced when there is an appropriate combination and cohesion of the adjoining elements. This requires a meeting of minds. The big partner in merger and acquisition should, for this reason, possess a liberal and generous attitude. All employees should be treated equally, fairly and in a dignified way. The management should not indulge discriminatory practices. It should show its concern for all employees and their well-being, irrespective of the fact whether they are old or new. This is not going to happen in a single day. The firm has to develop this type of culture right from beginning and before the decisions of managers and acquisitions. Because if this culture of open, liberal and generous thinking does not exist in the organisation, conflicts, disputes and quarrels may take place among employees working at different levels of management. Usually the decision of merger and takeover is made by top management; however, its consequences during implementation are experienced at all levels. An organisational culture developing a typical corporate elitism and indifference to outsiders; breed up a differentiating 'we' and 'they' attitude. These mental blocks may cause for groupism and later on fragmented working and personal relations. Thus after merger/acquisition, though assets are clubbed and shown collectively in balance sheet; the human resources of both companies are not suitably intermixed. Of course, the responsibility of accommodating all people and developing harmony and cohesion, rests with the bigger firm or senior partner. There these organisations before implementing a merger acquisition should develop a suitable corporate culture which values (1) Equal and fair treatment to all employees, (2) No discrimination among people on the basis of their personal background, (3) Open thinking and receptivity to new and useful ideas, (4) Respect for outsiders, (5) Honour of merit and contribution, (6) A friendly and accommodating atmosphere, (7) Flexible, liberal and generous outlook. These values and a corporate culture emphasising them is more suitable for mergers and acquisitions.

In case of joint ventures, new problems in addition to those observed in respect of mergers and acquisitions are required to be dealt with. Joint ventures are, usually, in the form of partnerships wherein two or more organisations carry out a specific project. Once the project is finished, joint venture disbands. So joint ventures mostly are temporary and the ownership of firms therein remains unchanged. **Peter Wright, Charles Pringle and Mark Kroll** view in 'Strategic Management' that even successful joint ventures may not last forever. Actually, corporate partnerships are formed for specific and time-bound objectives, which once achieved, leave little reason for the alliance to be continued. Thus joint ventures have a scheduled life cycle. This life cycle ends up either sooner on later. If joint ventures outlives, then it is required to be dissolved. So performance of existence is the remotest possibility in case of joint ventures. Again when changes in business environment occurs, the joint ventures have to be redesigned. Such things happen, even in case of joint ventures of transnationals and multinationals. So the cultural blending is bit different here. The partners in joint venture work together for temporary period and for specific goal. So a culture of cooperation, co-option and goal-orientation need to be developed. In case of mergers and acquisitions; there is an expectation of a total and complete amalgamation of physical and human resources for permanent period. If the partners in mergers and acquitions try to retain their independent identity and work and behavioural styles; then, these strategies will become ineffective. Because, here, long-term togetherness and unity is desired. Therefore, both firms should be so well intermixed, that in no respect should they appear or seem to be separate. However, joint ventures have a temporary and contractual relationships. It pools up distinctive capabilities and expects risk-reduction through sharing. Therefore a suitable culture for joint ventures is somewhat different. Both firms must respect each other, keep up their separate identity and work complementary to each other. They should pay attention to sharing and combining the strengths of each other and by doing this; eliminating the weaknesses of both. The resources, technology and experience of participants can be very well used collectively for market expansion and business development. This approach has to be developed and maintained in joint ventures. A focus on completion of the specific project and attainment of the goal or target is to be maintained throughout the life of joint-ventures. The culture suitable for joint ventures is that of collaboration instead of integration. Loose, flexible and task-related norms for functional and general behaviour are more useful. Thus joint ventures are a sort of 'trial-marriage' whose success depends on seeing and utilizing the merits of your co-partner and ignoring and covering up the drawbacks of each other.

A firm following a strategy of horizontal integration creates other firms in the same line of business. This strategy aims at related diversification. This occurs when existing firm creates another business unit in the same industry. Again there is another form of diversification which is called as conglomerate diversification. In this method the firm creates new business units which are unrelated to its original business. By diversification either in related or unrelated fields the firm can reduce the risk and enjoy the economies of scale, financial stability and increased profit. But unless a culture suitable for diversification is developed, the expansion in activities and operations may be bitterly reacted by the employees of the firm. The horizontal integration or concentric diversification is expansion of business in related areas. So there is the rise or increase in the volume of activities, though, many times the nature of activities do not undergo a drastic change. So the employees should be motivated to do more work of the same type and to some extent perform independently with self-responsibility. But in case of conglomerate diversification, besides the above things, employees should be taught to learn new things and be receptive to environmental changes. Conglomerate strategy is followed (1) to utilise different potential opportunities of profitable investments and (2) to achieve distinctive competitive advantage and with those, broaden the stability. Hence the firm is now doing the business which is totally separate and different from its original business. Unless the firm develops a suitable culture of receptivity and responsiveness to new learning; conglomerate diversification can not be practiced effectively. The organisation should create such a culture where the employees will positively accept the new business as a challenge and an opportunity for growth and not as a worrying problem of change, extra work and new learning. In fact, the employees should voluntarily come forward to learn new things. This should be looked as their capability development by the staff.

Vertical integration is another growth strategy in which new products, complementary to the existing product lines are added. Vertical integration may take any of the following forms, namely (a) Backward integration and (b) Forward integration. Backward integration occurs when the firm creates or acquires a business unit which supplies it raw materials, components and other inputs. A forward integration, on the other hand occurs when the firm creates or acquires a company which purchases its products. Backward integration connects the firm with the supplier of inputs and forward integration with the market. Sometimes a firm may opt for both, i.e., backward and forward integration simultaneously. Thus by vertical integration a firm links itself either with its suppliers or marketing intermediaries or with both. The greatest problem which such firms face is related to technology upgradation. The technology upgradation in any organisation in the backward link or forward link compels the firm to modify its own technology also. If the firm has a technology-savy culture; things will be bit simple. But if the situation is reverse and any proposal to change the existing technology is strongly reacted and opposed by management and staff, then the vertical integration will be less effective. So an organisational culture responsive to technology upgradation and modernisation is suitable for vertical integration. An organisation which constantly updates its technology, will face very little problem in this respect.

Retrenchment strategies have a different purpose and outlook than stability and growth strategies. Normally growth and stability strategies are adopted by organisations whose competitive position is satisfactory and such a position is going to enhance, most probably, in future. But if the competitive position of the firm is disappointing and the survival of the firm in future will be at stake; then, the firm opts for retrenchment strategy. So stability and growth strategies require an optimistic attitude, whereas the retrenchment strategy expects a realistic attitude more at the organisational level. Especially, when (1) the external business environment poses more threats before the company than opportunities, (2) the general economic conditions are poor, (3) the firm has several weaknesses and its operational efficiency is very low, (4) the competitive pressure, on one side is mounting up and on the other side the firm is lacking the latest technology and is not doing well then, the retrenchment strategy is suitable for the firm.

The commonly thought over retrenchment strategies include divestment and liquidation strategies. Under a divestment strategy the firm either sells out some of its business to another firm or closes a portion of its operations. A firm normally sells out those business units which are noncompetitive, unprofitable and unsuitable to the major business of the firm. Divestment is necessary to allow the remaining business to survive. So it is a sour decision having a sweet intention. Divestment requires a culture of realistic and practical thinking. If the organisation has an emotional and sentimental culture where things are valued and retained not for their utility to the organisations but for some irrational reasons or simply because those are associated with the organisation for a very long period, a divestment strategy cannot be effectively practiced. The inability to face severe competition in a particular business line or the more profitable opportunities in other business fields, or simply to abide by certain provisions of law; a firm may again opt for divestment. Whatever may be the reasons of divestment; the firm has to follow a typically radical and most practical approach in thinking and acting. Because then only the firm can make the bitter decisions which will be a part and parcel of this divestment strategy. For this purpose the firm will have to carve a culture in which its executives will always think with their head and not with their heart. Further, they will consider only those things which are most possible and probable and will not do any kind of imaginative thinking based on unreasonable optimism.

Liquidation strategy is, in fact, some steps ahead of divestment. It is considered as the extreme retrenchment strategy. It involves closing down an organisation and selling its assets. Usually when the rate of return is lowest as compared to the value of the assets or when the organisation is in such a trouble that it is wise to close down the business than to continue and aggravate the problem; then the firm adopts liquidation strategy. In case of partnership firms, when one of the partners retire then the partnership gets liquidated. In case of sole proprietary concern; when the proprietor wants to withdraw from the business; he liquidates the proprietary concern. In all liquidation cases, the consequences are very severe. This severity increases when large organisations liquidate their business. Employees lose jobs, creditors, suppliers, bankers, dealers, customers and such other stakeholders suffer a lot. The shareholders have to forego their share capital either in full or in part. Their investment diminish. The economic functions performed by the firm for the society are stopped. These and many more losses and sufferings are consequent upon a decision of liquidation. So nobody will prefer liquidation strategy unless its adoption is indispensable and inevitable. As the liquidation produces harmful effects, it is to be executed carefully and with maximum human concern. A culture of sympathy, concern and compassion must be developed while executing liquidation. This culture will care for the losers and sufferers and will generate ideas and plans for their rehabilitation. When the corporate culture has an element of caring and humanity, even the inevitable brutal decisions are also made in the softest way alongwith the supply of measures reducing its hazardous effects. The schemes of financial compensation and alternative jobs in other companies of the same business group are thought over only when the corporate culture has human values and a concern for the sufferings of all those weak people whose fate is decided by the strong and powerful members of the society.

Turnaround and transformation are those forms of retrenchment strategies which require a rather courageous approach. Internal efficiency can be improved by adopting a turnaround strategy. Its purpose is to transform an organisation into a learner and make more effectively its business. Turnaround means reversing the negative trend. Usually a firm adopts this strategy when (1) it is continuously incurring losses. (2) The demand, market share and sale of its products is declining rapidly. (3) It is facing a problem of increasing cash outflows and insufficient working capital. (4) Job dissatisfaction and employee turnover is very high. Turnaround strategy can be implemented by any of the following two approaches, namely, (1) surgical approach and (2) human resource development approach. Both these approaches require different types of work culture. In surgical approach improvements are brought by using threats, punishments, compulsions and forcible changes. It is a tough approach and as such the executives have to issue instructions for modifications and change, fire employees, replace machinery and equipment, fix responsibility and accountability of people and keep strict control on finance and accounts. This approach is more mechanistic than humanistic. It expects a task-centred leadership and managerial style. As against this the second approach of human resource development approach requires a persuasive work culture. It emphasises on encouraging the employees to modify their behaviour on their own, to work out solutions on the problems of the organisation, to suggest and invest new methods and techniques to transform the negative trend into a positive one. For this purpose the chief executive and other managers conduct a series of meeting, motivate people to diagnose and discuss the root causes of problems, involves them in preparing actions plans and development of methods and techniques and induce them to acquire new skills. Thus, the human resource development approach of turnaround strategy requires an inspirational culture; whereas, the surgical approach needs instructional culture. In instructional culture the executive and managers are predominant and the employees are at subordinate position. The superior or the boss orders and instructs and the followers obey. In inspirational culture, changes and modifications emerge from the bottom and are accepted and widely communicated by the upper level management. The employees are encouraged to offer suggestions and solutions, to acquire new skills and to develop new methods and techniques to transform the situation of negativities into positive results. Here the employees drive the management instead of the management pushing the employees. In short, the suitable cultures for both approaches are different from one another.

When a firm follows a transformation strategy, it makes major changes in its outlook and operations, usually, including moving from one kind of business to another. These changes in strategy are substantial. Unless a firm develops a culture having a thrust on flexibility and reforms. Change in outlook is difficult to bring than change in operations. Operational changes are comparatively easier and simpler to practice. Because they relate to tools, techniques and methods of doing a job only. However change in outlook requires comprehensive thinking. It includes an analysis of business environment and the present outlook of the management as well as synthesis of the alternative business opportunities and the modifications required in the style of decision making and functioning of the firm to utilise these alternative business opportunities. This process is deep end broader. It deals with not only the working of people as an organisation but with their collective thinking, as well. A change in business outlook requires at the outset a change in the concept of business itself. What the firm has thought as a good business earlier, is thoroughly assessed on the test of its validity and potentiality in the changing business environment. These activities are intellectual one and they need an atmosphere of freedom. An organisation which develops a culture of freedom to think and act (without any kind of fear and inhibition) for the betterment of the organisation imbibes the necessary flexibility and receptivity for transformational strategy.

Any generic strategy is useless unless people who are going to practice it, accept that strategy by heart. This is possible only when the organisation has developed a value-system which is supportive to the chosen strategy. Values are central to organisational culture. A suitable culture can make a strategy effective and fruitful. A mismatch in culture and strategy will push the organisation to a degenerative stage. Developing a suitable culture is difficult than selecting a strategy suitable to the culture of the organisation. Cultural development takes a long time and this process is gradual, systematic and concerted. So, it is better to select a suitable strategy which will match with the culture of the organisation.

It is important to remember the advice of **Barry Phagon** (Developing your Company Culture). Culture provides a platform for the actions of people. People have an access to wide range of behaviours. However, people choose that form of actions and behaviour which suits the specific platform, i.e., their culture. The organisational culture is how people and equipment work together in harmony. Culture is the glue which holds all parts of an organisation together. Culture works like oil which lubricates the organisation and keeps it functioning smoothly and continuously.

A culture which engages people and develops belongingness in return gets more involvement of employees in their respective jobs. In such a culture people bring their best to the organisation. They bring more of themselves to work. Present days are those of individualised corporations. **Sumitra Ghoshal and Christopher Bartlet** finds that an individualised corporation focus on the power of individuals as the drivers of value-creation in the company and on the importance of individuality in management. Till 1986, corporations were forcing their employees into an organisational model defined by policies, systems and constraints. They were carving out of people the so – called 'organisational men'. Modern organisations on the other hand, make themselves suitable to people. This opens up opportunities to do the best, awaken the potential of people and inspires them for excellence. The individuality in management and the deep human concern of the organisation encourage people to performance. Otherwise there is only the conformance. People have tremendous potential for productivity. This is the resource in the organisation which appreciates over time if it is put to proper use. Unlike the physical resources the human resources do not depreciate over time. The more the organisation utilises them the greater is the growth of their experience and expertise. Due to this, people can become the true assets of an organisation. However, this happens only when an organisation inculcates the human culture. If the organisation looks to people as costs, burdens and problems, the things start rottening up. By developing a culture of negative constraints and suspicion, the management itself initiates a process of organisational decomposition.

Dan Thomas talks about the five most important freedoms in Business Sense. He feels that when an organisation uses them it succeeds and when it does not use them it fails. These freedoms are as follows

(1) Choice of right business, (2) Creation of right strategy, (3) Implementation of right system, (4) Designing the right organisational structure, (5) Choice to get the right people.

These decisions take the organisation on the path of excellence. Right business is the one which has profit potential, growth potential and diversification potential. Right strategy is the one that will take the best advantage of its growth, profit and diversification potential in order to increase shareholder's wealth. Right system provides right information, in right form, at right time to right people so that they can make the best possible decisions. Right organisational structure is the one which will provide a framework in which management can have an access to the right information and use that information to implement the right strategy. Right people are those people having the combination of skills and motivation that will allow them to use the systems in the organisation to implement the business strategy effectively and efficiently.

Besides the above 5 elements, the organisation needs to develop a suitable culture for excellence. Culture exaggerates the required behavioural patterns and inhibits the undesirable one. Culture is like a circle. Its top half is composed of people and the bottom of it is composed of operations. The operations part of culture describes what we do and the human or people part of culture explains how we do the things. Many organisations in the same line of business may have similar operations. So the real opportunity to distinguish an organisation from its competitors lies in showing how they do the things. Their unique style of doing the operations similar to their competitors in the extraordinary or distinctive way gives the organisation its separate and charming identity. The way in which we make certain things; i.e., how we do them bring meaning to them. Tasks, anyhow, includes operations and actions. However the way in which the tasks are performed display their purpose, importance and utility. A simple act of greeting the customer when he enters the office of the organisation can either be performed mechanically or heartily. When it is done mechanically, it denotes the robotic formality being observed as a matter of office routine. When it is made wholeheartedly, it exhibits the involvement of the organisation in its customers. It indicates, how much the organisation values its customers and in what way it respects them. These willing gestures of welcome generates the warm relationship, which both parties realise completely.

The meaning which the style of performance brings to action lights on the values, thrust and attitude of people. Work is worship, is not simply a slogan to be put on a board at conspicuous places. Work becomes worship only when it is performed with that spirit and is felt so by other spectators. One's values become evident from his behaviour. Again one's attitudes reflect from his actions and reactions. The intensity and frequency of one's response reveals the nature and strength of his attitude. The repetition in similar behavioural responses indicates the thrust of the organisations. The way people do the things have motivational energy. If a person does his job in a disinterested way, displaying his indifference every now and then through actions and verbal communication, signaling his dislike of the job through frequent absence from duty, disobedience, slow speed, non completion of targets; his negative behaviour produces a demoralizing effect. Others maybe tempted to follow the same route. On the other hand, the people doing their work with commitment and concern for its results, develop a positive atmosphere. Such performers become role-models for others. If such people are more in number and hold influential positions in the organisations; the organisational climate is charged with positive energy. The organisation has to develop such a culture where positive motivation will strengthen and spread everywhere. Management experts, therefore, feel more commonly, that the real opportunity lies in how we do the things, rather than what we do. Functions in any organisation, though have a element of commonness; the style of doing these functions is organisation-specific. This style differentiates one organisation from another. It indicates the uniqueness of the organisation. It is often the major cause of success of the organisation in its field of operation.

Cultural Leaders: For the development of organisational culture, cultural leaders in the organisation, is a person who by example, balances the human values alongside work tasks. Cultural leaders exists at any level in the organisation. He need not be the top level manager or the CEO. He can be the first line supervisor in the production department also. The major job of cultural leaders is to make it clear, how people and operating issues can be held together. Normally, cultural leaders guide groups and systems and not individuals. Because it is sometime labourious, time-taking and impractical to provide guidance to each individual employee about the culture of the organisation. On the other hand, most often groups act as a whole in an understandable way. Especially new groups are like empty vessels and the leader fills them up with cultural values, norms, ideologies and behavioural patterns. Cultural leaders ask questions to groups and its members. E.g., how should we approach this problem? Such questions coach the group about the decision processes to be adopted. Cultural leader provides structure and direction for thinking, but does not supply ready-made answers and solutions to the problem. He removes the fear and defensiveness and encourage the group to make its own decision. For this purpose he creates an atmosphere of open discussion, interaction and matured relationship. He convinces them that the journey is safe. He provides security and clear direction to their efforts of decision making. Once the group realises its freedom of deciding on the issues concerned; it stops expecting to receive special knowledge and ready solution from its leader. Then the group behaviour depends on interactive relationship among its members. If the interaction is weak or stereotyped; then the competitive behaviour develops among members. This should be avoided by cultivating and nurturing the team decision-making. For this purpose the leader has to encourage and guide for the process of fusion. Under this process the members merge themselves in the group and develop a feeling that they are part and parcel of a great group, which can do anything. They join the euphoria of shared action.

To be a good and effective cultural leader one should not do too much, too fast. If the leader tries to force a change or hold a dominating position; then he cannot groom the desired culture. He should try to evolve the new suitable culture from the existing one. He should search out the groups which have like mindedness. He should encourage an open and more human culture. A leader must know that many problems in the organisations are system-oriented. But, unfortunately, people focus on events and not the processes which leads to these events. A cultural leader has to teach people to see to events as information inputs and focus on the work processes, departmental functions and functional relationships among work-groups as well as individual employees. When thrust is developed on charging the system to solve the problem, a kind of collective thinking, co-operation and faith starts breeding up. People then look to the problems of others as problem of self and attempt to search out solution for it on their own. This inspires and develops an attitude of continuous improvement and modification. Such an attitude is an essential element of the organisational culture for excellence.

Good Company and Great Company: There is always a difference between a good company and a great company. In Chapter I, a little discussion is made on this point while describing how a good organisation can become a great organisation. The major difference between the good and the great company is that of organisational culture. Culture describe the values commonly shared by all members of the organisation. In a great organisation, there is a culture of excellence which thrusts on an eternal journey of improvement and progress. Good company is happy when it accomplishes the predecided goal. A great company experiences continuously a divine dissatisfaction about its achievements. Once it reaches a particular target, immediately it gets inspired to think about a new target at a higher level. A great company always consistently elevates its goals. The continuous furtherance in the accomplishment of higher and higher goals is the essence of the culture of a great company. A company becomes great when it succeeds in excelling consistently its most outstanding past performance. It never stops at any particular destination; be it anything like quality, cost-leadership, market-leadership, etc. A great company continuously improves itself not due to any external pressure. In fact, a great company is already the best company in its line of business with notable achievements. But it still works to go far ahead and far higher. So it thinks about, what others call as unthinkable and brings those 'unthinkables' into reality. It has the self-illuminating culture. A great company is like a big river which flows relentlessly until it gets converted into an ocean.

❐❐❐

CHAPTER 5

LEADERSHIP

Leadership plays a significant role in improving and increasing organisational effectiveness. The culture of excellence needs efficient and effective leadership. Strategy and organisational culture are the cornerstones of excellence and leadership is the concrete of the tower of excellence.

For a very long time, the study of leadership was the subject matter of politics, history, economics and sociology. Business organisations were thought to require good managers and so management science had focused on the managerial development and managerial effectiveness. However, management scholars realised the need and importance of leadership, when they observed that several organisations are simply well managed but are not well led. Now, it is a well accepted fact, that leadership and managerial skill are two different things. The personality, perspective role and functions of leaders and managers are different. It cannot be presumed that when someone becomes a manager, he automatically acquires leadership capability also. Good managers may not be good leaders and so they need training about leadership skill. Modern organisations require effective leaders to survive and succeed in the present competitive environment.

Leadership and Managers

A manager may or may not possess the leadership qualities. Similarly a leader may not be holding the office of the manager. Such contradictions are the result of the misunderstanding that leaders and managers are one and the same and once a person is deputed as a manager; then, he simultaneously becomes a leader also. To remove this misunderstanding, we need to distinguish between leaders and managers. **Stephen P. Robbins** defines leadership as the ability to influence a group towards the achievement of goals. The source of this influence is formal or personal. If the leader is holding a managerial position then he gets the formal power to influence the behaviour of his subordinates. But many a time leadership emerges within a group and the leader does not have formal managerial authority, then influence is informal and personal. In fact, the source of influence does not matter much, in the concept of leadership. The concept focuses on the leader's ability to influence the group for the achievement of the common goals. This influenceability distinguishes a leader from a manager. A manager is defined as a person who has been authorised to carry out the managerial functions like planning, organising, co-ordinating, communicating, directing and controlling. Thus a manager becomes a manager by virtue of his position and he has to perform a specific set of functions. Anyone who is appointed as a manager, becomes a manager. On the other hand, the influenceability of the leader is his personality-trait. Someone becomes a leader because he possesses the leadership ability. A leader is never appointed or thrust on a group. The leadership emerges and blossoms up. It is the followers, who choose and make someone as their leader. And the followers, normally, select that person as their leader, whom, they consider as capable, fit and suitable for the leadership role. Therefore, there are hardly any ineffective leader, but there are many misfit and ineffective managers.

A manager uses the delegated authority. He gets the authority from his superiors. A leader gets the power from his followers. It is the consent and acceptance of the followers towards the leadership which makes the leader powerful. So, contrary to the famous assumption, in leadership, authority flows upward, rather than downward. As the leader starts getting more and more followers; his leadership strengthens, expands and enhances. A leader, always, has the followers and if he loses his followers; then, he no more remains a leader. So leadership lives moment by moment. If at any moment, people refuse to follow him; his leadership ends up instantaneously. Thus, leadership is a social phenomenon. Conversely, a manager does not have followers. A manager's authority or survival does not depend on followers. So long as the top-management wants the manager to hold the office; he remains a manager. The top-management of the organisation can terminate the manager, but not the leader. A leader is the favourite of the followers and so he has more commitment to his followers. A leader must fulfill the needs of his followers. Both managers and leaders have to meet the organisational goals, invariably. But while doing this leader pays attention to the needs of his followers whereas a manager does possess this outlook. A manager can plainly become 'His Master's Voice'. That is sufficient for him. He can act as the hard taskmaster. But a leader cannot afford this approach. He has to consider the human relationships. He has to maintain a proper balance between tasks and relationship. He has to accomplish the tasks while maintaining cordial relationship with employees. The leader therefore, has to be interactive all the way.

The leaders, usually, make appeal to the emotions of their followers. They treat emotions as the reservoir of motivation. Different studies on leadership have proved that effective leaders possess emotional intelligence. In fact, the presence of emotional intelligence distinguishes an effective leader from an ineffective one. Managers rely mostly on rational decision making. Leaders combine rationality and emotional strength together which increase their influenceability. Rationality sometimes limit the scope of action to solve a problem; though it can make a minute analysis of the problematic situation. Emotion drives make people to do certain things which are beyond their normal capacity. Emotions intensify actions. Strong positive emotions build determination which pulls together the complete potential of a person and focuses it on the target to be reached at. Emotionally driven people can do unthinkable things.

Peter Drucker and Warren Bennis pointed out that management is doing things right whereas leadership is doing right things. Management's efficiency lies in climbing the ladder of success; leadership determines whether the ladder is leaning against the right wall. Thus, management most of the time adopts a corrective approach. It focuses on the implementation aspect. Leadership adopts a creative approach. A leader, at the outset, chooses the right things and so the implementation of them unquestionably leads to success. Leaders, therefore, are said to carve the vision. **Kotter**, on this line of thinking, says that the primary function of the leader is to carve a vision of the organisation and a strategy for attaining it. By contrast, the job of a manager is to implement the vision.

Nature of Leadership

Leadership has been defined by different management scholars from different points. Following are some of the notable definitions of eminent scholars.

(1) **Keith Davis and J. W. Newstorm** (Human Behaviour at Work) **:** Leadership is the process of encouraging and helping others to work enthusiastically towards objectives.

(2) **Hemphill and Coons:** Leadership is the behaviour of an individual when he is directing the activities of a group towards a shared goal.

(3) **Jacobs:** Leadership is an interaction between persons in which one presents information of a sort and in such a manner suggested or desired.

(4) **J. L. Gray and F. A. Starke** (Organisational Behaviour Concepts and Applications)**:** Leadership is both a process and property. The process of leadership is the use of non-coercive influence to direct and co-ordinate the activities of the members of an organised group towards the accomplishment of group objectives. As a property, leadership is the set of qualities or characteristics attributed to those who are perceived to successfully employ such influence.

(5) **George R. Terry and S.G. Franklin** (Principle of Management)**:** Leadership is the relationship in which one person (the leader) influences others to work together willingly on related tasks to attain goals desired by the leader and or group.

These definitions highlight the following important points regarding leadership.

(i) Leadership is the ability of an individual to influence others.

(ii) Leadership involves interaction between two or more persons and so it is regarded as a group phenomenon.

(iii) The leadership influences and changes the behaviour of others. This change of behaviour is intended for achieving the shared goals.

(iv) Leadership adopts non-coercive means to change the behaviour of others.

(v) The leader possesses a set of qualities which he uses to influence others.

(vi) Leadership is studied and developed as a process as well as personal characteristic.

The famous leadership guru, **Warren G. Bennis** says that leadership is the capacity to translate vision into reality. This definition indicates two important characteristics of a leader. (1) Leader is a visionary person. (2) Leader has the managerial ability to convert the vision into reality. The first characteristic requires creative insightful thinking and foresight. The second characteristic requires the administrative capability to execute the plans. In other words a leaders possesses the ability to plan and execute. They do what they have planned and they plan for what is right to do. So leaders are dream makers and not simply dream player. A dream maker has the capability to bring his dream into reality. A dream player only sees and shows a dream. Thus only big slogans and large promises do not make leaders. The commitment to fulfill the promise and consistent efforts for the same creates and increases the credibility of a leader. And only such leaders get followers.

Bennis and B. Nanus conducted interviews of 90 outstanding leaders; of which 60 were corporate CEO and 30 from the public sector. On the basis of this study, they identified four areas of competencies in leadership, which are as follows (a) Attention through vision. (b) Meaning through communication. (c) Trust through positioning being predictable, making your position clear and keeping at it and (d) positive self-regard. These competencies are core for leadership effectiveness. **Bennis** views that the issue in leadership is not just of interpreting and envisioning the future; but being able to create the kind of meaning for people, the values that make sense to them and the trust in the system. So leaders should possess vision, ability to see the reality and the quality to get the people to follow them. The effective leadership is very well commented by **Peter Drucker**. Drucker writes in management challenges of 21st century, that effective leaders have to size up the situation, forge a new path to see where the puck is going and then have a message and vision that has meaning to the workforce. There has to be trust in the system.

In the remarkable essay 'managing the dream leadership in the 21st century', published in Journal of Organisational Change Management, in 1989, Warren Bennis has endeavoured to differentiate between managers and leaders. The main differences between their characteristics are as follows.

(1) Manager administers whereas leader innovates.

(2) Manager focuses on systems and structures and relies on control. Leader focuses on people and inspires trust.

(3) Managers have short-range view and leaders have long-range perspective.

(4) Manager imitates and keeps his eye on bottom line. Leader originates and keeps his eye on the horizon.

(5) Manager accepts *status quo* and always asks how to do and when to do things. Leader challenges the *status quo* and asks to himself what to do and why to do it.

(6) Manager is a classic soldier and emphasises on doing things right. Leader is his own person and emphasises on doing right things.

Bennis views that leaders conquer the context, the volatile, turbulent, ambiguous surroundings that sometimes seem to conspire against us and will surely suffocate us if we let them; while managers surrender to it. In the 21st century the need is of a new generation of leaders.

Robert Tannenbaum and F. Massarik defined leadership as interpersonal influence exercised in situations and directed through the communication process, towards the attainment of a specified goal or goals. Thus, they view leadership as a process rather than as an exclusive attribute of a prescribed role. The essence of leadership is interpersonal influence. This influence is created through communication. Tannenbaum observes that leadership is a function of the dynamic inter-relationship of (a) the personality characteristics of the leader, (b) the personality characteristics of the followers and (c) the characteristics of the situation.

Tannenbaum and Warren H. Schmidt suggested a continuum of leadership behaviour. They view that, leadership involves a variety of styles ranging from one that is highly boss-centred to one that is highly subordinate-centered.

These styles vary with the degree of authority a leader grants to subordinates. The important elements which influences a leader's style along this continuum are

(a) Forces in the leader: Forces in the leader's personality include his value system, confidence in subordinates, inclination towards leadership styles and feelings of security in uncertain situation.

(b) Forces in the subordinates: These forces affect the behaviour of the manager and include the expectations of the subordinates about their boss, need for independence, readiness to assume responsibility, tolerance for ambiguity, interest in problem, understanding of goals, knowledge and experience and expectation to share in decision making.

(c) Forces in the situation: These include forces like organisational values, traditions, nature of problem, time pressure, delegation of authority and unity among subordinates.

In fact the leadership style depends upon the maturity of the followers. Warren Bennis therefore, points out that effective leadership cannot exist without the full inclusion, initiative and co-operation of the employees. The more the followers trust the leader and obey his commands unanimously, the greater is the effectiveness of his leadership. Most of the group successes are attributed to leadership. Recent Gallup survey indicates that employees believe that leader guides the culture and creates situation where workers can be happy and successful.

Mutual influence process: Leadership is not unidirectional. No doubt, that the leader influences the followers. But, similarly, the followers too influence the leaders. Leadership is a mutually influencing process. A leader influences and changes the behaviour of his followers with the help of five different types of power which are as follows:

(1) **Reward power:** It refers to the leader's capacity to reward followers.

(2) **Coercive power:** It refers to the leader's capacity to punish followers.

(3) **Legitimate power:** It refers to the power which a leader possesses as a result of occupying a particular position or role in the organisation.

(4) **Expert power:** It refers to the power which a leader possesses as a result of his knowledge and expertise regarding the tasks to be performed by subordinates.

(5) **Referent power:** This power is dependent upon the extent to which the subordinates identify themselves with the leader, look upto him and wish to emulate the leader.

The followers too influence the leader. The major sources of their influence are as follows:

(i) Performance or response of subordinates.

(ii) The personal characteristics of subordinates.

(iii) The nature of the task to be performed.

(iv) Organisational policy and organisational climate.

(v) Peers and their influence on the leader

(vi) Influence of the superiors on the leader.

Important Historical Studies: Three important studies on leadership have helped to set the traditional and modern theories of leadership. These studies are as follows:

(a) **The Iowa Leadership Studies:** In 1930, at the University of Iowa, a series of pioneering leadership studies were conducted by **Ronald Lippit** and **Ralph K. White** under the general direction of **Kurt Lewin**. These studies were the first to analyse leadership from the standpoint of scientific methodology. They showed that different leadership styles can produce different and complex reactions from the same or similar group. They were also the first attempts to determine, experimentally, the effect of styles of leadership on a group.

In the initial studies, hobby clubs for ten year old boys were formed. Each club was submitted to three different styles of leadership, namely, authoritarian, democratic and *laissez-faire*. The experiments did not directly examine the effects of leadership styles on productivity. But they were designed to primarily examine patterns of aggressive behaviour. The autocratic leadership was reacted by aggressive and apathetic behavioural response by the group members. These responses were due to the frustration caused by autocratic leader. The number of aggressive acts were maximum, when the group was subjected to *laissez-faire* leadership. Democratically-led group fell between the one extremely aggressive group and four apathetic groups under the autocratic leader.

The leadership behaviour was typical. The autocratic leaders were directional and allowed no participation. They give individual attention while praising and criticising, but tried to be friendly or impersonal rather than openly hostile. Democratic leaders encouraged group discussion and decision making. They tried to be objective while praising on criticising. The *laissez-faire* leaders gave complete freedom to the group and provided no leadership at all.

(b) **The Ohio State Leadership Studies:** The Bureau of Business Research at Ohio State University conducted a series of studies on leadership at the end of the second World War. These studies started with a premise that satisfactory definition of leadership does not exist. The studies found that previous definitions of leadership were made in the context of good leadership. These studies wanted to study leadership regardless of its effectiveness. The studies tried to describe the leader's behaviour to analyse leadership in various groups and situations.

An interdisciplinary team of researchers from psychology, sociology and economics was formed. They used the Leader Behaviour Description Questionnaire (LBDQ) to analyse the leadership in numerous types of groups and situations. Studies of a variety of administrators were made. Air force commanders, civilian administrators in navy department, manufacturing supervisors, college administrators, school superintendents, executives of regional cooperatives, non-commissioned officers of army, leaders of students and civilian groups were studied. In the first step the LBDQ was administered in a variety of situations. The answers to these questionnaire was subjected to factor analysis to examine the description of leader behaviours. Two dimensions of leadership continually emerged from the questionnaire data. They were (1) consideration and (2) Initiating structure. Initiating structure refers to the task or goal-orientation of the leader and consideration refers to the recognition of individual needs and relationships. These two dimensions are separate and distinct from each other. The Ohio State Leadership Studies were the first to point out and emphasise the importance of both, the task and human dimensions in assessing leadership. This study reduced the gap between the strict task-orientation and the emphasis of human relations. The former was the outcome of scientific management and the latter emerged from the human relations school which was very popular during that period. Ohio Studies threw light that task-orientation and emphasis on human relations are used in combination by effective leaders. Only task-orientation or recognition of human relationship will not become fruitful. A leader has to inspire the people to achieve the shared goal with voluntary actions. The followers should volunteer to work hard to accomplish the goal. At the same time their relations with the leader should be friendly and cordial. If the leader cannot make people reach the target, he cannot be effective, If he is unconcerned with the needs of the followers; he will become unpopular and later ineffective. The voluntary and wholehearted response of the followers can be obtained if the leader recognises and respects human relations. Similarly, this collective and concerted response and action of the followers should be directed towards the goal accomplishment. Then only the leader will be described as effective. The two dimensional approach balancing the task and human relations have great utility in improving leadership effectiveness.

(c) **Michigan Leadership Studies:** At the same time Ohio State Studies were conducted, a group of researchers from the Survey Research Centre at the University of Michigan also began their studies of leadership. The original study was conducted at Prudential Insurance company. The researchers selected 12 high-low productivity pairs for examination. Each pair represented a high producing section and a low producing section. The other variables like type of work, conditions and methods were the same in each pair. The researchers conducted non-directive interviews with 24 section supervisors and 419 clerical workers. Following results were obtained.

(i) Supervisors of high producing sections were employee-centred and general in their supervisory styles.

(ii) Supervisors of low producing sections were production-centred and close in their supervisory styles.

(iii) Employee satisfaction was not directly related with productivity.

(iv) The Ohio State Studies and Michigan Studies on leadership made significant contribution in developing the concept and theory of leadership. Both studies observed two dimensions of leadership behaviour. Ohio state studies identified these two dimensions namely initiating structure and consideration. Initiating structure is described as the extent to which a leader is likely to define and structure his role and the roles of employees for goal attainment. It includes his following behaviour

(i) Organisation of work

(ii) Designing work relationship

(iii) Setting up of goals. A leader who is characterised as high in initiating structure does the following things:

(a) He assigns group members to particular tasks.

(b) He expects workers to maintain definite standards of performance.

(c) He emphasises the meeting of deadlines.

Consideration, the second dimension of leadership behaviour, observed in Ohio State Study is described as the extent to which a person is likely to have job relationships which are characterised by mutual trust, respect for employee's ideas and regard for their feelings. A leader high in consideration displays following behaviour.

(i) He shows concern for the follower's comfort, well-being, status and satisfaction.

(ii) He helps employees in solving their personal problems.

(iii) He treats all employees equally.

(iv) He is friendly and approachable.

(v) He emphasises on co-operation and consensus building and adopts a people-oriented leadership style.

The Michigan Study group also recognised two dimensions of leadership behaviour, namely, employee-orientation and production-orientation. The production-oriented leaders emphasise the task aspects of a job. Their main concern is the accomplishment of group's tasks. They treat group members as means to an end. It has observed that production-oriented leaders were associated with low group productivity and low job satisfaction. On the other hand, the employee-oriented leaders emphasised interpersonal relations. They took interest in the needs of their employees and accepted individual differences among members. These leaders were associated with higher group productivity and higher job satisfaction.

Scandinavian Studies on Leadership: The Iowa Studies, Ohio State Study and Michigan Study were conducted during 1930 to 1960. These were behavioural approaches to leadership which evolved during the time when the world was far more stable and predictable. Now the world has become more dynamic and the realities of today are significantly different than those of the past. From this viewpoint the researchers in Finland and Sweden conducted studies to reassess whether there are only two dimensions which capture the essence of leadership behaviour.

Scandinavian studies have a basic premise that, in a changing world the effective leaders would exhibit development-oriented behaviour. The development-oriented leaders value experimentation, seek new ideas and generate and implement change. These researchers reviewed that original Ohio Study included development items. E.g., leader originates new approaches to problems or leader encourages members to new activities, etc. But these items did not explain much about effective leadership at that time. Because in those days developing new ideas and implementing change were not critical. But, today in the dynamic environment things are different. The Scandinavian researchers are conducting new studies to see whether development orientation as the third dimension is related to leader's effectiveness. Positive evidences are found. The researchers found, from the study of sample leaders in Finland and Sweden, strong support for development oriented leader behaviour as a separate and independent dimension. In the 21st century this dimension may probably become more important for leader's effectiveness. Because it appeared that leaders who demonstrated development-orientation have more satisfied employees and are seen as more competent by followers.

TRADITIONAL THEORIES OF LEADERSHIP

(A) Trait Theories of Leadership

The trait theory evolved from the 'great person' theory of leadership. The great person theory states that some individuals are born with certain traits which allow them to become leaders. Thus leaders are born and not made. Eventually this great person theory gave way to more realistic traits approach. The Trait theories focus on individual characteristics of successful leaders. They state that leaders possess a set of traits which make them distinct from followers. Several surveys and research were conducted to identify and decide leadership traits. **Ralph Stogdill** (Handbook of Leadership) made a study of more than 5,000 leaders and concluded that the successful leaders have following qualities.

(1) A strong desire for accomplishment.
(2) Persistent pursuit of goals.
(3) Creativity and intelligence used to solve problems.
(4) Initiative applied to social situation.
(5) Self-assumed personality.
(6) Willingness to accept behavioural consequences.
(7) Low susceptibility to interpersonal stress.
(8) High tolerance of ambiguity.
(9) Ability to influence other people.
(10) Ability to structure social interactions.

According to **Robert Kartz** (Skills of an Effective Administrator) technical, conceptual and human skills are needed for effective management. **Gary Yukh** (Leadership in Organisations) views that creativity, organisation, persuasiveness, diplomacy and tactfulness, knowledge of the task and the ability to speak well are the qualities of a successful leader. The Five Factor Model (FFM) or **Big Five Theory** of personality describes the following five core traits of personality which can be equally useful for leadership. These are

(1) Conscientiousness.

(2) Emotional stability.

(3) Aggreeableness.

(4) Extraversion.

(5) Openness to experience.

The description characteristics of these core traits are given below:

(1) **Conscientiousness:** Dependable, hardworking, organized, self-disciplined, persistent, responsible.

(2) **Emotional Stability:** Calm, secure, happy, unworried.

(3) **Aggreeableness:** Cooperative, warm, caring, good-natured, courteous, trusting.

(4) **Extraversion:** Sociable, outgoing, talkative, assertive, gregarious.

(5) **Openness to experience:** Curious, intellectual, creative, cultured, artistically sensitive, flexible, imaginative.

Certain studies have concluded that emotional intelligence is a decisive characteristic of effective leaders. S.A. Kirkpatrik and E.A. Locke have described six traits which distinguish leaders from non-leaders. In their essay, Leadership – do traits matter', published in Academy of Management Executive, May 1991, they give following six distinctive traits of leaders.

(i) Ambition and energy.

(ii) Desire to lead.

(iii) Honesty and integrity.

(iv) Self-confidence.

(v) Intelligence.

(vi) Job relevant knowledge.

A research by **Dobbins, Longe, Dedrick** and **Clamons** concluded that the people who are high self-monitors are more likely to emerge as leaders than low self-monitors. High self-monitors are highly flexible in adjusting their behaviours in different situations.

John Adaire (Leadership Skills) states the following leadership qualities.

(1) Enthusiasm.

(2) Integrity.

(3) Toughness.

(4) Fairness.

(5) Warmth.

(6) Humility.

(7) Confidence.

Stanley Bing a practicing executive gives a list of seven habits of successful leader, which is as follows:

(1) Empower your inner child.

(2) Be slightly weird.

(3) Embrace compensation.

(4) Focus carefully.

(5) Speak openly.

(6) Don't even — get mad.

(7) Keep up on the latest development.

Bing humorously calls this list as seven habits of highly offensive people.

Now there is a modification in the trait approach. Instead of the study of leadership characteristics or skills, the study of leadership competencies has been made by **House, Gregarson, Morrison, Black, R. N. Aditya, Kirkpatrik, Locke,** etc. The key competencies related to effective leadership are found to be as follows:

(i) Drive, or the inner motivation to pursue goals.

(ii) Leadership motivation, which is the use of socialised power to influence others to succeed.

(iii) Integrity, which includes truthfulness and the will to translate words into deeds.

(iv) Self-confidence that leads others to feel confident, usually exhibited through various forms of impression management directed at employees.

(v) Intelligence, which is usually focused in the ability to process information, analyse alternative and discover opportunities.

(vi) Knowledge of business, the ideas generated then will help the company to survive and thrive.

(vii) Emotional intelligence provides self-monitoring, sensitivity and ability to adapt to circumstances as per need.

Evaluation of Trait Theories: Trait theories provided descriptive insight to the study of leadership. They could differentiate the leaders from the non-leaders. They were able to highlight the specific characteristics of an individual's personality which shape the leadership behaviour. They were also able to see the different roles a leader is expected to play, from the lens of his traits. Traits can predict the appearance of a leader and thereby, provide information about the qualities of a successful leader. This identification of leadership traits help organisations, institutions and societies to choose better leaders. Once we know, which qualities make a leader, we can select those people as our leaders who possess many of these qualities. Trait theories have also highlighted the natural leadership instinct. The natural leaders possess certain qualities which carry them to the leadership position. This fact has been very well argued by trait theorists. The trait theories have carried the attention of scholars to the influential relationship between one's total personality and his success on the job. A leader behaves like a leader, because he has leadership stuff. Unless we possess the merit, we cannot perform. Trait theories advocate this logic forcefully, when behavioural theories state that some typical behaviour make certain people leaders; a question can be raised, as to what makes people exhibit that typical, characteristic leadership behaviour? **James Ownes** argues that the manager's inner personality causes or spills over into his behaviour. This validates the utility and significance of trait theories.

In spite of the above merit, trait theories have been criticised severely by a number of management scholars. These points of criticism can be summarised as follows:

(1) The list of leadership traits is too long and there is no final conclusion about it. A consistent pattern has not emerged though hundreds of traits are identified.

(2) Trait theories do not explain the proportion in which a particular trait is required for the successful leadership. Further the psychological qualities are non-quantifiable.

(3) The basic assumption of trait theories that leaders are born is not acceptable in the present times. The leadership development programmes and the behavioural approach to leadership have proved that successful leadership can be nurtured by proper guidance and appropriate training.

(4) Research and surveys have found that leadership effectiveness does not depend on personality alonc. Tasks, followers, situation, organisation are other relevant factors which determine leader's effectiveness.

(5) It is observed that some of the unsuccessful leaders have the same or similar traits like successful leaders still they failed. This questions the validity of trait theory.

(6) The different traits do not have precise meaning. There is very little consensus about the meaning of any trait. Each trait is described differently by different people. This creates ambiguity and confusion.

(7) There are no universal traits that predict leadership in all situations. Traits appear to predict leadership only in selective situation.

(8) Traits predict behaviour in weak situations, rather than strong situations. Strong situations are defined as those situations in which there are strong behavioural norms, strong incentives for specific behaviour and clear expectations as to what behaviours are rewarded and punished. These situations do not give a leader to express his inherent predisposition tendency. In most of the present organisations, there is high level of formalisation. Further the organisational culture is also very strong. All these create strong situations and so the power of traits to predict leadership in organisations remain limited.

(9) Trait theories do not provide causal explanation. They do not precisely clarify the cause-effect relationship. For example, when it is said that successful leaders are confident, it does not tell any causal relationship. Does confidence build the leadership ability or does the success in leadership develops confidence? What is the cause and what is the effect?

(10) Traits do not guarantee effective leadership. If someone is accepted as a leader by others due to certain traits, he will not definitely get his group to achieve the goal. So ultimately the leader's behaviour becomes move decisive and significant than his traits or qualities.

(B) Behavioural Theories of Leadership

When trait theories were unable to provide satisfactory explanation of leadership effectiveness, a new approach was developed, which was popularised as behavioural approach to leadership. Trait theories emphasised on studying the personal characteristics of leaders and attempted to separate leaders from non-leaders. Behavioural theories focused on the study of how a leader behaves and tried to determine how various kinds of specific behaviour affect the performance and satisfaction of followers. Among the different behavioural theories, the Ohio State University Studies and the Michigan University Studies are the two important main behavioural theories. Both Studies are discussed at length earlier. The Ohio State University Studies intended to identify the major dimensions of leadership and wished to find out the effect of behaviour of a leader on the performance and satisfaction of his employees. The Studies identified the two dimensions of leadership behaviour, namely, the initiating structure and consideration. The initiating structure refers to the leader's behaviour, defines and organises the group tasks, assigns the task to employees and supervises their activities. The consideration refers to the leader's behaviour which is characterised by friendliness, respect, trust, openness, support and concern for the welfare of the employees.

The Ohio State Studies had the following findings.

(1) Consideration was positively related to low absenteeism and grievances. However, it was negatively or neutrally related to performance.

(2) Initiating structure was positively related to performance. But it was associated with negative consequences like absenteeism, grievances, etc.

(3) When considerations and structure were high, performance and satisfaction tended to be high. But in some cases, high productivity was associated with absenteeism and grievances.

The Ohio State Studies did not place initiating structure and consideration on a continuum. The Michigan Studies, on the other hand, placed leadership on a continuum. They identified two dimensions of leadership behaviour; namely production-orientation and employee-orientation. Employee-centred leaders encouraged the participation of employees in goal setting and work-related decisions. They ensured high performance by inspiring trust and respect among followers. The production-centred leaders, conversely, set rigid work standards, organised tasks down to the last detail and prescribed work methods. They closely supervised the performance of subordinates. Michigan Studies placed these two leadership dimensions on a continuum. At the left end is placed production-centred leadership and at the right end is placed employee-centred leadership. It was presumed that as the leader move from the left end of the line to the right end; then he is doing better as a leader. However, after deeper analysis and study; the researchers found that employee-orientation are two separate dimensions and so they cannot be put on a continuum. Actually three possibilities of leadership behaviour emerge.

(i) A leader may be high or low on any one of these two dimensions.

(ii) A leader may be low on both dimensions.

(iii) A leader may be high on both dimensions.

The main contribution of behavioural theories is that people can be trained to adopt appropriate leadership behaviour and thereby, they can become effective leaders. These theories focused on how leaders delegate the task, communicate with others and motivate the employees. But these theories could not establish a consistent relationship between leadership behaviour and group performance. These theories ignored the situational factors which influence the success or failure of a leader.

Managerial Grid : This theory emerged from the behavioural approach to leadership. **Blake** and **Mouton** developed a graphical portrayal of a two dimensional view of leadership styles. They proposed the managerial grid (or leadership grid) based on the styles of concern for people and concern for production. In fact these two dimensions represent the dimensions introduced by Ohio and Michigan Studies. The concern for production represent the initiating structure or production-orientation and the concern for people represent the consideration or employee-orientation.

Managerial grid is a 9 x 9 matrix having 81 different leadership styles based on concern for production and concern for people. The concern for production is shown on horizontal axis and concern for people on vertical axis. Thus, the grid has of possible positions along each axis, creating 81 different positions in which a leader's style may fall. The grid does not show results produced but, it indicates the dominating factors in the thinking process of the leader which are related to getting results. The grid identifies five basic styles of leadership; which are, in fact, the alternative combinations of concern for production and concern for people.

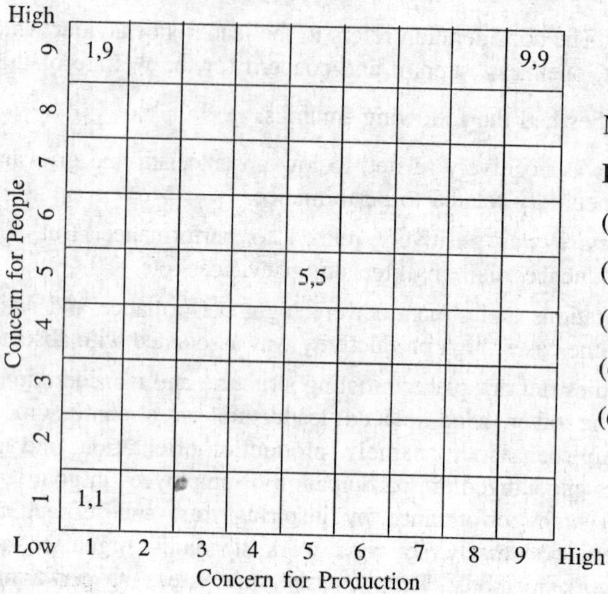

Managerial Grid

Five styles

(a) (1, 1)

(b) (9, 1)

(c) (5, 5)

(d) (1, 9)

(e) (9, 9)

Fig. 5.1 Managerial Grid

(a) Impoverished Leadership Style (1, 1): This style of leadership shows minimum concern for production as well as for people. The leader since has low concern for production and people; exerts minimum efforts to get the work done. The leader does not behave like a leader and does not play the leadership role actively. The leader leaves everything to the situation and makes lowest amount of efforts to sustain and retain the organisational membership and to get done the essential work. This style is similar to the *laissez-faire* style of management.

(b) Task Leadership (9,1): This style of leadership shows high concern for production but low concern for people. Production maximization is the only goal of such managers. They give utmost importance to production and productivity. Their behaviour is very authoritative. This style is similar to autocratic style of leadership. The leaders expects the employees to be obedient to his orders. So it is called authority-obedience style. Employee needs and satisfaction have the secondary important for managers following task leadership style.

(c) Middle of the road leadership style (5, 5): This style shows equal concern for production and people such leaders seek balance between the requirements of production and needs of people. Sometimes these managers are called the organisational men. They go along to get along maintaining and conforming to *status quo*.

(d) Country club leadership (1, 9): This style shows high concern for people and low concern for production. It is opposite to task leadership style. The leader emphasises more on friendly interpersonal relations, on meeting the needs of employees, on creating an atmosphere of mutual trust and respect. Good feelings towards followers are the hallmarks of such manager. The managers believe in employee efficiency.

(e) Team leadership (9, 9): This style shows high concern for production and people. It is most effective in all situations. Such leaders have democratic-orientation. This style is associated with high performance, high employee satisfaction, low labour absenteeism and low labour turnover. Though team leadership is presumed as the best style in all situations; the evidences in support of this claim are not much substantive.

The greatest utility of managerial grid is that it offers a better framework for conceptualising leadership styles. However, it does not provide any new information in clarifying the leadership quandary. The graphical presentation which this grid makes has simplied the study of leadership behaviour and made it easy to understand, as for the concept of different leadership styles go.

Likert's Four System of Leadership: Renis Likert and his associates, at the University of Michigan, studied the patterns and styles of leaders for thirty year. He suggested four systems of management, which are as follows:

System 1: Exploitative Authoritative Management - The leaders following this style are highly autocratic. They have little trust in subordinates. They make more use of negative motivation and occasionally they offer rewards. In such organisations decisions are made at the top and the communication is downward.

System 2: Benevolent Authoritative Management - These leaders are autocratic but hold paternalistic view. They trust the subordinates to some extent. They make use of reward for motivation. Such leaders prefer downward as well as upward communication.

System 3: Consultative Management - These leaders consult with subordinates and maintain the upward and downward communication flow. They have more trust in subordinates and use the ideas and opinions of subordinates while making decisions. They make use of positive motivation and allow subordinates to make some decisions.

System 4: Group Management - These leaders have complete trust in subordinates. They make use of positive motivation and downward and upward communications. They delegate decision power to subordinate and encourage higher subordinate participation. They use opinions of subordinates while making decisions.

Likert's studies had following conclusions :

(i) Managers applying system for approach achieved great success as leaders.

(ii) Companies managed by system for approach were most productive and efficient in their functioning.

Criticism: Likert's theory is useful to small groups but it is not that much useful to complete organisation. The research was conducted at lower level of organisation and so the findings may not be supported by the data regarding top level management. Likert suggested the use of matrix organisation which may result into the increase in role conflict. Again system 4 was used by profit-making companies. This cannot establish the hypothesis that the use of system 4 leads to profit-earning.

(C) Contingency Theories of Leadership

The researchers experienced that it is very difficult and complicated to predict leadership effectiveness than to identify a few traits or to describe preferable behaviour. The failure to obtain consistent results about prediction relating to leadership effectiveness led to contingency theories. Contingency theories are also called as situational theories. These theories have a basic proposition that the most effective behaviour for leaders to engage in, is contingent upon the characteristics of the situation in which the leader finds himself. So no theory or style of leadership is effective in all situations. A question such as whether employee-oriented leadership style is more or production-oriented, is really futile and meaningless. In fact, the right question will be, under what conditions will employee-oriented leadership be effective? Thus, situational variables are more important and decisive in leadership effectiveness. The situation directs as to which leadership-style should be used to create effectiveness. A particular leadership style effective in one situation may not be effective in another situation. Therefore, we cannot insist upon an all-time-effective leadership style. All leadership styles are equally valid and important and their utility and effectiveness depends upon the situation.

Among the contingency theories, Fiedler's theory, path-goal theory and situational leadership theory are more popular.

Fiedler's Contingency Theory: Fred Fiedler was the first person who developed a comprehensive contingency model of leadership. Fiedler's theory says that effective performance of the group depends upon a proper match between the style of the leader to interact with his subordinates and the degree to which the situation gives control and influence to the leader.

Fiedler's model has three important steps

(i) Determing the leadership style.

(ii) Defining the situation

(iii) Matching leaders and situations.

According to Fiedler a key factor in leadership success is the individual's basic leadership style. In order to find out the basic style of the leader Fiedler created a questionnaire called Least Preferred Co-worker (LPC) questionnaire. It intended to measure whether a leader is task-oriented or relationship-oriented. The questionnaire contained a set of 16 contrasting adjectives, such as, pleasant-unpleasant, open-guarded, efficient-inefficient, supportive-hostile, etc. The respondent (to the questionnaire) has to think of all the co-workers and has to describe that co-worker with whom he least enjoys working together, by rating him on a scale of 1 to 8 for each of the 16 sets of contrasting adjectives. Fiedler argues that on the basis of these responses, the person's basic leadership style can be identified. If the least preferred co-worker is described in relatively positive terms, with high LPC score; then the person (respondent) is interested in good personal relations with the co-worker. Thus a respondent describing his co-worker, with whom he is least able to work with, in positive terms would be titled as relationship-oriented by Fiedler. Conversely, if the least preferred co-worker is described in relatively unfavourable terms; then the respondent is treated as primarily interested in productivity and is titled as task-oriented. Fiedler's survey found that 84 per cent respondents score either high or low-range of LPC. Only 16 per cent were in the middle-range.

Fiedler views that an individual's leadership style is fixed. So if the situation requires a task-oriented leader whereas the person is relationship-oriented; then either modify the situation or change the leader.

Once the basic leadership style is identified, then the second step is defining the situation. Fiedler recognizes three contingency dimensions which define the situational factors determining leader's effectiveness. These are as follows:

(a) Leader member relations: The degree of confidence, trust and respect which the members have for their leader.

(b) Task structure: The degree to which the job-assignments are procedurised. (i.e., structured or unstructured)

(c) Position power: The degree of influence the leader has over power variables such as recruitment, promotion, salary-rise, disciplinary action, retrenchment, etc.

A situation is evaluated in terms of these three variables. So the leader-member relationship is either good or poor. The task structure is either high or low. And the power-position of the leader may be either strong or weak. According to Fiedler when the leader-member relationship is good, the job is highly structured and the power position of the leader is strong, then, the leader has more control.

The third step of the Fiedler model is matching the leader and situation. On the basis of LPC questionnaire and the above three contingency variables Fiedler proposes to make a match between the leader and the situation. Fiedler concludes that task-oriented leaders tend to perform better in situations which are very favourable and also in situations which are very unfavourable. On the other hand the relationship-oriented leaders perform better in moderately favourable situations. In other words, Fiedler says that task-oriented leaders perform best in situations of high and low control, whereas, the relationship-oriented leaders perform best in situations of moderate control.

If the situation-leader match is proper and suitable, then the leadership effectiveness is more. In order to bring the match and the effectiveness, there are two options

(i) Make the leader suitable to the situation, i.e., change the leader (if he is unsuitable) or

(ii) Make the situation suitable to the leader, i.e., change and modify the situation.

Now in the former cases if the situation is most favourable or unfavourable and if it is led by a relationship-oriented leader; then change him and give the situation under the command of a task-oriented leader. In the latter case, to change the situation; restructure the task or increase/decrease control power of the leader in respect of salary-increase, promotion and disciplinary action.

Fiedler contingency theory has a number of merits, which are as follows:

(i) Fiedler's model clearly explains the three important components of leadership-effectiveness, namely, the leader, the situation and the subordinates.

(ii) It provides a realistic and flexible approach to the issue of leadership effectiveness. In comparison to Fiedler's model the earlier research and theories appears to be naive.

(iii) Fiedler's model is useful for leadership training programme. Previously most of such programmes used to emphasise on trying to change and modify the personality of the leader which is very difficult, complicated and almost futile. Personality is the result of the grooming of the individual over a very long period. A limited-period training programme can very hardly alter completely someone's personality. Fiedler's model describe the concept of leader-situation match, which tells about the modification of situation to suit to the leader's style. This gave a new direction to leadership-training. Leadership-match is a programmed learning teenique that trains leader to modify the situation to fit to his personality. This technique is now widely used to train managers in different organisations.

However, several objections and lot of criticism has also been made on Fiedler's model. This criticism is as follows:

(i) The logic underlying LPC is ambiguous and confusing. LPC score does not reveal the leader's behaviour but only suggests his feelings about his least preferred co-worker. Further the respondent's LPC score was found unstable. Again questions are raised as to what LPC score really measures. It does not explain why a respondent who describes his least preferred co-worker in negative terms is considered as task-oriented and the other describing in positive terms is considered as relationship-oriented.

(ii) Some variables used in the model have unclear meaning. For example, it is difficult to label any task as structured or unstructured because these are relative terms and cannot be described in an absolute way. This and similar ambiguities develops errors in measurement. Practically, it becomes almost impossible to assess.

(iii) Some scholars view that Fiedler's model lacks the theoretical orientation. It is based on the research data than a theoretical scheme. It lacks the explanatory power, though it has a predictive value. It cannot explain why a particular leadership style is more desirable in a particular situation.

(iv) The model presumes that both the leader and the subordinates are adequately technically competent. The model does not pay attention to the actuality about the technical competence of the leader and his subordinates.

Though some of the criticism is justifiable, Fiedler's explanation about leadership effectiveness is still noteworthy. Fiedler says that in a favourable and unfavourable situation task-oriented leadership is effective. He further explains that a situation is favourable when all the three dimensions are high. So in this situation the leader is generally accepted and respected by his subordinates so leader-member relationship, the first dimension, is favourable. The task is structured and everything is spelled out, i.e., the second dimension of the situation is also high and if a great deal of authority and power is formally attributed to the leader's position then the third dimension is also high. These make the situation favourable. Fiedler also provides causation of his claim that task-oriented leadership is effective in favourable and unfavourable situations. So, accordingly, he says that in a favourable situation, the leader has power, informal backing, a relatively well-structured task and the group ready to be directed and expects to be told what to do. Therefore, task-oriented leaders become effective. Again in an unfavourable situation, there is no point in discussing anything with the subordinates, because the outcome will be zero as the subordinates dislike the leader and therefore, are non-co-operative and non-responsive. So the leader should focus on the task and decide by himself. Even if the leader makes a wrong decision, then also it is belter than no decision at all. Because in unfavourable situations there is a need for a decision to accomplish the task even without considering the happiness of anybody. Conversely in a moderately favourable or unfavourable situation, a relation-oriented, democratic leader is effective because he is able to win maximum support from the subordinates through discussion, interactive meetings, two-way communication and that way by strengthening the relations.

Through contingency leadership model, Fiedler has provided major breakthrough for leadership theory, research and practice. It is the first highly visible leadership theory to present the contingency approach. It emphasises the two most important determinants of leadership effectiveness, namely, situation and leader's characteristics. It stimulated a great deal of research and inspired formulation of alternative contingency theories.

Cognitive Research Theory: Recently **Fiedler** and **Joe Garcia** reconceptualised the contingency theory. They call this reconceptualisation as Cognitive Resource Theory. This theory focuses on the role of stress as a form of situational unfavourableness and how the intelligence and experience of the leader influence his reactions to stress. This theory treats stress as the enemy of rationality. Stress makes a leader difficult to think logically and analytically. Fiedler and Garcia found that intelligence of a leader correlates positively with performance under low stress but negatively under high stress. Thus in a stress-free situation, the intelligence of a leader will contribute more to increase the group performance. But in a stressful situation, its contribution is negative. Conversely, the experience of a leader correlates negatively with performance under low stress, but positively under high stress. So intelligent leaders perform better in low-stress situations and experienced leaders perform better in high-stress situations. Fiedler and Garcia concludes that the level of stress in a situation determines whether an individual's intelligence and experience will contribute to leadership performance. Thus, more intelligent leaders perform worse in high stress situation than less intelligent people. Similarly, more experienced leaders perform worse in 100 stress situations than their less experienced counterparts.

From the above theory, we can presume that intelligence acts as a useful cognitive resource under low stress situation and experience becomes an asset for a leader under high stress situation.

Situational Theory By Hersey and Blanchard

Paul Hersey and Keneth Blanchard combined the managerial grid and contingency theory and developed the situational theory. The theory suggests that leadership effectiveness depends upon the situation in which leadership is exercised. The theory adds 'maturity of followers' as a contingency variable. According to this theory, successful leadership requires adjusting the leader's emphasis on task-behaviour and relationship behaviour, according to the maturity of followers in performing their tasks. Maturity here is described as the desire of the followers for achievement, willingness to accept responsibility and task-related ability and experience. It is the level of development of the followers. This maturity is catagorised into four levels based on the ability and willingness of the followers to accept responsibility and complete their tasks. The followers who are unable and unwilling are catagorised as least mature and those who are able and willing are termed as most mature.

Hersey and Blanchard views that the relationship between the leader and followers moves through four phases which is kind of a life-cycle. As subordinates develop and mature, the leader has to change his style with each phase of development of followers. When the subordinate is a new recruit and joins the organisation for the first time, it is the initial stage. At initial stage high task orientation is the appropriate leadership style. At this stage the manager should give instructions to subordinates about the task to be completed and make them familiar with the organisational rules and procedures. At this stage the maturity level of the subordinates is lowest and hence they need direction. So a 'Telling style' which involves providing directions and instructions about task-performance and behaviour is appropriate. At this initial state, the ability and willingness to work of the subordinates is very low. And therefore, a non-directive manager may cause confusion and anxiety among subordinates. So a high task and low relationship directive telling style is useful when the maturity level of the subordinates is low due to newness.

As subordinates start learning their task and getting familiar with the organisation, the leader has to change his style. This is the second phase where the willingness of the subordinates is high but still their abilities are low. They still require directives. At the same time, the manager has become familiar with the subordinates. A little amount of trust and support will further enhance their efforts. So a manager need to follow the 'selling style' or 'coaching style' which involves supply of directives and support to the subordinates. A selling style is also described as high task-orientation and high relationship style.

In the third phase, the ability and achievement motivation of the subordinates is increased and subordinates actively begin to seek greater responsibility. Their maturity level is further enhanced. The subordinates no more require further direction. In fact, a close direction by the manager, will be highly resented by the subordinates. So a manager should no longer need to be direct. But still he has to be supportive. His support and considerate behaviour will strengthen the willingness of the subordinates for greater responsibility. So the participating style is suitable.

The fourth phase is the one when the maturity level of the subordinates is highest and so their readiness to accomplish, achieve and accept responsibility is at its peak. At this stage, the subordinates are more confident, experienced and self-directed. So the most appropriate leadership style in this phase is 'delegating style'. This style is described as the low task and low relations-orientation style. In this final phase the subordinates are 'on their own' and do not need or expect either directives or specific support. These styles are described in the following diagrams.

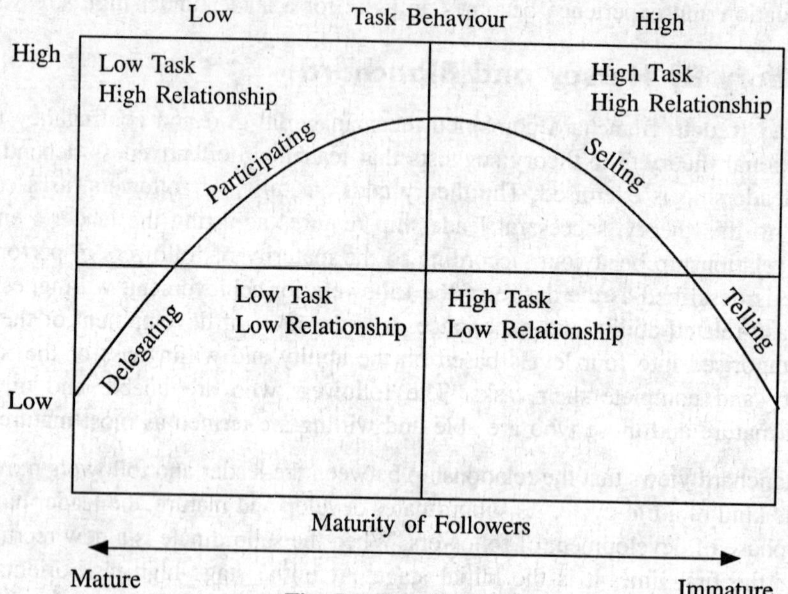

Fig. 5.2 Situational Theory

(1) Telling Style: High task and low relationship style. Also called Directive style. Effective for employees with ability and low willingness.

(2) Selling Style: High task and high relationship style. Also called Coaching style. Effective when employees have low ability and high willingness.

(3) Participating Style : Low task and high relationship style. Also known as Supportive style. Effective when employees have high ability to work but low willingness to accept responsibility. However, the employees are matured.

(4) Delegating Style : Low task and low relationship style. Effective when employees have high ability to work and high willingness to accept responsibility and act independently. Their maturity level is the highest.

Evaluation: Situational leadership theory is one of the more popular training models which is widely used in leadership training programmes. It recommends a flexible and dynamic leadership style. It continuously considers the ability and willingness of followers to decide the combination of task and relationship orientation. This helps the leader to adopt a suitable style under constantly changing conditions, which is the reality of the modern organisations. Hersey and Blanchard claims that situational leadership theory not only motivate employees to perform better, but also helps them to move to higher level of maturity.

However situational theory has the following weaknesses: (1) It is difficult to determine the maturity level of the subordinates. (2) It is presumed that the leadership style changes as per the maturity level of subordinates. However in a group how is it possible for a leader to adopt task orientation in respect of one employee and relationship orientation in respect of another employee. (3) The theory expects a flexible approach of the leader to his leadership style. Depending upon the situation he should go on changing the combination of task and relationship orientation. This may not be practically possible all the time. Once a leader starts following a particular style, it becomes somehow concretised in his personality. He gets habituated to think, decide and act in that style. So frequent changes in the style are very difficult to incorporate. No doubt, that, the leadership style should be adaptable to the changes in situation; but, how far is this practical and possible?

In spite of the limitations and disappointing research experience, situational leadership theory has its uniqueness. It has an intuitive appeal and it acknowledges the importance of follows. The theory builds a strong logic that the leader can compensate for the lack of ability and motivational limitations of the followers. So when the followers are unable and unwilling to do a task; then, the leader should give them clear and specific directions. When the followers are unable but willing, the leader should display high task orientation to compensate the followers lack of ability and high relationship orientation to enhance further their efforts. When the followers are able but unwilling, then the leader has to follow the supportive and participative style. If employees are able and willing, then the leader need not have to do much. He has to follow a *laissez-faire* leadership style. At this maturity level, the employees are on their own and so the delegating style becomes suitable.

Leader-Member Exchange Theory : The theory is also known as vertical-dyad linkage theory. The theory states that leader treats each subordinate in a different way. The leader and subordinate develops a two person or dyadic relationship. This relationship affects the behaviour of both. Over the time the leader develops an 'in-group' and 'out-group' of subordinates and establish different relations with them. He maintains special relationship with them. He maintains special relationship with the in group members. The in-group members are more trusted, get a disproportionate amount of the leader's attention and receive special privileges. It is seen that a leader chooses an in-group member because the person possesses a higher level of competence or has similar attitude and personality characteristics like the leader. Other followers fall into the 'out-group'. The out-group members get less time of the leader, receive fewer rewards from the leader and their relations with the leader are based on formal authority interactions.

Research evidences are supportive to this LMX theory. Leaders make differentiation among followers. The in-group members have higher performance rating, lower turnover intentions, greater satisfaction with the superior and higher overall satisfaction than the out-group members. The leader 'leads' the members of the in-group and supervise those of the out-group. The leader is more responsive to the needs of in-group than out-group. Thus the in-group has a high quality relationship with the leader and the out-group has a low quality relationship. Due to this high quality relationship, the in-group members assume greater job responsibility and make more contribution to their unit. The leader invests more of his resources in those who can perform well. Leader knows that the in-group members are more competent; he provides the special attention to them.

Path-Goal Theory of Leadership: This is one of the most respected approaches to leadership. The theory is developed by **Robert House** which was initially presented by **Martin Evans**. The theory states that it is the job of the leader to assist the followers in attaining their goals and to provide necessary direction and support to ensure that their goals are compatible with the overall objectives of the organisation. The leader has to use the structure, support and reward to create a work environment that helps the employees to reach the organisation's goal. Effective leaders clarify the path to achieve the goals and make the journey of the followers easier along the path by reducing the roadblocks. Thus the leader's job is to clarify the goals for the subordinates and set the path for realising the goals. These goals may be the work-goals or personal goals. The leader's behaviour is considered satisfactory when it increases the goal attainment of the subordinates and when it clarifies the path to these goals.

House identified four leadership styles, namely directive, supportive, participative and achievement-oriented. Directive leaders explain their expectations of performance of subordinates, they schedule the work to be done and give specific guidance on task accomplishment. Supportive leaders are friendly and show concern for the needs of the followers. Participative leaders consult with the subordinates and use their suggestions while making decisions and achievement-oriented leaders set challenging goals and expect that followers should perform at the highest level. House says that the same leader can display any of these four behaviours depending upon the situation. Different styles thus are used in different situations, by the same leader. Two situational factors are also identified. One is the personal characteristics of the subordinates and the other is the environmental pressures and demands facing the subordinates. In respect of the first situational factor, the path-goal theory states that the leader's behaviour is acceptable to the extent to which subordinates see such behaviour as an immediate source of satisfaction or as instrumental to future satisfaction. In respect of second situational factor, i.e., environmental pressure, the theory states that (1) the leader behaviour is motivational to the extent to which it satisfies the needs of the subordinate which are contingent on effective performance and (2) it complements the environment of subordinates by providing the coaching, guidance, support and rewards which are necessary for effective performance and which may be lacking in subordinates or in the environment.

The leader makes use of any of the four styles according to the situation and thereby influences the perception of the subordinate and motivate them. The leader makes the subordinate's path to goal as smooth as possible. He does this by making the following : (1) Recognising and arousing the needs of the subordinates for outcomes. (2) Increasing pay-off to subordinates for work-goal attainment. (3) Making the path to those pay-offs easier by coaching and direction. (4) Helping subordinates clarify expectancies. (5) Reducing frustration barriers. (6) Increasing the opportunities for personal satisfaction contigent on effective performance.

The path-goal theory is also criticised because research on it is not supportive. More research is required to test its validity and universality.

Leader Participation Model: This model is developed by **Victor Vroom** and **Philip Yetton** and it relates to leadership behaviour and participation in decision making. They argued that leader behaviour must adjust to reflect the task structure. Task structures have varying demands for routine and non-routine activities. The model provides a set of rules to determine the form and amount of participative decision making in different situations. The model was later revised by **Vroom** and **Arthur Jago**. They provided 12 contingency variables. However, the leader-participation model is complicated, unrealistic and omits the important situational variables such as stress, intelligence and experience.

Modern Theories of Leadership: Leadership is a topic of continuous discussion and debate. Trait, behavioural and contingency was found to be incomplete in certain respect. The tests conducted by traditional theories are judged as inappropriate and most of their results have not been replicated.

This necessitated the thinking of alternative theories and research methods. This resulted into emergence of a number of new theories in recent years. A brief discussion of these theories is made below.

(A) Charismatic Leadership: Charismatic leaders influence the followers by their personal abilities. Some people have such a tremendous personal ability with which they produce profound and extraordinary influence on followers. They are the charismatic leaders. The concept of charismatic leaders in not new old mythological stories speak about the charisma of great leaders of those times. However the modern development of the concept of charismatic leadership is attributed to the work of **Robert House**. House made an analysis of political and religious leaders and argued that the charismatic leaders have following five major characteristics: (1) Self-confidence (2) Confidence in subordinates. (3) High expectations for subordinates. (4) Ideological vision. (5) Use of personal example. House observed that the followers of charismatic leaders display extreme loyalty to the leader. They have tremendous confidence in the leader. They identify themselves with the leader and his mission. They emulate the leader's values and behaviour. They derive self-esteem from their relationship with the leader.

Bernard Bass extended the concept of charismatic leadership to business leaders, in recent years. He called Jack Welch and Bill Gates as charismatic leaders. He views that charismatic leaders have following skills and abilities: (1) Debating skill (2) Persuasive skill (3) Technical expertise (4) Ability to foster attitudinal, behavioural and emotional changes in followers. Charismatic leaders are described as wonderful heroes. They command the attention of followers. They persuade people successfully to do those things, which people rather would be disinclined to do. Followers do most unexpected things at the call of the charismatic leader. Charismatic leadership theory makes following two predictions. Because of the extreme influence on followers: (i) a charismatic leader will produce in followers performance beyond expectations and (ii) a charismatic leader can produce strong commitment in followers to the leader and his mission.

According to **Conger** and **Kanungo**, charisma is an attributional phenomenon and it varies with the situation. The leader traits which foster this charismatic attribution include self-confidence, impression-management skill, social sensitivity and empathy. Also the situations in which charismatic leadership will get promoted will either be a crisis requiring dramatic change or will be the one when followers are completely dissatisfied with *status quo*. Recent research, conducted by different scholars, on charismatic leadership have made following observations:

(1) The impact of charismatic leadership is enhanced when followers exhibit higher level of self-awareness and self-monitoring while observing the behaviour and activities of the leader.

(2) A charismatic leader who successfully implemented a technical change, suffered from political turmoil which was the side effect of the technical change. This shows that the studies of charismatic leadership must consider the context in which the leader operates and also the nature of the task or work to be performed.

These observations highlight the need for more research on charismatic leadership.

James M. Howell and Bruce J. Avolio have enlisted the ethical and unethical characteristics of charismatic leader in their essay, titled as, 'The Ethics of Charismatic Leadership – Submission or Liberation.' This observation shows the dark side of charismatic leadership which till then was ignored to a large extent. Those ethical and unethical characteristics of charismatic leaders are as follows:

Ethical Characteristics

(i) Uses power to serve others.

(ii) Aligns vision with follower needs and aspirations.

(iii) Considers and learns from criticism.

(iv) Stimulates followers to think independently and to question the leader's view.

(v) Open, two way communication.

(vi) Coaches, develops and supports followers; shares recognition with others.

(vii) Relies on internal moral standards to satisfy organisational and societal interests.

Unethical Characteristics

(i) Uses power only for personal gain or impact.

(ii) Promotes own personal vision.

(iii) Censures critical or opposing views.

(iv) Demands own decisions be accepted without questions.

(v) Insensitive to follower's needs.

(vi) One way communication.

(vii) Relies on convenient moral standards to satisfy the self-interests.

These observations show that if a leader does not have strong moral convinction then, his charisma may result into production of disastrous outcome. The extraordinary influence of the charismatic leader, if used unethically, will produce disproportionate harm and injury to the society. Therefore **Kambiz Maani and Cambell Benton** comments, that charismatic leaders deserve this label only if they create transformations in their organisations so that members are motivated to follow them and to seek organisation objectives not simply because they are ordered to do so and not merely because they calculate that such compliance is in their self-interest, but because they voluntarily identify with the organisation, its standards of conduct and willingly seek to fulfill its purpose. This transformation by charisma for a better cause is expected from the leader. The leader should use his charisma to give the followers a complete realisation of their role and the value of the goal which they are motivated to accomplish.

Conger and Kanungo argues that the followers observe certain behaviour of the leader and make attribution of heroic or extraordinary leadership abilities and this recognises the leader as a charismatic leader. They describe the following five characteristics of such leaders:

(i) Vision.

(ii) Willingness to take risk to achieve that vision.

(iii) Sensitivity to environmental constraints.

(iv) Sensitivity to followers' needs.

(v) Exhibition of extraordinary behaviour.

Conger and Kanungo say that these personal characteristics differentiate a charismatic leader from a non-charismatic one.

B. Shamir, R.J. House and M.B. Arthur explains the influence process of the charismatic leaders. It has following four steps.

(a) Articulation of vision.

(b) Communication of high performance expectations.

(c) Setting of new values.

(d) Making of self-sacrifice.

The influence process of a charismatic leader begins with articulation of appealing vision. This vision provides a sense of continuity for followers by linking the present with a better future of the organisation. Then the leader communicates high performance expectations to the followers and simultaneously expresses his confidence in them that they will attain the expected goals. Such a faith of the leader in followers enhances the self-esteem and self-confidence of the followers. Thereafter, the leader conveys to the followers, through his words and actions, a new set of values. By his own behaviour the leader sets an example before the followers to imitate. Finally the leader makes self-sacrifice and engages in unconventional behaviour. This demonstrates his courage and conviction about the vision.

Charismatic leadership and high level of performance and satisfaction among followers is correlated. This kind of observation was made by **House, Woycke** and **Fodor**. This high level of performance is due to the extra work efforts made by the followers. Followers voluntarily and willingly make these extra efforts because they like and respect their leader and feel and express greater satisfaction while working for the charismatic leader.

There is always a continuous debate on the point whether charismatic leaders are born or made? In other words, do people learn charismatic leadership or is charismatic leadership a born quality? A group of scholars which is in minority belives that charisma is an inborn quality and as such charismatic leaders are born. Charisma cannot be taught. Conversely, many experts hold the view that individuals can be suitable trained to exhibit charismatic behaviour and that way they can become charismatic leaders. From this viewpoint **R.J. Richardson and SK Thayer** propose a three step process by which a person can become a charismatic leader. This process is as follows:

(1) An individual needs to develop the aura of charisma by maintaining an optimistic view, using passion as a catalyst for generating enthusiasm and communicating not simply with words, but with the whole body.

(2) An individual, then should draw others in by creating a bond which inspires others to follow.

(3) An individual should, thereafter, bring out the potential in followers by tapping into their emotions.

Research about charismatic leadership finds that charismatic leaders are not always required. In following two situations charismatic leadership has been proved to be most appropriate.

(a) When the task of the followers have an ideological component, charismatic leadership is suitable.

(b) When the environment involves a high degree of uncertainty and stress, charismatic leaders are most appropriate to handle the situation.

(B) Transformational Leadership: In order to explain the concept of transformational leadership, we require to distinguish it from transactional leadership. The famous behavioural theories and contingency theories are concerned with transactional leaders. A **transactional leader** is the one who guides or motivates his followers in the direction of established goals by clarifying the role and task requirement. As against these transactional leaders, there are **transformational leaders** who inspire followers to transcend their own self-interests and who are capable of having a profound and extraordinary effect on followers. **Stephen Robbins** is of the opinion that transformational leaders pay attention to the developmental needs of the followers. They change the awareness of the followers by helping them to look at old problems in new ways. They are able to excite, arouse and inspire the followers to put extra efforts to achieve the group goals.

B.M. Bass gave the major characteristics of transactional and transformational leaders which are as follows.

Characteristics of transactional leaders

(1) Transactional leaders promise rewards for good performance of the followers. They recognise the followers accomplishments. They contract exchange of rewards for efforts.

(2) Transactional leaders follow active as well as passive management by exception. While adopting active management by exception, these leaders watch and search for deviations from rules and standards and take corrective action. When transactional leaders follow passive management by exceptions, they intervene only when the standards are not met.

(3) Transactional leaders sometimes adopt *laissez-faire* style of management. Then they avoid making decisions and abdicates responsibilities.

Characteristics of transformational leaders

(1) Transformational leaders have charisma. They provide vision and mission to the followers. Instil pride in followers. They get followers' trust and respect.

(2) Transformational leaders inspire followers. They communicate to followers high performance expectations. They express important purposes in simplest ways. They use symbols to focus the efforts of the followers.

(3) Transformational leaders promote intelligence, rationality and careful problem solving. By doing this, transformational leaders give intellectual stimulation.

(4) Transformational leaders provide personal attention to followers. They treat each employee individually and offer coaching and advice to them.

Many research studies have evidenced that transformational leadership is superior to transactional leadership. Transformational leadership have several positive outcomes like lower employee turnover rate, higher productivity and increased employee satisfaction. Studies in USA, Canada and Germany observed that transformational leaders are more effective than transactional leaders. However transformational and transactional leadership are not opposite approaches. In fact, transformational leadership is built on the top of transactional leadership. **B.M. Bass** observes that transformal leadership produces the level of followers efforts and performance much higher than that produced by transactional leaders. Again transformational leadership is more than charismatic leadership. **B.J. Avolio and B.M. Bass** make this distinction clear in the following way. The purely charismatic leader may want the followers to adopt the charismatic leader's world view and go no further. The transformational leader will attempt to instill in followers the ability to question not only established views, but eventually those established by the leader.

Transformational leadership has become more important today due to the dynamics of change. The business environment of today is extremely volatile and dynamic and therefore it poses the challenge of dramatic change and transformation before organisations for success and survival. The organisations which fail to make such successful transformation lagged behind in the competition and later their survival was at a stake. **J.M. Burns** explains transformational leadership is based more on the leader's shifting the values, beliefs and needs of the followers whereas transactional leadership involves an exchange relationship between the leader and followers. **B.M. Bass** goes a step ahead and comments that the transactional leadership is a prescription for mediocrity whereas transformational leadership leads to superior performance in the organisations facing demands for renewal and change. He suggests that fostering transformational leadership through policies of recruitment, selection, promotion, training and development will pay off in the effective performance of today's organisations. **Tichy and Devanna** conducted interviews of top executive of major companies and found that transformational leaders share the following characteristics: (i) They identify themselves as change agents. (ii) They are courageous. (iii) They believe in people. (iv) They are value driven. (v) They are lifelong learners. (vi) They have the ability to deal with complexity, ambiguity and uncertainty. (vii) They are visionaries.

James A.F. Stoner observes that transformational leaders possess distinct skills which are as follows:

(a) **Anticipatory skill:** This is the foresight into constantly changing environment.

(b) **Visionary skill:** It is a process of persuasion with example by which the leader induces a group to take action according to his purpose.

(c) **Value congruence skills:** It is the skill of a leader to be in touch with the employee's safety, economic, psychological, spiritual, sexual, asthetic and physical needs in order to engage people on the basis of shared motives, values and goals.

(d) **Empowerment skill:** It is the willingness of the leader to share his power with his followers and to do so effectively.

(e) **Self-understanding skill:** It is the skill to introspect and understand the own needs as well as the goals of the employees.

Prof. S.K. Chakraworthy views that the transformational leadership implies a process whereby an individual attempts to elevate his consciousness (chetana) so that various common place conflicts and dualities begin at higher levels of synthesis. So transformational leadership is able to change the organisational culture drastically and can introduce a new culture in the organisation.

(C) Visionary Leadership: Stephen Robbins defines visionary leadership as follows: Visionary leadership is the ability to create and articulate a realistic, crediable, attractive vision of the future for an organisation that grows out of and improves upon the present. The visionary leaders can take the organisation to a bright future. So **B. Nanus** expresses that if the vision is properly selected and implemented becomes so engergising that in-effect it jump-starts the future by calling forth the skills, talents and resources to make it happen.

Vision differs from direction. **P.C. Nutt and R.W. Backoff** explain that a vision has clear and compelling imagery that offers an innovative way to improve, which recognises and draws on traditions and connects to action that people can take to realise change. Vision taps the energy and emotions of people. A properly articulated vision creates the enthusiasm that people have for sporting events and other leisure-time activities. Vision brings this energy and commitment to the place of work. What vision does and how one can describe the proper vision are the questions raised when discussion on its importance is made. **Stephen Robbins** replies to all these questions precisely. According to him vision should be able to create possibilities that are inspirational, unique and offers a new order that can produce organisational distinction. A vision, in the view of Stephen Robbins, fails if it cannot offer a picture of the future which is clear and demonstratively better for the organisation and its members. The vision must be fit to the time and circumstances. A time-relevant and situation-suitable vision can only reflect the organisation's uniqueness. Vision should be perceived as challenging. It should induce and motivate people to make use of their full potential. But still it should be attainable and doable. Further vision should be understandable. Clear articulation and powerful imagery make the vision easy to grasp and accept.

Stephen Robbins observed that the visionary leaders possess three important characteristics which are related to the effectiveness of their visionary role. These qualities are as follows:

(1) The ability to explain the vision to others.

(2) The ability to express the vision through self-behaviour and not simply with words.

(3) The ability to extend the vision to different leadership context.

The leader has to explain the vision to the followers clearly and unambiguously in terms of actions required from them and the purpose of these actions. He uses oral and written communication for this. The leader makes his behaviour in accordance with his vision. He continuously behaves in that way to convey and reinforce the vision. Actions speak louder than words and as such leader's behaviour expresses and conveys his vision more strongly than his words. Similarly, the leader has to sequence activities so that the vision can be applied in a variety of situations.

Vision is the aim for the future. It is neither a dream, nor an optimism. It is a goal to be attained, a purpose to be served. Therefore, it has to be unambiguous, precise and achievable. If it is beyond the capacity to reach. It will simply produce frustration. If it is unclear, it will create confusion and misdirect the efforts and resources. No doubt, that the vision must be challenging. It should promote new ways of thinking and action. Still, it must have a sound rational and logical base. It should never be misconstrued as wild imagination. A visionary leader takes his followers to the future. He visualises the future and fixes the appropriate aim in future and so he becomes a visionary leader. The propriety of his vision is reflected in his popularity and effectiveness. If he is able to carve the right vision in the future; followers accept and respect him as a lighthouse. They follow him unquestionably. But the rightness and correctness of the vision is evidenced, only when things happen that way in future. The success in future decides the rightness of the vision. And so, how the visionary leader can influence other people in the present? This is a critical question. The uniqueness, unconventionality and rationality makes the vision attractive. However, in addition to this the conviction and commitment of the leader to his vision, adds glitter, glamour and weightage to the vision. The consistent behaviour and actions of the leader in accordance to his vision and confirming the vision, enhances the credibility of the leader as well as his vision. People, then trust the leader and perceive that he stands by his vision in all situations. They realise the truthfulness, accuracy and authenticity of the vision. This builds confidence about the vision and it widens and deepens the influence of the visionary leader. Any discrepancy or contradiction in the stated vision and behaviour of the leader disproves the validity of the vision and reduces the influence of the leader. Followers then do not believe in the leader. In fact, then the leader no more remains the leader, because he does not get followers. So it is imperative for the visionary leader to have conviction about the vision and to maintain congruence between the vision and behaviour. Then only can he produce a lasting effect on the followers.

Contemporary Issues in Leadership: Leadership and its effectiveness has been always a topic of continuous research, analysis and evaluation. From the famous postulate that leaders are born, to the approach that leadership is situational (i.e., circumstances decide who can be the leader), several viewpoints have been presented by eminent scholars. Traditional and modern theories have supplied lot of material for leadership studies and still there is much scope to prescribe the elements of leadership effectiveness. What makes the leaders and how the leaders become effective are the two prime questions which have been continuously and consistently posing intellectual challenge before the researchers. Further, a number of contemporary issues in leadership are also worth studying and researching. Because they are widening up the horizons of our understanding about leadership. A brief discussion about some of these issues is made in the following pages.

Action Leadership: A question is always raised whether leadership is a personal quality or a behavioural style. Does a person becomes a leader because he possesses certain qualities or does someone becomes a leader because he acts like a leader? This question has produced a new thought of action leadership. Leadership is a matter of action. A person becomes a leader, because he behaves like a leader. Simply because, a person possesses leadership qualities does not make him a leader. Leadership is in practice. Though a person has leadership-potential, unless he makes use of that potential and performs leadership action; he does not become a leader. Therefore, leadership is always in action or behaviour. So all leaders are action leaders. There cannot be any passive leader. Once a leader becomes passive, his leadership-cult automatically disappears.

A leader is supposed to lead the followers. The acceptance of the followers of the leader gives existence to his leadership. So leadership is not positional. It is the result of social consent. If this social consent is removed, leadership comes to an end. So leadership lives moment by moment. This social consent of the followers remains in force till the behaviour of the leader fulfills the expectations of the people. In essence the leadership behaviour is the only cause and the soul of the existence of leadership.

Team Leadership Role: In present days, creation and use of teams in organisations is becoming popular and common. So a leader has developed and manage effectively work teams. A team differs from a work group. A *group* is defined as a coming together of two or more members, who are independent and interactive with one another, to achieve a particular objectives through collective efforts. A *work group* is defined as a group that interacts primarily to share information and to make decisions to help each group member perform within his or her area of responsibility. A *work team* is defined as a group whose individual efforts result in a performance that is greater than the sum of the individual inputs. A work team generates positive synergy through coordinated efforts. And so the individual efforts in a team results in a performance level which is higher than the sum of the individual inputs. **John R. Katzenback and Douglas Smith** has clarified the difference between a work group and team in the context of the performance of both. They say that a work group's performance is a function of what its members do as individuals. A team's performance includes both individual results and what we call collective work products. A collective work product is what two or more members work on together. It reflects the joint, real contribution of team members. So the team has an individual as well as mutual accountability. It discusses, decides and does real work. The discussion in a team is open-ended, active and problem-solving.

Since the work group and teams have different nature; the leader has to play a distinct roles in teams and work groups. A work group needs a strong and clearly focussed leader whereas a team expects sharing from the leader. The leadership role in a team is that of the facilitation. A team leader is supposed to share his knowledge with his team members and then give them decision-freedom. So he should tell the members of the team everything that he knows and then let them make their own decisions. In a work group the leader and has to do many command and control type of things. This practice is inappropriate in teams. A leader has to sublimate his dominating style for the good of the team. A team leader has to imbibe the following abilities and skills: (i) Patience (ii) Sharing of information (iii) Trust on others (iv) Giving up self-authority (v) Understanding when to intervene. In order to become an effective team leader, the person must know keenly as when to intercede in team activity and when to leave his team alone. The interception and withdrawal of the leader in the team-work at the right moment add to the effectiveness of the team as well as the leader. Effective team leaders have mastered this balancing act. Sometimes the team needs the support and help of the leader and at other times it wants the autonomy. A good team leader is able to predict and judge accurately and precisely at what time he should actively help the team and when to free the team to decide and act independently. The decision to give enough autonomy to the team requires the attitude to part away with self-authority and to trust the ability of others.

R. S. Wellins, W.C. Byham and G.R. Dixon conducted a study of 20 big organisations which had reorganised themselves around teams. They found that all these team leaders had to assume certain common responsibilities which are as follows:

(a) Coaching. (b) Facilitating. (c) Handling the disciplinary problems. (d) Reviewing the team and individual performance. (e) Training and (f) Communication.

N. Steckler and N. Fondas describe the job of a team leader in a more meaningful way. According to them a team leader has to focus on following two priorities:

(i) To manage the external boundary of the team.

(ii) To facilitate the team process.

Stephen Robbins describes four roles of a team leader on the basis of the above views. These roles are given below:

(1) **Liaisoning** with external constituencies The other constituencies include upper management, other teams in the organisation, suppliers and customers. The team leader has to do liaisoning with these constituencies. His liaisoning role include the following tasks and functions.

(i) Representing self-team to other constituencies.

(ii) Securing the resources needed for own team.

(iii) Clarifying to own team, the expectations of others in respect of them.

(iv) Gathering information from outside and sharing it with the team members.

(2) Acting as the **troubleshooter** when the team faces a problem, the leader helps to sort it out by promoting discussions, lateral thinking and collective analysis of the same in meetings. The team problems usually are neither technical nor operational. Because most of the time, the team members have the functional skill, expertise and experience much more than the team leader. So they know how to do the task, very well. So the problems where the leader has to help the team are nontechnical and nonoperational. To solve such problems the leader encourage the team members to talk through the problem, asks them penetrating questions to provoke their thinking and analytical abilities, get for them the needed resources and thus, acts as a troubleshooter.

(3) Working as **conflict-manager :** The leader minimises the disruptive aspects of intra-team conflicts. For this purpose he induces the team members to search out the answers of the following questions, when disagreements surface.

(i) What is the source of the conflict?

(ii) Who is involved?

(iii) What are the issues?

(iv) What options are available for conflict resolution?

(v) What are the advantages and disadvantages of each option?

(4) Coaching : As a coach the team-leader has to clarify his expectations about the team members and their roles, teach them, offer them support and cheerlead them. The leader has to do everything which is necessary to improve the work performance.

Cross Cultural Leadership: A group of scholars believe that leadership is culturally bound. A leader must adapt his style to different national cultures. Because what works in one culture is not workable in another culture. In fact, a leader cannot choose his style at his will. His style is mostly influenced by the followers. The nature, culture and maturity level of the followers decide the suitability of the leadership style. So the leadership style is affected by the national culture of the followers. The leadership style is constrained by the cultural conditions that the followers have come to expect. As per the contingency approach the leaders need to adjust their style to the unique cultural aspects of a country. All countries do not have similar cultures. Some countries have high power distance cultures and some have low power distance cultures. In high power distance cultures, autocratic or manipulative leadership style is suitable. In low power distance cultures, participative and democratic leadership style is acceptable and appropriate. So depending upon the national culture, the leadership style should also change. There is no need and possibility of a universal leadership style.

In 1993, the Global Leadership and Organisational Behaviour Effectiveness research programme (GLOBE study) began. It is an ongoing crosscultural investigation of leadership and national culture. It collected data on approximately 18,000 in 825 organisations in 62 countries. It is the most comprehensive crosscultural leadership study. One important finding of GLOBE study is that there are some universal aspects of leadership. House and others observed that there are certain elements of transformational leadership which appear to be universal. These universal elements of transformational leadership are vision, foresight, providing encouragement, trustworthiness, dynamism, positiveness and proactivenes. The GLOBE team also found that effective business leaders in any country are expected by their subordinates to do the following three things

(i) To provide a powerful and proactive vision to guide the company into the future.

(ii) To stimulate all employees to fulfill the vision (with strong motivational skill) and

(iii) To implement the vision (with excellent planning skill)

Global competition and increasing influence of multinational organisations have the need for common technologies and management practices. This may make some aspects of leadership universally acceptable. GLOBE studies are extremely directional in this respect. The GLOBE team found 21 specific leader attributes and behaviours are universally viewed as contributing to leadership effectiveness. Eleven of these attributes were closely associated with global charismatic/value-based leadership. The same was true for team leadership and participative leadership. Similarly 35 other characteristics were identified as contributors to success in some cultures and impediments in other cultures. The general findings of the completed portion of GLOBE project are as under :

(i) Cultural dimensions do exist and those should be identified and measured.

(ii) Cultural differences can be studied through

(a) across cultures approach (etic approach) or

(b) within cultures approach (emic approach)

(iii) Cultural differences strongly influence the ways in which people think about their leaders

(iv) Cultural differences also influence the societal norms concerning the status, influence and privileges granted to the leader.

GLOBE studies suggested nine dimensions of cultures which differentiate societies and organisations. They are:

(1) **Power distance:** It is the degree to which members of collective unit expect power to be distributed equally.

(2) **Uncertainty avoidance:** It is the extent to which a society or organisation relies on norms, rules and procedures to alleviate the unpredictability of future events.

(3) **Human orientation:** The degree to which a society encourages and rewards individuals for being fair, altruistic, generous caring and kind to others.

(4) **Individualism/Collectivism:** The degree to which individuals are encouraged by societal institutions to be integrated into groups within organisations and society.

(5) **In-group collectivism:** In contrast to societal institutions, this dimension encompases the extent to which members of a society take pride in membership in small groups such as their families, circle of close friends and organisations in which they are employed.

(6) **Assertiveness:** The extent to which a society encourages people to be tough, confrontational, assertive and competitive versus modest and tender.

(7) **Gender egalitarianism:** The extent to which a society maximises gender role differences.

(8) **Future orientation:** The extent to which a society encourages and rewards future orientation behaviour such as planning, investing in the future and delaying gratification.

(9) **Performance orientation:** The degree to which a society encourages and rewards group members for performance improvement and excellence.

According to **Fred Luthans,** there are number of factors that potentially contribute to differences in effective leader processes across culture. He describes the major three of them in the following manner.

(a) **Personal Values :** These are found to shape the manager's perception of a situation, influence the analysis of alternative solutions and finally affect his decision. Similarly, the personal values of the followers also influence the leader and these values are different across culture.

(b) **Background of the Manager:** Educational background, social class and family status influence the managers a lot. These differ in different cultures.

(c) **Interpersonal skill:** Managers differ in interpersonal skills across cultures. Leaders hold different views about rules, procedures, deference of authority levels of dependence and independence, use of objectivity versus intuition, willingness to compromise and other interpersonal tactics.

Earlier to the famous GLOBE study, **Geert Hofstede** conducted a survey of more than 1,16,000 IBM employees in 40 countries about their work-related values. This is one of the most referenced approaches for analysing variations among cultures.

Hofstede found that managers and employees vary on five value dimensions of national culture, which are as follows:

(1) **Power distance:** The degree to which people in a country accept that power in institutions and organisations is distributed unequally. This is a national culture attribute. This power distance ranges from a relatively equal, i.e., low power distance to extremely unequal, i.e., high power distance.

(2) **Individualism versus Collectivism:** Individualism is a national culture attribute which describes the degree to which people prefer to act as individuals rather than members of a group.

Collectivism is a national culture attribute which describes a tight social framework in which people expect others in groups of which they are a part to look after them and protect them.

(3) **Quantity of life versus Quality of life:** It is a national culture attribute which describes the extent to which societal values are characterised by assertiveness and materialism.

Quality of life is a national culture attribute describing the degree to which people value relationships and show sensitivity and concern for the welfare of others. It emphasises relationships and concern for others.

(4) **Uncertainty avoidance:** It is the national culture attribute which describes the extent to which a society feels threatened by uncertain and ambiguous situations and tries to avoid them. It is the degree to which people in a country prefer structured situations against unstructured situations. If a country has a high score in respect of uncertainty avoidance; then it is seen that, people therein have an increased level of anxiety which is manifested in greater nervousness, stress and aggressiveness.

(5) **Long-term versus Short-term orientation:** A long-term orientation is a national attribute which emphasises the future, thrift and persistence. Against this, a short-term orientation is a national culture attribute which emphasises the past and present, respect for tradition and fulfilling social obligations.

Hofstede's research made following important conclusions:

(i) China and West Africa scored high on power distance. As against them, United States and Netherlands scored low.

(ii) Most Asian countries were more collectivist than individualistic.

(iii) United States ranked highest among all countries on individualism.

(iv) Germany and Hong Kong rated high on quantity of life; whereas Russia and Netherlands rated low on this dimension.

(v) France and Russia were high on uncertainty avoidance but Hong Kong and United States were low.

(vi) China and Hong Kong had long-term orientation whereas France and United States had short-term orientation.

These conclusions related to the period of 1970. The GLOBE study which started in 1993, made conclusions regarding the cultural differences on nine dimensions. The highlights of these conclusions are as follows.

(i) **Regarding assertiveness:** Sweden, New Zealand and Switzerland had low rating, Egypt, Ireland and Phillippines had moderate rating and Spain, U.S. and Greece had high rating.

(ii) **On the dimension of future orientation:** Denmark, Canada and Netherlands had high rating, Solvenia, Egypt and Ireland had moderate rating and Russia Argentina and Poland had low rating.

(iii) **Gender differentiation:** On this dimension Sweden, Denmark and Slovenia were rated low, Itraly, Brazil and Argentina moderate and South Korea, Egypt and Morocco high.

(iv) **Uncertainty avoidance:** On this dimension Russia, Hungary and Bolivia were rated low; U.S., Israel and Mexico moderate and Austria, Denmark and Germany high.

(v) **Power distance:** On this dimension Denmark, Netherlands and South Africa were rated low; England, France and Brazil moderate and Russia, Spain and Thailand high.

(vi) **Individualism/Collectivism:** On this dimension Denmark, Singapore and Japan were rated low on individualism and high in respect of collectivism; Hong Kong, U.S. and Egypt were moderate on both individualism and collectivism. Greece, Hungary and Germany were rated high on individualism and low on collectivism.

(vii) **In-group collectivism:** On this dimension, Denmark, Sweden and New Zealand were rated low; Japan, Israel and Qatar were rated as moderate and Egypt, China and Morocco high.

(viii) **Performance orientation:** On this dimension Russia, Argentina and Greece were rated low, Sweden, Israel and Spain moderate and U.S., Taiwan and New Zealand high.

(ix) **Human orientation:** On this dimension Germany, Spain and France were rated low, Hong Kong, Sweden and Taiwan moderate and Indonesia, Egypt and Malaysia as high.

A discussion on cross cultural leadership will be incomplete unless we study the contrasting attitudes of managers towards international operations. **Howard V. Perlmutter** identified three types of managerial attitudes towards international operations. They are labeled as ethnocentric attitude, geocentric attitude and polycentric attitude. Managers with ethnocentric attitude view that their home country's personnel and ways of doing things are the best. So they try to apply their home country procedures and evaluation criterion worldwide without any variation. Managers having polycentric attitude view that local managers in the host country know best how to run their own operations. So they rely more on local managers and offer them more freedom. Managers with the geocentric attitude hold a world-oriented view that draws upon the best talent around the globe. They consider the skill of the people and not their nationality while promoting them. They balance the local and worldwide objectives of their company in all aspects of its operations. They think globally and act locally. In the present competitive global business environment, managers with geocentric attitude are found to be more suitable.

Leadership for Excellence: In 1982, **Thomas J. Peters and Robert H. Waterman Jr.,** wrote a book titled In Search of Excellence. Both were management consultants and their book took the management world by storm. It topped the list of non-fiction best sellers for month and was translated in several foreign languages. The book tried to provide the explanation for the success of America's best-run companies. It tried to describe what made these corporations successful. Peters and Waterman has developed an unconventional approach to management. There approach is unconventional for following three reasons.

(i) They attacked conventional management theory and practice for being too conservative, rationalistic, analytical, unemotional, inflexible, negative and preoccupied 'with bigness.'

(ii) They replaced conventional management terminology (such as planning, MBO, control) with catch phrases collected from successful managers (such as Do it, Fix it, Try it or Management by wandering around)

(iii) They made their key points with stories and anecdotes rather than with objective, quatified data and facts.

Peters and Waterman employed a combination of subjective and objective criteria to identify the best managed companies in USA. After conducting extensive interviews at 36 excellent companies which had 20 years of such record of innovation and profitability; Peters and Waterman, isolated eight attributes of excellence. They said that all eight attributes were not present to the same degree in all excellent companies, but a preponderance of the eight was clearly visible and quite distinctive. These eight attributes of excellence and their key indicators as stated by Peters and Watermark are as follows:

(1) **A bias for action:** Key indicators are (a) Small-scale, easily managed experiments to build knowledge, interest and commitment. (b) Managers stay visible and personally involved in all areas through active communication and spontaneous management by wandering around.

(2) **Close to the customer:** Key indicators are (a) Customer satisfaction is practically an obsession. (b) Input from customers is sought throughout the product design-production-marketing cycle.

(3) **Autonomy and Entrepreneurship:** Key indicators are (a) Risk taking is encouraged and failure is tolerated. (b) Innovators are encouraged to champion their pet projects to see them through to completion. (c) Flexible structure permits the formation of 'skunk works' (small teams of zealous innovators working on a special project) (d) Lots of creative swings are encouraged to ensure successful products.

(4) **Productivity through people:** Key indicators are (a) Individuals are treated with respect and dignity. (b) Enthusiasm, trust and family feelings are fostered. (c) People are encouraged to have fun in meaningful accomplishments. (d) Work units are kept small and human.

(5) **Hands on, Value driven:** Key indicators are (a) A clear company philosophy is disseminated and followed. (b) Personal values are not buried, but they are discussed openly. (c) The organisations belief system is reinforced through frequently shared stories, myths and legends. (d) Leaders are positive role models.

(6) **Stick to the knitting:** Key indicators are (a) Management sticks to the business it knows best. (b) Emphasis is on internal growth and not on mergers.

(7) **Simple form Lean staff:** Key indicators are (a) Authority is decentralised as much as possible (b) Staff size at the headquarter is kept small and talent is pushed out to the field.

(8) **Simultaneous loose-tight properties:** Key indicators are (a) Tight overall strategic and financial control is counterbalanced by decentralized authority, autonomy and opportunities for creativity.

These eight attribute approach is criticised as Peters and Watermark ignored the important non-management variables like technology, finance, government policy and raw materials which are equally noteworthy for sustained corporate excellence. However, they have reminded managers to pay close attention to the basics such as new ideas, customers and employees. They found that excellent companies were all brilliant on the basics. So they view that tools did not substitute thinking, intellect did not overpower wisdom and analysis did not impede action.

The leadership for excellence therefore, should promote decentralised and value-driven organisation. It should encourage innovation and experimentation. It should be dedicated to human treatment of employees and should develop the organisational culture and practice of customer focus. The leader should work to keep things simple in the complex world. He should insist on top quality and make everyone persist for the same. He should be action-oriented, patient listener of followers views and customer-say. In this dynamic business world of today the excellence leader has to always welcome new ideas. Challenges and risks should not be looked at negatively. Failures and mistakes should be taken up as learning lessons. Trust, enthusiasm and family feelings should be strengthened, throughout the organisation.

Sometimes, the leader may face the problem of quick-fix mentality while following the views of Peters and Waterman. This, usually, happens when new ideas are welcome. Sometimes the leader, in order to encourage innovation, may overenthusiastically embrace appealing ideas without questioning and examining their validity and propriety in detail. This results into quick-fix mentality. It is this kind of mentality where a person arrives at a decision and fix the choice of an operation rather hectically. To avoid this quick-fix mentality **Michael A Hitt and R. Duane Ireland** have made five suggestions. They advice that managers should –

(i) Remain current with literature in the field particularly with journals that translate research into practice.

(ii) Ensure that concepts applied are based on science or at least on some form of rigorous documentation, rather than purely on advocacy.

(iii) Be willing to examine and implement new concepts, but first do so using pilot test with small units.

(iv) Be skeptical when simple solutions are offered, analyse them thoroughly.

(v) Constantly anticipate the effects of current actions and events on future results.

Brian Dumaine views that there are five golden management rules which have surviving power. They can be called as management wisdom beyond quick fixes. They are useful tips to be remembered by excellence leaders. These golden rules are as follows:

(i) Management is a practice (ii) People are a resource. (iii) Marketing and innovation are the key functions of a business. (iv) Discover what does well. (v) Quality pays for itself.

Servant Leadership: This term is coined by **Robert Greenleaf** in 1970. According to him great leaders act as servants. They put the needs of others, including employees, customers and community as their first priority. Servant leadership is not a theory. It is a way and philosophy of managing. Servant leadership focuses on increased services to others rather than to oneself. Servant leadership is a longer, transformational approach. It is not a quick-fix method or technique. It requires development of a mindset and value-system of prioritising the needs of others over the benefits of self. **L.C. Spears** give ten characteristics of servant leadership. They are

(i) **Listening:** Servant leaders carefully listen to the needs of others.

(ii) **Empathy:** Servant leaders try to empathise with the feelings and emotions of others.

(iii) **Healing:** Whenever failure or suffering occurs, the servant leaders try to make themselves and others as a whole.

(iv) **Awareness:** Servant leaders are keenly self-aware about their strengths and limitations.

(v) **Persuasion:** Servant leaders make use of persuasion while influencing others and making up decisions; rather than the use of positional authority.

(vi) **Conceptualisation:** Servant leaders spend considerable time and efforts to develop broad-based conceptual thinking. They balance short and long-term thoughts as well as day to day focus and conceptual orientation.

(vii) **Foresight:** Servant leaders are able to forsec the future outcomes of their current actions and situations.

(viii) **Stewardship:** Servant leaders assume themselves as stewards of other people and resources which they manage.

(ix) **Commitment to growth of people:** Servant leaders are commited to people beyond their immediate work.

(x) **Building community :** Servant leaders try to create a sense of community inside and outside the organisation.

While commeting on servant leadership, **Jim Stuart** says that leadership derives naturally from a commitment to service. When someone is practicing servant leadership, he will be said to be doing so, if his followers become wiser, healthier and more autonomous. Later they too become servant leaders. Servant leadership has a moral element. In fact, everything in business is basically for people and not for profit. Therefore, **George Merk II** of Merk and Co. made a rule for his company, that medicine is for people and not for profit. He believed that the purpose of a corporation is to do something useful and to do it very weill.

Shared Leadership – Angelo Kinicki and Robert Kreitner (Organisational Behaviour – Concepts, Skills and Practices) view that shared leadership entails a simultaneous ongoing mutual influence process in which individuals share responsibility for leading, regardless of formal roles and titles.

Conventional theories of leadership assume that leadership is a vertical and downward flowing process. It expects that leadership is concentrated in a single chain of command. On the other hand shared leadership means to share the leadership responsibility among two or more individuals in certain task environment. It is based on the postulate that people should share the information and should collaborate to get the work done. It highlights the need for a horizontal process of influence.

Shared leadership is particularly required when (a) people are working in a team. (b) people are involved in a complex project. (c) people are doing knowledge work which requires voluntary contributions of intellectual capital by skilled professionals.

Shared leaders is found to be useful for three kinds of tasks (i) Tasks which are highly interdependent. (ii) Tasks which require a great deal of creativity and (iii) Tasks that are highly complex. To develop shared leadership, the leader has to design the team, clarify the purpose, secure resources, manage the boundaries of the team, articulate vision, select team members and define team processes. The organisational systems should be supportive and positive to shared leadership. For example, training and development system should prepare the designated leaders and team members to engage shared leadership enthusiastically. Reward system should offer attractive rewards for sharing leadership responsibilities. Control system should articulate and demonstrate the value of shared leadership. Shared leadership is found to produce the positive effect on group cohesion, group citizenship and group effectiveness.

Level 5 Leadership: The concept of level 5 leadership is developed by **Jim Collins**. He described it in his best-seller book **Good to Great**. Collins conducted a longitudinal research study to search the answer of an important question, can a good company become a great company and if so how? So he identified a set of companies which shifted from good performance to great performance.

For this purpose, he defined great performance as cumulative stock returns at or below the general stock market for 15 years, punctuated by a transition point, then cumulative returns at least three times the market over the next 15 years. He identified 11 good to great companies, namely, Abbot, Circuit City, Fannie Mae, Gillette, Kimberely Clark, Kroger, Nucor, Phillip Morris, Pitney Bowes, Walgreens and Wells Fargo. He found that among the drivers of good to great performance; the key driver was level 5 leadership. Every company which experienced good to great performance was led by an individual possessing the level 5 leadership characteristics. These leaders were possessing humility and fearless will to succeed which was their prominent characteristic. Collins further gave the following hierarchy of leadership.

(1) **Level 1 Leadership: Highly capable individuals** – These leaders make productive contributions through talent, knowledge, skill and good work habits.

(2) **Level 2 Leadership: Contributing team member** – These leaders contribute their individual capabilities to the achievement of group objectives and work effectively with others in a group setting.

(3) **Level 3 Leadership: Competent manager** – These leaders organise people and resources towards the effective and efficient pursuit of predetermined objectives.

(4) **Level 4 Leadership: Effective leader** – These leaders catalyse commitment to and vigorous pursuit of a clear and compelling vision, stimulating higher performance standards.

(5) **Level 5 Leadership: Level 5 Executives** – These leaders build enduring greatness through a paradoxical blend of personal humility and professional will.

In fact a level 5 leader also possesses the characteristics of level 1 to 4 leaders. However what is outstanding and remarkable in his personality is profound humility and strongest determination. The people with ego and boastful tendencies can never become level 5 leaders.

Moral Leadership: For a very long time ethics and leadership were not collectively attended by researchers in large numbers. Most of the time the leadership in politics and business was evaluated on the criteria of its effectiveness, rather than its ethical implications. However, as the public life all over the world is facing the problems of corruption and misuse of power, a need to address the issue of moral leadership is deeply felt by the scholars and researchers. Especially when the big shots in politics and business were accused of employing the unethical practices in their lives at one time or another, the issue of ethics and leadership became the current topic of the day.

Ethics touches leadership at a number of junctures. For example, transformational leaders foster moral virtues when they attempt to change the attitude and behaviour of their followers. Charismatic leadership, too, has ethical components. An unethical charismatic leader use his charisma to enhance his power base. He misuses his influence on the followers to serve his own self-goals. As against this an ethical charismatic leader uses his charisma in a socially constructive way to serve others.

An important aspect of the leadership effectiveness is trust. Scholars now treat trust as the foundation of leadership effectiveness. However, a leader cannot develop trust in his followers unless he himself possesses logalty and integrity and practices the same in his behaviour. Leadership effectiveness needs to address the means that a leader uses in trying to achieve goals and the content of those goals. No doubt the goals and the content of the goals should be ethically desirable. However, in additions, the means to achieve these goals should also be ethically acceptable because bad means spoil good ends. Leadership needs to honour and accept ethics then only truly it will be effective.

Self-Leadership: It involves a set of processes through which individuals control their own behaviour. Research shows that self-leadership is possible. People can lead themselves. Super-leaders help their followers to lead themselves. They develop leadership capabilities in their followers by nurturing them in such a way that they no longer need to depend on their formal leaders for direction and motivation. **Stephen Robbins** make the following suggestions to leaders to create self-leaders from their followers.

(1) **Model self-leadership:** The leader needs to practice self-observation, self-direction, self-reinforcement and set challenging personal goals. He need to display this behaviour to his followers and should encourage them to rehearse it and then reproduce it.

(2) **Encourage employees to create self-set goals:** The leader has to encourage the employees to set goals for self which should be specific and quantitative.

(3) **Encourage the use of self-rewards to strengthen and increase desirable behaviour:** At the same time self punishment should be limited only to dishonest and destructive behaviour.

(4) **Create positive thought patterns:** Encourage employees to use mental imagery and self-talk to stimulate further self-motivation.

(5) **Create a climate of self-leadership:** Redesign the work to increase the natural rewards of a job and focus on these naturally rewarding features of the work to increase motivation.

(6) **Encourage self-criticism:** The leader should encourage the followers to critically evaluate their own performance.

There is an underlying assumption behind self-leadership. According to it people are capable and responsible. They can take initiative. If they are given proper support, they can monitor and control their own behaviour. So the external constraints of boss, rules and regulations can be removed.

Self-leadership is gaining popularity due to the emergence of self-managed teams. Self-managed teams are groups of normally 10 to 50 employees, who perform highly related or interdependent jobs and take on many of the responsibilities of the former supervisors. So a self-managed team does the job of planning and scheduling of work, assigning tasks to team members, collective control over the pace of work, making operating decisions, taking action on problems and working with suppliers and customers. A fully self-managed team selects its own members and the members of such a team evaluate the performance of each other. Thus, even in a fully self-managed team the supervisor is no more required. However such self-managed teams require self-directed individuals as its members. Because these teams emphasise on empowerment. If the people have spent their lives under a boss-centred leadership in organisations, then they suddenly cannot adjust to self-managed teams. Therefore self-leadership becomes a training and means to make transition from dependence to autonomy. This independence helps for a contributing membership of a self-managed team.

Online Leadership: Digital communication is a fact of the day. This has solved the problem of interacting with physically separated people. However, how can a manager lead the people who are geographically distinct from him. This is a new problem, which gave birth to online leadership. Today, in most of the companies, the manager and employees are linked with one another by electronics network rather than the geographical proximity, managers use e-mails, computers and modem to instruct and manage their groups. In this changed situation the leadership style has to be different. We know, that leadership is required to inspire and motivate people. A leader does this job through verbal and non-verbal communication. However, when employees are distant, dispersed and are connected to the manager by the means of digital communication, the possiility of using non-verbal communication is very dim. Online leadership inevitably has to depend on verbal communication which needs certain precautions to be taken up for its effectiveness. They are as follows:

(i) An online leader should remember that he cannot soften harsh words or sour decisions with smile or such comforting gestures.

(ii) An online leader should use full sentences while making digital messages. Short caps or phrases are seen as curt and threatening. So they may produce disappointing response.

(iii) The tone of the verbal message should correctly reflect the emotions of the formal or informal nature of the message should be correctly transmitted to the receiver. The online leader has to match his writing style with his interpersonal style. He should bring the warmth and feelings which appear in his interpersonal style to his writing style.

(iv) An online leader has to match his communication style with the audience. The style of communication with the superior has to be different from that with the staff. Use of jargons, abbreviations and the like should be properly made.

(v) An online leader will have to carefully think what kind of action his written communication will initiate from the receivers. His message should convey trust, status, task directives and emotional warmth to the followers. Words are powerful means. They hurt or heal. So read between the lines and know well that the others also will do the same.

Mentoring: It is a well-observed fact that many leaders create a mentoring relationship. A mentor is a senior employee who sponsors and supports a less experienced employee. In the views of **Stephen Robbins** mentoring includes coaching, counselling and sponsorship. As a coach, a mentor present ideas clearly, listen and empathise with the problems of their proteges. Mentor helps to develop their skills, share self-experience with them, acts as role models, shares contacts and provides guidance through the political maze of the organisation. A mentor vouches for a protege answers for him in the top circle of the organisation and introduces him to them. Some organisations have formal mentoring programmes. In these organisations mentors are officially assigned to new employees who spend a few weeks, with their mentors to learn from them the company–way of doing the business. In other organisations, where informal mentoring exists, senior managers senior managers personally select an employee and take him as a protege. According to **J.A. Wilson and N.S. Elman** the most effective mentoring relationship exists outside the immediate boss-subordinate interface. Because boss-subordinate relationship has an inherent conflict of interest and tension and therefore, meaningful and open communication which is essential for effective mentoring is hardly possible between a boss and his subordinate.

There are a number of benefits of mentoring to the leader as well as to the subordinate. They are as follows -

(1) Mentoring gives a leader an unfiltered access to the attitudes and feelings of the low rank employees.

(2) Protege is a fast source of news about the potential problem. Through mentoring the management gets timely information about potential problems.

(3) Mentoring provides personal satisfaction to the leader. As a mentor they get respect, opportunity to share their expertise and experience, a chance to play the role of elder member of the organisation. All this is personally rewarding.

(4) Mentoring provides a support–system to high potential employees. These employees get guidance, motivation, political understanding and career advancement. In this situation they are less likely to quit. Such employees develop a higher level of commitment.

However, sometimes all employees do not equally get a mentoring relationship. Mentors select those employees who have similar attitudes. Employees choose those mentors with whom they can communicate easily and identify themselves. It is observed that women and minority people are less likely to be chosen as proteges. Therefore, organisations should provide for formal mentoring so that each employee will get a chance to participate in mentoring relationship.

Attribution Theory of Leadership: This theory states that leadership is merely an attribution that people make about other individuals. Thus, people characterise leaders as having such traits as intelligence outgoing personality, strong verbal skills, aggressiveness, understanding and industriousness. According to attribution model, people perceive that effective leaders are consistent in their decisions. **Stephen Robbins** views that, following the attribution theory of leadership, what is important in being characterised as an effective leader is projecting the appearance of being a leader, rather than focusing on actual accomplishments. So those who wish for leadership try to develop the perception of others that they are smart, personable, verbally adept, aggressive, hardworking and consistent in their style, and by doing so, they increase the probability that others will view them as effective leaders.

Substitutes and Neutralisers to Leadership

Leadership theorists and supporters state that leaders influence the behaviour of followers. They sometimes give undue importance to leadership-impact on followers behaviour. This view states leaders are important. They always have an impact on followers outcome. They believe that employees are guided to goal-accomplishment solely because of the leader. However, data from numerous studies collectively indicate that in many situations leadership action is irrelevant. **S. Kerr and J.M. Jermier** state that certain individual jobs and organisational variables can act as substitutes for leadership or neutralise the effect of the influence of the leader on his followers. They further explain how the substitutes and neutralisers act. The neutralisers negate the leaders influence. The neutralisers make it impossible for leader behaviour to make any difference to followers' outcomes. Substitutes not only make the influence of the leader impossible but also unnecessary. They act as a replacement for the influence of the leader. So the substitutes make leader's behaviour redundant and unnecessary whereas the neutralisers prevent the leader from behaving in a certain way and sometimes counteract leader behaviour. These substitutes and neutralisers are found in the characteristics of subordinates, tasks and organisation. **Kerr and Jenifer** provides a detailed explanation as to how these characteristics act as substitutes and neutralisers for task or instrumental leadership as well as for supporting or relationship leadership. Thus experience, ability and training of the subordinates act as substitute for task leadership. Professional orientation of the subordinates acts as substitute for task and supportive leadership. Indifference of the subordinates towards organisational rewards neutralise task and supportive leadership. Structured and routine nature of task acts as substitute for task leadership. Similarly intrinsically satisfying task acts as a substitute for supportive leadership. Cohesive work group act as substitute for task and supportive leadership. Low power position of the leader acts as neutraliser for task and supportive leadership. Formalisation in the organisations acts as substitute for task leadership. Similarly inflexibility of the organisation neutralises task leadership. When the leader is physically isolated from subordinates, this physical isolation neutralises task and supportive leadership.

The concept of leader–substitutes is further analysed by management Scholars. **Kerr** and **Jermier** conducted field studies of police officers. They found that substitutes like feedback from the task performed had more impact on certain job-related activities than leader–behaviour. In another study, conducted by **Robertz H. Miles** and **M. M. Petty** it was found that formalisation acts as the leader-substitute. **Jon Howell** and **Peter Dorfman** found that professionals and non-professionals have different views. Professionals view that the intrinsically satisfying work tasks and organisational rewards are strong substitutes for leadership. **Robert P. Vecchio** (Organisational Behaviour) observe that the idea of leadership substitutes and neutralisers help to account for the largely mixed results of research on most leadership theories. Studies of leadership that ignore the effect of neutralisers and substitutes may fail to uncover the hypothesised relationships because the particular leadership process is irrelevant rather than because the theory is invalid.

Actually the idea of substitutes does not negate leadership. It highlights the boundary within which the leadership can achieve desired results from the subordinates.

Leadership in the new environment: Leadership roles are changing in the 21st century in the light of the changes in organisations and environment. **George G. Dess and Joseph C. Pickens** views there are five key leadership roles which will shape the managerial success in the next decade. They are (i) A strategy vision to motivate and inspire (ii) Empowering employees. (iii) Accumulation and sharing internal knowledge (iv) Gathering and integrating external information.(v) Challenging the *status quo* and enabling creativity.

Now the leaders have to change their local focus and make it global. They have to be open, inquisitive and innovative. They should care more for the quality of execution of an idea. Because even the beautiful ideas fail in the absence of careful purposive and timely implementation. The leader has to become a networker, a facilitator and a consensus builder. The old style of a lone ranger, commanding the people, 'follow me' is not suitable for the present days. Some scholars feel that the concept of managing has now become obsolete. Therefore young people look to it as an irrelevant, exhausting, unfashionable career choice. This perception is more common in highly developed and advanced nations.

Similarly the young people now joining the organisations have several different expectations from their leaders. They have different beliefs and value systems. This situation has highlighted the problem of Generation Xers and Baby Boomers. This Generation Xer's is composed of people who are born between 1965-1981. They are more demanding and possess greater mobility. If the organisation does not stand to their expectations, they simply quit and go elsewhere. These employees have learned very well to expect change and they accept it when they mentally need it. This generation has grown with the computer revolution. They experience the corporate downsizing and massive layoffs. These people therefore are more practical and flexible.

This Generation Xers are led by Baby Boomers who are the individuals born between 1945–1964. Baby boomers have greater organisational loyalty and obedience. They want to know what their boss want done. Accordingly they function to please their boss. They are thankful to their organisations for the job opportunity which the latter has given to them. The attitudes, beliefs and values of Generation Xers and Baby Boomers differ sharply. The Generation Xer's stay in an organisations as long as the organisation satisfies their needs and expectations and so long as they have fun and happiness in the job. Once they feel disappointed due to nonfulfillment of their expectations, they go to another organisation.

A higher level of job-mobility is observed in respect of them. So the major question is how the organisation can retain these Generation Xer's and make them work for it effectively. Management scholars make the following suggestions.

(1) Assign to Generation Xer's those types of tasks which are challenging and allow them to use their entrepreneurial instincts and their strong pragmatism.

(2) Create and develop the team concept. Increase your level of interaction with others and thus make work enjoyable.

(3) Give them chance to use their problem solving skills and by that way boost up their confidence.

(4) Explain them what work needs to be done and its probable outcome in terms of pros and cons. Also tell them the importance of their contribution and its relatedness with other areas of the organisation.

(5) Involve them in planning, accept their suggestions and ideas, bring meaning to their work.

(6) Tell them the rationale behind the instruction, pair them up with seniors, give them prompt feedback on their work, praise them for good work and show them, how to avoid mistakes and errors.

(7) Offer them counselling and guidance and tell them about the career path in the organisation.

Leading by Example: A leader has to inspire people for goal accomplishment. The best way to do this is by way of setting the example of self. The words of a leader do not carry any weightage unless they are supported by his own action. Followers have a usual tendency of observing the leader and assessing his behaviour in the light of his own actions. When the actions and words of the leader are congruent, then the impact of leadership is greater. A leader who first does what he expects others to do, motivates and guides the followers effectively. In fact a leader himself is an example. He becomes a role-model for others. His ideas, throughts and views are best learned by following and limitating him. However, the leadership behaviour must be worth following. Leadership is not simply in telling and convincing; It is more in doing, illustrating, self-modelling and thereby motivating.

Centurian leadership was the leadership by example. A centurian was a military leader in the Roman empire. Those leaders used to rise up to leadership due to their consistent valour and war performance. They were not positional leaders, i.e., leaders who are called so, due to their positions. They set example by their own performance and so were recognised as leaders. A centurian's sword was the first to touch the enemy as he led from the front with strength, honour and integrity. They were the true frontline leaders. A leader who marches ahead and takes the foremost position in crisis, receives honour and followership from people. Leading by example displays commitment of the leader to the chosen cause. only a great cause is not enough to motivate others, the leader's commitment to the cause encourages others to follow him.

Leading by example do not emphasise on telling, it straighway shows. Visuals produce relatively lasting effect than verbals. And when the leader uses himself for demonstration then ordinary people too are influenced and inspired in an extraordinary way. Because in leadership image is everything. A leader's image is built by his vision and strengthened and reinforced by his actions. Moral accountability is the foundation of leadership. Morality cannot be taught and learned by reading treatise on virtues. As **Aristotle** says that the spirit of mortality is awakened among individuals only through the witness and conduct of a moral person. The leader is always morally accountable to his followers, for their betterment and good fullfillment. The failure of followers in achieving the desired results is, in fact, ultimately the failure of the leader. The leader must possess the morality of accepting this obligation and express this through his conduct. Then only he can develop the culture of responsibility. Normally, people own the success and forgoes the failure. This tendency develops a system of passing on the bug. A leader can successfully intervene when he actually treats himself responsible for all wrongs and works for correcting and rectifying them. Then people learn responsibility and act with the same. An organisation of responsible people has great potential for performance and strength for success.

Leadership and Emotional Intelligence: Research is continuously made on finding out, what makes successful leaders. Though success in leadership cannot be attributed to any one factor, a large volume of evidence shows that almost all successful leaders possess emotional intelligence. It is therefore very important to understand the concept of emotional intelligence and how it adds to leadership effectiveness. However to learn about emotional intelligence we require to know about emotions first.

Emotions: Emotions are defined as intense feelings that are directed at someone or something. In fact, these terms are closely related. They are emotions, affect and moods. Affect covers a broad range of feelings which people experience. Moods are feelings which are less intense than emotions and which lack a contextual stimulus. Emotions are not a trait, but reactions to an object. They are object-specific and so contextual. For example one is happy or sad or angry due to something. That something is the object in respect of which a particular emotion is developed. when the focus on the contextual object is last, the emotion gets converted into mood. So we get angry due to some upsetting event. But when that upsetting event is over, still for the rest of the day, we feel disspirited. Now this negative feeling cannot be attributed to a single event. This feeling does not allow us to behave like a normal person. This affect state is described as mood.

Emotional Labour: It is described as a situation in which an employee expresses organisationally desired emotions during the interpersonal transactions. It is a related affect state. This concept of emotional labour is originally developed in relation to service jobs. But today this concept has become relevant in respect of every job. For example, Lawyers should look serious, teachers ethusiastic, sportmen energetic, researchers thoughtful, politicians social, bankers calculated etc. These emotions displayed by them are suitable for their jobs and organisations. Leaders are expected to draw on emotional labour to charge the troops.

Emotional labour requires a person to display such emotions which are not natural. Automatically it results in producing certain dysfunctional results. Like physical and mental labour, emotional labour too, comes for stress, tension and exhaustation. Especially when the employees are required to exihibit those emotions which are are incongruent to their natural feelings, the dysfunctional results of emotional labour are more in number. And in organisations such incidences where the felt emotions f an employee are different from the displayed emotions occur more frequently. Felt emotions are the dividual's actual emotions. Displayed emotions are the emotions which are organisationally quired and considered appropriate in a given job. Displayed emotions are learned emotions and not nate emotions. Many times the felt emotions of people are different from their displayed emotions d large is this discrepancy, greater is the stress experienced by the individual. So people need to arn to reduce this discrepancy and when it is not possible then to avoid and control its dysfunctional ffects. This is essential because, in organisations people exhibit such emotional behaviour which mask their true feelings. This is necessary to fulfill the demands of one's organisational roles and situational needs. All these circumstances have forced the people to learn and acquire emotional intelligence.

In fact emotions are a critical factor of employee behaviour. However till recently, management scholars and organisational behaviour experts paid very little attention to them. There are two reasons for this neglect:

(1) It is presumed that emotions are disruptive and hinder performance. This view is developed after considering the negative emotions like anger, distress. No doubt that negative emotions rarely stimulate performance and are usually destructive, still people have positive emotions also and they are constructive and contributory. In fact positive emotions become the reservoir of energy and will to work.

(2) There exists a myth of rationality which expects that organisations should be emotion free. After the introduction of scientific management, organisations were specifically designed to control emotions. It was presumed that a well run organisation is the one which successfully controls and eleminates the feelings like anger, jealousy, hatred, fear, grief, love, etc., from the workplace. Such emotions were treated as the antithesis of scientific management and the organisation were suggested to be kept from them. However, we can not delay the fact that human being are inseparable from emotions and employees bring their emotions to workplace. As such we cannot except an emotion-free organisation to exist. So long as people are the important components of any organisation, the organisational environment will have an influence on employee emotions to a certain extent. Similarly we can never eliminate emotions from the personalities of people. Infact, an emotionally frozen person is suffering from mental disorder. So having emotions and getting touched by them is a sign of good mental health. However, control over emotions is equally important. Outbreak of emotions in a sudden and more frequent manner is not good. It retards performance, spoils relationship and disturbs the behaviour of self and others. It negatively affects the work atmosphere. It reduces the level of concentration and lowers the level of employee productivity. Emotional arousal is for a short period, but the mood which it develops lasts for a relativaly longer period. Therefore people must learn to deal with emotions in a clever way. Well-managed emotions help whereas ill-managed emotions hurt.

Emotional Intelligence – Stephen Robbins defines emotional intelligence in the following words. Emotional intelligence (EI) refers to an assortment of non-cognitive skills, capabilities and competencies that influence a person's ability to succeed in coping with environmental demands and pressures.

Daniel Goleman a psychologist and author brought for the first time this term, emotion. intelligence, to a wide audience in 1995, in his famous book which had the same title. He applied t concept to business again for the first time in 1998, in his article in *Harvard Business Review*.

Emotional intelligence is composed of five dimensions. They are as follows:

(1) **Self–awareness:** This simply means being aware of what you are feeling self–awarenes defined by Goleman as the ability to recognise and understand your moods, emotions drives as well as their effect on others. Goleman states that the halmarks of self–awarei are self–confidence, realistic self–assessment and self–depreating sense of humour.

(2) **Self–management or self–regulation:** Self–management is described as the ability manage one's own emotion and impulses. Goleman has used the term self–regulation. Th later writers on this theme changed it as self–management. Goleman defines self–regulation, distruptive impulses and moods. It is in fact the propensity to suspend judgement and think before acting. He gives the hallmarks of self–regulation as trustworthiness and integrity, comfort with ambiguity and openness to change.

(3) **Self–motivation:** It is described as the ability to persist in the face of setbacks, failures. According to Goleman self–motivation is the passion to work for reasons that go beyond money or status. It is the propensity to pursue goals with energy and persistence. Its hallmarks are strong drive to achieve, optimism even in the face of failure and organisational commitment.

(4) **Empathy:** It is described as the ability to sense how others are feeling. Goleman views empathy as the ability to understand the emotional make-up of other people. It is the skill in treating people according to their emotional reactions. The hallmarks of empathy are expertise in building and retaining talent, cross-cultural relationship and sensitivity and service to clients and customers.

(5) **Social skill:** According to Goleman it is the proficiency in managing relationships and building networks. It is an ability to find common ground and support. It is the ability to handle the emotions of others. The hallmarks of social skill are effectiveness in leading change, persuasiveness, expertise in building and leading the teams.

Leadership and EI: Emotional intelligence (EI) and leadership is closely related. EI plays a very important role in job performance. Daniel Goleman conducted a survey of 200 large global companies and found that the truly effective leaders are distinguished by a high level of emotional intelligence. Goleman feels that though a person has an incisive mind, first class training and an endless supply of good ideas, without EI he will not become a great leader. In another survey conducted in respect of eleven. American presidents; they were evaluated on six qualities. Those qualities were communication, vision, organisation, political skill, cognitive skill and emotional intelligence. The key quality which differenciated the successful leaders from the unsuccessful one was emotional intelligence. The successful leaders were Roosevelt, Kennedy and Reagan. The unsuccessful leaders were Johnson. Carter and Nixon. All successful leaders are found to possess high degree of emotional intelligence. Different research conducted in this regard have following important observations.

(i) Emotional Intelligence (EI), Intelligent Quotient (IQ) and technical skill are the threshold capabilities for executive position. The threshold capabilities mean the entry level requirements.

(ii) All the most effective leaders have the high degree of emotional intelligence.

(iii) Emotional intelligence *sine quo non* of leadership. Without EI one cannot become a great leader.

(iv) A ratio of technical skill, IQ and EI is calculated as ingredients of excellent performance and it was proved that EI was twice as important as the others for jobs at all levels.

(v) EI plays an increasingly important role at the highest level of the company where the difference in technical skills are of negligible importance.

(vi) The star–performers at higher ranks of the management have more EI capabilities which are the reasors of their effectiveness.

(vii) At senior leadership positions, the 90 per cent of differences in the profile of star–performers is attributable to EI factor rather than cognitive abilities.

It is observed by a number of research scholars that all effective leaders use the emotional component to convey their message effectively to others. Many a time a message with an emotional content is accepted more easily by the subordinate than the dry message. Again a leader's behaviour which is full of emotions is more likely to energise the subordinates. The enthusiasm and activeness of a leader produces an inductive effect on his followers. The emotional elements are most useful when the leader has to buy the subordinates into the vision of their company's future. Moreover when the vision and mission statement is changed, again emotions can be powerful tools to convince and persuate the employee.

Modern management has to face such situations very often where ambignity, uncertainty and vagueness prevails. Goals are then vague. Change is faster and ineviable. And there are no definite presumptions which can provide premises for sound logical and rational thinking. Under these circumstances employees can be driven to higher level of performance, only when they are emotionally activated. Because when everything is unknown and unclear, then one has to use his own intellect to decide the right goal, the right path and the right action. This one does only when he/she is emotionally charged. Organisational commitment, job involvement, social responsibility, quality awareness, spirit of innovation, team spirit, etc., which we treat as important principals features of effective organisations are basically employee–emotions and nothing else. When these emotions are widely cultivated throughout the organisation and properly and continuously nurtured and strengthened, the organisation displays consistent outstanding performances. Effective leadership does this job successfully.

Can EI be learned? : Previously emotional intelligence was called as emotional maturity. It was observed that in most of the cases this emotional maturity grows with age. As people grow old, their emotionl maturity increases. Scientific research suggests that there is a genetic component to emotional intelligence, that is, emotional intelligence is a born quality. Similarly psychologists and developmental research indicate that nurturing plays a very important role in developing emotional intelligence. So it is seen that people are born with certain levels of empathy and they acquire it also as a result of life's experience. Training, too enhances EI. But such a training should consist of motivation, extended practice and feedback. Because analysis, concept–formation and logical–sequencing which is usually taught to people to develop rationality is very little useful in EI training. Practice and feedback acts as a very effective tool of teaching emotional intelligance. Again people learn emotional intelligence more efficiently in groups than as a single pupil. Because emotional intelligence is an interactive skill for the development of which we need to provide lot of scope for interaction. Similarly if training in EI is not given, then job–performance gets hampered.

Old behavioural habits become a great deal of hurdles in acquiring and enhancing emotional intelligence. In fact, customarily we are habituated to ignore, suppress and conceal emotions. The family and social influences perpetuate and foster this habit. Emotional expression is abused as weakness of personality. We presume that strong, iron–personalities do not display their emotions atleast. This kind of understanding develops a negative notion about emotional intelligence. Even some of the people feel that emotions and intelligance are two mutually distant terms. This type of view and mindset make people disinterested in learning acquiring and mastering emotional intelligence. Naturally rude, indifferent, curt behaviour is exhibited by many people. Most of the executives do not show that much concern for people which they particularly display about the task completion.

So rather a ruthless practice of extracting the work breeds up. Even though we talk so much about human relation. many times they are superficial and work-oriented. We do not relate to others at workplace in a purposeless but meaningful way. We show our concern for others when it is beneficial. In fact, many times organisations try to capitalise on human relations. So clever tricks instead of wise methods are employed. Emotional intelligence will not develop in a true way unless there is an honest purpose and sincere effort. Empathising can be successfully done only when we sublime ourselves and enter into other's personality for the time being. This is difficult but not impossible. If we really understand how others will think and feel in particular situations, we can better know why they react in the characteristic way.

Empathising increases our knowledge of others, but to deal with them, we need to know ourselves first. This demands an objective and realistic self–assessment. It is not simply a SWOT analysis of self. It is not also a typical awareness of self–existence. More than all this it is an evaluation study of the impact of self on others. In order to be an effective leader the aspirant therefore must know that what of him touches others and what troubles them. Then, self–management can be done in a desired way. Self–assessment gives a person a clear picture of himself from the viewpoint of self and others. But then the person must be ready to change his views of others, attitude and behaviour. Modern research on management practices shows that trust is that cornerstone of improved productivity, efficiency and employee–employer relationship mutual trust develops when the relationship is based on early concern, integrity and fidetity. A leader has to prove himself as a trustworthy person. For this, he should develop the habit of creating faith and maintaining faith. An attitude of skepticism becomes an obstake in this process. The old belief that all are cheats, unless they prove themselves otherwise, should be replaced by the practice of trusting others. Self–management is to be done in the light of self–awareness and empathy.

Self–motivation and social skills again are interlinked with self–awareness, self–management and empathy. The strong drive to achieve and optimism is the result of our knowledge of self and others. Without this knowledge they will become blind and void. Persuasiveness as a social skill will develop only when there exists optimism and achievement drive. One who wishes to achieve something great needs others to collaborate. If one is optimistic about future one will develop strong achievement drive. Then one will do everything and engage his full intelligence to persuate others. Also one will simultaneously work hard to build an integrated team and lead the same. In essence the five components of emotional intelligence are interlinked and interwoven. All components are supportive and complementary to each other.

To learn EI effectively one has to follow the action–plan as below.

(i) Develop the habit of introspection. Introspect your own behaviour. (ii) Practice empathy. (iii) Get a feedback. (iv) Allow people to criticise your deficiency in EI skill. Take this criticism positively and learn through it. (v) Improve and modify your behaviour accordingly. (vi) Again ask others to watch your behaviour and make suggestions. (vii) Practice this modified behaviour and gradually make it a regular habit. Never forget that there is a lot of scope for improvement. (viii) Keep on improving your listening ability. Because your skill of empathy largely depends on it.

Leadership and EI are closely related. This is now a well established fact. More precisely speaking higher level of EI will enhance leadership effectiveness. To know how much expertise and proficiency a leader has acquired in EI; we need to discuss again each component of EI and its reflection in behaviour.

(1) Self awareness and behaviour: Self awareness includes a deep understanding of one's own emotions, needs, drives, strengths and weaknesses. A leader with himself as well as with others. He is neither unrealistically hopeful nor over critical. A self–aware leader has an accurate assesment of his emotional make up. Similarly he has a high degree of understanding of how his emotions affect the feelings and job–performance of others. He can appropriately combine his values with the work–goals and thereby make the work pleasant and energising. A self–aware leader is never shy of talking about his own limitations and always welcomes the positive and constructive criticism of others. He is open about his own emotions and its impact on others. Similarly he knows quite well his capabilities and so does not accept the overstretching assignments. He takes the calculated risk and if necessary demands help from others. This realistic approach saves him from failures and builds confidence.

(2) Self–regulation or self–management behaviour: Self regulation or self–management needs an inner dialogue. It is a skill of knowing identifying and properly controlling one's feelings and moods. Self–awareness inform us, what type of emotional make–up we possess. Self–regulation tells us how we can utilise the same for better performance and behaviour. Self–management means successfully dealing with one's emotions and channelising them in the most useful ways. A leader with self–regulation can pose him himself as a calm and cool personality. He will appear as a resonable individual and create an atmosphere of trust and fairness. Automatically talented people will flock in the organisation. The productivity will increase and dirty politics which resorts to the frequently changing mood of the leader will reduce. Additionally, when the leader is well known for his coolness and emotional balance none of the subordinates want to be known as hot–tempered individuals. This develops positive impact on the employees' emotional behaviour. Display of negative emotions unreasonably is in fact a sign of bad leadership. Presently self–regulation is most essential for the leader due to the increasing competition and continuous change. The ambigulty and uncertainty which these two factors create have to be faced in a cool and balanced way. A leader should not become or create panic in such situations. This is only possible if the leader has mastered his own emotions. One who is easily blown away by emotions cannot take a stand to face the problems of uncertainty and ambignity. An emotionally balanced leader in such situations plainly collects maximum information about the changes, understand their needs and purposes, recognises their inevitability and indispensability and then systematically moves with the change and also carries his organisation through this transition smoothly. For internal management also self–regulation is of great use to the leader. Because many bad things and unwise decisions in organisations take place due to impulsive behaviour. Profit exaggeration, expenses padding, misuse of power for selfish ends are the common examples of the same. Normally, such behaviour is made by impulsive people. A person who can control his greed, temptation, fear and such other emotions, always applies his reason and intellect before making any action. Thoughtfulness and integrity are the other signs of self–management besides compability with the change and ambiguity.

(3) **Motivation and behaviour:** Effective leaders have high achievement motivation. They have a position for the work itself. They are interested in seeking out creative challenges. They have an urge for learning and feel great pride in a well done job. These leaders are optimistic and are always eager to explore new approaches to their work and they keep a way of tracking progress. Effective leaders displays an unflagging energy to do things in a better way.

Motivated leaders are like the torch of lights. They are self-illuminated and also illuminate the surrounding. Enthusiasm, optimism and work orientation has distributive effect. Similarly, pessimism, negativities and disclination to work too spreads up very fast among others. Normally, a leader becomes an idol for both these attributes and tendencies. Therefore, his emotional behaviour matters a lot in these situations. A self–motivated leader leads by example. He first does what is expected and then expects people to do it. So the people are charged with positive energy. In order to motivate others towards a goal, one must be motivated first. What one believes, one can convince it forcefully to others. What one truly values, one strives very hard to achieve. And then one also gathers the efforts of all his colleagues and subordinates and pulls their energies towards that goal. Leader's self–motivation does this important task.

Empathy and Behaviour : Empathising is described as putting the feet in others shoes. It is a process and skill of putting oneself in the position of others and truly realising the views, thoughts and feelings of them. It is not simply adopting these feelings of others and pleasing them. It is not simply posing the famous I am ok– you are ok type stance. It means thoughtfully considering employees feelings, along with other factors in the process of making intelligent decisions. The importance of empathy as a component of emotional intelligence is increasing due to three reasons : (i) The increasing use of teams. (ii) The rapid pace of globalisation (iii) The growing need to retain talent.

Teams need a leader who has a better and deeper understanding of human relations. Groups can be successfully led by hard taskmasters focussing on targets. But teams differ from groups on the points of cohesion, member's, interactions and relations as well as roles played by members. Teams can produce synergic effects. However, mastering the team development requires the skill of empathy. Unless the leader gets a complete grasp of the feelings of people, he will not be able to motivate them effectively. Teams sometimes become the tank of bubbling emotions. So getting a consensus on issues become difficult when emotions of members clash with one another. During the course of discussion at some moment, some members feel that they are ignored, some feel frustrated and some get irritated. These emotional vibrations though natural, may produce a diminishing effect on team performance. A leader with emotional intelligence is able to realise the complaints and frustrations quite earlier and encourage them to speak about it openly and thereby remedies it constructively. Empathising helps the leader to know the emotional make up of his team.

Another reason of increasing importance of empathy is globalisation. Globalisation has resulted into diversified workplace. People from different countries and culture join the organisations and so the work groups and teams become heterogenous. When people have different cultural backgrounds, the cross-cultural dialogue naturally becomes inevitable. Such dialogues have the risk of misunderstandings and miscues. Communication problems and misinterpretation is more common in cross–cultural interaction and therefore, empathy becomes essential. Empathy acts as an antidote. People with empathy are attuned to the subtleties of body language. They can understand the message even beyond the words. People with emapthy have ease in dealing with the audience having cultural and ethenic differences.

Empathy is useful in retention of talent which is becoming a bigger problem nowadays. Employee turnover rate of the organisation of 21st century is quite high. Especially in information technology sector this rate is considerable and requires attention from the top management. Again, when good people leave the organisation, they take away with them the knowledge and expertise which has helped the organisation to prosper. Similarly the newcomers taking the place of the old guys require further training and induction which adds to the cost of man–management. So in all respect it becomes wise and clever to make every possible effort to retain the talent. Empathy plays a useful role in this respect. A leader with empathy can successfully offer coaching and mentoring to these people. Good coach and mentor actually gets an entry in the brain of his subjects. He can recognise what is happening at the subconscious level of the others. Empathy develops this capablility. A leader with empathy can perceive more accurately, completely and precisely the feelings, expectations, disappointments and dispositions of others. So they can offer useful advice and feedback in such cases. Such leaders know therefore, when to push their followers ahead for performance and when to hold them back.

Social skill and behaviour: The first three components of emotional intelligence, namely, self–awareness, self–regulation and motivation are actually self–management skills. The last two components, namely, empathy and social skill are interactive skills. They are concerned with a person's ability to manage relationship with others. Social skill is described by **Goleman** as the friendliness with a purpose. It is a kind of relatedness with others for a persuasion to be made. It is being social with a cause. Social skill is not simply extrovert behaviour. Extrovert people have a habit of mixing with others. Even an introvert person can master this skill. It is a methodical approach of associating with others and then making them move forward in your desired direction. A leader with social skill develops a wide circle of acquaintances and he has a minute sense and a tact of finding out common ground with all kinds of people. He has a skill of building rapport. Such a leader does not socialise continuously. However, they know profoundly that great work cannot be done alone. So they always keep a network ready and when there is a need they keep that network in action. Thus, it is a skill of using one's social relations. A leader with social skill is an effective persuader. He can successfully manage the team and create synergy. Infact social skill is the outcome of other four dimensions of emotional intelligence. Unless one understands his own emotions, he can empathise the emotions of others and unless he develops empathy, he cannot successfully manage social relationship. Social skill is the tool with which the leader puts his emotional intelligence into practice.

Leading by feel: Emotional intelligence is the most important factor which distinguishes successful leaders from the unsuccessful one. Therefore, modern leadership literature speaks more about leading by feel. EI is the crucial factor of leadership, from the viewpoint of contemporary scholars. They state that leaders need to manage the mood of their organisations. The gifted leaders are found to have done this by using a mysterious combination of their psychological capabilities, which we now call as emotional intelligence (EI). These great leaders possessed empathy, intuition and self–awareness. They can read and regulate their own emotions and can intuitively grasp how others feel about them. These great leaders can gauge the emotional mood of their organisations. However a question is always put forward for discussion that, how does the successful leaders learn to use emotional intelligence and where does it come from? A good volume of management literature view that EI is the outcome of both, nature and nurture. By making systematic efforts, one can develop and improve his EI.

EI can be useful as well as risky and hazardous. If EI is used wisely and compassionately, then it can become a driving force for the organisation to achieve superior performance. But if EI is used malaciously then it manipulates the followers for personal gain of the leader and thereafter, it completely paralyses the entire organisation.

John D. Mayer a professor of psychology, says that emotional intelligence (EI) is the ability to accurately perceive your own emotions and those of others and to understand the signals that it sends about relationships and then to manage your own and others emotions. He separates EI from optimism, initiative and self–confidence and suggests to be most realistic to develop your ability of EI.

Daniel Goleman, who is the pioneer of EI movement suggests that a leader should never stop learning. He states that the art of sustained leadership lies in making others to produce superior work especially in tough times. When the pressure of the situation is tremendous, a leader needs the social capital to pull the best out of people around him. Goleman belives that EI can be learnt at any age. For this, one needs right information, right guidance and right support. The right information in this regard means the information about their strengths and limitations. Such an information should be the result of the candid assessment of the leader by the people who know him very well and whose opinions are trusted and respected by the leader. The guidance which the leader needs to develop EI is a developmental plan which uses the naturally occurring workplace encounters as the laboratory for learning. The right support means someone to talk to when the leader is practicing the art of handling different situations. He needs someone to discuss what to do, when he is blown up by others and also he needs the trainer, who will teach him how to learn from the setbacks. Goleman feels that a leader developing and cultivating these resources and making a continuous practice can develop EI skills which will last longer.

Collin Barret who worked as president and COO of Southwest Airlines, shares his own experience about EI. He views that people are generally born with a predisposition for emotional awareness. He suggests that closely watch your own language and also that of others. Language to him means verbal as well as body language. He says that he always watches the body language and the style of interaction of other people. He prefers calm people around him, who simply by raising their eyebrows suggest him to lower his passion and then he will be listened more. Barret further tells that whenever he makes arguments he tries to be most factual and dispassionate.

Adrea Jung the C.E.O. of Avon products emphasise on seeking frank feedback from others to develop EI. **Richard Boytzis** who is a professor of Organisational Behaviour, says that EI can be developed, if one strongly wants to develop it. In his opinion, the real hurdle in developing EI is lack of motivation. If one develops a desire to change himself, one can definitely change himself. He further states that the motivation to develop EI capabilities should be positive motivitation, driven by positive hope and aspiration. As against this negative motivation comes out of fear of caution that over emphasising empathy or overusing the teamwork may not be desirable.

Steven Gustain a psychologist and autism expert introduces RDI approach to develop EI skill. RDI means Relationship Development Intervention. He explains that RDI begins with a belief that people can be taught to value relationship and to seek out interactions which are not merely transactional. The therapy has been developed for the autistic people, but it is useful for the others also to learn and develop EI. People with autism lack EI. They are not interested in connecting themselves emotionally with others. RDI approach teach people to enjoy the shared experience. The people who lack EI maintain only transactional relationships. They have an approach, that I will deal with you because there is something I want from you. This tractional perspective about interactions lead to emotional dryness and may convert a person into a psychopath. A psychopath is one who is rather afraid of any emotional relationship and so does not get involved in others. RDI uses cognitive exercises and activities to learn specific behaviours enhancing EI. In normal cases a baby of around 10 months starts developing the capacity of social referencing. This involves taking into account the emotions of others and then accordingly designing self–actions as to respond to them. From neuro–imagin some critical neural pathways are laid down among all structures in the limbic system which regulates emotions and motivation. Autistic children do not develop these pathways.

From the views of all these experts it is quite clear that emotional intelligence can be learned and put to practice for superior performance. However, at individual level its evaluation is comparatively easier than the same at group and organisational level. Sensitivity should spread through out the organisation. An awareness at all levels of emotionally driven behaviour of self and others is a must for creating an organisation which has emotional intelligence.

Excellence Triology :

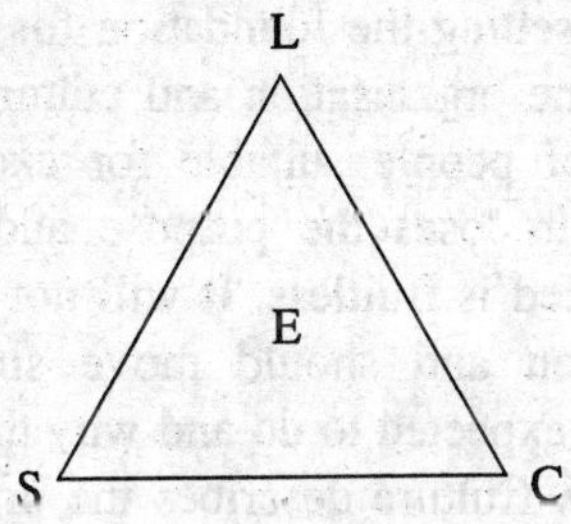

E – Excellence

L – Leadership

S – Strategy

C – Culture

Fig. 5.3 Excellence Triology

Corporate excellence is not a matter of a single day. It requires consistent policy and sustained efforts. It is the result of an appropriate combination of suitable strategy, responsive culture and effective leadership. This is the triology for excellence. Only an intelligent strategy, an aggressive leadership or a homogenous culture alone cannot take the organisation on the path of excellence. Similarly excellence is not a destination. One should not presume that once he reaches this point which he calls as excellence, his journey is over and he can relax there for the rest of his life. Moreover excellence is not a target or a goal, that once it is achieved it can be possessed and owned forever. In fact, excellence is your way of thinking. It is the style of functioning. It is an approach either of a person or an organisation towards its purpose or an organisation towards its purpose of existence and performance. The philosophy of excellence focuses therefore, on continuous and consistent improvement. It is a way of developoing an all–time programme outlook. In an organisation which is progress and improvement becomes a rule, a normal regular rouline rather than a special programme.

This progress and improvement is in all areas of operations such as product–quality, cost reduction, resources–utilisation, healthy management practices, customer care and service, wealth and profit maximisation, corporate governance, social responsibility activities, etc. So this requires good strategy, culture and leadership.

At the helm of this excellence triology is leadership and the foundation is built by strategy and culture. Leadership creates suitable strategy and culture. A leader plays a significant role in developing a suitable strategy and carving out an appropriate culture. He has to further make the blending of them. For creating excellence, the leader has to pinpoint cetain steps of his thoughts and actions which are an follows:

(a) **The start-up stage:** At this stage he has to develop the suitable strategic alternatives and organise the culture for excellence.

(b) **The growth stage:** At this stage the leader has to determine the strategy suitable for the organisation and hold the strategy and culture together.

(c) **Evolution stage:** At this stage the leader has to fine tune the strategy and culture and carefully and make best strategy–culture alloy.

(d) **Crisis:** Whenever the situation takes an unexpected and undesired turn, then the leader has to radically alter the strategy as well as the culture after a careful analysis and evaluation of prevailing circumstances.

A detailed discussion relating to the above points had been made in the chapters on strategy and culture. The point of discussion here is that the leader is the driving force for excellence. Effective leadership can create an organisation for excellence. But if the leadership is poor and incapable even an excellent organisation will deterwiorate and ultimately will diminish.

Strategy and culture are the two pillars setting the foundation for excellence. Strategy develops actions which gives a performance edge to the organisation and culture develops values and norms which shapes the mindset and behaviours of people suitable for excellence. An action which is unguided by the value system is rootless. In loses the purpose and meaning. It becomes void. Similarly, a value system which is not practiced is fruitless. It will not yield any outcome. Thoughts and actions should have the same direction and should move simultaneously. People in the organisation should know, as to what they are expected to do and why they should do it. The principle and practice should be interwoven beautifully. Culture describes the principles and strategy explains the practice. When an organisation prepares the quality checks, the people therein must fully realise what does it mean by matching and maintaining. When the organisation wants to differentiate its products, then it has to incalculate innovation as a value. The strategy culture alloy develops the strong foundation for excellence.

Excellence cannot be created and developed by pushing people towards it. It needs to light up the spirit which will induce and encourage the sponteneous action for excellence. Leadership, strategy and culture collectively develops and keep lasting the spirit for excellence. Inspiration changes the personality of an individual. Incentives direct and dictate the suitable behaviour. Inspiration motivates people to decide and design on their own what can be the suitable behaviour. No doubt that excellent organisations set norms of performance and behaviour. But at the same time they allow people to deploy the same by themselves. The leadership, strategy and culture in such organisations provide enough scope for people to take initiative, be creative and enhance the worth of their organisation.

People are the real assets of excellent organisation. Because at the core of leadership, strategy and culture; there are people and none else. People develop effective leadership, design competitive strategies and carve out culture for excellence. Infosys founder–chairman Mr. Narayanmurthi reveals the secret of the success of his company in the following words; – In Infosys, the most important word is 'we' and the least inportant word is 'I' – This denotes the team spirit and collectivism which is developed in the organisation systematically. It then results into subordination and sublimation of individual interest to general interest. This type of thinking and actions are the output of leadership, strategy and culture. The leadership promotes the sense of sacrifice and commitment by setting its own example. A leader, typically, becomes the friend, philosopher and guide for the followers. The actions and views of the leader becomes a manual for the followers. The values are better understood from the leaders behaviour. The culture offers shared meaning of the values. Culture creates the atmosphere for desired behaviour. If self–sacrifice is the desired value, then it need to be percolated and accepted at all levels in the organisation. It should become a common and collective perception of all people. Culture does this task leader influences the culture and also gets influenced by it. Similarly leader and culture both, have an impact on strategy and again strategy too affects leadership style and culture of the organisation. When these three elements namely, strategy, culture and leadership are turned to each other and play complementary roles, the results are noteworthy. Otherwise the desired organisational performance and the actual one differs significantly.

Leaders as stated earlier, make strategies. At the same time, the leadership culture should be suitable for the strategy implementation. For example, a turnaround strategy needs dynamic and aggressive leadership whereas a stability strategy requires a leader with a calm and cool approach and balancing attitude. A leader with the suitable mortality can effectively implement the chosen strategy. After all a strategy brings success to the organisation when it is correctly and appropriately exection. Simply, making of good strategies does not guarantee success. It is their execution, which matters most. The organisations building a competitive edge are always found to be doing extremely well in strategy–implementation. For example, how you make cost–cutting to become a cost leader is more important. In which ways you differentiate your products and position strongly in the market gives you an edge over your competitors. The entire question is that of detailing. All these minute details that become the critical points are to be attended prudentially. This needs the suitable culture. Because strategy implementation needs participation of all members of the organisation. Everyone plays a useful role, whether small or big. Negligance to small things may form, finally, big deficiencies. A suitable culture activates and energises people to do everything required by the strategy wholeheartedly. Leader contributes to this culture development and culture strategy make the leader to choose that course of behaviour and action which is most required in those situation. When it is necessary to develop the vision of the organisation, the leader has to act as a visionary leader. When charismatic behaviour is essential to motivate and induce the people the leader has to display effectively his personality charisna.

When the situation needs people to transcend their limits, develop inventive thinking and make creative contribution to the organisation, the leader has to play the role of the transformational leader. If in any of these situations, a particular leader is not able to exhibit the required, desirable, leadership behaviour. then, this old leader should be replaced by a new one who is suitable and can offer effective leadership under those specific circumstances. Because it is effective leadership which is more important than the question of effectiveness of the leader. And the effective leadership must always be there for the organisational success.

In short, for achieving excellence leadership, strategy and culture has to act in concert. All the three elements are inter depended as well as inter–influences leadership affects strategy and leadeship. Again strategy has an impact on leadership and culture. So the three collectivly produce the desired results. Excellence triology explains this inter–relatedness of leadership, strategy and culture. It suggests that the efforts for excellence should be complete and comprehensive and this is possible only when leadership, strategy and culture are attuned to one another.

❑❑❑

CHAPTER 6

CREATING EXCELLENCE IN THE PROCESS – TOOLS AND TECHNIQUES FOR EXCELLENCE

Creating excellence in the organisation requires policy, procedures and programmes for the same. From small details to the big goal setting, everything should be driven by the philosophy of excellence. Infact, creating excellence requires a lot of continuous improvement in processes and people. These two Ps, namely process and people, have a significant impact on organisational performance and effectiveness. Organisational performance lowers because either the people are wrong or the processes are defective. In the people holding different positions in the organisation are incapable of handling the tasks and the responsibilities assigned to them, then the organisation will suffer from not only low productivity and efficiency but also from disharmony, conflict, wastage and under-utilisation of resources as well as reduced business reputation and loss of goodwill. So to make an excellent organisation, the people working therein must possess the skills for creating, developing, acquiring and retaining excellence, throughout. This is the subject-matter of the this chapter. This chapter focuses on the discussion about the tools and techniques for improving the processes and creating excellence thereby.

A process, in the simplest sense, is the way of doing a task. It is composed of a number of operations and each operation consecutively leads to completion of the task. Many a time completed task is not upto the mark, because the process is incorrect or defective. It means that either we choose a wrong way of doing a job or we commit several mistakes in doing that job. In any of these situations, the final output is unsatisfactory work and non-competitive performance. So we have to pay close attention to work-processes and see that they are error-free. If we cannot develop such ideal work-processes, then we should have to develop a corrective system which will anticipate, trace and point out the errors and mistakes at the point of their origin and provide immediately for the rectification actions. The tools and techniques of process excellence serve this purpose. The major, most popular and widely used tools and techniques in this regard are-

(1) Total Quality Management (TQM).

(2) Quality Standards and ISO Series.

(3) Kaizen way of thinking.

(4) Six Sigma.

Each one of them is discussed at length in the following pages.

Total Quality Management (TQM)

Lee Iacocca the famous expert of quality-management has said that quality and productivity are the two sides of the same coin. Everything one does for quality, improves his productivity also. These words carry lots of wisdom and experience. For many years there had been a misconception that quality is a costly affair. Small organisations therefore cannot afford quality. However, it is now a well established fact that quality improves productivity, efficiency, effectiveness and ultimately financial returns. Productivity relates to the input-output ratio. When with minimum input, maximum output is produced, productivity is to be said higher. Normally, this term is used in respect of physical resources, e.g., machine-productivity. Efficiency to certain extent, is synonymous to productivity. The term efficiency is used in respect of human resources, usually. **Kreitner** defines efficiency as a central element in the process management which balances the amount of resources used to achieve an objective against what was actually accomplished.

Thus, when the ratio of benefits to cost is more favorable, there is greater efficiency. **Weihrich** and **Koontz** views efficiency as the achievement of ends with the least amount of resources. Thus, it is the ability of minimising the use of resources in achieving organisational objectives. **Peter Drucker** says that the efficiency means doing things right. So efficiency does not include, only economising the use of resources but also making the correct actions and avoiding errors and mistakes. Similarly **Peter Drucker** defines effectiveness also. He says that effectiveness means doing the right things. It is, therefore, concerned with achievement of objectives in a prompt manner. It involves choosing the right goals and determing the appropriate objectives. Effectiveness is more related to the goals and results than the cost and utilisation of resources economically.

When an organisation wishes to improve its quality, in the first instance, it becomes most essential to decide what is meant by quality. **Philip Crosby** says that quality is conformance to requirements. Another quality expert, **John Stewart,** a consultant at McKinsey observes that there is no single definition of quality. Quality is a sense of appreciation that something is better than something. The concept of quality changes from generation to generation. Quality varies by facts of human activity. **Stoner and Gilbert** are of the opinion that quality in the work place has gone beyond creating better than average product at a good price. Now it refers to achieving increasingly better products and services at progressively more competitive prices. This includes doing things right at the first time, rather than, making and correcting mistakes.

The above three definitions provide perspective thinking about the concept of quality. Quality is not an absolute term. It is relative. It is subjective. The concept of quality upgrades over a time. Quality cannot be described only from the point of view of the user. The fulfillment or conformance to requirements does not simply mean the production or technical requirements. It means fulfillment of utility requirements also. In other words, the products should stand to the quality concept of the manufacturer as well as consumers. Actually, the viewpoints of the customers in respect of quality are more important than those of the producers because when the customer appreciate the product, then the product quality gets recognised. Similarly this appreciation has an element of comparison. The quality of one product is better than another. This is how, normally customers describe their quality concept. So when a particular product has features which are superior than other products, then only, the customer feels that the products possesses quality. Again the customers expectations regarding quality changes in their lifetime and from generation to generation. Therefore, consistently producing better goods and services and continuously upgrading them becomes an essential aspect of maintaining and developing the quality. What customers felt as quality yesterday, may not be the same today and tomorrow his quality expectations might have progressed far ahead. Therefore, evergoing improvements is the core of the quality concept. Exactly, this is the central theme of excellence. Excellence needs improvements forever and quality also expects the same. So the efforts for quality leads to excellence.

Quality has another dimension, which is financial. The quality products must be availed at competitive prices. If the price is higher, the customers' notion of quality will change. Therefore, a quality-product must possess an affordable and reasonable price which should be attractive and competitive if compared with the product-prices of others. Competitive pricing is possible when a company keeps a strict control on its costs. It has to produce the goods and services of a satisfactory quality at minimum cost. This is possible if the company avoids mistakes and errors as well as wastages of all kinds. It should learn to do every operation right at the first time. The cost of correcting mistakes and rectifying errors adds up to the total cost. And if, this is a repeated practice, the costs mount up obviously. Therefore once, we start eliminating, reducing and avoiding mistakes and errors, the cost-control and cost-reduction process begins automatically. Similarly, when wastage of all kinds, such as, material-wastage, labour-wastage, time-wastage, monetary-wastage and likewise, again cost-reduction is effected. With minimum physical and non-physical resources, when we turn out the maximum output, then we derive two sets of benefits. First, we achieve cost reduction and second, we make optimum utilisation of resources. Every improvement in performance is thus cost-effective. So productivity/efficiency and cost control are the two sides of same coin. When we look to the definition of quality, we observe that there is need for more precision. Crosby's definition of quality is more general in nature. Quality experts, now, have refined Crosby's general perspective by identifying five different types of product-quality which are as follows-

(1) **Transcendent quality** - It is the inherent value or innate excellence which is apparent to the individual. It is the perception of the individual regarding quality of a particular product. It is subjective in nature. The best example of this quality is the incidence of watching a piece of art. When in a museum, people watch the art piece, they react in several different ways. There is lot of variations in their views regarding the artistic quality and beauty of these pieces of art. Each one has a unique perception. This is transcendent quality. As such, we always say, that beauty lies in the eyes of the beholder. Usually, transcendent quality relates to aesthetic things. The pieces of art, decorative things, ornamental things are said to possess this transcendent quality.

(2) **Product-based quality** - We expect, in respect of each and every product, that it should possess certain attributes. When these attributes are absent in the product, we say that the product does not possess the quality. For example, we except the fruits do not possess quality. We expect that the refill should have a smooth ink-flow. If it is absent, then we remark that the refill does not have the quality. We expect the candies to be sweet. If they are otherwise, they are not the quality-candies. Thus product-quality is the presence of a particular/stated attribute in the product. If this attribute is absent, then goods do not possess what is called product-quality and if it is present, then, we say, that the goods possess product-based quality. The presence or absence of a given product-attribute is the primary determinant of product-based quality. Many a time this quality is described as the adjective of the product. For example, soft tissues, rough sandpapers, sweet candy, fresh vegetables and fruits, flawless glass, etc.

(3) **User-based quality** - This concept of quality, uses the customers viewpoint to test its existence. It is described as the quality of a product which is determined by its ability to get the expectations of users. If the product serves the purpose for which it is purchased by the customer in a satisfactory way, then the product is said to possess user-based quality. In order to test, whether a product possesses this type of quality, two simple questions should be asked –

(a) Does the product possesses the ability to get the job done for which it is purchased?

(b) Is the job done in a reliable way by the product?

In other words, has the product fulfilled the purpose of its purchase and has it served the purpose in a reliable manner.

(4) **Manufacturing-based quality** - **Philip Crosby,** while defining the concept of quality emphasised on the point of conformance to requirements. The concept of manufacturing-based quality corresponds to this Crosby's definition. We know that each product has its design-specifications or blueprint. Now, how well the actual product conforms to its design specifications decides the manufacturing-based quality of the product. According to **Keither,** the closer is the match between the intended product and the actual one, the higher is the manufacturing-based quality.

(5) **Value-based quality** - Value-based quality is supposed exist in a product, when the customers feel that they have a good return of their money spent in buying the product. At the heart of this concept of quality is the cost-benefit relationship. If the benefits derived from the product are greater than the price paid for the same or the cost for acquiring the same, the product is said to possess the value-based quality. However, the value-based quality is subjective because the cost-benefit relationship is a matter of personal perception and preference so the marketing experts state that the concept of value-based quality is nebulous. Every customer value is simply giving customers what they want at a price which they consider fair. With this viewpoint many companies adopt a low price strategy to attract more customers and to convince them that they get higher benefits from the products than the price (cost) which they pay for the same.

Quality of Services - The above five types of quality mostly related to goods or tangible products. Services are intangible products. As such the quality of services require separate consideration. Services differ from goods in several ways. But the most important differentiating fact regarding services is relating to the sequence of production, distribution (marketing) and consumption. Goods are produced first, then they are distributed or marketed and then they are consumed. So the buyers get a chance to inspect the goods and their quality before purchasing them. Services on the other hand are demanded first, then produced and are consumed by the buyers and thereafter their marketing takes place. Thus, the buyers consume or experience the service first and then checks out its quality. So the quality of a service becomes a complicated issue to decide, due the different perceptions of the buyers, the non-standardisation of a service-product, the lack of chance to assess the quality before purchase which otherwise would reduce and soften the perceptual differences, the non-repetitive indegeneous skill of the service-providers in many instances. However, service quality is becoming an important issue, nowadays, due to the rapid expansion of the service-sector. The earlier notion regarding service quality states that services are usually customer-driven and as such pleasing the customer with the service is the only way of indicating the service-quality. This view, though focusses an important element of quality-determination process, still it is vague to a great extent. No doubt, that quality is what customers view as quality. So customers' perceptions play a very important role in deciding, defining and describing the product-quality. But the term 'pleasing the customer' is not precisely enough to decide accurately the degree of service quality and also its dimensions. Does pleasing means satisfying the customers? Then the present service quality experts disagree on this point. They argue that service quality does not simply mean satisfying the customer. It should convey something more than that. So they explain that the real challenge before service providers today is to anticipate and exceed the customers expectations. **Michael Quinlan,** the Chief Executive Officer of

McDonald has clarified this point very nicely in the words given below. He says that in the 70s we focussed on serving the customers, in 80s we emphasised satisfying and now in the 90s our goal is to exceed customers expectations. Thus, quality of service has a varying meaning. Modern management experts believe that virtually every organisation is a service organisation and so from this point of view also quality of service is a matter of study and analysis. **Kreitner** in this regard suggests that organisations need to understand and manage following the five distinctive characteristics of a service.

(1) In case of services, customers participate directly in the production process.

(2) Services are consumed immediately and cannot be stored.

(3) Services are provided where and when the customer desires.

(4) Services tend to be labour-intensive.

(5) Services are intangible.

In fact, customers are more intimately involved in the service delivery process and so, to decide service-quality, customers' perception should be taken as a correction. The level of customer satisfaction, therefore, will state how much quality a particular service possesses. A compression of this satisfaction level of different customers, informs how much superior is the quality of one product over the other. Research at Texas AandM University have uncovered important and valuable insights about customer-perception, regarding service-quality. The researchers surveyed hundreds of customers of different types of service organisations and brought to the light following five dimensions of service-quality: (a) Tangibility or intangibility (b) Reliability (c) Responsiveness (d) Assurance (e) Empathy. This five dimensions are concerned with the service-provider. Tangibility/intangibility refers to physical facilities, equipment and appearance of service personnel. Reliability refers to the ability to perform the desired service in a dependable, accurate and consistent manner. Responsiveness refers to the service-providers willingness to supply prompt service and help the customers. Assurance refers to the service providers knowledge, courtesy and ability to convey trust and confidence. Empathy refers to the caring and individualised attention offered by the service provider to the customers. The study revealed that reliability was the most important dimension of service quality regardless of the type of service involved. In present days, also the Texas dimensions are used for assessing the quality of a service. The respondents are asked to rate each of the five dimensions on a scale of 10 points. By this method the treatment which they received from the service establishments under survey is evaluated. One end of the scale denotes poorest service and the other end denotes the best service. The total of the score of these factors describe the customers perceptions regarding quality of that service. If the total score is below ten, the quality of service is poor and the treatment given to the customers can be described as cruel and unusual punishment. If the total score is between 11 and 20, then a question can be raised whether this activity can be truly called a service or not. If the score is between 21 and 30 then the quality of the service is rated as average. But then we know that people don't want an average service. If the total score is 31 to 40 the service is described as close only counts in horseshoes. And if the total score is 41 to 50, the service provider is described as the service hall of fame candidate.

So after knowing different aspects of the concept of quality, we turn to the concept of total quality management (TQM). TQM is a broad concept and has wider approach to quality. TQM does not simply think about product quality but the total quality of work in the organiastion. Therefore, **Marshall Shashkin and Keneth Kiser** define TQM as creating an organisational culture committed to the continuous improvement of skills, teamwork, processes, product, service quality and customer satisfaction. Another consultant on quality, **Richard Schonberger** views TQM as a continuous, customer-centred, employee-driven improvement. Thus TQM emphasises on continuous improvement. This improvement is not expected in product alone but almost in each and every operation and every aspect of organisational functioning. Further such improvements should be customer-centred and employee-driven. So the very purpose of developing a TQM culture is to enhance and increasing consistently the customer's satisfaction. Customer is the cause and purpose of business. Consumption is the beginning of production. So every business has to take care of its customers continuously. No one affords to neglect the needs and the expectations of customers at any moment of time. Over the period, the customers expectations and so also their perception of quality changes. This change is again an ongoing process. Naturally, the organisations, too, have to undertake a quality improvement programme on a permanent basis. This is another important aspect of TQM. All quality improvement efforts should have a focus on customers. They should be so made as to give enhanced satisfaction to the customers. This customer may be external or internal. An external customer is the buyer of the product of the organisation whereas the internal customer is the employee in the same organisation working in another department.

In fact TQM has introduced this new concept of internal customer. Organisational work is divided into tasks, operations and activities which are performed by different people, work groups and departments. That results into a flow of work from one person to another person. When each employee is participating in the work-process, doing a specific task, his performance influences that of others and also gets influenced by others. For example, if A,B and C are the three employees doing the consecutive operations, then the performance of each of them is interdependent. A's negligence to quality affects adversely. B's performance and carelessness makes C to suffer. Thus, the mistakes, errors, defects and deficiencies have a carrying forward type of effect. TQM, therefore, suggests the concept of internal customer. It says that each employee, work group and department should treat the other as its customer as far as it work is concerned. And so when the work passes from one employee to another, it should take care as if it is going in the hands of a customer. This orientation will bring a new outlook to defect-free, error-free, conscious and prudential performance. So each person and group in the organisation will attend to all the niceties of their work in the almost careful way. This creates an atmosphere of quality-consciousness.

Another important aspect to TQM is that it should be employee-driven. The urge for quality improvement should not be thrust upon the employees by the top management. On the other hand, it should emerge from the employees themselves. The employees should strongly feel the need for quality development and quality improvement. Irrespective of the cadre and level, each employee should have an alertness for quality and should actively participate in the development of quality. The management should create, development and sustain a suitable environment for the same.

TQM is a matter of organisational culture. Because it is deeply embedded in every aspect of organisational life. Organisational culture encompasses all the assumptions which employees make for thinking and acting. When something is treated as a core value of the organisational culture, then all members of the organisational culture presume that everyone will follow these core values in his thoughts and actions. As such all time of thinking and acting will resort to those care values. Automatically a personal commitment to the core value develops and everybody starts imbibing it in his behaviour and performance. When quality becomes a core value of the organisational culture systematic continuous improvement, as its effect, becomes an everyday matter for each and every member of the organisation. Quality improvement then becomes, a habit, a routine activity rather than a special, one-time, eventual task. In such an atmosphere people look to the efforts for quality as just the way they do things there. Thus quality-making becomes a normal thing. Consciously and unconsciously all efforts of all people in the organisation are directed towards creation and development of quality in each and every activity which they undertake either singularly or collectively. One who does not imbibe these values, motions, attitudes and work habits, automatically becomes an odd person and is easily identified. The same thing happens with a non-conforming work group. Tough actions can be decided against such elements as a part of the system correction. In an organisation with quality culture, non-quality performance becomes an exception and a very rare incidence. Ultimately quality is inbuilt in every decision and action in the organisation. On the other hand in an organisation with dissimilar culture, thoughts and efforts for quality are discrete, isolated, sporadic and temporary. There is no consistency in the thoughts and actions for quality. Mostly efforts for quality remain at the individual levels and they do not have a collective impact. So such organisations cannot be said to follow the TQM philosophy.

TQM has certain prerequisites. In order to develop the TQM culture and system, the organisation must pay attention to quality triology. Quality triology has three basic elements. They are (a) Quality planning (b) Quality control (c) Continuous quality improvement. Quality planning aims at fulfilling customers' expectations. It tends to establish a customer-driven standard. Quality control aims at ensuring the delivery of the product or service at lowest internal cost and time. Quality control tries to conform to the standard. Quality improvement leads to perfection and so it challenges the existing standards to upgrade it. Quality improvement efforts should eliminate and reduce defects, errors and mistakes on an incremental basis. Every such incremental increase in quality will lead to quality improvement and zero defect operation. In fact, quality intends to offer fullest satisfaction of customers' requirements. Customers' requirements are their needs. These are the primary expectations of a customer in respect of the products and services which he desires to consume. The TQM has to attend to the customers requirements perfectly. The customers primarily expect that (i) The product or service must have a precise specification. (ii) The product or service must conform to the given specification accurately. (iii) The product or service should possess reliability. (iv) The product or service should offer the best return for the money which the customer spends. (v) The product or service should be delivered to the customer in time.

Therefore **Gilbert and Stoner** say that TQM is the organisational cultural commitment to satisfy the customers through the use of an integrated system of tools, techniques and training. It involves the continuous improvement of oraganisational process, resulting in high quality products and services.

Kreitner also has a similar view. He says that TQM is the creation of an organiastional culture committed to the continuous improvement of skills, teamwork, processes, product and service quality and customer satisfaction. Thus quality is an important value of an organisational culture. Once a quality culture is developed, the efforts for quality improvement start spontaneously and continuously. When organisations create and develop quality-culture, quality gets rooted deeply in the minds of people. It becomes their attitude and there begins the successful implementation of TQM. Further quality-improvement requires progressive thinking and an inventing mind. So **Dr. Frank P. Carruba,** the Chief Technical Officer at Philips says that quality has to begin in research. Naturally, unless research for quality begins, quality-production is not possible. Because expectations about quality are always on an ascending scale and therefore unless research is conducted on producing better products and services, the purpose to TQM cannot be accomplished.

According to **Prof. S.A. Sherlekar** TQM needs an integrated system of tools, techniques and training to satisfy total customers needs and desires. So this involves - (i) reorganising the management system (ii) reengineering the process of production and distribution and (iii) radical changes in the organisational structures and processes. These continuous improvements results in quality creation and development. Reengineering consists of radical thinking and reorganisation of work-processes to create value for customers. The organisation has to review its strategies, plans, procedures, policies and practices and modify them to suit to the changing circumstances.

TQM is a way of life. It cannot be taken up as a magical formula of transformation. It is an activity. It is a style of functioning. It is an approach to work. It is a pattern of thinking. It should become not only an ideology but a practice of making, doing, behaving, treating and living the work life. TQM has its seeds in the philosophy of excellence. The consistent and collective efforts to create excellence automatically produce TQM. Similarly imbibing the TQM philosophy and style of functioning leads to creation of excellence in the organisation. TQM expects quality in almost all areas of business and organisation, such as technology and resources, functional management, organisational leadership, social responsibility, activities, etc. For successful TQM, top management should provide strong, capable and quality conscious leadership at all levels of the organisation. TQM anticipates participation and involvement of each and everybody in the organisation in the process of improvement and upgradation. At all levels in the organisation, there should be a deep urge and continuous efforts for TQM. TQM can not be injected from outside. It should be groomed internally. Similarly it needs a holistic approach. The organisation should be considered as a complete whole and every aspect of the organisational work should be analysed and evaluated for improvement. TQM develops a quality-atmosphere.

TQM does not hold any unrealistic expectations or impractical assumptions. Quality-building is not achievable in a single day. It is an outcome of long-term planning and substantial efforts. TQM, therefore, insists on constituency and continuity in the efforts for improvement. It develops a new realisation in the organisation. It makes a new awakening. When this happens, a self-motivation develops among the people in the organisation for upgradation of quality. Then efforts for quality at all levels of the organisation starts, rather spontaneously. When people working at the lowest to the top level are encouraged and allowed to participate in quality-management, it becomes a movement and later creates a quality-culture. Quality-conscious organisations do not restrict the efforts for quality only at specific levels. They do limit thinking for quality only to special groups or people at higher levels of management. From operating level to the policymaking level everybody's views are considered and their contribution in quality-improvement is encouraged. TQM develops a quality perception in the organisation, at the initial stage. Without such a perception, people will not even think for actions suitable for quality creation and development. **Kreitner** suggests following four principles of TQM –

(i) Do it right the first time.

(ii) Be customer-centred.

(iii) Make continuous improvement a way of life.

(iv) Build teamwork and empowerment.

Quality management does not expect to rectify and correct the things. It has a proactive approach. It suggests to make the right product at the first instance. TQM sets the procedures and operations in such a way that quality building in the product starts from the stage of product designing itself. This approach is more economical in two ways- (1) It eliminates the cost of correction and rectification of errors and mistakes as well as duplication of work. (2) It avoids the wastages and losses due to rejection of substandard products. This new approach of doing right things focusses on catching the errors at their source thus eliminating and avoiding them. Now the quality is looked as a personal responsibility. It is not a departmental or institutional responsibility. When quality is treated as personal responsibility, it comes to the operating level. Then the first man working at the lowest level of the organisational management who actually performs the task and operations essential for making a product is involved in the quality. Thus, quality becomes an integral part of all work. TQM does not take quality in lumpsum. It motivates, creates and monitors quality in detail and minutes. TQM suggests comprehensive training in processes and tools for quality improvements should be given to the employees. Then only will they display their inclination to accept personal responsibility for quality creation and quality development.

The second principle of TQM is to become customer-centred. TQM organisations deals with two types of customers, namely, internal customers and external customers. Internal organisations who depend on say, your work to do their work. This is due to the interdependence of work. So, anyone in your organisation who cannot do a good job unless you do a good job. Thus, every member of an organisation becomes an internal customer of the other member as he or she is dependent on each other either directly or indirectly. The concept of an internal customer develops in organisations a new outlook and approach to work and colleague relations. It brings a greater alertness and caution among employees when they are doing their jobs. This ensures quality in performance. When every small or big task in the organisation is performed with great care, accuracy and precision, quality pervades and prevails in the organisation.

External customers are outsiders who purchase the products of the company. They are the cause and purpose of the existence and functioning of the organisation. The organisation must and has to produce what its customers desire. It has to deliver always that what its customers expect. Thus, the organisation has to become customer-centered. For this purpose, it has to do the following:

(i) Anticipate the needs of its customers.
(ii) Listen to the customers intelligently.
(iii) Learn and master the ways and means to satisfy the customers.
(iv) Respond to the customers quickly, courteously, properly and responsibly.

In order to prepare yourself to offer the best service to your customers, you must develop the anticipatory thinking style. You must be able to predict what the customers will require and what will please them. This needs empathising. Still, sometimes we cannot accurately guess what our customers truly expect. So we need to listen to them carefully and intelligently. We must attend to their desires, complaints and opinions as guidelines and suggestions for improvements. Quality improvement is a continuous process. The different ways and alternatives to develop and sustain quality should be consistently thought about and practiced. Quality should become the mindset and routine behaviour of the people in the organisation. Because what matters most in TQM is the appropriate behaviour and not simply the good intentions.

Continuous improvement, which is the central pillar of TQM, means improving the complete work system by constantly improving the little details. And this is an endless job. The Kaizen practitioners in Japan, believe that quality is a process of continuous and consistent improvement. They say that quality is an eternal journey and not a final destination. Therefore, the TQM managers always have to measure and improve performance. They are not naively assuming that quality means zero defect and zero defect means perfection. On the other hand, they are supposed to search for actual and potential trouble spots. And when it is located, initiate the corrective action. Continuity in improvement demands consistency in efforts for better quality. So what you do good today, make it better tomorrow and best thereafter. This process should continue progressively forever. Similarly, speed of operations should also increase. Quality lies in doing a better job in less time span. The sluggishness in performance is against the notion of quality. Performing slowly actually means retarding the quality process. Correctness in decisions and actions cannot be an excuse to delay in both. TQM presumes best performance within a short time. Because your customers will not wait simply because you will give him a better offer after a prolonged time. Neither your competitors will give you chance because you are better, though late. Moreover cost of operations is one more aspect of quality performance. TQM says that quality and productivity are the two faces of the same coin. Quality in performance avoids wastages, economises the use of resources and thus, reduces the cost. The cost reduction is not at the expense of quality and neither is the quality achieved at the expense of higher cost. So for cost reduction efficiency and effectiveness must be maintained in the organisational working. Efficiency ensures a more favourable output to input ratio and effectiveness is achieved when the desired outcome and results are obtained. One more aspect of continuous improvement for quality is greater flexibility. This flexibility is exhibited when an organisation gives a very fast response to changing customer demands and new technology. Thus, the continuous improvement for TQM must do the following activities to the minimum.

(i) Enhance consistently the utility and service value of your products.

(ii) Speed up all your operating cycles such as product development cycle, order processing cycle, customers' grievances process, credit collection process, etc.

(iii) Respond promptly to changing customer needs, market competition, development in technology and other factors of business environment.

(iv) To reduce cost and avoid wastages, eliminate needless steps, duplication and rectification, non-value adding activities and reworking. Do everything right at the first time.

Empowerment - Quality is not a single person affair. It should be a concern of each and every member of the organisation. Otherwise the broad outlook and efforts for quality will not develop. Quality does not expect decreet and temporary attempts in isolation. TQM needs a holistic and concerted efforts for quality-development, quality-improvement and quality-maintenance. This is possible only if teamwork is developed and empowerment is made. **Kreitner** defines the concept of empowerment in the following words. Empowerment means making employees full partners in the decision making process and giving them the necessary tools and rewards. To make empowerment successful the organisation needs to do the following –

(i) Train the employees how to use the power correctly and cleverly.

(ii) Provide them all the necessary and relevant information to make decisions judiciously and prudentially.

(iii) Supply them the best tools for information collection and decision making.

(iv) Involve them fully in key decisions. Do not limit them only to marginal decision making.

(v) Reward them fairly for the good results and outcomes of their decisions.

In many organisations there is a situation of pseudo-empowerment. This happens because either the employees are incapable or the manager is authoritarian. Empowerment requires the suitable atmosphere. It is not a single activity. It is a style of organisational functioning. And such a style to become acceptable to all levels of the oragnisation require nurturing. Therefore, empowerment is compared to a growing seed. The complete process of farming and cultivation is responsible for the seed to take the form and shape of a plant and then progressively a tree. **Stephen R. Covey** (The Principle-centred Leadership) provides the comprehensive thinking on this issue. He considers four important factors which affect the success of empowerment. They are as follows - (a) The skill base of the individual. (b) Culture of empowerment. (c) Empowerment opportunities (d) The character development of the individual and his emotional maturity. Each of these four factors have again certain major subfactors which influence the success of empowerment.

The skills of the individual are according to Covey, of three types- Technical skills, Team and communication skills and Self-management skills. Similarly, the culture of empowerment depends upon – (i) Mutual trust (ii) Win-win relationships (iii) Open communication (iv) Access to key information (v) Rewards for initiative and cooperation. These are the subfactors of the culture of empowerment. Unless the organisation pays enough attention to them it will not create such a culture. The third factor of successful empowerment, namely, empowerment opportunities depend upon the following elements - (1) Delegation of authority (2) Participative goal setting (3) Self-managed teams (4) Freedom to experiment. If such empowerment opportunities are available and are utilised properly, then chances of success of empowerment are higher.

The fourth factor responsible for successful empowerment, according to Covey, is the character development and emotional maturity of the individual. It has following subfactors – (i) Honesty (ii) Trustworthiness (iii) Commitment (iv) Desire to learn and grow (v) Willingness to adapt and change (vi) Personal responsibility and accountability.

So empowerment cannot work without a supporting situation. This supporting situation is developed by the above mentioned factors and subfactors influencing the success of empowerment.

The discussion on the four principles of TQM cannot be complete unless the importance of team and teamwork is considered.

Teams - Groups and teams are different from one another in many respect. A team is more than just a group. **Jon Kazzenbach and Douglas Smith,** the management consultants at McKinsey and company, view that using the terms group and team interchangeably is a mistake. They define the term team as a small number of people with complementary skills who are committed to a common purpose, performance goals and approach for which they hold themselves mutually accountable. Thus, a team is a more cohesive, responsible, purposeful and performing group. In order to convert a group into a team, following things need to be done.

(i) Leadership should be made a shared activity.

(ii) Accountability should be individual and collective.

(iii) The group should develop its own goal/mission.

(iv) Problem solving should not be a part-time activity but should be made a way of life.

(v) Effectiveness is to be measured by the collective outcomes and products of the group.

The theory of group development describes the stages of its development such as forming, storming, norming, performing and adjourning. Actually, teams can be termed as the task groups which have reached the performing stage. According to **Katzenbach and Smith,** the essence of a team is common commitment with this, the team becomes a powerful unit of collective performance. Many of the groups cannot become the real teams because of two reasons –

(i) They suffer from a conflict over power and authority. When the members of a group are fighting over the issue of, whose power and authority is what, then the common commitment cannot develop. As a result the group cannot become a team.

(ii) The group has unstable interpersonal relations. In such a situation the members of the group will never experience any relatedness, belongings and collective accountability. In the absence of these elements a group cannot become a team.

Stephen Robbins points out the difference between a group and a team very nicely. He says that a work group interacts primarily to share information and make decisions to each member and perform within his or her area of responsibility. So it has no need or opportunity to engage in collective work that requires joint efforts. The performance of a group, therefore, is the summation of the contribution of each member. A group cannot create the positive synergy. A work team on the other hand generates the positive synergy through co-ordinated efforts. So the efforts of team members produce a level of performance which is greater than the sum of the individual inputs. If we compare a work group with a team, we observe the following things.

(1) The goal of a work group is to share the information whereas that of a team is to make a collective performance.

(2) A work group is neutral on the point of synergy but a team produces positive synergy.

(3) The accountability in a work group is individual but the same in the team is individual and collective (mutual).

(4) The skills of the members of a team are complementary and those of group members are random and varied.

Types of Teams - There are four most common types of teams which are as follows-

(1) Problem solving teams - These teams have 5 to 12 members who work in the same department. They have weekly meetings. Members share ideas or offer suggestions on how work-processes and methods can be improved. Quality circles in Japan are the best example of problem solving teams. Normally, these teams recommend the solution and very rarely have they the power to implement their suggestions.

(2) Self-managed work teams - These are composed of 10 to 15 members. They perform highly-related or interdependent jobs and take on themselves the responsibilities of their former supervisor. Thus, these teams undertake

(i) The work of planning and scheduling.

(ii) The work of task-assignment to members.

(iii) The work of control on performance.

(iv) The work of taking suitable action on problems.

(v) The work of selection of their own staff.

(vi) The work of evaluation of each other's performance.

(3) Cross-functional teams - These are the teams composed of employees from different work areas having the same hierarchial level who come together to accomplish a task. In fact, taskforce and committees are cross-functional teams. Cross-functional teams allow people from diverse areas to share their knowledge, develop and exchange new ideas and solve complex problems.

(4) Virtual teams - These are of recent origin. These teams have members who are physically dispersed. But virtual teams make use of computer technology to tie them together to accomplish a task. Though there is no face to face communication among the members, still the virtual teams do everything which the conventional teams do such as information-sharing, decision making and problem solving. For this purpose the virtual teams use e-mail, video conferencing and wide-area networks.

What TQM Needs - TQM is based on the theory of continuous improvement. Because zero defect work or perfection can become an ideology but not reality. As we learn more and more about our work, we feel that our past performance is not perfect and there is scope for improvement in one way or another. This is always true. Because, everywhere there is always a scope for improvement. So TQM as well as Kaizen works on the theme of continuous improvement. TQM believes that there are four general avenues for continuous improvement. These are –

(a) Improved and more consistent products and service quality.

(b) Faster work-cycle times. These cycles range from product development to order processing.

(c) Greater flexibility. It means there should be faster response to changing customer demands and new technology.

(d) Lower cost and less wastage. For this purpose eliminate scrap, unnecessary work-procedures, reworking and non-value adding activities.

TQM focusses on quality improvement by avoiding wastages and cutting unnecessary cost. TQM tries to prove that efficiency and economy, quality and thrift is possible simultaneously. It discards the restrictive notion that a gain on the parameter of quality is followed by a loss on the frontier of cost. TQM demands creativity and diligent efforts. It does not allow trade-off. TQM has customer-orientation. To become customer-centred TQM makes following suggestions to organisations.

(i) Greet the customers courteously.

(ii) Respond to the customers promptly.

(iii) Ask politely about the customer's preferences.

(iv) Assist customers in making decisions and selections.

(v) Speak softly but clearly to customers.

(vi) Call customers by name.

(vii) Provide customers correct product information.

(viii) Make employee appraisal and evaluation on the basis of customer service.

(ix) Reward employees for being customer-responsive, service-oriented and efficient.

(x) Cultivate the philosophy that customer is the purpose of our business and by serving the customer, we are actually serving ourselves.

TQM Tools - Several tools have been developed by quality-experts to improve the product quality and organisational performance. Following tools of TQM are more popular and widely used.

(A) Benchmarking – William H. Baker explains the concept of benchmarking as the practice of identifying, studying and building upon the best practices in one's industry or in the world. It is a process of finding the best available product features, processes and services and using them as standards for improving a company's own products, processes and services. Thus, benchmarking involves comparison of own products and processes with the very best in the world. This comparison provides an opportunity to introspect as well as the outlook to build and sustain quality. So, benchmarking is not mere irritation. It is much broader and deeper as well. Through benchmarking a company is not trying to follow the best practices which are already established by someone else, but it tries to create and develop its own quality-credentials by making a realistic analysis of the existing best quality.

Effective benchmarking starts with the customers. Customers' involvement helps the benchmarking process to pick up the right direction. Normally the organisations which successfully used benchmarking activated this process with customers' suggestions. For example, Ford did not build its world-class hot-selling automobile Taurus, simply, out of imagination in eighties. It collected the suggestions from customers and compiled nearly 400 features of a car which these customers treated as most important. Then, they surveyed the cars which were best in respect of each such features. Ford thus, searched out the best in each feature and tried to match and even top these best of the competition. The outcome of this consistent hard work was Taurus.

So we can state the following stages for effective and efficient benchmarking.

(i) Ask the customers, which are the most important product-features from their viewpoint.

(ii) Enlist these features and search out the products.

(iii) Make such products or services that will match or top the best of this competition.

Two basic types of benchmarking is observed –

(a) Benchmarking within the industry.

(b) Benchmarking across the industry.

When an organisation relies on the standards of its direct competitors for benchmarking, then it is described as benchmarking within the industry. The above case of Ford company is the example of benchmarking within the industry. Benchmarking acres the industry takes place when a company uses the standards of another company doing a dissimilar business to improve its performance, in respect of certain functions. The famous case of across the industry benchmarking is that of Xerox + L.L.Bean. Xerox learned the method of order processing function by studying Bean's mail order business. Xerox improved its order-processing function by studying L.L.Bean's widely respected mail order operations. Actually both companies are in different businesses. But their order filling processes are similar. Both companies handles such products which vary in size and shape widely. Therefore, most of the work has to be done manually by hands, but was able to pick up orders three times faster than Xerox. So Xerox minutely studied the operations of Bean. Bean did not use exotic methods. It emphasised and adopted the method of stocking high volume items close to packing stations. This strategy was known as 'high volume-short walk' strategy. Bean had got this beautiful idea from the suggestions of its employees. Xerox learned this lesson from Bean and followed the same method. By doing this Xerox could cut off its warehousing cost by 10 per cent.

From the examples of Ford, Xerox and Bean, it is observed that the best business-practices are developed by carefully and seriously listening to your customers as well as employees. Ford listened to their customers and Bean to their employees.

Limitations of Benchmarking - The study conducted by **Ernst** and **Young**, an accounting and consulting firm and the American Quality Foundation about international best quality practices found that benchmarking does not work well for every organisation. It observed that there is a strong relation between the financial performance of a company and its success at benchmarking against the world-class role-models. A number of similar limitations of benchmarking which became widest through research studies and actual practices of different organisations are as follows –

Benchmarking is found to work well for high performing companies. But for moderately successful companies, benchmarking does not make any real difference. Similarly, companies with low financial results reported negative experiences with benchmarking. Management scholars explain its causation in the following way. Low performing companies do not have the quality infrastructure ready to support the organisation-wide change necessary to eliminate the best. Therefore, quality experts suggest that instead of benchmarking, the low performing companies should focus on nurturing cross-functional teams, training and empowering workers. Especially, such companies who deal with customers directly, should adopt the earlier said methods to improve their performance on quality count.

The companies which had a frustrating experience with benchmarking made a common mistake. They selected inappropriate role models to benchmark against. They compared themselves against unattainable competitors. If an average company tries to compare and compete with a world class leader in that business area, the resulting experience, naturally will be most frustrating. In this comparison, such a company will find itself highly deficient in almost each aspect and area of operation. The result will be a wholesome disillusionment in the organisation. So it is most essential in benchmarking to choose an appropriate competitor. Such a competitor is the one whose performance level is attainable for our company. Thus, a company on the tenth position should select the company on the ninth or eighth position as its role model for benchmarking and a company on the second position should select the one on the top as its role model. If our role models are perfectly ideal entities, then, we simply start worshipping them and do not follow their route of improvement or imbibe their efforts and commitment to progress. As a result we remain where we are and the entire exercise of benchmarking becomes fruitless and futile. **Jeremy Main** provides tips as Benchmarks's Guide for successful benchmarking. Those tips are as follows–

(1) Don't go on a fishing expedition. Pick up a specific area in which you wish to improve. Then do a lot of homework. Study your own process thoroughly and minutely. Then choose a company which handles this process very well and benchmark your company against it.

(2) Send out the people who will have to make the changes. The people involved in the change process need to see it for themselves. If senior executives go outside, visit the role model organisation, come back and tell about benchmarking to the 'owners' of the process; then it will not help much. Because those who do, had not seen the ideal processing and those who saw it are not going to do the actual work. Therefore, there remains a discrepancy in perception and practice. What is perceived as right benchmarking is not practiced and what is actually implemented might not be according to the accurate perception of the ideal. To avoid such ambiguities, deficiencies and discrepancies, the performers and not the advisors should be sent outside to make a complete understanding of the functioning of the role model. However, care must be taken to keep the visitor-team small and visit duration short.

(3) Be prepared to exchange information, so you should answer each and every question which you asked the other company. You should not conceal any information about yourself otherwise suspicion and misunderstandings will develop.

(4) Avoid legal problems. Focus the discussion on existing products, business practices, human resources and customer satisfaction. These are the areas of improvement through benchmarking and exchange of information in respect of these topics take place smoothly.

But do enquire or try to learn about new products of the other company, price fixation methods, market allocation, strategies and similar issues because these issues may involve legal complications.

(5) Respect the confidentiality of the data you obtain. The companies sharing their information with you, will never like the same to reach their competitors. So maintain its confidentiality. This will also prove the fidelity in relationship with the benchmarked company.

(B) TQM Process Improvement Tools - Many times the quality deterioration occurs due to defective, erroneous or redundant processes. Therefore, TQM suggests process improvement and the development of productive processes. Again TQM insists on continuous improvement and continuous improvement requires lot of measurement. Because unless we measure, we do not understand what, where and how much we are lacking. Similarly, if we do not know our deficiencies, we cannot design an improvement programme. Therefore TQM managers make use of the following graphical and statistical process improvement tools, very often.

(1) Flow Chart - A flow chart displays decisions and activities sequentially. It is a graphic presentation of activities and decisions. Standard flow charts use symbols. These symbols are as follows- (a) The symbol of a box shows activities or events. (b) The symbol of a diamond shows key decision and (c) The symbol of an oval shows starting and end points. So usually a flow looks like the following figure.

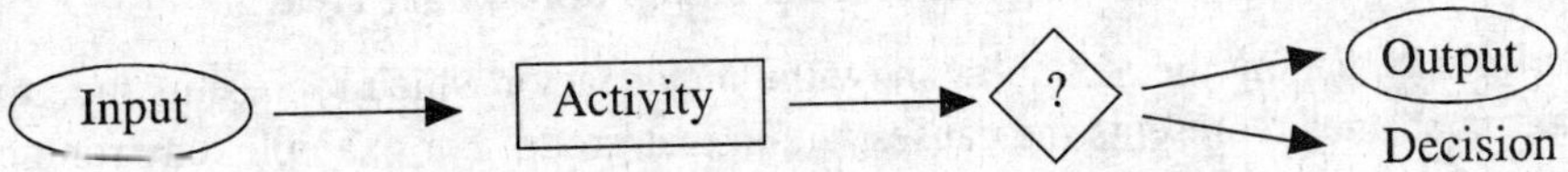

Fig. 6.1 TQM Process Improvement Tools

TQM teams observed three major advantages of flow charts, namely, (i) Increased efficiency (ii) Reduced cost and (iii) Elimination of wastage.

Flow charts make work-simplification by eliminating the wasteful steps and activities. It is also useful for sequencing. Sequencing is a process of arranging events in the order of their actual or desired occurrence. Managers in almost all specialised areas and working at different levels of management can use flow charts to identify and properly sequence important events and decisions. In fact, flow chart encourages analytical thinking. It inspires the managers to consider all relevant links as well as their proper sequence in a particular situation.

However flow charts suffer from two major disadvantages. They are -

(i) Flow chart does not indicate the time dimension. Therefore, it cannot display and inform the different time required to complete each step and make each decision.

(ii) Flow chart is not practically useful to complex situations in which several activities take place at once.

However, in essence, flow charts make the diagramatic display of activities in a simplified way. See the above diagram and the point becomes clear. The oval box shows the starting and end points. The starting point is also called as input and end point as output.

(2) Cause-effect Diagram - It displays diagrammatically the cause-effect analysis. It is also called as the fishbone diagram, because it roughly looks like a fish skeleton. The famous Japanese quality expert Kaoru Ishikawa popularised this method of diagramming and so these diagrams are also called as Ishikawa diagrams.

Fishbone diagrams help the TQM managers to visualise important cause-effect relationships. These diagrams are used to organise and show visually the possible cause of a problem or event. When an event takes place or a problem arises, it is the result of a number of causes which had acted severally as well as collectively. The major factors to which these cause relate are five in number, namely People, Material, Machines, Methods and Environment. A positive or negative effects occurs because either the environment is favourable or adverse, material is standard or substandard, adequate and available or non-available and inadequate; machines are suitable, sufficient and operative or unsuitable, insufficient and non-operative and the people handling the situation are a capable and willing or unwilling and incapable. Thus all such causes are responsible for a particular event. Following diagram will explain this fishbone style of displaying the cause effect relationship.

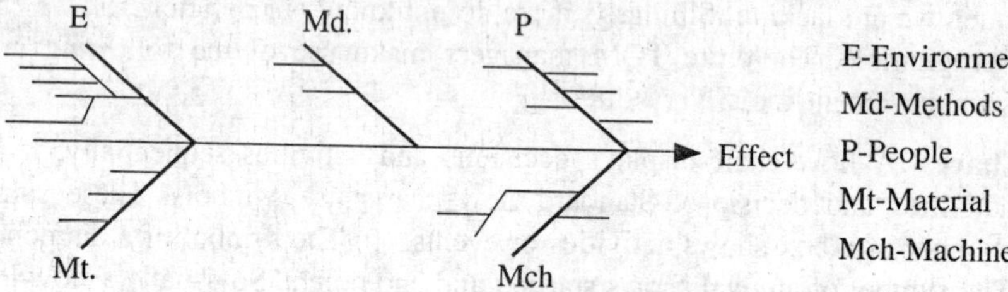

Fig. 6.2 Cause effect relationship of fish bone style

The dark lines heading the alphabets show the major factor which represents the group of causes and the small inner lines represents the causes within that group. For example, environment is a major cause of a particular output/effect. However, there are certain environmental elements which develop the supportive or nonsupportive environment. For example to develop TQM in an organisation environment plays a crucial role. The environment has two aspects, physical and non-physical. Physical environment creates working condition the elements of which are light, ventilation, temperature, physical facilities and amenities, etc. Non-physical environment relates to the work-culture which is composed of several elements such as shared values, beliefs, work-attitude, learning, etc. So each line in the fishbone diagram represents a cluster of causes and so can be dissected vertically as well as horizontally to indicate the specific causes contributing to the creation of a particular form of environment – Diagramatically all this appear like a fishbone skeleton.

Similar to environment, the other major factors like methods, people, materials and machines are also the cluster of causes. Fishbone diagram helps to systematically analyse all the pertinent causes of a particular effect and thereby, can develop suitable control means and methods to produce a desired outcome.

(3) Pareto Analysis - The famous quality experts **Joseph Juran** popularised this technique of Pareto Analysis. It involves constructing a bar chart. This bar chart indicates which problem needs most attention. In actual practice all problems are not of equal importance. Similarly, all people or events do not produce the same volume of impact. Italian economist **Vilfredo Pareto** (1848-1923) found out that there exists an eighty-twenty pattern in the wordly situations. That is 20 per cent of people or event are responsible for producing 80 per cent of results or impacts. Therefore by focussing on these twenty per cent things we can efficiently improve the situation significantly. In other words, an organisation can concentrate on certain selective few things which bring a big difference in the quality of performance and thereby, make a significant improvement.

Pareto analysis is a technique for separating the major problems from the minor problems. It looks for the 20 per cent possible causes which will lead to 80 per cent of problems. Thus, in every organisation there are relatively few people or events which account for maximum results and outcomes. So focus on these most effective, selective elements which mainly cause for quality and deterioration. By doing this the organisation can improve its quality significantly. The TQM efforts become successful when we consider the crucial elements in the organisation which cause the biggest difference. These elements are never in large numbers but still the magnitude of their impact on quality is very big. In the Pareto bar chart, the tallest bar represents these crucial elements which cause the common problems. So they require proper and prompt attention. The Pareto bar chart looks as follows.

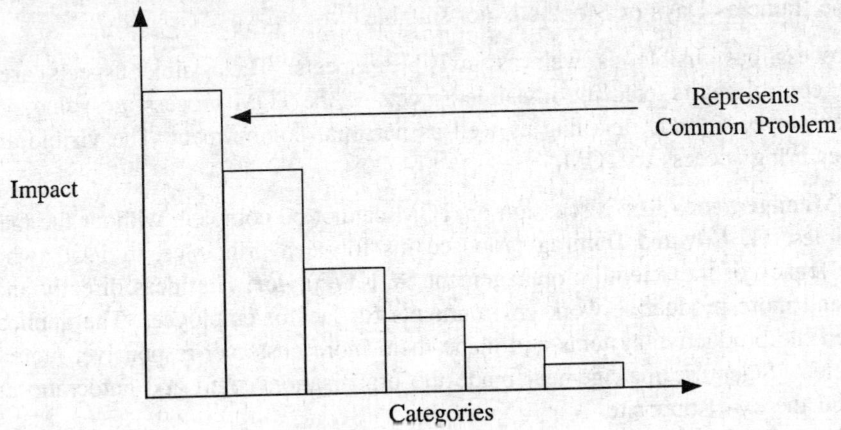

Fig. 6.3 Pareto bar chart

(4) Control Charts - This is a statistical method of quality control. It is economical and is useful for repetitive operations. A control chart is defined as the visual aid showing acceptable and unacceptable variations from the norms for repetitive operations. It helps to monitor the actual quality versus the desired quality measurements during repetitive operations. It is useful to keep key quality measurements within the acceptable range. The method of control chart is as follows-

To maintain the quality of a process, first the upper control limit and the lower control limit is fixed. Then the output of this process within these limits is treated as the output with the acceptable quality. A random measurement is made of the process output for quality checks and its results are graphically plotted on a chart which is called the control chart. Let us consider the following example in this regards-

Suppose the process relates to drilling and there is a job drilling hole of 5cm on 5,000 metal pieces. Now, in the first instance an upper and lower control limits are required to be fixed. Suppose the upper control limit is 5.1cm and the lower control limit is fixed as 4.9cm. This means that the holes having the measurements within this range will be treated as the processing of acceptable quality. Then the random measurements of the output are made during the process and they are plotted on the control charts. The process-operator has a simple visual aid which flags the control-limit violations and signals the need for a corrective action. Accordingly the operator makes the corrective action for quality maintenance and improvement, such as, cleaning or sharpening or replacing the drill.

This method of quality control is less expensive than rejecting the wrongly processed output completely.

Besides the above popular tools, histogram, scatter diagram and run charts are also used as TQM tools. Histogram is a bar chart which shows whether repeated measurements of a given quality characteristic conform to a standard bell shaped curve.

Deviations from standard need corrections. Scatter diagram is used to plot the correlation between two variables. Similarly, the run chart tracks the frequency of a given variable over time. It is also called a time-series chart or trend chart. Though these tools have specific utility, quality-experts feel that tools are necessary but not sufficient for TQM. TQM is a wider and continuous process of improvement. **Kreitner** holds the view that successful TQM requires long-term organisation-wide drive for continuous improvement. Therefore, an organisation should fix the time frame for TQM as years. The time frame as Days or Months is not suitable.

TQM process has visible as well as invisible aspects. The visible aspects are tools like benchmarking, control charts, etc. The invisible aspects of the TQM process are value-system of the organisation, employee attitude, learning as well as personal commitment. The visible and invisible aspects together bring success to TQM.

Deming Management - The discussion on TQM cannot be complete without the mentioning of Deming principles. **W. Edward Deming** proposed his fourteen principles, in 1950, which directly challenged the legacy of the scientific management by **F.W.Taylor**. His ideas directly and indirectly creates better and more productive work environments for lacs of employees. The application of his ideas revitalised the productive systems and made them more customer-responsive, more democratic and more efficient. Scientific management made the organisations rigid and autocratic and Deming management did the exact opposite.

Deming is respected as one of the major quality leaders. His 14 principles are the guidelines to top managers for quality improvement in their organisations. Deming believed that for TQM, an organisation has to change its philosophy because TQM means quality in everything. Therefore, his 14 principles should be understood as the total and comprehensive philosophy of management. These 14 points aim at altering the behaviour of managers and employees so that the organisations applying them will become a low-cost high-quality and highly productive suppliers of goods and services. Deming expects, that to sustain and improve quality, the organisation should honor and support the contribution of all its members.

A key imperative of Deming management is to learn to live without enemies. This is a transformation of the mindset. Deming explains that fear acts as a barrier to quality-improvement and so he suggests to drive out the fear. He questions the validity of the assumption that high quality means increased price and rejects the same. He says that constancy of purpose coupled with statistical quality control and joy in the work will lower the cost and drive the quality upward. Demings views that the manager should not merely detect the causes of failure but he is supposed to rectify the same. A manager, in Deming's view should seek out the causes of failure and correct them before the failure actually occurs. Deming is recognised as a revolutionary management scholar. The important aspects of his management philosophy are as follows.

(a) Quality improvement drives the entire economy. Deming feels that everybody wins when quality improves. Higher quality leads to more jobs. Quality improvement drives out wastage and inefficiency. It induces higher productivity, greater market share, new business and employment opportunities. How everyone can benefit from improved quality is explained by Deming in the following chart.

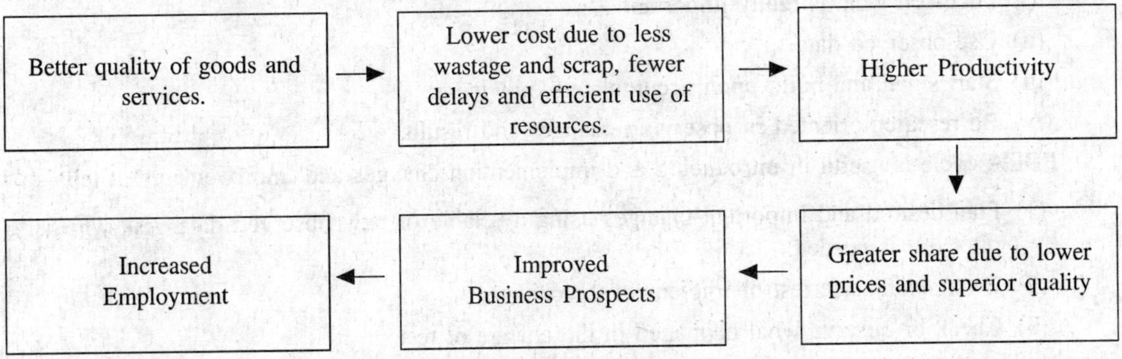

Fig. 6.4 Quality Improvement

(b) **Customers always come first -** In 1986, Deming wrote in his most influential text titled as Out of Crisis, that consumer is the most important part of the production line, So quality should be aimed at the present and future needs of the consumer. This view precisely explains the purpose of any action and decision of any employees of the organisation. Many a time quality of a product or service is decided by the customer. The capacity of the product to satisfy the needs of customer is viewed as quality and higher is this capacity, better is the quality of the product or service. Therefore, Deming adopts a most practical approach by relating TQM with customers need satisfaction. The view of Deming is his outward looking. Different from scientific management which is inward looking. As such it focuses on creating and increasing the efficiency regardless of customers. Deming pinpoints the purpose of creating efficiency and quality and that is customers satisfaction. This was revolutionary in 1950.

(c) **Do not blame the person, fix the system -** Deming does not blame people for low quality of output. He criticises the usual practice of finding out somebody for mistakes, defects and deficiencies and placing the entire blame on him. On the other hand, Deming insists on fixing the problems and redesigning the system. He emphathetically argues that people can and will turn out superior quality, if the system is redesigned to permit them to do so. Deming's argument has a research base. His research convinced him that the system is typically responsible for 85 per cent of substandard quality. System, according to him, means management, work rules, technology, organisational structure and culture. For TQM Demings suggests that the manager should treat the employees as internal customers. He should listen to them and should respond to their ideas and suggestions for improvement. Deming explains that the person who actually makes the job knows its intricacies and niceties much better than the supervisor and manager and so his ideas and suggestions can be more fruitful for TQM.

(d) **Plan-Do-Check-Act -** One important aspect of Deming management is the making of informed decisions. Deming says that the managers should base his decisions on data. More the decisions are based on data, greater is their accuracy, utility and practicality. Deming recommends a vehicle for this process, which is popularly called as the PDCA cycle. The PDCA cycle has 4 aspects namely Plan, Do, Check and Act. According to this cycle whenever decisions and actions are to be made then the first step should be planning. Then doing the task, then checking the results and then acting for rectifications and improvements. This PDCA cycle according to Kreitner gives the following tips to managers.

(i) Focus on what is really important.

(ii) Use observed data.

(iii) Start small and build upon accumulated knowledge.

(iv) Be research-oriented in observing changes and results.

PDCA cycle is useful in introducing and implementing changes and improvements. It tells -

(1) Plan desired and important changes using available or new observed data. Ask whether a pilot test is needed.

(2) Do a small-scale test or implement the change.

(3) Check or observe what happened in the change or test.

(4) Act after studying the results. Act on the lessons learned. Think if any predictions be made as a basis for new methods.

At the heart and soul of Deming management are his fourteen points or principles. They are as follows-

(i) **Constant purpose -** Strive for continuous improvement in products and services so that you can be competitive. Competitive survival is possible when the organisation can create joy in work and keep control on quality.

(ii) **New philosophy -** Deming explains that management should make wiser use of all resources. This awakening about the realities of new economic age is must.

(iii) **Give up quality by inspection -** Deming suggests to build the quality in products right from the beginning. He feels that inspecting and rejecting the faulty products is unnecessary.

(iv) **Avoid the constant search for lowest-cost suppliers -** The practice of each time searching out a supplier quoting the lowest price is not suitable for TQM. Deming tells to build long-term, loyal and trusting relationships with a single supplier.

(v) **Seek continuous** improvement in production processes for greater productivity and low cost.

(vi) **Train everyone -** It is necessary that the employees must have clear idea of how to do their job. Informal learning should be avoided and formal training to everyone should be provided.

(vii) **Provide real leadership -** Real leadership involves providing individualised help.

(viii) **Drive fear out of workplace -** According to Deming no one can put his best performance unless he feels secure. Employees continue to do wrong things when they are afraid of asking questions about why and how. Secure means not afraid to ask questions and express ideas. When job-security is lacking, quality improvement is very difficult to make.

(ix) **Promote teamwork -** In the views of Deming customer satisfaction should be the common goal of the working of all departments and functional specialists. So remove the barriers and develop team spirit.

(x) **Avoid slogans and targets -** Demings insists on avoiding slogans like zero defect, pride in quality, etc, because he views that for real quality improvement, the manager should provide leadership and make system improvement continuously. Because according to Deming system is largely responsible for product quality. If the manager blames the people that do not control the system, then this will only breed the resentment. So correct the system, help for the individual measure and improve productive processes for TQM.

(xi) Get Rid of Numerical Quotas - Deming strongly rejects the idea of MBO, numerical quotas and statistical goals. Because once employees start pursuing the numeral quotas aggressively, then they start neglecting quality, continuous improvement and cost reduction. This attitude of employees paralyses the TQM efforts.

(xii) Remove barriers that stifle the pride in workmanship - Deming views that the pride of workmanship is most essential for quality and improvement. As such he points out the barriers that stifle the pride in workmanship, are as follows- (a) Poor management (b) Inadequate instructions (c) Faulty equipment (d) Pressure to achieve numerical goals.

(xiii) Education and self-improvement are key - Deming management argues that greater knowledge means greater opportunity. Education enhances career opportunities. Deming management links personal career growth with quality improvement efforts. So Deming says that continuous improvement should be the number one career objective of everyone in the organisation.

(xiv) The transformations is everyone's job - Deming management involves in the transformation process of upper, middle and lower levels of management. Upper management converts the new philosophy into flow charts and training and declare system aim. Middle management implements the 14 points under the direction of top management and lower management will form inter-discipline teams targeting specific inhibitors to performance. When entire organisation works together, the quality starts developing.

Contribution of Joseph Juran - Juran wrote a book on quality control which is titled as the Handbook of Quality Control. Juran worked with **William Schewart** and was involved in developing the concepts of statistical process control. The credit of quality triology goes to Juran. He developed the concept and showed that it is similar to financial planning, control and profit improvement. Quality triology includes quality planning, quality control and quality improvement.

Some of Juran's ideas of quality improvement are close to those of Deming. However, Juran disagrees with Deming on the issue of amount of change in management approach necessary to create a total quality system. Deming believed that the focus on quality requires a revolution so he supplies a philosophy for guiding the big change efforts. Juran on the other hand, views that a change in the quality can be made like any other shift in the organisation. Thus, quality improvement does not necessarily require a change and modification in the entire set-up. By usuing the current framework of the organisation, the decisions and actions for change in quality and improvement is possible. So unlike Deming who insists on important changes for quality, Juran advises great managerial efforts for quality enhancement.

Contribution of Kaoru Ishikawa - Ishikawa is recognised for his contribution in respect of quality circles. The concept of quality circles development in Japan in 1960 and around. Quality circles are voluntary problems solving groups committed to improve quality and reduce cost. Each such group consists of five to ten employees belonging to the same work area. They meet regularly to discuss and devise the ways and means to improve quality and reduce cost. Normally, the quality circles hold meetings every week. The usual duration of these meetings is one to two hours. Such meetings are conducted during company hours. Quality circles emphasise on voluntary participation of members. They try to make use of the creative potential of employees. Usually quality circles function in the following way-

(i) Members of quality circles collect and analyse the data in respect of different issues relating to work, quality and productivity. Then they weed out the trivial issues and focus on major issues.

(ii) The quality circles generate innovative ideas to solve the problems and improve the quality productivity through the brainstorming sessions of its members.

(iii) After adequate debate and discussion on different ideas and alternative solutions, the members of the quality circles forge consensus decisions and these decisions are communicated effectively to all concerned.

Quality circles have following three major benefits – (i) Direct cost saving. (ii) Improvement in the relationship between workers and management. (iii) Increased employee commitment.

However certain precautions are necessary for introducing quality circles. They are as follows-

(i) The quality circles should not be dictated by management. They should be voluntary groups of employees who have a lot of concern for quality.

(ii) Quality circles should emerge in an evolutionary manner. They should not come out revolutionarily. A revolution has the feature of a sudden outbreak or happening. Evolution is slow, gradual well directed process. It involves development. In fact, most of the time evolution is developmental. Therefore, this evolutionary development of quality circles has following major aspects-

(A) Employee training (B) Supportive supervision and (C) Team building

(iii) Training of members is an important factor deciding the success and effectiveness of quality circles. Initially, the members of the quality circles should be given the basic techniques of problems solving. Similarly, at least, one member should be given extra training in leadership. Again, a few more members should also be trained as facilitators. These facilitators will help the members to organise the groups. They should also encourage the employees to think, talk, listen and care as members of a team. This is necessary to dislike and diminish the employee habit of isolated performance of a job.

Usually, the foreman of the work group plays the role of the leader. He guides, assists and encourages the quality circle. He is responsible for development and successful working of the quality circle. However, he should not participate in the discussion of the members. Mostly, the quality control and productivity improvement techniques are discussed in the meetings of quality circles. Quality circles not only identify the problems but also make recommendations to management and watch their execution.

Quality circles can improve the quality successfully when its members offer wholehearted cooperation and participation. A steering committee should be formed to decide the policy regarding quality circles and to determine their pattern of working. Intensive training about the working of quality circles should be given to the members and facilitators. A code of conduct for the members is a must and should be strictly followed. Quality circles should report to the management periodically, the problems and its solutions which are discussed therein. The management, too, should consider the suggestions of quality circles seriously and implement them sincerely. Otherwise quality circles will lose their importance, validity and utility. In fact, quality circles relieve the employees from their routine, repetitive and monotonous tasks and give them the opportunity to use their creative intelligence. Quality circles encourage insightful thinking, team spirit, confidence, loyalty, self-respect among the workers to develop and similarly enhance productivity, quality, better utilisation of resources and reduction of cost and wastage.

Besides quality circles, Ishikawa introduced the concept of internal customers. He argued that all quality efforts should be directed towards customers. He emphasised and focussed on the concept of customers. His views explain that unless and until we feel that our work output is going to be offered to customers, we will never become serious about its quality. Unless we perceive that the receiver of our output is our customer and we are his supplier, we cannot become cautious and careful about our offering. The concept of custodianship immediately changes our mindset and develops quality-orientation in us. Ishikawa applies the concept of customers and applies it in the interdepartmental dealings which constitute the internal work-procedures and work-flows in an organisation. So he suggests that the output of one department should be given to another department in such a way and with such a work and quality perception that as if this another department is the customer of the first one. This approach of 'internal customer', develops interdepartmental communication, service-attitude and co-operation. It breaks down the bureaucratic mentality and perceptions. It removes and finishes the selfish and narrow outlook and attitude of looking only to the benefits and interests of our department even at the cost of other departments. The interdepartmental conflicts automatically end up when one department looks to another department as its customer and promptly serves it also. Internal custodianship enlightens employees about the purpose of their decisions and actions. They realise for what and for whom do they work. When they understand that their work-output is of great use and value to others, they work with the highest sense of responsibility. Because, then, they know that their work will produce either satisfaction or dissatisfaction among its receivers and accordingly it will bring for them either the rewards and recognitions or the curses and criticism. Naturally quality consciousness and responsibility start grooming up.

International Quality Study (IQS) - Ernst and **Young**, along with the American Quality Foundation conducted study on international quality practices. The researchers examined 500 organisations and nearly 900 management practices to determine as to which extent which organisations employ these practices and what is their impact on organisational output. The selected organisations were from the industrially leading nations such as Canada, USA, Germany and Japan. Similarly the participating organisations were from a variety of industries such as automobile, computer equipment and supplies, commercial banking and acute care hospitals. The study revealed the following –

(1) There is no one best approach to quality improvement for all organisations. Rather, a situational or contingency approach is warranted.

(2) Different quality initiatives are appropriate for differently performing companies. So for low, medium and high performing companies, the quality measures have to be different.

(3) The model which has a crawl-walk-run method of quality improvement, informs the companies where and how to begin.

(4) IQS demonstrates systematically, how the hapazardly implemented quality practices at once end up in disappointment and cynicism about quality movement. The model suggests a bite by bite approach for quality improvement.

IQS model fixes three important criteria of organisational performance, such as profitability, productivity and quality. It recommends different quality emphasis for high-performing, medium-performing and low-performing companies. It views that quality emphasis and performance should be suitably interlinked, then only the quality improvement can take place in the right direction and for accomplishment of the right goals.

The quality emphasis by IQS are as follows-

(A) Quality emphasis recommended for high-performing companies -

(1) Market research and world-class benchmarking.

(2) Innovation and creativity.

(3) Technology enhancement.

(4) Employee empowerment and self-managed teams.

(5) Teamwork among senior managers.

(B) Medium-performing companies -

(1) Process simplification and cycle time reduction.

(2) Strategic planning for quality.

(3) Teamwork among middle managers and departments.

(4) Relationship with suppliers.

(C) Low-performing companies -

(1) Development and delivery of reliable products/services.

(2) Training in customer relationship.

(3) Training in basic problem solving.

(4) Cost cutting and elimination of non-value adding activities.

(5) Customer involvement in cross functional teams.

Quality in Service Organisations - Ron Zemke and Dick Schaaf, the specialists in service quality identified and profiled 101 service organisations in United States which were widely respected. They pointed out that successful service organisations do the following.

(i) They listened, understood and responded to the evolving needs and constantly shifting expectations of customers.

(ii) They establish a clear vision about superior service, communicate it to all employees and ensure that service quality is positively and personally important to everyone in the organisation.

(iii) They establish concrete standards of service quality and regularly measure their performance against those standards.

(iv) They hire good people, train them carefully and extensively and empower them on behalf of customers.

(v) They recognise and reward service accomplishments on individual and group basis and celebrate their success.

Kaizen – Kaizen is the Japanese word which means change for better. Kaizen is a technique of total quality management. Kaizen aims at quality improvement on continuous basis. Kaizen argues that progress is possible everyday. Each day provides opportunity for improvement and progress. This approach of continuous and consistent improvement makes Kaizen different and distinctive. Kaizen expects such a continuous improvement not only in work life, but also in personal and social life. Kaizen involves managers as well as workers in the process of continuous improvement. Kaizen has the following characteristics.

(i) Kaizen is a process of gradual improvement.

(ii) Kaizen is a people-oriented and process-oriented movement.

(iii) Kaizen is equivalent to total quality management.

(iv) Kaizen includes problem identification and solution.

Kaizen emphasises on long-term and permanent effect of improvement. It involves small and gradual improvements on continuous basis. It does not believe in making sudden and dramatic changes which usually happen in the western companies. Kaizen says that the philosophy of continuous improvement should be properly and fully internalised by the people. Improvement should become a way of everyday living of people. It should become the part of personality of them. This is possible when the improvement process is gradual involving small changes and continuous.

Kaizen tries to develop better work methods and procedures with an objective of enhancing quality and reducing cost. For this purpose people should be made to think in that direction. Particularly the operating level employees can develop beautiful and practically usable ideas in this respect. So Kaizen involves all people in the process of improvement. On this point Kaizen differs from innovation. Innovation involves, contrary to Kaizen, only a few top managerial personnel in the process of designing the improvement programme.

Kaizen is a broad concept. It is not confined only to the efforts of improving product quality. It is equivalent to Total Quality Management (TQM). It works for overall improvement. In companies it aims at improving the complete work life. Therefore, it includes efforts to enhance productivity, quality, automation, discipline, customer-awareness, product development, innovation, workers' participation in management and such other elements which lead to better management practices. As such Kaizen covers a variety of activities, which can be grouped into three categories.

(a) Customer-awareness activities, quality control activities, robotics, quality circles and suggestion scheme.

(b) Kanban/Just in time inventory management, quality improvement activities, zero-defect production, timely production (just in time production), activities related to small work groups.

(c) Automation, productivity improvement, labour management, development of co-operation and harmony, productive maintenance and prevention of error.

Kaizen rejects and hates the attitude of self-contentment. It focuses on attitude of identification and solution. Everyday improvement and continuous progress is the spirit of Kaizen. So Kaizen builds awareness among employees about problems, encourages people to reject *status quo* and trains them in the development of solutions. Kaizen is based on the philosophy of excellence. It is employed at managerial group and individual employee level.

Kaizen at Managerial Level – Infact management is responsible for creating and developing an atmospheres of quality awareness and improvement and so it is the first pillar of Kaizen. Management should develop suitable strategy and atmosphere for continuous improvement. It should boost up the morale of the employees for progress and improvement. Kaizen philosophy expects that managers should devote fifty per cent of his time for improvement activities. Normally, Kaizen at managerial level deals with the following problems-

(i) Labour movements, wasteful activities and wastage of human energy.

(ii) Problems relating to production, processing and material handling.

(iii) Just in time inventory management and automation.

(iv) Systems improvement.

Kaizen is all pervasive. It touches all every aspect of the organisation and each activity in the organisation. It attempts to improve all functional systems of the organisation such as planning and control, decision making, organisation and information management. Kaizen first considers the way of making an operation and then introduces necessary modifications and improvements therein. Kaizen gives the message to employees – use your intelligence and not money. It clarifies and proves that improvement and progress is the outcome of creativity and inventive thinking and so cannot be attributable to spending. More expenditure does not assure greater progress and higher profits. Fertile brains and operating hands make improvements.

Kaizen at the managerial or organisational level strives to accomplish the following objectives.

(i) To achieve highest quality with optimum efficiency.

(ii) To adopt just in time management.

(iii) To eliminate labourious and strenuous operations, through work simplifications and process improvement.

(iv) To develop and use suitable technology, equipment, machinery and tools to increase the level of efficiency and quality.

(v) To develop and adopt the practice of open thinking and questioning for continuous improvement.

(vi) To develop teamwork and cooperation.

Kaizen at Group Level - At group level, Kaizen is implemented through small groups and their activities like quality circles, productivity councils, zero-error groups, suggestion-schemes, security and safety measure groups, MBO method group, etc. These groups are formed to fulfill different objectives. The groups may be temporary or permanent. When they are temporary, they usually take shape of an *ad hoc* committee or temporary task group, which have specific problem assigned to them, and provide solution thereon. Once the purpose of the group is served, the group is dissolved thereafter. On the other hand, a permanent group has to follow a particular procedure for problem identification and solution. It is as follows –

(i) Identification of the problem area

(ii) Searching out the reasons of the problem

(iii) Consequences of the problem.

(iv) Developing alternative solutions for the problem.

(v) Testing and evaluating the utility and effectiveness of these alternatives during their trial implementation.

(vi) Establishing for revision, modification and improvement.

The group-members collectively offer the solution and suggests the decisive action to the management.

When the work is organised through such small groups, it produces the following advantages –

(i) Development of team spirit and co-operation

(ii) Group members understand their jobs/roles and allocate duties among themselves in better ways. Effective co-ordination and communication is possible.

(iii) Development and increase in morale

(iv) Workers learn new skills and knowledge and group activities and collective working.

(v) Group becomes self-dependent and start solving the problem independently. This relieves the management from solving the operational level problems.

(vi) Labour-management relations improve.

Kaizen at personal level - This involves suggestion scheme as its important ingredient. It suggests smart working instead of hard working. It considers the suggestions of the workers for improvement. These suggestions relate to workers own job, use of raw material power and other resources, work-environment, machinery, equipment and processes, work-procedures and routines, product quality, customer services and customer relations as well as new products. Suggestion scheme has the following advantages –

(i) It builds awareness among workers about Kaizen.

(ii) Employees get a chance to discuss with their foremen about the working conditions in their department.

(iii) Communication among employees improve.

(iv) Employees help managements to solve problems.

(v) Two way communication between workers and management develops.

(vi) Employees get opportunity for ,self-development.

Kaizen at personal level is successful when employees enthusiastically participate in the suggestion-scheme. For this purpose the management should create positive atmosphere. It should encourage the employees and appreciate their suggestions. It should provide necessary training in this regard. The analytical and creative thinking of the employees should be developed and induced. Their suggestions should be seriously and studiously considered by management and accepted wherever possible.

Japanese management has made the best utilisation of suggestion schemes. Usually it accepts those suggestions of workers which

(i) Simplify the work procedures

(ii) Reduce cost, wastages and work

(iii) Increase the safety and security in work

(iv) Improve the quality of work

(v) Make savings in time and money

(vi) Make the work more productive

Distinction between Kaizen and Innovation

Improvement and progress is the need for survival and growth. This rule applies to individuals as well as, to organisations, also. There are two basic approaches to improvement. One is Kaizen and another is Innovation. The Kaizen way of improvement is followed by Japanese corporations and it consists of small and gradual changes on a continuous basis for improvement. It involves rapid, sudden and dramatic changes for improvement. Innovation includes - (a) big technological changes (b) acceptance of modern management, and (c) modern production techniques. - The difference between Kaizen and Innovation can be clarified with the help of following points –

(1) Kaizen emphasises on long-term and permanent improvement whereas Innovation expects dramatic change for short-term improvement.

(2) Kaizen is a continuous process of improvement. Innovation is discrete and intermittent.

(3) Kaizen involve small changes which are gradual and continuous. Innovation consists large changes which are dramatic. However, they are introduced abruptly.

(4) Kaizen involves each and everybody in the organisation in the process of improvement. Innovation involves only a few or a particular group of employees in the process of improvement.

(5) Kaizen perceives innovation as a collective activity and so emphasises on teamwork. Innovation uses individual ideas and personal efforts for improvement. Unlike Kaizen which encourages group thinking. Innovation does not encourage group ideas and team creativity. On the other hand, it depends mostly on individual imagination and creativity.

(6) Kaizen has a thrust on repairs and revisions, maintenance and modifications. It includes upgradation and enhancement. Innovation, on the other hand, displaces the old ideas and practices and introduces the radical and new one. It dismantles the old system and replaces it by the new one. Innovation, unlike Kaizen, does not believe in improving the existing system for better performance and results. The basis of innovation is technological improvement and development of new technology. As against this Kaizen focuses on human element and attempts to improve the performance of managers and workers. Because Kaizen strongly believes that development and progress of any kind is the result of consistent and sustained human efforts and not due to technology alone. As such, Kaizen advises therefore, for improvement use your brains and not money. For improvement Kaizen uses the traditional and modern techniques in combination. It says that modern tools and techniques, often, emerge from traditional knowledge. Innovation, on the contrary, insists on discarding old ideas and knowledge. It argues that unless old ideas and practices are abandoned and discarded, new ideas and practices will not find a place for their introduction. The ideological base of Kaizen is the famous Zen philosophy of Japan. Kaizen assumes that the present day technology, practices and methods are the modified version of the traditional knowledge.

(7) Kaizen does not require huge capital investment. It emphasises on creative thinking and the involvement of people. Innovation presumes that improvement is a capital intensive activity and it requires therefore huge capital investment.

(8) Kaizen perpetuates small changes for improvement. Kaizen feels that improvement should be people-driven. Innovation is basically technology-driven. So many times the innovated practices and methods are later ignored and discontinued. So innovation sometimes loses its spirit and remains simply as a formality.

(9) Innovation has the objective of increasing the profitability of the organisation. On the other hand, Kaizen aims at improving the total quality. It tries to achieve excellence.

(10) Experts view that Kaizen is useful for moderately and gradually growing economies, whereas innovation is useful for fast growing economies.

ISO Quality Standards - ISO is the International Organisation for Standardisation. It was established in 1947' to develop common standards in many areas at international level. It is located in Switzerland. Its members come from the standardisation bodies in well over ninety countries. ISO first published its quality assurance and quality management standards in 1987 and in 1994, republished its updated version. These quality standards are referred as ISO 9000 standards. These ISO 9000 standards apply to all kinds of organisations and in all kinds of areas. These include manufacturing, processing, forestry, computers, services, retailing, banking, construction, insurance, health care, research, publishing, shipping, agriculture, aviation, government, education, biotechnology, tourism, consultancy, etc. Presently ISO 9000 has become most popular in Europe, USA and everywhere around the globe. Because -

(i) ISO 9000 controls quality and simultaneously saves money.
(ii) Customers expect ISO 9000.
(iii) Competitors prove their superiority by using ISO 9000.

The international standardisation is must for almost all organisations. It is needed due to the following reasons –

(i) There is a worldwide progress in trade liberalisation.
(ii) Today, no industry can claim to be independent. There is interpenetration of sectors.
(iii) Global standards are fastly developing for the emerging technologies.
(iv) Communication and completion has increased tremendously.
(v) Developing countries require standardisation infrastructure for productivity improvement.

ISO 9000 is a certificate stating that your factory, office, laboratory or organisation has met the quality management requirements determined by the International Organisation for Standardisation. It is awarded by an independent auditor after testing the factory, office, laboratory or organisation and verifying whether they qualify to the standards set by ISO in respect of quality management. ISO 9000 is to be looked as a set of generally accepted evaluation principles for documenting quality procedures. Nowadays, ISO standards have become an internationally recognised system which is comprehensible for buyers and sellers. ISO certificate gives a competitive advantage. In the view of quality expert **Ronald Henkoff,** ISO is not an acronym in any language. It is an official nickname, derived from the Greek word '*isos*'. Isos means equal.

ISO 9000 applies to all types of organisations irrespective of their size or nature of work. It helps organisations to achieve standards of quality that are recognised and respected throughout the world. The greatest virtue of ISO 9000 is its universality.

ISO quality standards are based on the following important equation which describes and interprets the concept of quality. Quality means characteristics. Every product (including services) has certain characteristics. These characteristics are derived from stated or implied needs. The set of these special need-oriented characteristics make up the quality of the product. Like a product, a process, person, activity, system, machine, service, department, organisation also has a quality in the sense that all these entities possess certain characteristics. Thus, every entity has characteristics and so some type of quality. This quality should be upto the mark so that it can satisfy the specific need of the customer. In other words every entity must possess the required quality or quantity requirement. These quality requirements lead to standards. Though, ISO does not define the term standard, it uses the term standard to suggest the concept of an expectation, obligation, requirement or norm which ISO wants organisations to accept. There is an another definition of the term standard which suits the concept of standard by ISO. Standards are documented agreements containing technical specifications or other precise criteria to be used consistently as rules, guidelines, definitions or characteristics to ensure that materials, products, services and processes are fit for their purpose. Thus according to the notion of ISO – Quality = Characteristics = Requirements = Standards.

ISO views that a wide variety of elements influence the quality of company's products or services. So these elements should be controlled. For this purpose quality system should be developed. A quality system is a network of processes made up of elements. These elements include responsibilities, authorities, relationships, functions, plans, procedures, practices, processes and resources. The purpose of establishing a quality system is to fulfill quality management requirements and to assure that customer receives quality products and services. The quality system is composed of quality assurance which controls the work and management process. Quality assurance is composed of activities whose purpose is to demonstrate that an entity meets all quality requirements. Quality assurance activities develop the confidence in the managers and workers in respect of compliance of all quality requirements.

The quality system of an organisation consists of the following-

(i) **Quality Leadership Programme** - It controls the management process of the company.

(ii) **Quality Design Programme** - It controls the company's process of quality design.

(iii) **Quality Purchasing Programme** - Controls quality purchasing process of the company.

(iv) **Quality Contracts Programme** - Controls contract process.

(v) **Quality Production Programme** - Controls production process.

(vi) **Quality Inventory Programme** - Controls inventory management process of the company.

(vii) **Quality Inspection Process** - Controls company's process of testing and inspection.

(viii) **Quality Nonconformance Programme** - Controls nonconformance process of the company.

(ix) **Quality Measurement Programme** - Controls company's measurement process programme.

(x) **Quality Service Programme** - Controls service process

(xi) **Company's Quality Audit Programme** - Controls internal audit process of the company.

(xii) **Quality Training Programme** - Controls company's training process.

Each of these twelve quality requirements stated above can be further subdivided into ten additional requirements, which are as follows -

(i) Policy requirements (ii) Planning requirements (iii) Procedural requirements (iv) Instructional requirements (v) Personnel requirements (vi) Organisational requirements (vii) Documentation requirements (viii) Record keeping requirements (ix) Technological requirements (x) Resources requirements.

The first set of 12 requirements indicate as to which functional areas need to be controlled. Similarly, the second set of requirements specify as to how this control can be exercised within these 12 requirements. This second set indicates the form of requirement. In other words the first set can be described as programme requirements and second set as process requirements. Because the first set tells us what quality programmes should be developed and the second set informs which tools, techniques, methods and processes should be developed within each quality programme prescribed by the first programme set.

ISO 9000 requires a company to document its processes and quality systems. It should assure that all employees understands and follow the guidelines of these documents and continuously check and monitor its quality system with the help of internal and external auditors. Also with their suggestions necessary modifications in the system should be incorporated.

There are three standards, namely, ISO 9000, ISO 9002 and ISO 9003. A company can develop quality-system that meets the quality-requirements specified by one of these ISO standards. Among ese standards ISO 9001 is the roadmap for the ISO 9000 family of publications. It explains briefly hat each ISO publication is about and also discusses some concepts and general theoretical points. his 9001 is a quality assurance model made up of 20 set of quality system requirements. This model pplies to organisations that design, develop, produce, install and service products. The quality-system requirements of 9001 are as follows-

(1) Management Responsibilities -

(i) Define the policy of the organisation regarding quality.

(ii) Define the organisational structure that you will need in order to manage your quality system.

(iii) Define quality system responsibilities, give personnel the necessary authority to carry out these responsibilities and that the interaction among these personnel are clearly specified.

(iv) Identify and provide required resources to people for managing and verifying the work of quality system.

(v) Appoint a senior executive to manage your quality system, give him authority and define procedure to be used for reviewing the quality system.

(2) Quality System Requirements -

(i) Develop a quality system and also its manual.

(ii) Develop and implement quality system consistent with your quality policy.

(iii) Develop quality plans showing your intention to fulfill quality system requirements. Such a quality plan should be about products, processes, projects and customer contracts.

(3) Contract Review Requirements -

(i) Develop and document procedures to co-ordinate the review of sales orders and customer contracts. Make sure that customers are included in the review process.

(ii) Ensure that all contractual requirements are acceptable.

(iii) Develop procedures specifying the amendments in customer contracts and their communications throughout the organisation.

(iv) Develop a record keeping system to review the customer's orders and contracts.

(4) Product Design Requirements -

(i) Develop and document procedures to control the product design and development process. Also develop procedures for product design and development.

(ii) Identify the groups to be involved routinely in the product design and development process.

(iii) Develop procedures to identify, document and review design input requirements. Also ensure that design laws, ambiguities, contradictions and deficiencies are resolved.

(iv) Develop procedures to verify and control product design output and to ensure that designed output meets the needs of the customers.

(v) Ensure that all product design modifications are documented, reviewed and formally authorised before their circulation and implementation of changes.

(5) Document and Data Control -

(i) Develop procedures to control quality system documents and data and changes therein.

(ii) Develop procedures to review, approve and manage quality systems data and documents.

(6) Purchasing Requirements -

(i) Develop procedures to control selection of subcontractors, use of purchasing data and verification of purchased products.

(ii) Ensure that purchase order documents precisely describe what the organisation wants to buy.

(7) Customer Supplied Products -

(i) Examine the products to confirm that right items were shipped without loss/damage.

(ii) Prevent product loss, misuse, damage or deterioration through proper storage and security.

(iii) Clarify who is responsible for maintenance and control of the products when they are in your possession.

(8) Product Identification and Tracing -

(i) Identify and document procedures from purchase of supplies to servicing, through every stage like handling, storage, production, delivery, etc.

(9) Process Control Requirements -

(i) Develop and document procedures to plan, monitor and control your production, installation and servicing processes.

(ii) Design a record keeping system monitoring and controlling process personnel and equipment.

(10) Product Inspection and Testing -

(i) Develop procedures to inspect, test and verify incoming, in process and final products meet all specified requirements.

(ii) Ensure that incoming products are not used until they are verified on the criteria of specific requirements.

(iii) Ensure that work in progress meet all the requirements before specified.

(iv) Develop amd make the staff use documentation for testing and inspection activities.

(11) Control of Inspection Equipment -

(i) Develop the procedures to control, calibrate and maintain the inspection, measurement and test equipment which demonstrate that your products conform to specified requirements.

(ii) Ensure that your equipment are secure, appropriate and effective.

(12) Inspection and Test Status of Products -

(i) Ensure that each product passes through the required test and inspection and identified as pass or fail.

(ii) Document the test status of each product throughout the production, installation and servicing process.

(iii) Use and sell only those products which have passed all tests and inspections.

(13) Control of Non-conforming Products -

(i) Develop procedures to prevent use of non-conforming products.

(ii) Develop procedures to record, review, retest and rework the non-conforming products.

(14) Corrective and Preventive Action

(i) Develop procedures to prevent and correct the non-conformities without delay.

(ii) Ensure that potential non-conformities are routinely detected and prevented.

(15) Handling, Storage and Delivery -

(i) Develop such product handling methods and procedures which prevents product damage and deterioration.

(ii) Designate secure areas to store and protect products.

(iii) Develop procedures to preserve and issue products, detect damage or deterioration in them.

(16) Control of Quality Records -

(i) Define and identify the quality information to be collected.

(ii) Develop a quality record keeping system and procedures to maintain and control it.

(17) Internal Quality Audit Requirement

Develop internal quality audit procedures-

(i) To determine the compliance of quality activities and results with written quality plans, procedures and programmes.

(ii) To evaluate the performance of your quality system.

(iii) To verify the effectiveness of your corrective action.

(iv) To plan audit activities and to record the audit results, corrective action and its consequences.

(18) Training Requirements -

Develop quality training procedures -

(i) To identify the need for quality system training.

(ii) To ensure that quality training is provided to the needful and people are able to perform the quality system jobs.

(iii) To make everyone understand how the quality system works and to keep accurate and appropriate training records.

(19) Servicing Requirements -

Develop and document quality service procedures, to verify the quality of product service and reporting it.

(20) Statistical Techniques -

Select the statistical techniques to establish, control and verify process capabilities and product characteristics and ensure that these procedures are documented.

Besides ISO 9001, there is 9002 and 9003 also. In ISO 9002 quality assurance model which is composed of quality requirements similar to ISO 9001. ISO 9001 and ISO 9002 has that same set of quality requirements with a small exception that ISO 9002 omits product design requirements against 20 contained in ISO 9001 model. Again ISO 9003 has a set of 16 quality requirements. All of them are same of those of ISO 9001. However ISO 9003 omits 4 quality requirements of ISO 9001 which are as follows -

(i) Product design requirements.
(ii) Purchasing requirements.
(iii) Process control requirements.
(iv) Servicing requirements.

ISO 9000 has a number of benefits, which prove its importance. They are as follows -

(i) Documentation of processes takes place.
(ii) A greater quality awareness is developed among employees.
(iii) Increased productivity and positive change in the culture of the organisation.
(iv) Installation of an overall quality system.
(v) ISO 9000 certificate provides the company a competitive edge and advantage over its competitors.
(vi) Customer's requirements are met.
(vii) ISO 9000 provides a higher perceived quality and possible greater customer satisfaction.

However, a number of management scholars point out the limitations of ISO 9000 and criticise it in the following way.

(i) ISO 9000 neither evaluates the efficiency of the operation, nor product quality, nor improvement trends.
(ii) ISO 9000 does not ensure quality products and services. It does not insist on continuous improvement. It does not empower employees or develop team work.
(iii) It does not require companies to show that they know how to reduce their operation cycle time, cut inventories and speed up deliveries. ISO virtually ignores the mantra of modern quality management.
(iv) ISO companies need not have to demonstrate that now their customers are happier than they used to be.
(v) Richard Buetow, Director of corporate quality at Motorola comments that with ISO 9000 you can still have terrible processes and products. You can certify a manufacturer that

makes life-jackets from concrete, as long as, those jackets are made according to the documented procedures and the company provides the next kit with instructions on how to complain about defects. This is absurd.

In spite of these limitations, it is a notable fact that ISO focuses on the adherence to thr practices specified by the company. Its purpose is to assure the customers that certain practices and documentations are in conformance with the quality system identified by the firm. ISO 9000 provides the documentation to show customers how the company trains employees, test its products and corrects problems. In a global market the purchasing agents are interested in seeing the proof that the vendor company has a documented quality system, which is followed strictly.

SIX SIGMA - Sigma is a Greek letter which is written as 'σ': It is used to describe standard deviation. Standard deviation is a measure of variation. Six sigma is seen as the most powerful breakthrough management tool ever devised.

Six sigma is a business process which allows companies to drastically improve the bottomline by designing and monitoring everyday business activities in ways that minimise wastage and use of resources while increasing customers' satisfaction. Six sigma guides companies into making fewer mistakes in everything they do. It also guides companies in eliminating losses in quality at the earliest possible occurrence.

Actually six sigma is broader than a quality control programme. Quality control programme have always focussed on detecting and correcting the industrial, commercial and design defects. Six sigma goes beyond this. It provides specific methods to recreate the process. So that defects and errors never arise in the first place. Six sigma initiative helps the companies to increase the market share, decrease costs and grow profit margins. By usuing business strategies six sigma produces superior financial results. These business strategies receive the company and help it to march ahead of its competitors in terms of increased market share and profitability.

Sigma is a measure of variation within a process. A process is a set of activities which work on same input to give a particular output. Sigma measures as to how much good or bad is the performance of a process. It measures how many mistakes a company makes while doing whatever it does from manufacturing to delivery.

Six sigma is the sigma level of performance a company is aimed at. When a company is working at six sigma level, it is making only 3.4 defects/errors per million opportunities. So, at six sigma level, the company achieves 99.99966 per cent good quality. Thus to achieve the six sigma level, a process should not produce more than 3.4 defects per million opportunities. The statistical representation of six sigma describes quantitatively how a process is performing. A six sigma defect is defined as anything outside customers' specifications. A six sigma opportunity is the total quantity of chances for a defect. In simplest sense, six sigma is a measure of quality that strives for near perfection. Six sigma is a disciplined, data driven approach and methodology for eliminating defects in any process from manufacturing to marketing and from products to service. Six sigma is not a hapazard do better programme. It is a management philosophy which focuses on eliminating mistakes, wastages and reworking. It gives people well defined roles and a clear structure for their tasks. Six sigma combine people-power with process-power. It has the primary goal to improve the financial bottom-line. It strives to improve quality, make customers happy and add money to bottomlines.

Benefits of Six Sigma - Six sigma offers the following major benefits to organisations.

(i) Increased productivity.

(ii) Reduction in operating cycle time.

(iii) Reduction in defects, errors and mistakes.

(iv) High quality level of products and services.

(v) Dramatic improvement in the bottomline.

(vi) Standardised improvement methodology for organisations.

(vii) A set of tools and techniques to simplify improvement efforts.

(viii) Greater customer satisfaction.

(ix) A combination of people-power and process-power for improvement.

The fundamental objective of sigma methodology is the implementation of a measurement-based strategy that focuses on process improvement and variation reduction. Six sigma approach emphasises on -

(i) Use of data.

(ii) The identification of root cause of the issue.

(iii) Systematic analysis.

(iv) Involvement of people close to the problem in solving it.

(v) Customer satisfaction.

Usually, six sigma entails five key steps which are as follows -

(a) **Define** - Identifying the customer requirements, clarifying the problems and setting the goal.

(b) **Measure** - Select what needs to be measured. Identify information sources and data.

(c) **Analyse** - Develop hypotheses, Identify the key variables and root causes.

(d) **Improve** - Generate solutions and put them into action. Either modify the existing system or process or develop new one. Quality costs as well as benefits.

(e) **Control** - Develop monitoring process for continuous high quality performance.

The above five steps form the six sigma methodology which is known as DMAIC, i.e. Define, Measure, Analyse, Improve and Control - DMAIC is an improvement system for the existing processes, which look for incremental improvement. Besides this, there is another six sigma methodology which is used to develop new process or products at six sigma quality level. It is known as DMADV improvement system which means Define, Measure, Analyse, Design and Verify. This DMADV can also be employed if a current process requires more than just the incremental improvement.

Six sigma process makes use of black belts, green belts, master black belts and champions. These are the employees who participate in the implementation of six sigma methodologies. Black belts are those people who completely understand the application of statistics to business problems. Green belts are those people or six sigma leaders who form teams and work on improvement projects in their own areas. At the highest level are the Master Black Belts. They have technical process proficiency. They are the people who train and mentor other belts. Further, in six sigma terminology, the top management people or functional leaders are known as Champions. They are the people who ensure smooth progress of six sigma projects.

Six sigma is useful to companies in different ways. Companies can set performance goals with the help of six sigma for individuals as well as for the entire organisation. Dramatic improvement in existing processes is possible with the help of six sigma. More specifically six sigma can -

(i) Make processes more rigorous, by using data and by making operating decisions in time.

(ii) Cultivate customer loyalty by delivering superior value.

(iii) Strengthen and reward team work.

(iv) Easily clearly and empirically measure even the most complex performance.

(v) Achieve quantum leaps in product performance.

(vi) Accustom managers to operate in fast moving internal business environment.

(vii) Displays marked place conditions outside the company.

(viii) Reduce variations in service processes such as time from order to delivery.

(ix) Provides a high quality service experience.

(x) Improves financial performance through cost saving from projects and expanded operating margins.

Six sigma methodology gives us three important messages -

(i) We can improve our performance, if we can analyse it. We can precisely make the analysis of what we can measure. And we can measure what we can define correctly. So the path to improvement is Define - Measure - Analyse - Improve - Control. In other words, we measure what we value or what we care about. When we start measuring our performance, we begin to improve the same.

(ii) Time plan is very important. Stick a date to everything. If we try to work without deadlines, nothing will be got done. Lithergy, indiscipline and inaccuracy will prevail in the organisation and will badly hamper the organisational performance.

(iii) Be specific in job-allotment. Assign a very specific job to each individuals in your team. Define clearly the responsibility and accountability. This will remove and avoid confusion and duplication. It will remove and avoid confusion and duplication. It will decide the direction of work and will also guarantee the successful completion of work and efficient and accurate performance.

The popularity of six sigma is increasing day by day. Companies are accepting six sigma because it improves teh profitability as well as quality an efficiency. Prior to six sigma, quality programmes bringing improvements had no visible impact on the company's net margin. With the implementation of six sigma, profit margin grows by 20 per cent every year, with each sigma shift (upto 4.8 to 5 sigma). Infact, six sigma breakthrough strategy broadens the definition of quality to include economic value and practical utility to both, the company and the consumer. According to this definition, quality is a state in which value entitlement is realised for the customer and provider in every aspects of the business relationship. This definition of quality focuses on value entitlement. Value represents the economic worth as well as practical utility of the product for the company and customers. Similarly, entitlement for the company means to have a rightful level of expectation to produce quality products at the highest possible profits. And entitlement for the expectation to buy high-quality products at the lowest possible cost. Six sigma provides maximum value to company and customers. It provides increased profit to companies and high quality products at low cost to customers.

Six sigma is a performance target that applies to a single critical to quality characteristic (CTQ) and not to the total product. Six sigma means that within a single product the average opportunity for a defect of a CTQ is only 3.4 defects per million opportunities. Six sigma does not mean that 3.4 products out of million are defective. Therefore, experts of six sigma never state that a product is six sigma, rather they say that the average opportunity for non-conformance within a product is six sigma. The higher the sigma level, the less likely a process will produce defects. Each sigma results into creation of an exponential reduction in defects. Consequently as sigma increases, product reliability improves at a disproportionate rate. As a result of this, the need for inspection and testing of products automatically diminishes. Similarly, cost reduction decrease in the operating cycle time and increase in the customer satisfaction are the other benefits. Six sigma level is nearly the perfection in the process.

Six Sigma Breakthrough Strategy - There are eight steps of the breakthrough strategy to achieve six sigma performance in a process, division or company. These eight stages are Recognize, Define, Measure, Analyse, Improve, Control, Standardise and Integrate. Every organisation has three basic levels. The highest level is the business level. The second level is the operations level and the third is the process level. The breakthrough strategy applies to each level of the company and achieves different results which is complementary to each other. The success of six sigma depends on the extent to which it transforms each of this level and thereby, improves the overall quality and profitability of the organisation.

We can have a six sigma roadmap which has four categories. And in each category falls the two out of eight primary components of the breakthrough strategy. This whole chart appears as follows -

(1) **Identification stage -** Objective - to identify the key business issues - The breakthrough strategy phases - (i) Recognize (ii) Define

(2) **Characterisation stage -** Objective - to understand current performance levels - The breakthrough strategy phases - (i) Measure (ii) Analyse

(3) **Optimisation stage -** Objective - to achieve breakthrough improvement - breakthrough strategy phase - (i) Improve (ii) Control

(4) **Institutionalisation stage -** Objective - to transform the day to day business methods and means - The breakthrough strategy - (i) Standardise (ii) Integrate

A detailed discussion of these stages is as follows -

(1) **Identification Stage -** This is the stage where a company begins to understand the fundamental concept begins to understand the fundamental concept of six sigma. It also knows about the breakthrough strategy as a problem solving methodology with a unique set of tools. At this stage key business issues are identified. Actually a company's business growth depends on how it meets the expectations of its customers about quality, price and prompt delivery. Now a company's ability to satisfy its customers depends on the process capability. A process is any activity of group of activities that take an input, adds value to it and provides an output to customers. These processes are of different kinds such as manufacturing, sales, administrative, service process, etc. If there occurs a variation in the process, it has a direct impact on cost, operation cycle time and number of defects. All these adversely affect the level and magnitude of customers' satisfaction. Identification allows the organisation to recognise how their processes affect profitability and then define the elements critical to business processes.

(2) **Characterisation Stage -** Characterisation aims at understanding the current performance levels. It has two components, measuring and analysing. At this stage characteristics critical to quality are described and measured. Characterisation points out the goals which a company should aspire to achieve. It fixes a baseline or a benchmark and provides a starting point for measuring improvements. At this stage an action plan is created to close the gap between the current performance. At this stage the six sigma black belts select one or more of the key characteristics of the products and then create a detailed description of every step in the process. The black belts then make the necessary measurements, record the results on process control cards and estimate the short-term and long-term process capability.

(3) **Optimisation Stage -** Optimisation stage is aimed at achieving the breakthrough improvement. It has two components, namely, improve and control. Optimisation chalks out the steps to be taken to improve process and reduce the major sources of variations. To identify the key process variables, certain statistical experiments are conducted. Black belts use this data to fix the control points for process improvement. At the optimisation level, the vital and important variables, which have the greatest impact are determined. Usuing various types of analysis black belts determine the variables which exert the highest influence. Optimisation uses the knowledge gained through analysis for process improvement. Optimisation controls and improves the key variables which have the greatest impact on the important characteristics of the products. This is done by modification of the process, development of better process limits, and selection of better material and equipment. As a result of these improvements, there is an increase in the profitability, customers' satisfaction and shareholders' value.

(4) **Institutionalisation Stage -** At this stage the application of results of the complete breakthrough strategy are woven into the company's culture. There are two phases of institutionalisations: One is standardisation and another is integration. With these two phases the company brings the six sigma into its daily routine. The standardisation phase ties together many six sigma projects within a business and works to identify best practices and standardise them within and across businesses. Standardisation of processes brings effectiveness. Because it uses those methods and processes which are optimised and are successful. Integration modifies the management processes of the organisation by taking advantage of the best practices identified through six sigma projects.

Breakthrough Strategy at Process Level - The breakthrough strategy at process level is described in a nutshell as RDMAICSI, i.e.,

R - Recognise functional problems that link to operational issues.

D - Define the processes that contribute to the functional problem.

M - Measure the capability of each process that offers operational leverage.

A - Analyse the data to assess prevalent patterns and trends.

I - Improve the key product/service characteristics created by key processes.

C - Control the process variables that exert undue influence.

S - Standardise the methods and processes that produce best in class performance.

I - Integrate standard methods and processes into the design cycle.

A detailed discussion of each step is as follows -

(i) **Recognizing Functional Problems -** Process problems are hierarchial in nature. They are interconnected to operational issues. Operational issues are tied to the support systems. And ultimately support system are linked to business issues like customers' satisfaction, profitability and shareholder's value. It is essential to understand this hierarchial nature.

(ii) **Define the Process -** Functional problems are of three types - (a) Product problems (b) Service-related problems (c) Transactional problems - These problems are developed by the process which create products, services or transactions. Infact all processes consist of a series of steps events or activities. These steps are usually repetitive and maximise the labour or material efficiency and effectiveness. Independently, none of these steps can create any output. Normally, organisation focus on outputs and ignore and avoid the comparison of processes. Process-maping is not done regularly. Similarly processes are not linked to common operational issues and problems. Too much critical processes are never mapped and linked. When a problem arises in a process, sporadically teams are called to solve the problem. But in the absence of process mapping the problems continue as unrecognised. On the other hand by way of process-mapping, a company can create data-flow map. It can see how this information affects accounting, material acquisition, engineering and such other processes. Process-mapping itself can lead to improvement.

(iii) **Measuring Process Capability -** Many organisations do not know the capability of their processes. They do not measure how well a process is performing. As a result they are unware of their business capability. Actually process capability impacts every aspect of the business. A poor process leads to quality problems, affecting operating cycle time, inventory and employee morale. In order to understand the process capability, the organisation should do the following -

Organisation should do the following -

(a) Break apart the elements of a process.

(b) Identify the critical characteristics.

(c) Define map-related process.

(d) Understand the capability of process.

(e) Discover the weak links.

(f) Upgrade the capability of the process.

(iv) **Analyse the Data -** Data are collected to decide the relationship among the factors in the process and to determine the direction of improvements. This phase of analysis determines how well or how poorly the process is performing currently and identifies the possible root cause of variations in quality. This data analysis can reveal the basic nature and the behavior of the process. It shows the capability and stability of the process over a period of time. It also tells us the physical limits of a process. If the inherent capability is poor, then black belt project is terminated and if the analysis shows potential for improvement, the project can progress to the next phase.

(v) **Improving Key Characteristics -** Improving a product means improving the process. So the Black Belts focus on the critical to quality characteristics in a product and then make efforts to improve the capability of such characteristics. For this purpose, They screen the variables having greatest impact on the process. The Black-belts improve the critical to quality characteristics by following the methods given below -

(a) Isolate the key variables.

(b) Establish the limits of acceptable variations and

(c) Control the factors affecting these limits.

The capability of CTQ characteristics is the result of machine capability, material capability, human capability and management capability. Now to improve the capability of a CTQ, we have to understand CTQ and define its performance objectives. So, firstly, define the scale of measurement such as centimetres, grams, etc., of that of a CTQ. Secondly, identify and assess the performance standards. Thirdly, decide the parameters to be change and also decide the extent to which they should be changed to achieve the desired goals. These three steps translate the practical problems of improving the CTQ capability into a statistical problem. Thus a process and CTQ can be changed by specific amounts.

(vi) Controlling the Key Process Variables - After improving the process Black Belts must implement measures which will control the key variables within their operating limits.

(vii) Standardise the Methods - One of the key principles of Design for Six Sigma (DFSS) is to make use of existing components, processes and practices which have proved to be the best in class. At this stage the standard methods and processes are integrated into the design cycle. It is often easier and economical to make changes in the design itself than to make equivalent changes in the process. It is always unwise to create new processes for every new design or evaluation of an existing design.

Implementation and Deployment of Six Sigma - The company has to decide as to how to focus and deploy the Six Sigma Breakthrough Strategy to address the key business priorities and strategy issues. All the strategies for implementation and deployment must flow down from the executive leadership. For the successful implementation of six sigma following important things should be developed -

(1) Highly visible management commitment. The employees should experience that the leadership is active.

(2) A measurement system to track the progress. By this tangible picture of the efforts of the organisation is provided and also the accountability for initiative is clarified.

(3) Internal and external benchmarking of the products, services and processes of the organisation. This brings an emotional touch when actual and real market position of the company is discussed.

(4) Stretch goals for the people to change the processes to get the work done. Then people do not simply tweak the existing process. This speeds up the improvement process.

(5) Educate all levels of the organisation. Train people.

(6) Tell success stories to demonstrate the application and results of six sigma breakthrough strategy.

(7) Develop Champions and Black Belts to promote the initiatives and to provide planning, teaching, coaching and consulting for people at different levels of the organisation.

Stages of Six Sigma Implementation - There are usually six sigma stages of implementation, which are as follows-

(i) Discover - Recognise the need for six sigma and explore its potential impact on your company.

(ii) **Decide** - Executive leadership approves the six sigma initiative and then define the purpose and scope of six sigma.

(iii) **Organise** - Establish financial targets, set time lines, Train senior executives as well as the deployment champions.

(iv) **Initiative** - Create deployment plans for metrics, communications, human resources, training of Black Belts, funding for Black Belt projects.

(v) **Deploy** - Train Project Champions and Black Belts.

(vi) **Sustain** - Train six sigma Green Belts and process improvement Team Leaders.

The stages of the six sigma implementation comprehends all activities such as identifying the need, purpose and scope of six sigma, establishing the time and financial targets and plan training, communication, etc., actually training the six sigma players, etc. All these lead to a purposeful and effective implementation of six sigma.

Creating Six Sigma Focus - The six sigma implementation is deeply influenced by the way of focus which a company develops. A company can choose any of the following alternatives.

(1) **Focus on project cost saving** - A company which has a focus on cost saving, selects those projects which have a potential of reducing the fixed and variable cost. This approach has limitations as it does not consider the project's effect on the root drivers of process capability.

(2) **Focus on the deliverable** - Such a focus makes the company concentrate on product defects and their removal. However it is short-sighted because it considers the product-defect and not the process or system which makes the products.

(3) **Focus on process** - Here the focus is on the process capability. This approach is described as the best one, because it attacks the root causes of product defects and customer dissatisfaction. According to this approach a company identifies processes which are critical to value and which operate at low sigma levels. However, this approach requires strong cross-functional co-ordination. Because correction in one process in a particular department has application on the other departments of the same company.

(4) **Focus on the Problems** - Normally, six sigma projects focus on root causes and inputs and not on outputs or problems and symptoms. But some companies develop six sigma projects focussing on problems affecting sales and customers' satisfaction. Accordingly they make efforts to solve such problems and increase the product sale.

SIX SIGMA ROLES AND RESPONSIBILITIES -

(1) **Executive Management** - It must inspire, own, fund and drive the six sigma initiative. It establishes the corporate level goals and targets and determines the time frame of performance expectations. It decides the six sigma focus also.

(2) **Senior Champion** - It is a corporate level strategy position. Senior champion is fully responsible for the day to day corporate level management of six sigma. He directly reports to the office of the president of the company. He should possess the leadership qualities and must be capable of doing the right thing right now.

(3) **Deployment Champion** - It is a strategic business unit (SBU) level position. They are responsible for the development and execution of six sigma implementation and deployment

plans. They also look after the efficiency and effectiveness of the six sigma support system. They report to senior champions and area vice president.

(4) **Project Champions -** It is business unit level position with tactical importance. He is responsible for identification, selection, execution and follow up of six sigma Black belt projects. They are 'trial bosses' who drive the six sigma initiative. Their leadership must be strong, sound, consistent and prevalent. They develop and see over the details of implementation and deployment plan.

(5) **Deployment Master Black Belts -** This position requires high technical orientation and is posted at business-unit level. They are responsible for long-range technical vision of six sigma. They develop technical road map and work technically across functional areas and businesses. They ensure that six sigma technologies, methods, procedures and tools and their knowledge is translated into training materials, manuals and operational documents. They spread the seeds of six sigma.

(6) **Project Master Black Belts -** They work at business unit level. They are transfer of six sigma knowledge to Black Belts. They act as teachers of six sigma. They also work as mentors. They need strong stage presence, credible leadership ability and sound technical knowledge.

(7) **Project Black Belts -** They are on site experts and are described as Black Belts. They are responsible for project-execution and realisation of the targeted benefits. They develop and lead cross functional process improvement teams. They utilise and disseminate the six sigma tools and methods. They advise the middle management on formulation and implementation of process improvement plans.

(8) **Process Owners -** They are actually line managers. They ensure process improvements.

(9) **Six Sigma Green Belts -** They work in specific areas and take on mini-projects.

(10) **Project Team Members -** They provide project-specific cross-functional support. Under the guidance of Black Belts, they can gather and analyse data and help to sustain the gains created by six sigma.

Mikel Harry and Richard Shroeder provides the typical initial stages of implementation and deployment of six sigma, which are as follows -

(i) Generate executive leadership interest in six sigma.
(ii) Conduct six sigma executive briefing.
(iii) Decide to move forward with six sigma implementation.
(iv) Conduct six sigma Champion Training.
(v) Select the first cluster of businesses for six sigma implementation.
(vi) Identify Black Belt candidates for training.
(vii) Conduct six sigma Black Belt training.
(viii) Conduct standard six sigma process review.
(ix) Make second assessment of implementation.
(x) Make decision to expand the initiative.
(xi) Review six sigma deployment schedule.
(xii) Integrate lessons learned into strategy.

Mikel Harry and Richard Shroeder also gives details of the roles to be performed by six sigma players. They are as follows -

(A) Champions - (1) Create the vision of six sigma for the company. (2) Define the path to implement six sigma across the organisation. (3) Develop a comprehensive training plan for implementing the breakthrough strategy. (4) Carefully select the high impact projects. (5) Support development of statistical thinking. (6) Recognise people for their efforts. (7) Make Black Belts to focus properly. (8) Make sure that project opportunities are acted upon by the organisational leadership. (9) Realise the gains by supporting six sigma projects through allocation of resources and removal of roadblocks. (10) Implement Black Belt recommendation.

(B) Master Black Belts - (1) Develop and deliver training to various levels of the organisation. (2) Understand the big business picture. (3) Assist in project identification. (4) Coach and support Black Belts in project work. (5) Take on leadership of major programmes. (6) Participate in project reviews and offer technical expertise. (7) Facilitate sharing of best practices across the corporation.

(C) Black Belts - (1) Acts as breakthrough strategy experts and stimulate the champions. (2) Lead and direct the teams in project execution. (3) Identify the barriers and report progress to appropriate leadership levels. (4) Mnage project risk and prepare a detailed project assessment during measurement phase. (5) Determine the most effective tools to apply and ensure that the results are sustained. (6) Teach and coach the six sigma breakthrough strategy methods and tools.

(D) Green Belts - (1) Employees throughout the organisation executing six sigma as a part of their overall jobs. (2) Focus on project related to their day to day work. (3) Lead small scale improvement projects within their respective area. (4) Help to deploy the success of six sigma techniques. (5) Do the legwork in gathering data and executing experiments in support of a Black Belt project.

Black Belts play a very important and useful role in six sigma projects. They possess the knowledge and skills to implement, sustain and lesd a highly focused six sigma initiative. They characterise and optimise key processes which here influence on the business. They identify and execute projects which will reduce errors and defects in the industrial and commercial processes as well as producta and services. Black Belts solve problems by identifying and focusing on the key factors at the causation. In fact the term 'Black Belts' first coined by **Mikel** in 1980. It was used for those project leaders who were trained in statistical problem solving. The term was taken from the physical sport of Karate. Similar to Karate, six sigma, too, requires mental discipline and systematic and intensive training. Black Belts have to develop patience, persuasion, creation and imagination. Black Belts need not only the intellectual ability and drive but also the desire and tenacity to rethink and relearn the business. Black Belts are important because -

(i) They dramatically raise an organisation's sigma level and simultaneously deliver financial gain to the bottom line.

(ii) They stimulate management thinking by posing new ways of doing things.

(iii) They challenge conventional wisdom by demonstrating successful applications of new methodologies.

(iv) They seek out and pilot new tools, create innovative strategies and train others to follow in their fool steps.

(v) They take responsibility for achieving financial results.

Black Belts have to perform the following tasks -

(a) Mentoring - Develop a network of six sigma individuals.

(b) Teaching - Provide formal training of employees in new tools and strategies.

(c) Coaching - Supply one to one support to people.

(d) Transfering - Pass on new tools and strategies through training, workshops, case studies and symposiums.

(e) Discovering - Find application opportunities for the six sigma strategies and tools internally and externally.

(f) Identifying - Highlight business opportunities through partnership with other organisations.

(g) Influencing - Sell the organisation on the use of six sigma strategies and tools.

Effective Black Belt leaders possess the following characteristics -

(1) Ability to understand the big picture of the business.

(2) Focus on results and committed to excel.

(3) Possess excellent communication skill.

(4) Capable of consulting, mentoring and coaching and allows failures and mistakes with a recovery plan.

(5) Possess creative, critical and out of box intellect and views criticism as a pushing force to step forward.

(6) Drives change by challenging traditional wisdom, developing new methods, tools and strategies and accept the responsibility for choices.

(7) Unites and inspires a team to a core purpose and encourages commitment, dedication and teamwork.

(8) Empathises, acts decisively and promotes win-win solutions.

(9) Anticipates and confronts problems early and corrects them.

(10) Manages effectively even with limited resources.

(11) More concerned with business success than personal gain.

Black Belts have to become risk-takers. They need to possess the leadership skills and to teach employees to analyse and control their work processes. Their greatest challenge is to make everybody internalise and practice the new behavior. For this purpose they must sustain extraordinary level of energy and focus.

Six Sigma in the service industry - Infact service constitutes a large portion of a company's cost. Service industry contains many invisible processes and its products are not tangible. A service transaction has a number of process steps. Six sigma methodology breaks service transactions into individual process steps in order to create greater efficiency at lower costs. The time of operations (operating cycle time) and customers' satisfaction are the two important components affecting the quality of services and costs. By measuring the operating cycle time, a cost can be attached to each operation. Similarly, six sigma strategy can view statistically customer requirements and then quantitatively evaluate how well the customers' expectations are being met.

Thus six sigma can improve cycle time and customers' satisfaction.

❑❑❑

CHAPTER 7

EXCELLENCE SKILLS

Excellence is philosophy. It is a kind of mindset. It is a way of doing everything in life. It is a habit. It becomes a character. It is a style of living the life. Corporate or organisational excellence is the results of collective excellence of the people in the organisations are composed of people. Great organisations are made so by the people working therein. When people continuously and consistently excel in their work, organisation marches ahead on the path of excellence. Excellent organisations have thus excellent people. In other words, personal excellence is the cornerstone of organisational excellencc. However, personal excellence cannot be an effortless gift. To achieve excellence, one has to develop himself in the appropriate form and order. For this purpose one has to acquire and imbibe certain skills. Some of these important skills necessary for excellence are discussed at length below.

Creative Insight - The terms creative insight, creative thinking, creativity are used to denote the same meaning and creativity leads to innovation. It is a kind of thinking which generates new ideas, new products, new patterns, etc. The essence of creativity is its outcome which is a new thing. The novelty of the outcome decides, in fact, the strength of creativity. Therefore, creativity as a process is mainly known by its results. **Kreitner** describes creativity as the reorganisation of experience into new configurations. **Sidney J. Parnes** in his essay in *Futurist* (18th August, 1984), titled as, Learning Creative Behavior, explains the concept of creativity in the following manner. Creativity is a function of knowledge, imagination and evaluation. The greater our knowledge, the more ideas, patterns or combinations we can achieve. But merely having the knowledge does not guarantee the formation of new patterns, the bits and pieces must be shaken up and interrelated in new ways. Then the embryonic ideas must be evaluated and developed into usable ideas. Thus, creativity needs knowledge, ability, imaginativeness and evaluativeness. The three in combination develop the creative ability. Knowledge develops understanding. Ignorance leads to wild and irrational thinking and imagination. Imagination based on knowledge, generates ideas having potential to solve some problem or provide some useful benefits. Such results of imagination need to be tested and retested on the criteria of their practical application and need satisfaction. The outcome of creative thinking must be real, useful and fulfilling. This distinguishes creativity from mad ideas. Creativity is an ability whereas insanity is a disability. An insane also thinks differently and comes out with unusual ideas. But such ideas do not carry logic, reality and utility. Creative people, though, think differently and propose something unconventional, it has substantial capacity of problem solving. So creativity always solves one problem or other by making use of some kind of unconventional thinking and by developing new tools techniques, methods and resources for the same.

In order to understand more about creative thinking, let us go to the background and learn the concept and process of thinking. Thinking consists of the cognitive rearrangement of both, the information from the environment and the symbols stored in long-term memory. Thinking processes information during the period between a stimulus event and the response to it. Thus, thinking as set of cognitive processes mediate stimuli and responses. In the process of thinking we often make use of words and language. So thinking and language are closely related. Language-symbols have sophisticated the human thinking which is absent in the thinking of animals. Besides language, another type of symbols used in thinking are images. Images in the first instance are in the form of incomplete, abstract pictures. They are constructed as complete pictures from elements stored in long-term memory.

Our thinking can be classified into two broad categories, such as, Austic thinking and Directed thinking. Austic thinking is highly private and makes use of symbols which have very personal meaning. Dreams are the example of austic thinking. On the other hand, Directed thinking is aimed at solving the problem or creating something new. Normally, problem solving thinking is goal directed and is motivated by the need to reduce the discrepancy between one state of affairs and another. A problem arises when there is a conflict or difference between two situations and we, simultaneously, wish to attain a particular goal. In other words, something we want to do and the situation does not permit us for the same. Thus arises a problem. So in the process of problem solving, we try to reduce the discrepancy between the goal and the situation. For this purpose our thinking process makes use of two important things, one, the information stored in our long-term memory and two, our here and now perception of the problem situation. Our memory tells what is done in similar situations elsewhere and what can therefore be done. Our perception of the problem situation gives us the knowledge about the gravity and magnitude of the problem and also the limitations within which we have to operate. Thus, we came to know what we can do as well as what we cannot do. All this thinking is rule-based. These rules relate to the logical analysis of the information. Thus, in most of the situations, our problem solving thinking is guided by the rules of logic and the processing of information available. Many times it becomes so mechanical, that it loses the liveliness and purpose-full thinking. It develops certain mental blocks and produces regimentation in devising solutions. So sometimes, negative attitude, inactivity and helplessness springs up from such thinking. A 'can't do anything' mentality gets developed. Especially when the problem is unusual, emerged for the first time and is not tackled earlier, the attitude to adjust with the problem, limit one's activities and patiently suffering becomes habitual. Infact problem solving, thinking is basically aimed at producing a solution the problem and not simply understanding and coping with the problem. Giving up a goal or a noble cause because of a non-permissible situation is a defeatist attitude. Problem solving thinking should act as the trouble shooter not as the trouble-acceptor. Therefore if rule-based thinking cannot find out a solution, then change the rules, develop new rules, make new configurations but any how find out a solution to the problem. Make out of box thinking. Human brain has tremendous fertility. The development of human civilisation and culture is the result of out of box thinking from time to time. Discoveries, inventions, research and development of knowledge in different disciplines is largely attributable to creative thinking or out of box thinking. If human beings were not creative, then they would never have survived and progressed over the centuries.

Creative thinking tries to create something new. Creative thinking produces new and unique solutions. However, creativity is subtle and may be experienced in the insignificant day to day working. Such micro level creative solutions lead to organisational progress. In fact, creative thinking involves a considerable amount of unconscious arrangement of symbols. In the first stage creative thinking makes little progress, but then new ideas gradually starts bubbling up suddenly, may to due to the fortituous set of circumstances. Though these ideas come to the conscious level suddenly, much of thinking is already done on them unconsciously, earlier. This sudden appearance of new ideas is called insight. A number of creative people say that when conscious thinking on some problem is becoming fruitless, insight appears suddenly, when they are doing something which is completely unrelated to that problem. The best example of this creative insight is that of Archimedes, the great scientist and mathematician of the past. He got the idea about the method of deciding the weight of an unknown solid material, while he was taking a bath. When he immersed his body into the bath tub, the water splashed out. And therefrom he realised that when some solid material is immersed into water (liquid), the volume of water spilling outside is equal to the weight of the solid. The famous principle of Archimedes is the result of insightful thinking. But, it is very clear that insight does not really appear out of nothing. Actually, it gets developed and blossoms up in those fields which are thoroughly prepared by study of the various aspects of the problem. Insight should be tested systematically trace whether it will offer definitely a solution to the problem.

Stages in Creative Thinking - Graham Wallace studied the steps in creative thinking. He found that, there are individual differences in the ways creative people thought, however there was a recurring pattern. According to one approach, creative thinking proceeds through following five stages.

(1) Preparation.
(2) Incubation.
(3) Illumination.
(4) Evaluation.
(5) Revision.

In preparation stage, the thinker formulates the problem and collects the facts and materials considered necessary for the solution of new kind. Then, many times, it happens, that the problem can not be solved in spite of concentrated efforts for weeks or months together. Then the thinker either deliberately or involuntarily turns away from the problem. This initiates stage two, i.e., Incubation.

During the stage of incubation, some of the ideas which were interfering with the solution tend to fade. The past experiences of the thinker also provide clues. However, the thinker does not realise it at that time. Similarly, the unconscious thought process involved in creative thinking also works during the incubation.

Illumination, the third stage occurs, with its insight experience. So this stage is sometimes described as 'Aha'. From incubation to illumination, the journey is with the help of insight.

At the fourth stage of evaluation, the solution appeared through illumination is tested to find out whether it can solve the problem satisfactorily or not. It the solution is unsatisfactory, then, the thinker has to restart again from stage me, i.e., preparation. In other words, if. If the insight is unsatisfactory, then the creative thinker has to begin again from the preparation stage. Sometime, the insight is satisfactory, however, the solution needs some modification. Some solutions, similarly, are good for minor problems. Then revision, stage five is reached. Revision is the stage where the solution occurring through insight is modified, amended and made fit to tackle the problem successfully.

Nature of Creative Thinking - In 1967, Guilford constructed a test to measure the creativity in people. This work became the background and seed bed for development of two important concepts, namely, (a) convergent thinking and (b) divergent thinking. Convergent thinking is concerned, mostly, with a particular end result. Here, the thinker gathers information relevant to the problem. Then he proceeds further by using problem solving rules to work out the right solution. Convergent thinking produces an outcome to a solution, which is usually previously arrived at by someone else. Normally, when people think creatively, they do not make use of convergent thinking.

In divergent thinking, varieties of thought are involved. Creative thinking uses divergent type of thinking. Divergent thinking combines convergent thinking and austic thinking. The creative thinker uses convergent thinking to gather information and thoughts as building materials for the ultimate creative solution. At the same time, the person drifts into austic thinking or free association in which the thought-symbols have private meaning. In this process of austic thinking some useful ideas emerge which would have been missed in strictly concentrating on the problem.

Characteristics of Creative thinker - It is observed several times, that many creative people are talented in some special way. They have typical special abilities which are useful in searching new ideas. They have following important characteristics.

(1) Diligence and strong motivation to work for solving the problem.

(2) Give preference to complexity and some degree of apparent imbalance in phenomena.

(3) More independent in their judgment.

(4) Reject suppression as a control of impulse.

(5) Psychologically more complex.

(6) More self-assertive and dominant.

(7) Dislike policing themselves and others.

(8) Never restricts thinking to few thoughts and have greater personal scope.

(9) Usually resist conventional approaches.

(10) Dare to present and follow rebellious and non-conforming thoughts

(11) Lot of interest in artistic, literary and aesthetic matters.

(12) Sometimes inclined to individualistic interpretation and expression.

(13) Less positive to decide the things by customs and consensus.

(14) Entertain impulses and ideas in the thinking process.

(15) Possess inventive mind.

(16) Are liberal, adventurous, open, discrete and original in approach.

(17) Are interpretative, sensitive, tolerant, imaginative, candid, casual and usually do not become diffusive.

(18) Their approach to problem solving and development of ideas is contingent, flexible, variable and non-monotonous, unstructured and playful.

(19) Their views and thoughts are optimistic, qualitative, radical, expansive, unrestrained, genuine, artistic and aesthetic.

(20) They are quick, sophisticated, self-seeking, vague and self-oriented.

Mental Locks - Some of our attitudes stifle our creativity. Those attitudes have been described as mental blocks by the creativity specialist **Roger von Oech**. These mental locks inhibit our creativity. When these mental locks are conquered, the creativity can be utilised to its fullest potential. The major mental locks listed by **Roger Von Oech** are as follows.

(1) Looking for the right answer A problem may have a number of right answers. It is simply a matter of perspectives.

(2) Always trying to be logical. Logic does not always prevail. Because human emotions, organisational inconsistencies, ambiguity, contradiction hit back at the logic.

(3) Strictly following the rules. Rules sometimes restrict the scope and chances of improvement of creativity. So to improve the things, we need to question the arbitrary limits on thinking and behaviour.

(4) Insisting on practicals. The impractical answers to 'what-if' type of questions can become the stepping stones to creative insights.

(5) Avoiding ambiguity – When one insists, too much, on objectivity and specificity; it stifles creativity.

(6) Fearing and avoiding failure – Mistakes, failures are the lessons to learn new, useful and right things. If one is afraid of failures and tries to avoid it all the time, then one will never make experiments and thus, the creativity within oneself wills not get the required exposure.

(7) For getting how to play – In adulthood the playful experimentation of childhood disappears.

(8) Becoming too specialised Too much specialisation leads to acute and narrow outlook and thinking. More analysis sometimes restricts the fertility of the creative ideas.

(9) Not wanting to look foolish One should not always pose to look intelligent. Sometimes seemingly foolish questions enhance our understanding and it also fosters creativity. Humour can release tension and unlock creative energies.

(10) Saying I am not creative – Many times we presume that we are not creative. But by nurturing small and apparently insignificant ideas we can convince ourselves that we are indeed creative.

Creative Problem Solving - Huber describes problem solving as a conscious process of bringing the actual situation closer to the desired situation. According to **Kreitner,** managerial problem solving consists of a four step sequence as follows,

(a) Identifying the problem.

(b) Generating alternative solutions.

(c) Selecting a solution.

(d) Implementing and evaluating solution.

(a) Identifying the problem. Correct and complete problem identification is necessary for developing a workable solution. Many people have the tendency to rush for finding out a solution before thoroughly understanding the problem. **Peter Drucker** says that the most common source of mistakes in management decisions is emphasis on finding the right answers rather than the right questions. It we put the right question, then only there is possibility of a right answer.

Actually a problem is the gap between the actual and desired state of affairs. And problem solving is the process which closes this gap. In the effort to identify and define the problem following errors are usually made which need to be avoided.

(i) Defining the problem according to possible solution.

(ii) Focusing on narrow, low-priority areas and minor problems.

(iii) Diagnosing the problems in terms of their symptoms.

(b) **Generating Alternative Solution** - This is a creative step in problem solving. However, we do not allow the creativity to blossom up. **Adams** observes that the natural response to a problem seems to be get rid of it by finding an answer and often taking the first answer that occurs and pursuing it because of one's reluctance to spend the time and mental efforts needed to conjure up a rich storehouse of alternatives from which to choose. Thus, we do not use this creative step purposefully. We, simply, rush for a reply and avoid thinking over the alternative solutions which sharpens and strengthens creativity. However, in order to generate solutions, one should develop patience, analytical skills and also intuitive thinking. Following are some of the popular and useful techniques which stimulate individual and group creativity.

(i) **Brainstorming** - In brainstorming emphasis is given on allowing and recording ideas in nonjudgmental setting. This is a group technique. Once all ideas are recorded, then at the later stage, they are critically evaluated and then suitable ideas are selected.

(ii) **Free association** - In this technique, analogies and symbols are used to foster unconventional thinking, e.g., a weekly production/sales target may be treated as a big wooden log which is to be moved to a desired destination. How? Maybe by cutting it into smaller pieces and carrying the same or rolling it or pulling it with some energy, etc. Symbolising the problem may induce one to think about a variety of solutions.

(iii) **Edisonian** - This technique involves trial and error experimentation. It is named after the most renowned scientist Thomas Edison, whose tedious and persistent research resulted in inventing a durable light bulb filament.

(iv) **Attribute listing** - In this technique ideal characteristics of a given object are collected and screened for useful insights.

(v) **Scientific method** - Scientific method is a very systematic approach which includes normally the following steps, as the most important one. Systematic testing of hypothesis, manipulation of variables, situational control, careful measurement of results.

(vi) **Creative leap** - In this technique, at the first stage an idealistic solution is developed on problem and then necessary working is made thereon to design a feasible solution.

(c) **Selecting a Solution** - Normally, everyone thinks of searching out the best solution. But best solution may not be practically searchable and available due to different constraints. So we have to develop a solution that is realistic, efficient and effective. **Russell Ackoff** a management specialist views that three things can be done about solving the problems, such as, Resolving, Solving and Dissolving.

In resolving the problem, a course of action good enough to meet the minimum constraints is selected. This practice is known as satisfice. Satisfice is described as the practice of settling for solutions that are good enough rather than the best possible. Ackoff observes that most of the managers rely on problem resolving. However, satisficing is a shortsighted and passive technique. It does not emphasise on growth and improvement.

Problem solving is another way of dealing with the problem. Here the selection of best solution is made. Manager having a problem solving approach follow the technique of optimising. In optimising managers make the scientific observation and quantitative measurement and thereby, systematically research all creative solutions and then select the one with the best combination of benefits.

Problem dissolution is one more way to deal with the problem. A problem is dissolved when the situation in which it occurs is changed so that the problem does not exist any further. The problem dissolvers follow the technique of idealising. In idealising the nature of the system in which a problem exists is changed. Problem dissolvers emphasise on getting the job done for this purpose they make use of any combination of quantitative and nonquantitative tools and techniques.

In managing an organisation, problem solving is actually an endless activity. As **Ackoff** says it rightly, that, every treatment of a problem generates new problems. However, it is a matter of perception. A problem seems to be problematic only when we feel that it is a hurdle. If we look at it as a challenge to our potentials and capabilities, it provides in immense scope to prove our mettle. Because in every problem lies an opportunity for growth and improvement only problems push us to march ahead on the path of continuous improvement. They induce us for the continuous quest for excellence.

Creative Insight and Strategy Selection - In the views of **Kreitner,** strategic management is the ongoing process of ensuring a competitively superior fit between an organisation and it's changing environment. Effective strategic management requires thinking strategically. And here the manager with creative insight has a superiority over others. Because much success of strategic management depends upon selection of an appropriate strategy. To select a suitable strategy the manager has to do the following important things.

(a) To make the situational analysis and

(b) To prepare the capability profile of the organisation.

Situational analysis is described as a technique for matching the strengths and weaknesses with environmental opportunities and treats to determine the organisation's right niche. This matching process is not any way easy. Because this process has the purpose of identifying the suitability of the organisation. In other words, it tries of find out, what the organisation can do in the best manner. So the strategist has to visualise at the mental level a move of rapidly changing events. It is not a case of taking the snapshots of the organisation and its environment regarding certain specific events and thereby to make some prediction. This requires a creative mindset. Because, here, the task is to find out a match between unfolded opportunities and the resources which are yet to be acquired. Market forecasting, trend analysis, study of recent innovations, study of demographic shifts and labour availability are some of the tools of situational analysis. However, each of these tools need the creative insight for making their best use. The numerical data regarding factors of environment is only descriptive unless the strategist has creative insight, he will not be able to understand what the environment is exactly indicating. Because what appears to be a threat on the surface, can be converted into an opportunity, if it is seen with an appropriate angle. Many a time it simply becomes a matter of perspective. And our perspectives are the outcome of our creative insight. Thus, creative insight plays a very significant role in situational analysis.

Capability profile is the identification of the strengths and weaknesses of the organisation and that way, actually it is a subprocess of situational analysis. It makes management to look inward. In the present era of intense competition for the organisations of 21st century, according to a number of management scholars, following capabilities become the key capabilities.

(1) Quick response to market.

(2) Rapid production and delivery.

(3) Continuous cost reduction.

(4) Fast product development.

(5) Consistent improvement and upgradation of process and human resources.

(6) Greater flexibility of operations.

Besides situational analysis and developing the key capabilities, strategic thinking, seeing things in motion and making sense out of a cloudy and uncertain future by seeing the interdependence of key factors. Such an insightful thinking and vision requires more than the passing awareness of major and important political, economic, social, legal and technological trends and events. The creative and analytical thinking collectively trace the inter-relationship among different environmental factors and their changing configuration. This creative insight enables the manager to envision his organisation in the context of world trends and their interdependence. This also enables the manager to focus on the emerging opportunities and obstacles as well as the possible ways and means to respond to them. Creative thinking is necessary to provide to the organisation a clear strategic direction. Such a direction is very difficult in the present times due to increasing world competition, rising costs of operations and diminishing resources. This explicitly underlines the importance and need for creative thinking. Therefore modern scholars of strategic management, now talk about creative strategic thinking instead of the previous concept of only strategic thinking.

Though creative strategic thinking is a special gift to some managers as an inborn quality, it can be learned through practice also. The following four tools have a great utility in this respect:

(i) Concepts of synergy.

(ii) Product life cycle.

(iii) Porter's generic strategies.

(iv) Business ecosystem (This is a new perspective).

(1) Synergy - The concept of synergy states that the whole is greater than the sum of its parts. According to **Kreitner** synergy occurs when two or more variables interact to produce an effect greater than the sum of the effects of the variables acting independently. Some people mathematically describe synergy as 2+2=5. Usually there are four types of synergistic effect namely, market synergy, cost synergy, technological synergy and management synergy. Each kind of synergy boosts up strategic thinking and the organisational health.

Market Synergy - When one product or service strengthens the sale of one or more products or services, we say that market synergy is achieved. For example, installation of ATM in a supermarket or shopping mall-or a stall of gift-cards at a flowershop.

Cost Synergy - This kind of synergy will occur when two or more products are designed by the same engineer, produced in the same factory, distributed or sold through the same sales channel. Cost synergy can occur in almost every dimension of activity. Similarly, by recycling the by-products and waste, we can obtain cost synergy.

Technological Synergy - This synergy is achieved by transfer of technology from are application to another. This opens up new markets. The same product with a little modification can become useful for some other purpose. This is technological synergy. It avoids the expenditure of developing a totally new product for another new market.

Management Synergy - This type of synergy is achieved when a management team becomes more productive because its members have complementary skills. If their skills are identical, then there occurs a repetition of strengths and weaknesses. But when members have complementary skills, the weakness of each one is covered up by the strength of another.

(2) Product Life Cycle - Product life cycle makes a graphic representation of the sequential rise and fall of the product's sales and profit. PLC is a very useful tool for strategists who accept contingency approach to management. Product life cycle (PLC) has four main stages, namely, introduction, growth, maturity and decline. Some marketing scholars believe that there is pre-commercialisation stage prior to the introduction stage. At this stage the basic strategy is innovation. Market forecasting, new product development, test marketing, personnel training will be the strategic functions and concerns at this stage. At the introduction stage, the basic strategy is infiltration. Developing supplier relationship, financial planning, scaling up production and marketing operations are the strategic concerns at this stage. At the growth stage, advancement is the basic strategy and studying competitors and making competitive innovations, seeking economies of scale in production, building brand preferences and product loyalty are the related strategic functions. At the maturity stage, dependence is the basic strategy. Cost-cutting, product updating, tapping neglected market segments and emphasising customer-service are the strategic concern at maturity stage. Decline is the last stage of PLC, where, the basic strategy is withdrawal. Scaling down production and marketing, trimming inventories, reassigning personnel, cutting the promotional costs, competing on the basis of price, planning for termination of the product or product line, are the functions relating to the withdrawal strategy at the decline stage.

PLC and creative strategic thinking has a success combination. The basic strategy at the different stages of PLC is to be strategy by using the creative strategic thinking. PLC tells us the product's position in the market. It informs us whether the product is a baby product (introduction stage), star product (growing stage), cash-cow (maturity stage) or a tame-dog (decline stage). Accordingly, the strategist has to apply his creative mind to work out a suitable strategy which will after the most effective treatment at all levels to think strategically at its varying time frames. A strategy at introduction or growth need to be changed at maturity or decline. This develops flexible and diversified thinking. PLC not only encourages creativity in strategic thinking but brings variety in creativity. It breaks down the routine patterns in creative thinking and makes the strategist to seek out the new and effective ways and means to handle each time the situation in different manner. It teaches the managers to upgrade their strategies continuously, instead of presuming that they have obtained the final answers to which they can conveniently stick up. This process sows the seeds of the creativity culture which is the significant contribution of PLC.

(3) Porter's Generic Competitive Strategies - In 1980, **Michael Porter** developed a model of competitive strategies. His model evolved four generic strategies, namely,

(i) Cost leadership.

(ii) Differentiation.

(iii) Cost focus and

(iv) Focused differentiation.

Porter's generic strategies help the manager to think strategically. Managers following the strategy of cost leadership, try to keep the costs low and also accordingly the prices lower than competitors. Cost leadership strategy mostly focus on improvement in productivity. Similarly, differentiation strategy has a concern to provide the unique products. According to Porter, differentiation is the ability to provide unique and superior value to the buyer in terms of product quality, special

features or after-sale service. Organisations following the cost focus strategy keep a strict control on cost and price of its products in a particular market. Similarly, focused differentiations strategy involves achieving a competitive edge by delivering a superior product/service to a limited audience.

For creative strategic thinking, Porter's model acts as a useful helping tool. These four generic strategies provide the input to develop a thinking to get the most anticipated competitive advantage. How and where to apply cost leadership or differentiation or focus is the subject for creative thinking. In order to cut down the costs and offer the lowest price or to offer some special and unique value to the customers, the strategist will have to apply his creative ability to devise and develop the new ways and means to serve this purpose. The methods and techniques to be followed in this regard should be not repetitive and inimitable. The creative use of Porter's model gives the organisation a route to success.

(4) Business Ecosystem - James Moore (The Death of Competition – Leadership and Strategy in the Age of Business Ecosystems) defines the concept of business ecosystem in the following words, - It is an economic community of organisations and all their stakeholders including suppliers and customers. The model of business-ecosystem supplied a new thought to modern strategic management and it is as follows. Organisations have to be equally good at cooperating as at competing. Cooperation and competition are the two faces of the same coin. It is many times observed that within a dominant business ecosystem, key organisations cooperate and compete to achieve both their individual and collective goals. An example of this cooperation is the relationship between Microsoft and Intel. The worldwide known, winter technology is the combination of Microsoft Windows software and Intel microprocessor. This technology dominated the market of personal computers. The modern cooperation in two or more business organisations is like this. In fact, ecosystem is the term which is related to nature. Ecosystem has the arrangement for interrelated and interdependent elements. The elements of an ecosystem has mutual cooperation and coexistence. This concept of ecosystem is applied to business. Business ecosystem has provided a new perspective to strategic management. For a very long period the words strategy and competition were treated as closely related. But, now the business ecologists suggest that there needs cooperation to certain extent even among the toughest competitors. According to Moore, the major factor which limits the spread of innovation today is the inability to command cooperation across broad diverse communities of players who must become intimate parts of a far-reaching process of coevaluation. Thus, capital, technology or lack of good ideas are not the prominent hurdles in the spread up of innovation. If the coevolution does not take place, then the success will be far away. No company can do anything alone and so it has to search out a strategic partner to work with. The creative thinking ability of the strategist can develop measures to develop and speed up this process of coevaluation. It is, in fact, a crucial decision to select one's strategic partner. It not only influences the long-term future of the organisation but simultaneously may raise some important questions about the existence and image of the organisation. What for are you there in the business and where are you going? Such questions can be satisfactorily answered only if you have creative insight and with that you develop the solutions for them.

Sensitivity – A Skill for Excellence

Sensitivity may be described as the quality of being receptive and responsive to the people as well as to the surroundings. A sensitive person is more efficient in catching the messages of the happenings around him. The sensitivity as managerial ability has to be studied in two contexts.

(1) Sensitivity towards people.

(2) Sensitivity towards business environment.

Sensitivity in respect of people is the ability of the executive to perceive and understand the needs, emotions and behavioural responses of people and act accordingly. A sensitive executive is in a better position to know why people react in the characteristic manner and how they can be tackled successfully. However, sensitivity is completely shrewdness. A shrewd person also can predict the reactions of people but then he has manipulative intentions. On the other hand, a sensitive executive possesses empathy, sympathy and reasonability. With empathy, the person can understand the position of the individual passing through a particular situation. With sympathy the person can think compassionately and treat others in a soft and merciful way. And with the reasonability the person can make decisions and actions in respect of others, which are most appropriate, needful and balanced in that situation. A sensitive executive has the emotional and rational maturity. He is neither blunt, nor rigid in behaving with others.

Sensitivity towards people helps the executive to bring greater effectiveness in human resources management. In helps, on one side, in handling efficiently the human resources and on the other side, in opening up a broad spectrum of avenues for the fullest development of their potentials. Because sensitivity induces oneself to behave with others in the way in which he wants himself to be behaved by others. This tendency automatically enhances the responsibility in the executive in dealing with the human element in the organisation. Actually human beings are the most delicate, explosive as well as volatile factor in the organisation. Any mistake in the policy or practice of people-management has a long-lasting adverse impact on the total efficiency and effectiveness of the organisation. Therefore, a good number of management scholars believe that non-management is the core of management and is in fact the total management. Thus, sensitivity towards people becomes a significant quality of the executive. In the present days of globalisation, the sensitivity becomes an essential quality again due to the issues like workforce diversity, cultural differences, and complexity of global operations. People having different social, economic and cultural background join the organisations. Similarly, the proportion of women in the workforce is on a rising scale. Naturally, modern organisations have a cosmopolitan staff having a variety of expectations, perception and attitudes in respect of jobs and organisations. Under such circumstances sensitivity is the key to understand the nature of this workforce diversity. It also develops the views and approaches of the executives in smoothening the problems related thereto. Cultural differences is another issue of global corporations. Different cultures nurture different value-systems which have strong influence on the behavior and performance of the people. Again there may be minority groups in the organisations. In such situations, sensitivity brings balance and maturity in decisions. The executive has to take care that he is not unjust. Unfair and partial in respect of any group. He should not promote the culture and value-system of one type at the cost of another. The complexity of global operations is related to technical as well as social and behavioral aspects. Particularly relating to the social and behavioral elements, the sensitivity of the executive has the potential for solutions.

Improving Sensitivity towards People. To improve the sensitivity towards people, the executive has to practice continuously empathy as well as sympathy. Sympathising will teach him to be compassionate and considerate with others. Empathising will develop in him the ability and habit of seeing and understanding the other side of the situation. It helps to know a problem from others point of view. It teaches to experience a situation by being the other person. It gives the feel of the experiences of others. Besides sympathy and empathy, these are the following techniques which are useful in improving sensitivity.

(c) Ulterior Transaction - The third type of social transactions are ulterior transactions. In such type of social transaction one person holds two ego positions. One ego is apparent whereas the other ego state is implicit but more effective and active. This implicit ego state is real and expects suitable behaviour response to turn the transaction into a complementary transaction. For example, a boss apparently holds the audit ego and pretends that he expects the subordinates to talk and work freely and independently. Actually he may want his subordinates to submit themselves to him all the time. Thus, his real ego state will be that of a parent. His parent ego will be satisfied if the subordinates hold the child ego and then only the transaction becomes complementary. If the subordinates presume that the boss is holding the adult ego as he displays it, then they are mistaking and the transaction becomes crossed.

Transactional analysis teaches a person how to respond to people holding different ego state in different ways, how to identify and predict their real ego state. This improves and develops the ability to sensitise. Once a person is able to sense the behavior of others, then he can devise better behavioural response for the same. Transactional analysis provides tips to make the social transactions complementary. The habit of diagnosing the ego state of other person acts as a useful tool and technique for improving and sharpening the sensitivity. Ultimately only the resistive executive can offer a suitable behavioral response and make every transaction complementary.

Life Positions: Life positions and their analysis is another important tool, besides transactional analysis, for developing and improving sensitivity. Most of the time we look to our for fights and consider everything as a gain or loss. We look to each situation as win-lose condition. That is, either we are winning or losing. The study of life positions broadens our perspective and increases our level of sensitivity.

There are actually four life positions and each one of us tends to exhibit any one of them. These life positions influence our behavioral responses and normally they get developed in our early childhood and stay with us throughout our life. Therefore, they are called life positions. One life position tends to dominate the behavior of a person, however other life positions may be exhibited from time to time in specific situations. So, a person holds one life position at a time, but it is not the only one taken forever.

Life position stems up from a combination of two viewpoints,

(i) How people view themselves and

(ii) How do they view other people in general. Diagrammatically, the four life positions are as follows.

Views about self	Views about others: Negative	Views about others: Positive
Positive	I am OK you are not OK	I am OK you are OK
Negative	I am not OK you are not OK	I am not OK you are OK

Fig. 7.1 Views about others

On the X axis are shown views about others and on Y axis are shown views about self. Accordingly, there are four quadrants. The upper two quadrants express positive views about self and lower tow quadrants express negative views about self. Similarly, left two quadrants express negative views about others and right two quadrants express positive views about others. Thus these four quadrants describe four life positions. A brief explanation of them is as follows

(a) **I am OK, You are not OK -** This is a kind of life positions wherein the person holds positive views about self and negative views about others. Such a person has a typically selfish approach. He always considers only of his self-interest and that too at the cost of others. He looks of everything in life as a win-lose situation. He feels that he has to defeat others to win the life-battles. He thinks that he can win, if he makes others lose. Thus he measures all things in the form of gain and loss. When he is making a gain, the other party is making a loss and *vice-versa*. People holding this life position are extremely and unreasonably competitive. As a result they cannot be in tune with others. They are unable to make with others friendly, cordial and co-operative long-term relations. Very often they are having conflicting relations with others.

(b) **I am not Ok, You are not OK -** This life position is known as lose-lose situation. People having this approach are negative in thoughts and destructive in attitude. They do not have sportsmanship. They have an ill mind. They cannot tolerate the defeat of self and victory of others. Therefore, they have a philosophy that if they cannot win, then, they will not allow others to win. In that case, they will destroy the thing. They will spoil the situation, destruct the benefits, finish the transaction by extincting the parties. In simple words such people think that if they cannot win, then, they will spoil the game. If they do not get the benefits, then they will damage and ruin the system in such a way that nobody will be able to get those advantages thereafter. If they cannot enjoy, then they will obstruct the joyful life of others. The best example of such a mentality is the case of one sided love and murder-suicide phenomenon. Sometimes we hear or read the news where a boy is in love with a girl and when she does not respond to her, he kills here and commits suicide. This is the lose-lose mentality. This is simply a case of mental disorder. People having this attitude and approach are frustrated, negative, pessimistic, extremely selfish, destructive and violent.

There is an another pattern of behaviour resulting from the lose-lose approach and attitude. It displays a nervous, pessimistic, frightened and depressed mentality and outlook of the person. These people, being nervous, mentally sick and too tense are always in the negative mood. They themselves are disturbed and depressed. As such they cannot see the positive good things around them. They see in everything the problem and neglect its pleasing aspects. Every relationship is a trouble for them and they do not feel and think about its worth and warmth. Every social transaction adds to their worries and they suspect about its workability. These people have a problem inside, because which they feel that they are surrounded by problems, worries, difficulties and all kinds of unpleasant people and tasks. This develops in them pessimism and inactivity. They start becoming unhappy all the time. And since they are negative and completely engrossed in their negative thoughts and feeling, they do not pay attention to the needs of others. They remain aloof and unrelated. They become nonresponsive to positivists, and non-cooperative and act as agents of frustration and depression.

(c) **I am not OK, You are OK -** This is a typical attitude of self-sacrifice. People with this approach are ready to offer to others the benefits, even at the cost of their own loss. They may suffer the hardship for the betterment of others. This spirit of sacrifice and neglecting the self for the sake of others is in principle very good. But in actual practice this may lead to an unbalanced and unreasonable personality. Such people may be driven by the attitude and habit of sacrifice to such an extent that sometimes, they may be sacrificing for a wrong cause and for wrong people. Their thought of sacrifice unknowingly may get transformed into the attitude to surrender and the tendency for restoring a situation in its good form, such people may be withdrawing from the same and thus giving a walkover to aggressive and interrupting tendencies. This approach is indicator of the no sensitivity towards self and oversensitivity towards others including wrongdoers. Therefore, this life position is also described as lose-win altitude.

People with lose-win approach are ready to accept defeat and allow the other party to win. If this approach is practiced thoughtfully and reasonably, it will smoothen the social transactions and develop good relations. But if followed unjudiciously then it may breed aggressive, invasive and interruptive tendencies. Therefore, application of this outlook requires caution and carefulness. This approach is sweet in theory and sour in practice for common people.

(d) **I am OK, You are Ok -** People having this type of approach and attitude look for mutual benefits. They search out solutions which can satisfy all parties. This type of thinking is also called win-win approach. Such people never look to life and different situations as having conflicting and competing interests. They feel that by way of co-operation, collaboration and positive thinking we can develop solution which will be beneficial to all the concerned parties. The best example of this approach relates to distribution of profit among the workers and owners. Now the narrow view is that labor and management always have the contrasting and conflicting interests and therefore, they are always at tug of war. The major issue of dispute between them is the distribution of profit. Workers want more bonus and owners expect more dividends. If rate of bonus is increased, rate of dividend decreases and *vice versa*. This happens due to limited profit. Win-win style of thinking suggests that make more business, thereby earn more profit and that way offer attractive and satisfactory dividend as well as bonus. Win-win outlook, thus, believes in expansion, progress, advancement and development.

People with win-win type of thinking have positive attitude and sensible behaviour. They are able to balance the urge for competition as well as co-operation. Naturally their social transactions and relationship with people are fruitful and healthy.

Life Positions and Sensitivity - An understanding and awareness of different life positions help to develop and sharpen one's sensitivity. The knowledge of life positions help us to understand the behavioural philosophy of different people. Thereby, we can differentiate them as competitive, negative, sacrificing and co-operative persons. Accordingly we can design the suitable behavioural responses for the people belonging to different categories.

Similarly, study of the life positions develop our understanding of the causation of behaviour of people. This makes us thing about other people in a more mature, responsible and sympathetic way. There we do not bluntly neglect or discard people as eccentric, impractical, brutal and so not worthy of keeping any kind of relationship. On the contrary, when we study the life positions, are able to analyse their mindset and behavioural reactions more systematically. This gives us powerful input to our behavioural strategy in respect of such people on a positive and sensible foundations.

Life positions can be altered and modified by using proper methods and techniques. As their understanding enhances our sensitivity, with it we can handle such people more smoothly and in a troubles way. Actually, when we know the reasons of a particular action, we can remedy those reasons and thereby, correct the action responses. Life positions and their study gives new dimensions to sensitivity. Then the sensitivity becomes a combination of head and heart, i.e., intelligence and emotions. The person is compassionate and sympathetic due to his deep and wide knowledge of human nature, thinking style and life philosophy. His softness and considerate response is not instinctual and temporary but thoughtful and consistent. Such type of sensitivity is rational and not eventual.

Johari Window and Personality Quadrants

Famous behavioural scientists **Joseph Loft** and **Harry Ingham** developed the concept of personality quadrants. Which is known as Johari window. Diagrammatically, Johari window displays the four distinct aspects of every personality in the form of four personality quadrants. It is as follows.

	The Person is Known by Others	The Person is not Known by Others
The person knows about self →	1 Open Self	2 Hidden Self
The Person doesn't know about self →	3 Blind Self	4 Undiscovered Self

Fig. 7.2 Johari Window

Johari window is based on four important observations about self-personality. They are:

(a) Some of our personality aspects, traits or characteristics are known to us.

(b) Similarly, some of personality aspects are such about which we do not have any knowledge.

(c) Some of our personality aspects are known to others.

(d) Similarly, others do not have knowledge about some of our personality characteristics.

These four observations lead to four possibilities or situations, which are as follows.

(1) Some of our personality aspects are known to ourselves as well as to others.

(2) Some of our personality traits are known to ourselves but others do not have any knowledge of the same.

(3) Some of our personality characteristics are known to others, but we are completely unaware of the same.

(4) Some of our personality components are such that neither we nor others have any knowledge about them.

Accordingly, there are four quadrants of our personality called as, open self, hidden self, blind self and undiscovered self. Their brief description is given below.

(A) Open self - This part of our personality is composed of all those personality aspects which are known to ourselves as well as to others. It is also called as public area. Since people know this part of our personality very well, there is mutual understanding, friendship and openness in relationships and social transactions. When people know each others very well, the possibility of conflicts and disputes is very minimum. Actually, when people are ignorant about each other's characteristics, then they try to become defensive and their interactions with each other is not smooth, progressive and fruitful. Therefore, everyone has to broaden this part of his personality to become compatible and considerate.

(B) **Hidden Self -** This part of our personality is composed of all those characteristics of ourselves which are known to us but not to others. So this part is called private or secret area. As some of our qualities as well as limitations are not known to others, there are possibilities of misunderstandings and interpersonal conflicts usually when a person does not have any idea of the reactions of others about his values, attitudes, beliefs and capabilities, he tries to hide them out of the fear of the probability of negative reaction and annoyance of others.

(C) **Blind Self -** This part of our personality contains all our such traits or characteristics about which people have knowledge, but unfortunately we are completely unaware of. Therefore, it is called as blind self. Especially, we are unaware of our drawbacks, weaknesses, limitations and most of those characteristics of ourselves which may become the causes of disturbance and disappointment for others. Naturally, we do not understand why people do not respond to us in the way we expect them. Sometimes, unknowingly and innocently we hurt people. Actually, at such instances, we do not have any intention or purpose to disturb or annoy them. But still it happens because of this blind self. As we start knowing more and more about our characteristics included in blind self, then this part of our personality starts narrowing down.

(D) **Undiscovered Self -** This part of our personality is composed of all those characteristics of ourselves about which we are ignorant and so also others too are ignorant. Naturally, this quadrant becomes an explosive area since none of us have any idea or prediction or analysis of the positive and negative traits included in this quadrant of our personality. This area is composed of our potential qualities and deficiencies.

Johari window and personality quadrants help us to understand ourselves much better. It also helps us to improve our interaction with each other. The knowledge of hidden, blind and undiscovered self, alerts us about our strengths and weaknesses which need to be attended seriously and dealt with systematically. Our sensitivity sharpens only when we have a complete idea of our total personality and how others are looking to us. Once we know ourselves, it is easier to analyse the responses of others to us.

Johari Window and Development of Sensitivity

Johari window teaches us how to introspect ourselves systematically. This helps to develop sensitivity. The 'open self' quadrant of our personality includes all our good and bad features which are public. Naturally, there is a predictability regarding the behaviour and responses attributed to the characteristics included in this quadrant. Such a behaviour can be modified also if it is not producing the expected effect, e.g., If a person knows that he is short-tempered and others, too, know this well, then he can try to control his anger and others will also become cautious while dealing with him. He will take care to improve his level of patience and that way maintain smooth interaction. He will know why people avoid him or remain reserved when dealing with him. Open self develops our conscious behaviour. However, the real problem arises due to our hidden self, blind self and undiscovered self. Misunderstandings, wrong interpretation, biased presumptions, unreasonable expectations causing interpersonal conflicts and insensitive behaviour with others are due to reasons attributable to the personality aspects of these quadrants. These quadrants include all such personality aspects ourselves in respect of which either we or others or both are ignorant either completely or to a certain extent. But we do not know that these quadrants are also the indispensible part of our personality. Johari window makes us aware about their existence and this works as the first step towards the development of sensitivity. Especially, many times we purposefully or unknowingly neglect our personality deficiencies. That makes the real problem. Johari window helps us to see to ourselves from others' viewpoint. So we can modify our behavior to expand our open self. If we let people know all those of our good characteristics which remained concealed in hidden self and learn from them our cutting corners, drawbacks and defects situated in blind self, we can become more conscious and careful in treating others with sensibility and sensitivity. Johari window teaches how to make a complete self-analysis. It not only attends the known part of our personality but also awakens us about the undiscovered self which is composed of all those characteristics of ourselves which neither we nor others know to any extent.

Some Small Tips for Improving Sensitivity

(1) Develop the habit of empathising. Try to put yourself in the position and situation of others. By this way, you can better understand the causes of their actions and reactions. This will help you to give to others a more considerate and careful response.

(2) Reward people for their good doings immediately. But while punishing them, think twice. Then you will realise that they can be forgiven also.

(3) Introspect yourself. Nobody is perfect in this world. The negative responses of people may be due to the deficiencies in yourself. Therefore improve yourself first, before improving others.

(4) Human behaviour is dynamic. It is never static and constant. Sometimes, the stress in the situation may also cause people to behave in an unexpected way. Therefore, analyse the situation before evaluating and assessing people's behaviour. Never forget that good people in bad condition may cause to produce disappointing behavioural response. Then the situation is responsible.

(5) Positivities and negativities exist in all people. People act as their conductors. So you will get what you ask for.

(6) Mind well that sensitive persons do not labelise others. They believe in one to one communication and relations. They consider people as individuals with variations in capabilities, characteristics and expectations. At the same time they are fully aware of the group effect on individual behaviour.

(7) A sensitive executive prefers to play the role of a member of the team. He never treats him as a special person and never separates himself from his followers. Under such circumstances, there is a meeting between the leader and followers.

Sensitivity towards Business Environment

Sensitivity towards environment is equally important as that towards people. Because business environment too is dynamic and is subject to a variety of several factors. The major factors creating an impact on business environment are political condition, economic circumstances, demographic factors, culture, social elements, scientific and technological advancement, global changes and the system of law and regulatory framework. Any change in any of these factors or their compositions, alters the business situation. It either creates new opportunities for business expansion and growth or it imposes threats on the existence and survival of the business organisation and therefore alertness towards them is very much necessary for smooth and progressive functioning of the organisation.

For example, a change in the economic and industrial policy either may open up new horizons of business expansion or it may raise new challenges and increase the risk for a business. After 1990, when India adopted the policy of liberalisation, privatisation and globalisation of business industry, it created opportunities as well as threats for Indian business organisations. Similarly the change in the demographic composition also has also affected the previous business assumptions. The increases in the size of population in Asian countries have expanded the market therein. At the same time the rise in the proportion of young people have increased the demand for the latest product versions, fashionable designs and new products. The markets in these countries therefore, are called young markets. Moreover, globalisation has widened the choice for consumption and broadened the scope for the marketability of different products. Now, therefore the business organisations and their strategy-makers have to think about the existing and potential demand in the global market, and maintaining the balance in the global demand and supply, developing the international quality standards for products and performance, and preparing the self for the global competition. In fact, an executive with a high level of business sensitivity, only, can perceive, understand, assimilate and act upon these changes and challenges.

The political stability, awakening and awareness, the political system, the party in power and its ideology also influences the conditions for business. Political instability, coalition government, confused and impractical and unreasonable ideology, develops an atmosphere of uncertainty, bewilderment, controversies and misunderstandings. It hinders the progress and paralyses the process of development. There we earnestly need sensitivity. Because sensitivity is our only ability to feel the effect of externalities in advance. With it, we can anticipate the probable repercussions and prepare ourselves to face them constructively and carefully. The same happens with the scientific and technological advancement which is at its peak in the present times. **Peter Drucker** describes it as the 'Age of discontinuity'. This pace of development of science and technology has caused for a fast outdating and obsolescence of existing products. A sensitive executive can see and smell this changing scenario of business. Sometimes the innovation in products and services have a very small and non-conspicuous beginning. But within a short period of time it catches momentum and produces a far and deep reaching impact. Innovation always has an accelerating effect, which needs to be sensed appropriately and promptly. Sensitivity has a great utility in this respect.

Sensitivity helps a person to excel as a human being and also as a professional or businessman. Sensitivity teaches and induces to maintain healthy and meaningful human relationship. Then only long-term and respectful and responsive relations get developed and sustained. Similarly, the sensitivity towards business environment helps the person to predict most accurately the forthcoming changes and to become proactive in respect of them.

Vision – A Skill for Excellence

Vision is the combination of foresight, outlook, creative thinking, futuristic view, logical predictability, modernity and proactivism. Vision does not mean dreaming. It does not mean thinking simply optimistically. It means elevating the thinking from the available information to the probabilities of the future. It is a way of shaping the future with outstanding thoughts related to future contingencies. Vision enables you to think far ahead of others. Business vision is described as a powerful statement of what the business can and will be in future. It is a comprehensive analysis and prediction involving deep thinking about the following five major points:

(i) The basic purpose of our business.
(ii) Our strengths and weaknesses which are core.
(iii) The most probable future changes.
(iv) Our expected and desired position in future business world.
(v) The plan, programme, tools, techniques and strategies to acquire the desired future position.

Vision back–refers to direction, but is not the same as direction. **P.C. Nutt and R.W. Backoff** comments in their article 'crafting vision' in *Journal of Management Enquiry* (Dec. 1997), that a vision has a compelling and clear imagery that offers an innovative way to improve, which recognises and draws on traditions and connects to actions that people can take to realise the change. Vision taps the emotions and energy of people. A properly articulated vision creates the enthusiasm that people have for sporting events and other leisure-time activities and brings this same energy and commitment to the workplace. **B. Nanus** (Visionary Leadership) views that the properly selected and implemented vision is so energising that it jump-starts the future by calling forth, the skills, talents and resources to make it happen. **Charles Handy,** while commenting on effective visionary leadership have pointed out five conditions.

(1) The vision has to be different. It has to reframe the known, scene, to reconceptualise the obvious, connect the previously unconnected, dream a dream.
(2) The vision must make sense to others. It should be seen as challenging, but capable of achievement.
(3) It must be understandable and capable of sticking in people's mind.
(4) The trader must exemplify the vision by his own behaviour and evident commitment.
(5) If the vision is to be implemented it must be one that is shared.

People with vision know very well, where they are going and what exactly they want to achieve. They have the power of directing all their fellowmen reach their destination. Therefore, in order to develop the vision, ask yourself, all the time, where you want to be at the end of each decade and compare that with your present position. In fact a visionary has the ability to foresee the benefits to carry out the change despite obstacles. This differentiates the visionary from the conservatives as well as the pragmatists. Actually, the conservatives resist the change. They prefer the *status quo*. They are, mostly, afraid of unseen and unknown. Therefore, they stick up to the customs and traditions and set the work routine on the basis of the past experience and established norms. Apart from them are the pragmatists. They are practical and live in the present. However, they have the tendency to accept the change only when it is proved beneficial and reasonable. That is why they never become pioneers. They do not play the role of a beginner or trendsetter. Pragmatists will accept innovation, only if, it is proved as workable by somebody else. Different from the pragmatists and the conservatives are the visionaries. They dare to become the first person to introduce the change. Further they are capable of implementing the desired change successfully and reap out its rich benefits. When they think of any change and decide to put it into practice, it is not a blind, whimsical or instinctual decision. It is based on their logical thinking, clear-cut foresight and the ability to analyse and remedy the future probabilities systematically. For them, the future is visible. They can visualise the future and set the correct path become successful in fighting with the future-odds and utilising the future-favours emerges from their core capability of logical analysis and creative thinking.

How to Develop Your Vision - In fact, vision is an inborn quality. A true visionary is born once in a century. However, everybody, to certain extent, can possess and develop vision. For this purpose, one has to do the following:

(1) Your vision is your aim in future. So, define, what you are aiming to achieve in future.

(2) Compare your present position with your aim. Assess what you are today and what you are desirous of.

(3) Map out, what you will need, to bridge the gap between your present position and your desired position in future.

(4) Express your vision in the form of a statement to communicate to everyone in the organisation the long-term aim and the principle underlying the vision. This develops a clear understanding about your vision and makes it implementation easier and smoother.

(5) The vision expressed in the form of statement is called the mission. Break up your mission statement into operating plans.

(6) Each of these operating plan must have a goal. So fix the goals.

(7) From the goals, to achieve them; fix the specific targets and set out the deadlines to fulfill them.

(8) Provide resources and facilities to the staff for the implementation.

Important tips for development and implementation of vision

(a) Write down your ambitions and revise them periodically. Your aims and goals are strongly influenced by your ambition.

(b) If your vision seems unattainable, then do not give it up. Simply, intensify your efforts. Many times the goals appear as unattainable because we focus on our limitations and do not trust our potentials.

(c) Keep the mission statement which expresses your vision brief, clear and descriptive.

(d) Before finalising your mission statement, it is better to discuss it with other directors on the board. This works as a scrutiny process to check out the possibilities of confusion, controversy, contradiction and conflict of interest if any which may arise later due to the mission statement.

Key properties of vision - Mostly, the business vision is developed by the promoters of the organisation. It may be possible, that, their vision gets influenced by existing condition and specific challenges. Over the time, the conditions change, new challenges emerge, old ideas become obsolete and need for new ways and styles of thinking is felt strongly. Under such circumstances the vision and mission statement may lose its glitter and uniqueness. Therefore, the vision must be the outcome of deep and comprehensive thinking. The long lasting and ever unique vision possesses the following properties.

(1) The vision must be inspirational.

(2) The vision must be value-centered.

(3) The vision must be realisable.

(4) The vision must be capable of powerful imagery and articulation.

(5) The vision must clearly demonstrate the path for a better future.

(6) The vision must be fit in any time frame and situation.

(7) The vision must be unique.

The capability of the visionary leader to inspire the followers by his outstanding and astonishing vision is very important. In fact the vision statement should be so powerful that it should energise and activate the people by appealing to their enthusiasm and potentialities. This is more possible when the vision is value-centered and realisable. The value-system is, most of the time, a strong force that drives a person to decide and act. The goals and objectives which are compatible with our values and beliefs are more attractive and motivating than those lacking this element. Similarly, the realisation possibility of the vision strengthens the confidence and enhances the magnitude of efforts, for the implementation of vision. The first three characteristics of an outstanding vision, namely inspiration capability, value-centredness and reliability develops the next four characteristics. The vision demonstrating the better future, having appropriateness with time and situation and possessing uniqueness is the one which has the first three properties. The capacity of powerful imagery and articulation is also related to the values which the vision, illuminates and by them the inspiration it provides. An enlightening vision does not simply state clearly the aim to be reached at, but, at the same time prescribes the path to that destination. The imagery aspect of the vision brings to it visibility and the fitness in the time frame and situation develops relevance of the vision. These two again adds to its reliability. The uniqueness of a vision is the result of these, all earlier, six properties. All these properties are interrelated and their existence develops a unique vision in total. Then it can picturise and truly demonstrate the desirable future. If the vision cannot create a picture of the future, then it fails to motivate the people. When people understand that the vision is attainable, it is challenging and doable, then people will earnestly accept it and make sincere efforts to implement it.

A leader has to communicate his vision to his followers and make them act accordingly. For this purpose he has to do three basic things.

(i) Explain the vision to followers clearly, in terms of required action and aims through oral and written communication.

(ii) Behave in such a way that it continuously communicate and reinforce the vision.

(iii) Sequence the activities required for the implementation of vision.

The most important aspect of the effective implementation of a vision is the leader's behaviour and detailing of actions suitable for the vision-implement. Through own behaviour the leader can set an example for others. Further his behaviour will recall and reinforce the vision consistently. This has a positive effect on the employees. In addition to this provide the details of actions required to implement the vision. This involves explaining to them the following three things

(i) What the employees should do.

(ii) How they can do that.

(iii) Why they are required to do it.

Thus, when it comes to detailing the vision and directing the employees, the leader should tell the followers the nature, form and kind of actions they should make. Again he should inform to them the methods, tools and techniques for better performance. At the same time, he should describe to them the consecutive objectives of these actions and in what way the accomplishment of these objectives will lead, progressively, to the implementation of the vision.

Vision and Change Management - Many management scholars explain the need of the vision in the context and on the background of change management. Though change is inevitable and certain in the life of an individual and organisation, we must prepare ourselves for the changes in future, in advance. That is why vision is necessary. Because vision acts as a central pillar for a planned change. The change programme which intends, to make a better future emerges from the vision of the leader. What needs to be changed, how and what new principles and practices should be introduced are all included in the vision. That is why the term vision is broader and deeper in meaning and sense that the terms foresight, forecast, prediction, futuristic view, insightful thinking, progressive outlook, etc. All these become the components of vision and still there remains a lot of undescribed meaning in the term. Vision is not confined simply to seeing the future but is more concerned with making a better future. This naturally involves planned change. Such a change programme has three important aspects.

(a) Unfreezing.
(b) Changing.
(c) Refreezing.

The leader has to incorporate this process systematically, prudentially, reasonably, logically and above all very very smoothly.

(i) Unfreezing		(a) What	(d) Where
(ii) Changing	→	(b) How	(e) Why
(iii) Refreezing		(c) When	

Planned change is the result of the most appropriate and relevant vision. At every stage of the change process the vision of the leader has to play a very decisive and determinative role. The change process has three stages, namely, the unfreezing stage, the changing stage and the refreezing stage, the changing stage and the refreezing stage. The unfreezing stage is concerned with discarding the old behavior. It is a process of detachment from the past. It is the rejection and elimination of the old habits, work-methods, outlooks, techniques as well as perception. However, when the leader expects, from the followers, the avoidance, elimination and haulting the old practices, then, he has to provide them the details, which are based on his vision. He should tell them,

(i) What/Which old practices should tell them,
(ii) When those things have to be stopped?
(iii) Why those habits are to be stopped?

The vision of the leader is the guiding force behind these rejections. The unfreezing process based on the vision, supplies the answers to the above questions, which are definite, purposeful and well focused. Perhaps, sometimes, it is unwise to discard all past practices. Therefore, the leader has to select the obsolete practices which are to be discarded, since they are incompatible and obstructive to the future progress which is desired. The purpose and the particulars of elimination should be communicated to all employees, so that, the employees can give their meaningful and wholehearted cooperation. Similarly the time of incorporating the change is another important issue. The leader has to decide the correct time for discarding the old habits and introducing the new one. This decision again has the future orientation. In the light of the speed of changing conditions of future business and circumstances, the leader has to decide the time for change. As the correct predictability of future circumstances is the most difficult and complicated matter, the leaders vision has a great utility in this respect. Vision does not simply visualise the future, but pictures it also. In the process of picturisation, vision directs and dictates the necessary steps and actions for a desirable future. With the vision the leader is not only able to see the future but also can shape a better future. This making a better future with the help of the vision is, in fact, the essence of change management. Therefore, the time of unfreezing the old habits and practices replacing and changing them with the new one, has to be closely related to the leaders' vision.

The stage of unfreezing is followed by the stage of changing. Actually change process is a continuous process and as such the three stages unfreezing, changing and refreezing are intermixed and interdependent to a great extent. Naturally, the moment at which the old practice gets discarded, the new practice has to be introduced. This process of displacement and replacement has to become smooth and consecutive. It can be made so, if the employees are explained the necessity and rationale behind the change programme. The resistance to change arises because of the fear and misunderstanding. Once the people understand that the change is for the betterment of all, then they readily accept and participate in the change programme. The rationale of change should emerge from the leader's visions. It is the leader which provides the strong foundation of ideology for the planned change. This ideology is always future-oriented and has the logic development of a system for the transformation of the organisation in order to enhance its future compatibility.

During the refreezing stage, the refreezing stage, the reforms and newly introduced practices are repeatedly undertaken. This is done with a view to concretise and reinforce the changed behaviour. Refreezing makes the changed working styles and methods habitual. When people are familiar of habitual with the changed norms, styles and patterns of behaviour and performance, then a new organisation starts developing in place of the old one. However, most of the time, this process is gradual. Changing and refreezing has to be made systematically and step by step. It should be evolutionary as well as revolutionary. Here also the leader's vision plays a great role in providing direction on how to make change and refreeze the same, vision gives direction as well as momentum to change management. Leader's vision is the guiding force behind the organisational change and transformation.

Versatility - Versatility results from broad interests. A versatile leader is a person with multiple abilities, diversified skill and knowledge of almost each and every field. In other words, a versatile leader is jack of all trades and master of at least a few of them. Thus versatility develops an all-round personality of the leader. When a person is leading his organisation on the path of excellence, then, he needs to develop and possess versatility to overcome the unpredictable, eventual obstacles successfully and convert all threats into opportunities.

Management, in fact, is a limiters science. Nobody can set rigid, constant and all time fixed strategies and policies for managing an organisation. Because, organisation exist in dynamic external environment. Similarly, internally also, organisations experience a continuous change. In such a condition, the leader has to anticipate, predict, perceive and prepare reasonably for these changes. This needs the leader to possess broad interest, keen observation and wide knowledge. Because change takes place in different spheres of activities in a number of ways. But ultimately it produces an impact on the lives of people in one way or another. This results into a revision in their needs, lifestyles, work-expectations; job-attitudes, market and consumption as well as magnitude and intensity of competition. Effective management is possible only when a person has the capability to deal with such revisionary human behaviour proactively and utilise it every time for improving the organisational performance and bettering the organisational prospects. At the same the philosophy of excellence also expects the organisations to make continuous learning and improve themselves. Such an improvement should not be caused alone by the pressure of the external environment but due to own urge and attitude spread throughout the organisation for consistent improvement. Naturally, an organisation working and striving for excellence needs to possess strong activism and tremendous dynamism. It should become a vibrant organisation. It should not only accept the threats as challenges and convert them into opportunities, but should step forward to search out the new challenges and convert them into new spheres of business activities. In this respect, the role of the leader is of great importance. He has to act as the driving force behind organisation all thinking and functioning. And only a versatile leader can do this appropriately.

Threats to Opportunities - A versatile leader is capable of converting the threats into opportunities. This is possible to him, because of his two very special characteristics, namely a deep understanding of human behaviour and acute planning of resources. The knowledge of human behaviour relates more specifically to two important aspects such as knowledge of customers' behaviour and knowledge of employees' behaviour. Again the planning of resources is concerned with the physical, monetary, human and time resources. Let us discuss each of these aspects one by one.

The knowledge of human behaviour as customers and employees, is the foundation of effective management. A manager who precisely knows market and his own staff is able to control the situations more positively. In the present days of severe competition at global level, an organisation has to be market-focused **Tom Peters,** therefore, says that an organisation must have obsession with responsiveness to customers. He suggests that the total customers responsiveness can be created by doing the following

(i) Specialising in product and services.
(ii) Creating niches in the market.
(iii) Making product differentiation and thereby creating uniqueness.
(iv) Providing top quality and superior service.
(v) Becoming internalist.
(vi) Launching a customer revolution.

The knowledge and deep understanding of the market helps a lot in doing all the above. A versatile manager has a good knowledge of customers' perception, attitude, behaviour and changing preferences. Similarly he has the analytical ability to assess the degree of competition and its causes. With all this, a versatile manager is able to pinpoint the relative position of the organisation and thereby can design an effective strategy.

A versatile manager is also an expert in human resources management. Knowledge of human behaviour is most essential for successfully managing the people. A versatile manager has a good amount of people skill. He deputes the right person for the right job. Besides this job allocation, a versatile manager with the help of his knowledge and human psychology and inter-personal dynamics, can initiate and develop the relationship with right people. **John C Maxwell,** (Winning with People) provides the following tips in the regard.

(i) People are interested in the person, who is interested in them.

(ii) Believing the best in people usually brings the best out of people.

(iii) We can lift people up or take them down in our relationship with them.

(iv) Trust is the foundation of all relationships.

(v) All relationships need cultivation.

(vi) The journey with others is slower than the journey alone.

Henry Mintzberg has described ten basic roles which a manager has to perform to fulfill truly his obligation as a manager. Actually, the meaningful accomplishment of these roles evidenced the versatility of the manager, Mintzberg classifies these roles into three groups, such as, interpersonal roles, informational roles and decisional roles. The grouping, itself, suggests how much diversified these roles are and how do they expect the multitasking ability from a manager.

A brief discussion about these roles is as follows.

(A) Interpersonal Roles.

(1) **Figurehead** - The manager is symbolic head who is required to perform a number of routine duties of a legal or social nature. Naturally he has to conduct ceremonies, handle solicitations and status requests.

(2) **Leader** - The manager has to motivate and direct his subordinates. He has to set goals and clarify the path to reach to them.

(3) **Liaison** - The manager has to keep a contact with the outside world on continuous basis. He has to be in touch with the people who provide him useful information and can do certain favors.

(B) Informational Roles.

(1) **Monitor** - The manager has to receive a wide variety of information and act as the nerve centre for internal and external information about the organization and its business.

(2) **Disseminator** - Manager has to supply the relevant information to the concerned people and groups. This keeps all sections well-informed and thus helps them to do their jobs more efficiently and accurately. Lack of information causes confusion and weakens down the confidence of information.

(3) **Spokesperson** - The manager has to supply some information regarding the organisation's plans, policies, actions and results to the outsiders. This is an image building activity also. Many a time the chief executive officer (CEO) is the chief reputation officer (CRO)

(C) Decisional Roles.

(1) **Entrepreneur** - The manager has to search out opportunities in the business environment to start new projects and to make improvement in the existing projects. With this view, he has to design and initiate the project, monitor their implementation and see that they get launched successfully.

(2) **Disturbance Handler** - Manager has to conduct session with subordinates to discuss and analyse disturbances and crises and also initiate corrective actions.

(3) **Resource Allocator** - Manager has to decide the resources allocation among tasks and work groups on the basis of logical and progressive criterion. He has to handle budgeting, allocation, scheduling, requests for authorisation, etc.

(4) **Negotiator** - Manager, has to handle the contract negotiations and is responsible for representing the organisation at major negotiations.

The different roles which mints be expects from a manager are diversified and demand at least working knowledge (if not advanced one) of finance, human relations, economics, marketing, law, public relations, psychology, sociology, production and operations management, etc. Naturally versatility is must. Only a versatile manager can acquire such a diversified knowledge from a variety of disciplines. With this inventory the manager is able to convert the threats into opportunities. The planning, foresight and development of an appropriate strategy is mostly related to the diversified and multilevel thinking of the manager. A sound knowledge base enables him to do all these different tasks systematically and successfully. To develop and then utilise the characteristic of versatility, the Manager has to do the following

(1) Be open and receptive to the environment. Because the business environment imposes threats and opens up opportunities of progress also.

(2) Enhance curiosity, strengthen the urge to learn and widen the areas of interest. This will help to develop the multidisciplinary knowledge base.

(3) Develop lateral thinking. Analyse the situation factually and then think of a number of alternative solutions. The if-then way of thinking helps to search out substitute solutions in good number. The more the number of substitutes are available, the higher is the possibility of a right solution.

(4) Always try to make out of box thinking versatility develops through experiments, unconventional thinking and interaction with people having diversified experience.

(5) Versatality is an outcome of your reading, experiencing, observation, analysis and learning. Therefore never leave any chance to do these things. They develop knowledge-base.

(6) Versatality develops positive thinking. Positive thinking develops the mind set to look to threats as challenges to prove one self. This broadens the outlook towards the opportunities. Then every threat becomes an opportunity and every problem becomes a challenge. Barriers and obstructions cannot prevent the progress of versatile people. Because they have illuminating ideas and flexible approach with which they can pass through any situation.

Focus - Focus develops concentration. A focussed leader is more precise and acute in his thinking and actions. Focus brings sharpness and selectivity in them. Versatality causes for extensive thinking and focus persists on intensive thinking. Focus develops specificity and to the point approach in thoughts and action. Focus makes a disciplined performance. It ensures economical, efficient and productive utilisation of resources and eliminates the possibilities of wastages, duplications, errors, randomness and chaos.

For excelling, focus is essential, as it streamlines the operations and brings a result-oriented approach in management. Efficiency and effectiveness, both, can be achieved when the organisation brings focus in their working. Actually the importance of focus is well recognised, when **Michael Porter** described the concept of competitive advantage. He describes the three generic strategies as :

(1) Overall cost leadership strategy.

(2) Differentiation strategy and

(3) Focussed strategy.

In case of a focussed strategy, the company concentrates on special group of customers or a particular product line or a specific geographic region or other aspects that become the most important and must attend part of the company's efforts. The focus strategy is developed to achieve a particular target most efficiently and successfully. It presumes that a narrow specific target can be accomplished more effectively than a broad one. The definiteness and precision which is interweaver in a broad one. The definiteness and precision which is interwoven in a focussed strategy makes the leader and the entire organisation to think and act realistically and prudently. From the views of **Michael Porter** emerged the need and utility of being focussed. Focus, thus, becomes an integral part of the philosophy of excellence. Because excellence is not a matter of description and analysis but it incorporates a process of doing which involves a step by step progress, improvement and advancement on a continuous and consistent basis. This is possible only when there is a definite purpose and precision. Haphazard actions and too wide and general goals may develop uncertainty of outcome and unorganised directionless performance. As such, when the executive adopts a focussed cost leadership, then, he selects certain number of markets where he follows this strategy. Especially in markets, where the competition is intense and the customers are fashionable and prefer selective consumption, the focused differentiation strategy brings success and benefits to the organisation. Thus, focus develops a target-based and result-oriented approach. A focussed leader, in all his doings, is more purposive and practical. That ensures the progress on definite lines.

Focus in strategic thinking cultivates the thinking and analysis of core competencies. **Gary Hamel and C. K. Prahlad** views core competence as central value creating capability of an organisation. It is a collective learning in an organisation on how to co-ordinate diverse production skills and integrate multiple streams of technologies. A company from their viewpoint is a portfolio of core competencies and not a basket of businesses. Actually, the concept of core competence involves the harmonisation of streams of technology, organisation of work and delivery of value. Once a company attends to the development of core competence, its competitive strength increases on a continuous basis. Even the creation and development of core competencies requires focus and reversely, core competence will ensure focused performance and progress. Focus and core competence have thus the reciprocal relationship. In other words, it is better to concentrate on those things which we can do in the best possible way and leave the rest of the things to others. This will result into the optimum utilisation of resources in the most productive manner. Similarly, let us identify what we can do in the best way. This requires analysis and as easement of our potential and conversion of some of our best potential capabilities into our strengths.

Focussed thinking makes analysis as well as synthesis. It makes assessment and also assertion. It develops selectivity in thinking and actions. A focussed leader is accumulative and also rejective in his approach. He accumulates what supports and supplements his efforts to reach the goal and he rejects all those ideas and activities which deviates him from his target.

Focus and change management - Focus must be maintained in introducing change. A focussed change management makes possible the organisational development in the proper spirit and style. In fact, organisational development is focused and well planned change management programme. The organisational intervention strategies which constitute the integral part of the organisational development programme are actually the focussed efforts of change and improvement. They describe what needs to be changed and how it can be done. Interventions constitute the action thrust of organisational development (O.D.)

Robert Blake and **John Mouton** described a list of major interventions in terms of their underlying theme, which are as follows.

(1) **Discrepancy Intervention** - It calls attention to a contradiction in action or attitudes which needs exploration.

(2) **Theory Intervention** - The focus is on the explanation of present behaviour and assumptions underlying the same. For this purpose the knowledge and theory of behaviour science is used.

(3) **Procedural Intervention** - It is critical enquiry and evaluation of how things are done and aims at scrutinising whether the best methods are used.

(4) **Relationship Intervention** - Here the focus is on the enquiry and assessment of interpersonal relationship. Particularly, the causes of strong negative feelings are explored and resolved.

(5) **Experimentation Intervention** - Two different action plans are examined, to study their probable consequences. This helps for a more suitable choice of an action plans which fits to the organisations needs.

(6) **Dilemma Intervention** - An imposed or emergent dilemma is used to examine the possible choice involved and the underlying assumptions.

(7) **Perspective Intervention** - It concentrates on the assessment of actions and target. It tries to watch whether the actions are still on the road to target. For this purpose it draws away attention from the immediate actions and demands and allows a look at the historical background and future objectives.

(8) **Organisation Structure Intervention** - It focuses an examination of the structural causes of organisational ineffectiveness.

(9) **Cultural Intervention** - It assesses in a direct way the traditions, precedents and practices. These constitute the fabric of organisation's culture.

Thus organisational interventions are the focussed attempt to improve organisational effectiveness. It focus is lost, the change and development program will become unorganised and undirected. The entire planned change involves a series of activities with a focus on assessment and modification of different aspects of the organisation with a step by step approach.

Becoming a Focussed Leader. Focus can be developed as personality trait. To develop this ability, make use of the following tips.

(i) Develop the habit of concentration. Increase involvement in the subject-matter at the mental level. The more one starts thinking about a thing, the greater involvement, he starts feeling about the same.

(ii) Always keep a target-oriented approach. Think in terms of goals and accordingly streamline your decisions and actions accordingly.

(iii) Split a broad objective into specific goals, divide the goals into fixed target. Then make precise efforts to accomplish the targets, one by one.

(iv) Analyse resources and responsibilities to be fulfilled. Develop work-priorities on the basis of urgency and importance. Relegate resources accordingly.

(v) Always try to find out the root cause of a problem or the core part of a situation. Deal with it in a systematic manner. The rest of the things get revised consequentially.

(vi) Use the technique of delegation and decentralisation. Thereby you can devote your time and energy for core activities and goals and can assign the routine, repetitive and peripherial matters to others.

(vii) Develop a positive bias for time-management. Fix the deadlines for all your commitments in personal and professional life. This will reciprocally make you more focused.

Patience - Patience is another important and essential leadership quality for excellence. Patience develops both persistence and tolerance. Excellence, since, is an unending journey of improvement and progress; continuous effort for upgradation and enhancement becomes an essentiality for the same. Persistence, therefore, becomes one of the basic requisites. Tolerance is necessary, to endure with calm, the reactions and resistance to the reform-process. Unless transformation and reformation of habits, attitudes, methods and practices at the work place are made; the suitable environment for excellence cannot be developed. Naturally the change-process initiated with this view may find hurdles and obstacles every now and then. Tolerance is the only quality with which one survives during adversities and all odd times.

Patience builds tenacity and integrity. When things are favorable and smooth; an ordinary manager too can move forward. But when the going get tough, then, only the tough get going. This toughness is found only in extraordinary people who are very much determined to reach to the goal and accomplish the objectives in spite of all difficulties, odds and hardships. Patience develops this capability. Patience teaches to become calm and considerate. This gives the strength to withstand the pressure of the intense competition and the increasing stress of the fast changing circumstances within which the organisation operates. Impatience results into unstudied and hurried decisions.

The consequences of such decisions are often bitter and bad. **Peter Drucker** calls the present age as the Age of Discontinuity. Confusion and uncertainty prevails everywhere. The changes taking place all round are abrupt, fast, multilevel and diversified. They are not step by step and sequential. One change in a specific area produces chain of changes in a number of related as well as unrelated areas. Thus the complexities of changes are many a time very difficult to predict. So, it is then wise to face these uncertainties with a cool and balanced mind and find out a reasonable solution on each and every problem. Patience is the foundation of this type of mindset.

Patience is necessary for healthy and cordial relations with others. Such relationship can create the bonding and commitment for the hard work for excellence. Excellence can be achieved through people only. Technology and resources raise the efficiency level of the people. But it can't replace the creative and committed people which are at the backbone of the organisation. Nurturing such people requires patience. **John C. Maxwell** says that for the friendship of two, the patience of one is essential. **Arnold Glassglow** views that the key to everything is patience. You get the chicken by hatching the eggs and not by smashing it. Of course, for creating and managing excellence, the processes and efforts directed towards it must be long lasting. Excellence cannot be achieved with a piecemeal approach and intermitant activities. It is a nonstop long journey. **Glenn Clerk** observes, that, if you wish to travel far and fast, then travel light. He suggests to take of all your envies, jealousies, selfishness and unforgiveness. This reduces your luggage and makes you free to enter into a relationship more fruitfully.

Patience is required for a leader, because it is most expected of him by the followers. In fact, patience of the leader is more useful to his followers to perform steeply and steadily. As **Aristotle** comments that the greatest virtues are those which are most useful to other persons. Thus with patience the leader becomes more acceptable. This acceptability of the leader to his followers acts as the driving force for the development of the loyalty among the followers. Actually, the journey with others is slower than the journey alone. Patience makes us understand this. Patience leads this journey to a fruitful destination.

Developing Patience - John C. Maxwell suggests a six step action plan to develop patience and thereby improve relationships. It is as follows.

(1) Prioritise patience as virtue worthy of developing.

(2) Understand that it takes time to build good relationships.

(3) Patience is based on exchange principle. Exchange is the essence of all relationships.

(4) Realise that people have problems and they create problems too. So do not anticipate easy going.

(5) Identify areas where people need patience from you. Develop those areas.

(6) Remember that all relationships have the give-up give-ins and give and take. Give-ups means there are things which one likes to do, but should not do it this time. Give-ins means there are things which one does not like to do but should do it this time. Give and take means that there are things which we do for one another at this time.

Many times, people look to patience not as a good quality, but, as a drawback of the person. Patience is considered as the weakness of a person. It is misconstrued as the inability to retaliate. It is misunderstood as passivity. Therefore, conscious efforts to develop patience are very rarely made. We always think of improving and enhancing competitiveness. But we forget that in order to be truly competitive, we have to be ungrudgingly receptive and tolerant too. Especially when the situation is too much unfavourable and we do not have either a control or solution on it and further it is simply a matter of our capacity to withstand the odds and adversities, our patience can only rescue us from such eventual deadlocks and help us to go further. Our relationship with others can flourish and sweeten only due to our patience. Because, nobody is perfect and one can search out hundreds of deficiencies and demerits in others, it he so desires, but, then, the result will be strain, pain and no gain of in any form. Our success can be achieved only with others. Through them and with their help and co-operation can we improve the conditions and master the circumstances.

Actually, the leadership styles can be broadly classified into two categories, namely task-oriented leadership style and relationship-oriented leadership style. Both styles need more patience. To decide the allocation of tasks minutely and controlling by close supervision, also needs patience. Because such things cannot be hurriedly made. Allocation of duties and observation and control of performance has to be made objectively and in a balanced way. This too requires patience. Similarly the relationship style has patience as its foundation. Relationship can be developed and fostered through the gardening principle. All relationships, according to this principle need cultivations. Now cultivation and nurturing is also a matter patience. We cannot cultivate a lasting and fruitful relationship in a single day. We have to wait for the right response to our offer. We have to allow others assess and evaluate our proposals. Sometimes, we have to repeat our offers. All these things tare time-consuming. Their goal is to win the trust of the people. And this is a relatively lengthier process. A task-oriented approach has a transactionary motive. Once the task is over, the concern for the other party ends up. But relationship style intends to create a permanent bonding. This is possible only when both parties have fully understood each other's views. Therefore relationship needs extra time and special efforts for their development and nourishment. Patience is then the pedestal for this relationship.

In a dynamic and turbulent business environment, patience of the leader has a special significance. When an organisation possess through the bad times, it is the patience of the leader which is most useful. As there is saying that when the going get tough, then, the tough get going. The leader's toughness is exhibited through his calm and composed behaviour in critical and difficult situations. If the leader becomes panicky, then the followers lose their courage completely. This simply worsens the situation. The cool posture of the leader gives emotional support and confidence to the followers that the situation is under control and recovery is possible. In fact, the patience of the leader becomes strength to withstand comfortably the pressures and tensions of the adverse conditions.

Patience has another dimension. A leader with patience can face the criticism and abuses with balance and can reply them in a reasonable and clever way. Such replies should be through progressive and developmental actions. This is essential because actions always speak louder than words. A leader with patience only can take criticism as an evaluation of his work and can use it to remove the deficiencies. From the criticism he can fitter the issues requiring more attention as well as the expectations of the audience in respect of improvement and progress. That clarifies his path to the goal of excellence. It also helps him to set his priorities and develop his focus on areas of public interest.

Positive Thinking: Positive thinking is a sum total of optimism, achievement drive, perseverance and openness. All this develops positive attitude which is very much essential for a long journey of development, improvement and progress. Positive thinking is the tonic to work for excellence. Excellence demands lot of hard work, pain, involvement and sacrifices. All these may cause to develop negative feelings and reactions among people. The continuous and abundant exertion which becomes must in the journey towards excellence may develop the thoughts of deprivation and despair. But then the positive thinking of the leader with which he can create and cultivate the positive attitude among the people, makes a difference. A leader with positive thinking is not a day-dreamer. No doubt, he is optimistic. But his optimism does not emerge from the wishful thinking of a better tomorrow. His optimism is reality-oriented. It has a strong foundation of his achievement drive and an elevated support of his perseverance and openness.

Positive thinking and positive attitude to a common man are the same, though, technically the former is the cause and the later is the result. So let us use them interchangeably.

A person having positive attitude looks to failures as stepping stones to success. They take failures as lessons for improvement for them, problems, difficulties and hardships are the opportunities to test self-capabilities and develop new skills and strengths. Positive thinking makes a person move ahead all the time. It teaches that hurdles and obstacles can be removed, road-blockages are temporary and if there is no further path; then one can create a new path and continue his journey. This is needed for achieving excellence. Excellence is the approach of consistent improvement and progress. In fact, there is nothing which cannot be improved. Simply, we require to develop this perspective and practices suitable to this perspective and practices suitable to it. This process involves experimentation. People are afraid of experimenting due to the risks of mistakes and failures which are associated with it. Positive attitude treats mistakes and errors as cost of learning. The right answer is found out when all wrong alternatives are eliminated. Screening and testing ought to be done. The chance factor should also be considered. Sometimes even after a systematic and logical analysis of all related factors, eventual failure occurs. But that too help to understand the previously unknown and unforeseen elements which have narrowed down the path to success. In future we can remove these bottlenecks too. Because the experiments broaden our horizons of understanding. This is positive thinking. Only positive attitude can build within us the courage to step ahead.

When we compare the successful people with the ordinary, we find that the skills, abilities and expertise in both of them are little or more the same. The biggest difference in them is that of attitude. Successful people always have the positive attitude. They look to setbacks as stepping stones and learning exercises. This approach sustains their enthusiasm and energy to make further efforts. People with positive attitude are patient, humble and optimistic. They endure are patient, humble and optimistic. They endure the bad times with a hope of good future. They modestly accept the reality, but at the continuously to improve the conditions. They hope to carve a better future with the help of their patience and humble efforts.

This expectation of a positive outcome and good future has the roots in their faith on sincere, thoughtful, disciplined and consistent efforts and hardwork. Actually the valuable things are achieved only through struggle through storms and floods and floats him to the harbour safely and successfully. Our thinking creates our own environment. Negative thinking develops tension, fright, resentment and loser's attitude. Obviously then, such people do not put in the required volume of efforts and always try to run away from the situation. They always try to find out excuses for giving up. Negative people blame the circumstances. But they forget that most of the time we are the masters of our environment. In fact, we are what we think of ourselves. If we develop and possess self-defeating negative attitude then we may cause to cultivate an organisational climate of despair, lethargy and inefficiency. The negative attitude of the leader causes for the degeneration and downfall of the organisation. It discourages and demoralises the people and cause to descend the organisational effectiveness.

A leader with positive attitude become instrumental in

(i) Developing cordial relations and congenial work-environment.

(ii) Increasing productivity and improving quality.

(iii) Building loyalty and fostering teamspirit.

(iv) Reducing stress and solving work as well as personality-related problems.

Positive attitude has a culminating effect. The positive attitude of the leader spreads among the followers also. It energises the organisation and ignites the work-spirit among its members. However development of positive attitude is a systematic exercise. Though some people are born with this quality, there are lot of others who can develop this through well planned can develop this through well planned conscious efforts. Some important and useful conscious efforts. Some important and useful tips in this respect are as follows

(1) **Always keep yourself away from negative influences and negative people –** Some people complain while some contribute. Complainers blame others and find out excuses, for their nonperformance. Contributors make every possible effort to solve the problem, overcome difficulties, give positive results. They play the role of trouble shooters too. So be in the company of contributors. **Mark Twain** says that one should keep himself away from those people who belittle your ambition. So stay away from negative people who not only discourage you but also weaken your confidence and courage to do new and good things.

(2) **Look, always to the positive side of everything -** Remember the blessings and forget the hardship. Every venture carries risk. But it can bring success and progress also. To develop positive attitude one has to focus on the possibility of positive outcome and benefits. It acts as a motivational force. One has to see the good qualities of others. Do not count their faults and deficiencies. Beware of their limitations, but concentrate on their different abilities. Think how you make their best use for your organisation. Great work can be done only through dedicated and disciplined people and teamwork. So make people feel that they have something in them which they can utilise for all and thereby become special person. Enthusiasm can be developed not through on small achievements and convincing them about their potential for great work. In short, cherish the success; forget the failure.

(3) **Start your day with a positive thought -** If the day starts with a worry or tension or a negative thought. It affects the complete day-work. The morning-thought usually sets the

tone of the day. It keeps us in a good mood throughout. The tradition of morning prayer and evening prayer may have this purpose too besides spirituality. Positive morning thought has an energizing and activating effect. It builds the right frame of our mind which becomes useful to face the problems and difficulties in the whole day. Morning time is always recommended as the best time for studies. Because in the morning our mind is fresh and more receptive after the sound sleep at night. Naturally the morning thought has greater retention and effectiveness.

(4) **Develop love for the things you need to do** - Our likes and dislikes often affect our performance. Things which we like to do are done fast and with priority. The opposite happens about the work disliked. Therefore to develop positive attitude about all those work and activities which are must, we need to develop love for them. We have to convince our self that we like this work. Rationally and emotionally we have to involve ourselves in such activities. Our love develops passion for them and then naturally our involvement in them increases. Who likes study or exercise? But once we start loving, we do it regularly without any complaint.

To love the work we need to do two things

(1) Convince yourself about the benefits of doing such work.

(2) Make a habit of doing the same as self interests are basic and prime, we get attracted towards things which benefit us in one way or other. Similarly we live by habits. Once something become habitual to us, we do it regularly without any excuse. If we can't do it even for a single day due to unavoidable circumstances, we become restless.

(5) **Hate the attitude of procrastination and postponement** - People who procrastinate often are trapped into negative attitude. When we postpone the task, actually we provide the space for emergence of excuses for nonperformance. We start analysing it from different angles and too much analysis leads to action-paralysis. The person turns to be inactive.

Therefore to develop positive attitude, have a strong bias for action. Do not waste time in making too much analysis. Do not procrastinate. Do it right now. A completed task is always fulfilling and energising. It acts as a motivator itself. Action-biased people are more positive than analytical one. Remember actions may or may not produce desired outcome. But inaction, for all times, does not definitely produce any outcome. So it is better to act with 50 per cent possibility of success than to remain inactive with 100 per cent certainty of failure.

(6) **Be grateful for your blessings** - Whenever we start any work, there are well-wishers as well as skeptics around us. The well wishers offer blessings and greetings and the skeptics raise hundreds of questions and doubts. Count always your blessings and gratefully remember them. They will keep you positively charged. They give you emotional strength and remove the anxiety and stress. This stimulates you to think and act positively and fearlessly.

(7) **Develop and maintain self-esteem** - Our self-esteem is our self image. It is the way we feel about ourselves. It is a combination of self-respect self-pride and self-honour. Our self-esteem, many times cause us to behave responsible. We do not like to be disrespected in our own eyes. Naturally therefore we try to do as many noteworthy things as possible. The people with strong self-esteem, do normally the positive and mutually beneficial activities. Because they want to be recognized and respected by others. Development of self esteem has retrospectively a developmental esteem on positive attitude.

(8) **Become a continuous learner** - Learning opens up new horizons of opportunities. It broadens our thinking and develops receptivity. It encourages us to make experiments. This nouristies and flourishes the positive attitude. Ignorance narrows down our thinking. It develops fear about the unknown. It creates negativities in our personality. This results into making of a timid, coward, escapist individual. Such a person does not dare to face any challenge. He cannot innovate. And so he cannot make any progress. The fact is that ignorance keeps us in darkness and habituates us with darkness, so education is must to move forward. Learning not only gives us the ability to progress but also inculcates within us the attitude supportive to progress. People with positive attitude are actually continuous learners. They learn from the past, from the books, from the experiences of other and also from their own mistakes. Their attitude to learn from everybody and from almost everything sharpens their intelligence and generate in them lot of positive energy. This energy is mostly useful for excelling the work and the working.

Trust - Trust is the foundation of all long-term, purposeful and fruitful relationships. **George McDonald** says that it is a greater compliment to be trusted than to be loved. Lack of trust results into suspicion, dispute and disharmony. It may cause to create chaos. Trust acts as the binding force to keep people together. However trust starts with our self. Those who cannot trust themselves cannot trust others. The skeptics are actually mentally unhealthy people. They doubt the integrity of all. Trusting other is a sign of positive feeling about others and healthy mind. This is necessary because trust is like a savings a/c in a bank. Unless we make deposits therein we cannot make withdrawals. Therefore to make others trustworthy to us; we need to trust them first. If we start behaviour, then their plain and spontaneous responses too can be wrongly interpreted and negatively biased.

Trusting other, though, is the first step in the development of trust, it cannot be done blindly. We cannot trust each and all. But we can systematically develop the atmosphere wherein trust becomes a normal phenomenon and distrust is an exception. Such an atmosphere has a positive impact on the productivity and morale of the people. In order to create an atmosphere of trust we need to develop certain systems and mechanism. The important steps in this regards are as follows

(1) Develop transparency in decisions and dealings with all people.

(2) Treat all employees fairly, equally and indiscriminately. Prize and penalty must be based on justifiable cause and criterion.

(3) Establish standard procedures for performance and its evaluation.

(4) Development of two way, open, formal communication. Gossip, back-biting, private communication should be strictly avoided and discouraged.

(5) Develop team-spirit. Make people get habituated to work in teams. Teach and train them to link up their work and performance with others. Create alliances among departments and sections.

(6) Nurture methodically cordial relations and healthy practices among employees and employer.

Distrust in organisation is of two types.

(a) Distrust in vertical relationship and

(b) Distrust in horizontal relationship.

The distrust in vertical relationship is the lack of mutual faith between the employee and employer, the subordinate and superior, the junior and senior and the workers and management. This distrust may be on individual level as well as group level. Again the distrust in horizontal relationship is the absence of faith among employees working at the same level of management. It may also be between two individual employees or between two or more work-groups of employees

However distrust at any level and in kind of relationship has always a retarding. Effect on the organisational performance and effectiveness. The major causes of distrust in organisational relationship are follows

(1) Dishonesty in performance.

(2) Conflict of interest and greed of bigger share.

(3) Resources inadequacy and stressful situations.

(4) Exploitative practices and manipulations.

(5) Intense internal completion and lack of the spirit of co-operation.

In most of the cases dishonesty, insincerity, non-integrity and disloyalty becomes the cause of distrust. A person who dose not keep up his promise loses his reliability and credibility. Similarly a non-performing employee is always looked with a suspicious eye. He is closely watched to screen out his inability or unwillingness to perform. If he lacks the capacity then he needs work-training. But if he is avoiding cleverly the job and is reluctant to perform; then his tendering a attitude becomes the subject matter of assessment. His loyalty is questioned.

Conflict of interest and greed for comparatively bigger share at individual and group level cause distrust. **F.W. Taylor** has said it long back, that the prominent cause of dispute a between the management and workers is the distribution of profit. How much profit should be given as dividend and how much as the bonus, becomes the fighting issue. Workers therefore always suspect that their wages are less than contribution to the organisation and management feels that workers do not give the output in proportion to what they receive from the organisation. Each party wish to snatch a greater share of benefits and suspects that the other party is in genuine. This distrust gets fostered when the management starts employing exploitative practices and the workers too indulge in manipulation. Strict adherence to rules, heavy quota, rigid work routine are some of the management practices which are restrictive and stiffly regulative in nature. Their hidden purpose is to disallow the worker to enjoy leisure and relaxation. These practices resemble to what **McGregor** called as Theory X assumptions. Once we presume that people dislike the work and try to avoid it and so we have to compel, our management strategy is consequentially founded on distrust. In that situation workers may make manipulation in target-completion, rules-observation, etc. They never think of bringing quality in their performance or utilizing their potential which will not be counted for their personal growth.

Distrust in organisational relations may creep in when resources are inadequate and the situation is immensely stressful. This distrust widens when employees and their sections start competing intensely with each other for showing their extraordinary performance. Resources crunch and competitive spirit induces people to conceal the information from one another. It may relate to procedure, availability and access to resources, methods and techniques of making their optimum utilization, etc. To beat others, employees and their groups use private communication, secretive communication, gossip, cornering technique which am plies the effect of distrust. It the result of the strategy employed by departments and workgroups in their mutual dealings. Wild competition kills the spirit of co-operation. If only the victory is a matter of concern and the ways and means used to win are ignored then unethical and illicit practices and propositions become acceptable and excusable. This allows the distrust to grow and spread fact. All such factors lead to formation of a stressful situation. When people are under stress, their communication with each other does not remain open and plain. Each one has a fear that the other person may use his talk for self benefit of the other or to pinpoint the weakness of the dialogue maker. Under such circumstances distrust becomes deep-rooted and openness and transparency are criticised as bookish and impractical ideas.

Confidentiality and secrecy is an important aspect of administration. This is essential to protect the organisation and its working from the ill-intentions and interference. In every organisation, there are few, selective persons who are the most confidential people in the organisation. They are most loyal and their integrity is unquestionable. But at the same time there are hundred of other who too are working in their respective sections and departments with all sincerity. It is not necessary to suspect their integrity unless such a typical incidence takes place. Unfortunately there happens a partition of employees as trustworthy and untrustworthy without any reasonable ground or assessment of the people. This develops a tendency to think in terms of 'we-the loyal' and 'they-the disloyal'- and make separation accordingly. Such a division results into creation of an atmosphere of distrust and partition. Therefore there should always be a policy of open communication, transparency and integration. The confidential work should be handled by those who are entitled to do it by the virtue of their position. Thus the maintenance of secrecy automatically becomes a matter of the professional obligation. Instead of treating some people as confidential persons, if we entrust the responsibilities relating to confidentiality to certain designations, then we can develop a more systematic, formalised and professional approach to this issues.

To develop trust, we need to do the following.

(1) Remember that trust begins with ourself. First we have to become trustworthy to make others become trustworthy to us.

(2) Understand that trust cannot be compartmentalised. Trust is a matter of a person's character. Integrity is an important personality trait. And a person with integrity shows it in all his behaviour everywhere. Thus, a trustworthy person can not be honest with one and dishonest with another. So trust is to be developed as a personality quality and not as simply a technique or strategy.

(3) If somebody breaks up your trust, in the first instance, forgive him/her. But do not forget the incidence. Your forgivance may make the person to repent for his wrong-doings. Simultaneously, give him gradual opportunities to improve him self. His development will be from a distrusting personality to a trustworthy employee. The method to convert him will be as follows.

   (a) Explain to him that the violation should never happen again.

   (b) Remember his better work and tell him about the same. This will have a twofold effect. He will understand your goodness and will also feel ashamed of his misbehaviour.

   (c) To improve, give him chance, step by step to prove that he has now become honest and reliable. Test this positive development by assigning to him jobs carrying a small of amount of secrecy or importance. Once he successfully completes them with all sincerity and honesty, then assign to him more crucial and important jobs. However, at each such level there should be an indirect or implicit testing of the improvement in his loyalty and commitment.

The main objective of this exercise is to strengthen the reliability and sincerity of the loyal employees also to improve the level of honesty and responsibility of the 'black sheeps' among the employees. The point is to institutionalise the trust. This is possible when almost all employees have become sincere and honest and do their jobs in the most efficient and responsible way and similarly the management responsible way and similarly the management responds to their integrity and honors it in some way or other. Development of trust is a mutual task. Both parties must be fair and honest in their dealing with each other. However the role and responsibility of the employees in this regard is pivotal and more contributory. Management can be responsive transparent and generous it the employees are honest, productive and co-operative. The sincerity of the employees increases the management's concern for them. At the same time, the management should also make special efforts to develop and nurture a climate and culture of trust. Through training and practices it should communicate, convince and confirm its emphasis on trust. A system of reward and punishment for the desirable and undesirable behaviour, too, can be of a great help in this regard.

Warren Benis states that integrity is the basis of trust. It is the one quality which cannot be acquired but must be earned. Thus it is not we who decide ourselves as trustworthy. But the other people such as our peers, superiors, subordinates, coworkers etc assess and decide how much honest, believable and dependable we are. They confer on us the title of 'the trustworthy person' after making our evaluation in different situations and from different angles. It is their perception of our selves. We earn the trust of others by our consistent honest behaviour and developing trust is not a piecemeal activity or single intermittent incidental behaviour. Trust is developed and restored only with deeds and not with flowery words or big slogans.

William Boast and **Benjamin Martin** explains that trust is established when words and deeds are congruent. Trust also develops when people feel safe and secure.

Many times we observe that good thoughts and ideas are shot down and ridiculed. Then people feel unsafe to generate innovative and productive ideas and thoughts. Similarly unnecessary evaluation and excessive criticism leads to breeding up of defensive climate. Initiative, pioneering, leadership and enterprising attitude gets discouraged. Everybody wish to set the boundaries and perform his duties within that typical framework. In such situations, each one starts suspecting the other. Everybody, then, wants to play safe and avoid the criticism and low grading. As a result, the organisation becomes stagnant and there is a retarding effect on its growth and development. One of the important aspect of trust is the creation of an open, fearless, stimulating environment. Trust encourages people to use their full potential and do well. If the people feel frightened, shy and reluctant to take up the adventurous task, presume self responsibility and become growth and progress-oriented, the culture and climate of trust is not instilled and developed in its true sense. Therefore, instead of making the evaluative comments, instead of making the evaluative comments; provide to the employees the description provide to the employees the description regarding expected level of performance and behaviour. Express your feeling of caring and involvement. Show your willingness actively and consistently to listen, understand and utilise the perspectives of people. Always remember the following three principles and practice them regularly

(a) Trust begins with yourself.

(b) Trust cannot be compartmentalised.

(c) Trust is like a bank account. In order to make the withdrawals, you need to make the deposits first.

□□□

BIBLIOGRAPHY

(1) **Management** - Robert Kreitner

(2) **Business Policy and Strategic Management** - Azhar Kazmi

(3) **Management** - Stoner, Freeman Gilbert

(4) **Organisational Behaviour - Concepts, Controversies and Applications** - Stephen P. Robbins

(5) **Organisational Behaviour** - Fred Luthans

(6) **Fundamentals of Management** - Ricky W. Griffin

(7) **Leadership and Organisation** - R. Tannenbaun, I. R. Weschler and F. Massarik

(8) **Management Challenges for the 21st Century** - Peter Drucker

(9) **The New Managerial Grid** - Robert R. Blake and Jane S. Mounton

(10) **The Adaptive Corporation** - Alvin Toffler

(11) **Business Ethics** - Dr. A. K. Gavai

(12) **Modern Management Practices** - Dr. A. K. Gavai

(13) **Business Policy and Strategic Management** - P. Subba Rao

(14) **Exploring Corporate Strategy** - Genny Johnson, Kevan Scholes

(15) **The Nature of Managerial Work** - Henry Mintzberg

(16) **You can win** - Shiv Khera

(17) **In Search of Excellence** - Thomas J. Peters and Robert H. Waterman Jr.